The Marketing Casebook

Cases and Concepts

Second edition

Sally Dibb and
Lyndon Simkin

THOMSON
LEARNING™   Australia • Canada • Mexico • Singapore • Spain • United Kingdom • United States

THOMSON
LEARNING

The Marketing Casebook: Cases and Concepts – 2nd edition

Copyright © 2001 Sally Dibb and Lyndon Simkin

Thomson Learning ™ is a trademark used herein under licence.

For more information, contact Thomson Learning, Berkshire House, 168–173 High Holborn, London, WC1V 7AA or visit us on the World Wide Web at: http: //thomson learning.co.uk

British Library Cataloguing-in-Publication Data
A catalogue record for this book is available from the British Library

ISBN 1–86152–624–5

First edition published 1994 and reprinted 1996 by Routledge, London
Simultaneously published in the USA and Canada by Routledge, New York
Reprinted in 1999 by International Thomson Business Press
Second edition published 2001 by Thomson Learning

Typeset by Saxon Graphics Limited, Derby
Printed in the UK by TJ International, Padstow, Cornwall

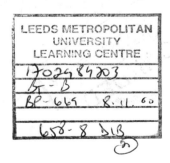

Contents

Part I   How to tackle case study analysis and presentations   **9**

Part II   Short cases for discussion   **23**

Tables

Figures

About the Authors

Sally Dibb and Lyndon Simkin have been at the leading UK university management centre, Warwick Business School, since the mid-1980s, teaching undergraduates, MBAs – full-time, part-time and distance learning – and executives the basics of marketing, advanced strategic marketing, buyer behaviour, marketing communications and marketing research. Sally and Lyndon's research focuses on services marketing, market segmentation, marketing planning, retail modelling, marketing communications and teaching methods, in which areas they have published extensively in the academic journals in the UK and USA. Consultancy principally addresses marketing planning and target market strategies in a host of UK and North American blue chip businesses. Married, Sally and Lyndon live in Kenilworth with their four children, Becky, James, Abby and Miranda Mae.

In addition to being joint authors of *The Marketing Casebook: Cases and Concepts*, they produce the market leading *Marketing: Concepts and Strategies* (Boston: Houghton Mifflin, now in its fourth edition) with US marketing colleagues Bill Pride and OC Ferrell, as well as the practitioner-oriented *The Market Segmentation Workbook* and *The Marketing Planning Workbook* (both London: Thomson Learning), aimed at assisting marketing managers to re-assess their target markets and understand the complexities of marketing planning. These workbooks were based on their consultancy experiences with organizations as diverse as Andersen Consulting, DRA (MoD), Forte, ICI, JCB, Jet, McDonald's, PowerGen, Raytheon, Standard Chartered, Tesco and Zeneca.

Acknowledgements

In preparing this edition of *The Marketing Casebook: Cases and Concepts* we would like to acknowledge the help and support of:

Esra Arson
John Bradley and JCB
David Bunworth and Aer Lingus
Rebecca Dibb-Simkin
Caroline Farquhar
Peter Jackson and Adsearch
Jervis Johnson and Games Workshop
Susan Kahn and Houghton Mifflin
Jens Maier and David Harris
Roger Moggs and Brookes & Vernons
Claire Murphy
Marcelo Rocha
Chris Vere
John Wringe and Lansdown Conquest

Long suffering Sheila Frost and Janet Biddle.

All our students, former and current, our consultancy contacts and colleagues at Warwick Business School.

Sources

Part II

'Sainsbury's sets up helpline to quash fears over GM foods', *Marketing Week,* February 18 1999, p. 9; Alexandra Jardine, 'GM scare strains retailers', *Marketing*, February 18 1999, p. 7; 'Public resist GM food', *Marketing*, February 25 1999, p. 4; Julia Hinde, 'GM circus comes to town', *The Times Higher*, March 12 1999, p. 20 & p. 60; Richenda Wilson, 'Race against time', *Marketing Week*, January 21 1999, pp. 51–53; Roger Baird, 'Winning formula', *Marketing Week*, March 4 1999, pp. 37–38; Richard Foster, 'Why sponsors need to negotiate the rule book', *Marketing Week*, February 25 1999, p. 16; 'NSPCC Aims to Convert Abuse Anger into Cash', *Marketing*, 25 March 1999, pp. 37–38; Jade Garrett, 'Charities Snub Shock Tactics for Subtle Approach' *Campaign*, 26 March 1999, p. 10; 'Spotlight Charity', *Marketing Week*, 17 December 1998, pp. 28–29; 'Charities Unite in Donor Appeal', *Marketing*, 14 January 1999, p. 4; BUPA; 'BUPA looks for better health', Claire Murphy, *Marketing*, December 3 1998, p. 21; 'BUPA axes O&M for direct focus', Lisa Campbell, *Marketing*, November 26 1998, p. 1; *Fragrance Fabrics and Essential Oils and Their 'Well Being' Qualities*, Courtaulds Jersey Underwear; Courtaulds Textiles, Nottingham; Sian Phillips, 'Space Invaders', *Hotline,* Winter 1998/99, pp. 16–19; David Reed, 'Fuel Injection', *Marketing Week*, 4 February 1999, pp. 37–42; Matthew Reed, 'Online sales go uptempo', *Marketing*, 7 January 1999, pp. 23–24; Philip Rooke, 'Production must take backseat on the Internet', *Marketing Week*, 11 March 1999, p. 30; 'Why Net music is poised to hit the high notes', *Marketing Week*, 25 February 1999, p. 40; http://www.boxman.co.uk; 'Progressive not McDesperate', Letters, *Marketing Week*, 22 April 1999, p. 32; 'Aroma therapy', *Marketing Week*, 8 April 1999, pp. 28–29; Ian Darby, 'Big Mac blunder hits McDonald's', *Marketing*, 7 January 1999, p. 1; Claire Murphy, 'How McDonald's conquered the UK', *Marketing*, 18 February, pp. 30–31.

Part III

David Bunworth, Aer Lingus; Bernie Cahill, chairman of Aer Lingus; Aer Lingus *Annual Reports*; Aer Lingus Media Relations, 1999; Aer Lingus web site; John Bradley; JCB Sales & Marketing; JCB Parts; Roger Moggs, Brookes & Vernons; *The JCB Experience*, JCB; Legoland UK; Charles Darwent, 'Lego's billion-dollar brickworks', *Management Today*, September 1995, pp. 64–68; 'Legoland rejigs team', *Marketing*, 4 March 1999, p. 5; Richard Morais, 'Babes in toyland?', Forbes,

3 January 1994, pp. 70–71; 'A faint squeak from Euro-Mickey', *The Economist*, 29 July 1995, p. 56; Jeff Ferry and Richard Hooper, 'The great game of infant-motion', *Director*, September 1995, pp. 30–38. 'Legoland upgrades its online presence', *Marketing*, 1 April 1999, p. 15; 'Lego hires Motive to devise strategy for £20m media', *Marketing Week*, 10 September 1998; Adam Penenberg, 'Letting go of Lego', *Forbes*, 9 August 1999, pp. 122–124; 'First-ever net loss is recorded by Lego on decreasing sales', *The Asian Wall Street Journal*, 12 May 1999, p. 2; Robert Frank, 'Lego will try demolition, reconstruction', *The Asian Wall Street Journal*, 22 Jan 1999, p. 25; Cora Daniels, 'Lego's Star Wars robot: another great way to kill time in Silicon Valley', *Fortune*, 7 June 1999, p. 190; Joseph Pereira, 'Toys: Lego's robot set for kids grabs crowds for grown-ups', *The Wall Street Journal*, 10 December 1998, p. B1; Stephen Wildstrom, 'Lego's little mind-builder', *Business Week*, 12 October 1998, p. 20; Robert Frank, 'Toys: facing a loss, Lego narrates a sad toy story', *The Wall Street Journal*, 22 January 1999, p. B1; Laura Liebeck, 'Retailers to feel the force of all things Star Wars', *Discount Store News*, 8 February 1999, pp. 45, 50; Cecile Corral, 'The 'Star Wars' licensing empire strikes back', *Discount Store News*, 7 June 1999, pp. 27, 46, http: //www.lego.com; Pivco, Oslo; David Owen, PowerGen; Peter Jackson, Adsearch; *What Car?;* Crispin Haywood; http://www.aqmd.gov/monthly/white.html; http://www.ford.com/electricvehicle/qvm.html; http:/www.bsi.ch/vel/velen01.htm; *Retail Business; Euromonitor; Statistisches Bundesamt; Gesellschaft fur Konsum; Markt und Absatzforschung;* David Harris, Metal Box; Jens Maier, Warwick Business Consultants; *Packaging News*; Kodak; Kodak Norge; Norges Markedsdata; Barry Quinn; Conoco UK; http: //www.safeway.co.uk; 'Shell unveils new "green" petrol', *Marketing*, 10 December 1998, p. 2; Francesca Newland, 'Jet to ditch new fore-court design', *Marketing Week*, 2 April 1998, p. 9; Victoria Medhurst, 'Jet back after long ad silence', *Marketing*, 19 February 1998, p. 6; Claire Conley, 'BP taps into retail seam to fuel profit', *Marketing Week*, 12 February 1998, pp. 20–21; Claire Murphy, 'Anything to petrol but price?', *Marketing*, 10 December 1998, p. 19; NOP/Mintel; David Benady, 'Loyalty offer threatens to shatter petrol price truce', *Marketing Week*, 5 June 1997, p. 8; Mintel, 'Petrol forecourt retailing', *Retail Intelligence Report*, September 1997, Jonathan Singleton, 'Development of petrol retailing in the United Kingdom', *Journal of the Market Research Society*, 40 (1), pp. 13–23; *Petroleum Reviewer*; Datamonitor; The Marketing Pocket Books, NTC; Fitzwilton, Ireland; Waterford Ltd; Caroline Farquhar; KeyNote Publications; Debenhams, Coventry; TGI Friday's; Whitbread plc; Ahold; Marcelo Rocha; Heineken, Netherlands; Jervis Johnson and Games Workshop; the *Games Workshop Newsletter* and *White Dwarf* publications; James Dibb-Simkin; Games Workshop branch staff in Coventry and Leamington Spa; Esra Arson; Claire Murphy; Nestle Turkey; Unilever; Campanile Hotels; Travelodge; Granada plc; Travel Inn; Whitbread Hotels; ABN AMRO; *The Banker/Financial Times*; Salomon Brothers; Barclays de Zoete Wedd; *Business Week; Institutional Investor; Chester Zoo Life*; Chris Vere and Chester Zoo; English Tourism Council; British Tourist Authority; The Henley Centre; Target Group Index/BMRB; *HMSO Social Trends; HMSO Employment Gazette*; Carrefour, France; M. Laurent Noel, 'Carrefour has Czech mate', *Chain Store Age*, August 1999, 75 (8), pp. 44–48; Courtaulds Textiles plc; BUPA; Boxman.

Special thanks must be paid to the leading trade magazines *Campaign, Marketing* and *Marketing Week*. Also to the wonderful source for marketing information, the *Marketing Pocket Books* published by NTC and The Advertising Association.

The shorter cases in Part II owe much to the development of the fourth edition of our mainstream marketing textbook, *Marketing: Concepts and Strategies*, Boston: Houghton Mifflin.

Preface

In 1994 the first edition of *The Marketing Casebook: Cases and Concepts* was an innovative product. Most published cases discussed anonymous producers of widgets or disguised the brands to the point of obscurity. We decided to write about genuine brands, real companies and markets relevant to students undertaking undergraduate business studies degrees or MBAs. Our own MBAs at Warwick Business School, particularly those studying via distance learning or part-time routes, regularly requested concise revision-oriented overviews of the key marketing concepts. As experienced marketing lecturers and the authors of one of the best selling marketing textbooks – *Marketing: Concepts and Strategies* (Boston: Houghton Mifflin) – we were able to produce such overviews. *The Marketing Casebook: Cases and Concepts* was duly conceived – a mix of real-world cases with theory summary notes, plus guidance on addressing the cases, using the theory notes, further reading and understanding key marketing terms.

The Marketing Casebook: Cases and Concepts is designed to illustrate the key concepts in marketing theory through a series of case studies and theory notes. By examining the way marketing works in practice, the reader is drawn into the problems and questions facing marketing practitioners in their everyday lives. *The Marketing Casebook: Cases and Concepts* is structured to help develop students' understanding of marketing with specific focus on plenary seminar discussions and examinations.

The cases have been used by tutors in Asia-Pacific, North America, Africa and throughout Europe. Marketers in many of the featured businesses have been quizzed on a variety of marketing issues by students tackling Chartered Institute of Marketing diplomas or business school degrees, and by marketing practitioners participating on in-company training programmes. This level of interest has persuaded us to up-date *The Marketing Casebook: Cases and Concepts*.

The new edition has been totally overhauled. Each theory note has up-to-date concepts and suggestions for further reading. There are additional theory notes examining direct marketing and ethical decision-making in marketing, while relationship marketing, the Internet, green issues and competitive strategy are also included. There are a few favourite cases retained from the first edition. Only one, classic packaging case Stepcan, remains unaltered. The others have been revised, up-dated and re-structured. New cases include Aer Lingus's drive for competitive advantage, Lego's brand extension, the CityBee electric car, the hardships of petrol forecourt retailing, Dutch retailer Royal Ahold's social responsibility, wargaming-to-toy Games Workshop's rapid rise, the Turkish ice-cream wars, budget hotels' branding and Carrefour's global fortunes. The up-dated cases include JCB's diggers, Kodak Norge's film products, Waterford crystal, TGI Friday's American diners, Heineken's refreshing expansion, ABN AMRO's global banking, and Chester Zoo's intense competition.

In addition to the new full-length cases, Part II now presents a selection of narrowly themed short caselets intended for plenary discussion or examination revision guidance. These include the ethical issues of GM foods, motor sport Formula 1's fight to retain tobacco sponsorship, the NSPCC's use of marketing campaigns, health insurer BUPA, the development of innovative 'smelly' fabrics, surprising advertising, Boxman's Internet retailing and McDonald's operational controls.

As with the first edition of *The Marketing Casebook: Cases and Concepts* the key themes of each case are clearly illustrated in the book's *Introduction*, while each case is thoroughly cross-referenced for ease of use with the most relevant theory notes.

Part I   How to Tackle Case Study Analysis and Presentations
Part II   Short Cases for Discussion
Part III   Full Cases
Part IV   Theory Notes
Part V   Glossary of Key Terms
Part VI   Further Readings

Producing this version of *The Marketing Casebook: Cases and Concepts* coincided with latest addition to our family, baby Miranda Mae, so it proved to be a juggling act of responsibilities and time! We hope you enjoy the new edition.

Sally Dibb
Lyndon Simkin

Introduction

The Marketing Casebook: Cases and Concepts presents a selection of short cases intended for plenary session discussion or to aid examination revision and a large selection of full-length teaching cases which are proven in the business school seminar environment. These cases may also be read in conjunction with the accompanying theory notes to provide detailed insights into the deployment of marketing and application of the discipline's core concepts. The set of included theory notes covers the essential concepts of marketing analysis, marketing strategy and marketing management.

The cases lend themselves to syndicate group discussions for students tackling marketing diplomas, undergraduate degrees and MBAs. A set of suggested questions is provided for each case. When combined with the theory note overviews of core marketing concepts, the cases ensure *The Marketing Casebook: Cases and Concepts* becomes an effective text for self-tuition or for examination revision.

Teach yourself	Cases; theory note overviews; explanation; further readings.
Diversity of styles	Mix of short and long cases; choice of cases with a narrow focus or multi-themed cases.
All arenas of marketing	Consumer, services and industrial business-to-business products and markets.
International coverage	Asia-Pacific, France, Ireland, the Netherlands, North America, Norway, South America and Turkey.
Variety of case themes	Marketing analysis, marketing strategy and marketing management; topical issues; successes and failures; practical insights.
A complete resource	Cases, readings, theory, references, glossary, instructions for tackling cases and presentations.

For Tutors

For lecturers and trainers there is an *Instructor's Manual* with case issue solutions, additional insights, suggestions for teaching and contact details for further information. The *Instructor's Manual* is only available on the web at the following address: http://www.thomsonlearning.co.uk. The cases have been selected to provide a choice of in-depth discussion, quick overview examination or revision style use. Part II's cases are the short, narrowly focused plenary-oriented cases. Part III contains the more extensive and complex cases. The matrix below summarizes the key topics examined by each case. The theory notes are used by many tutors as lecture handouts, subject to ALCS copyright permissions.

Matrix of Case Issues

Short Cases — Part II

	1	2	3	4	5	6	7	8	9	10	11	12	13	14	15	16	17
GM Foods																	X
F1		X															
NSPCC											X						
BUPA											X		X				
Smelly Fabrics								X					X	X			
Surprising Ads											X						
Boxman									X			X					
McDonald's	X																

Full-Length Cases — Part III

	1	2	3	4	5	6	7	8	9	10	11	12	13	14	15	16	17
Aer Lingus			X	X		X	X						X	X			
JCB			X					X			X			X	X	X	
Lego			X		X			X								X	
CityBee		X	X	X												X	
Stepcan		X				X	X			X				X		X	
Kodak			X	X		X			X					X		X	
Petrol		X	X				X			X				X			
Waterford			X	X		X		X									
TGI Friday's			X			X	X				X		X				
Royal Ahold		X														X	X
Heineken		X					X									X	
Games Workshop			X						X		X	X				X	
Turkish Ice		X														X	
Budget Hotels						X		X					X				
ABN AMRO						X							X				
Chester Zoo						X				X	X		X			X	
Carrefour						X	X									X	

1   What Is Marketing
2   The Marketing Environment and Competition
3   Buying Behaviour
4   Marketing Research
5   Forecasting
6   Market Segmentation
7   Competitive Strategy
8   The Marketing Mix: Products and Product Management
9   The Marketing Mix: Place - Distribution & Marketing Channels
10   The Marketing Mix: Pricing
11   The Marketing Mix: Promotion
12   Direct Marketing and the Internet
13   The Marketing of Services
14   Industrial, Business-to-Business Marketing
15   Marketing Planning
16   International Marketing
17   Ethics and Social Responsibility in Marketing

Case Content Summaries

Part II of *The Marketing Casebook: Cases and Concepts* presents a selection of narrowly themed short caselets intended for plenary discussion or examination revision guidance. These include the ethical issues of GM foods, Formula 1's fight to retain tobacco sponsorship, the NSPCC's use of marketing campaigns, health insurer BUPA, the development of innovative smelly fabrics, surprising advertising, Boxman's Internet retailing and McDonald's operational controls.

Part III's full-length cases examine brands and companies engaged in all aspects of marketing – consumer goods, services and industrial business-to-business – in a selection of territories, including Asia-Pacific, France, Ireland, the Netherlands, North America, Norway, South America and Turkey. The longer cases are:

> **Aer Lingus** is a service business that has utilized marketing to rejuvenate its fortunes, researching customers' expectations and their perceptions of competitors, customizing its marketing mix programmes to reflect the needs of its principal target markets, while enhancing the standing of its brand in an increasingly competitive marketplace.

> The **JCB** story is one of success for a large, privately owned UK engineering company. The case highlights reasons for this success on an international scale, featuring JCB's branding, positioning, marketing planning and promotional strategies. JCB's product innovation and attention to customer service are also explained. The difficulties of selling and marketing in industrial markets are more than evident.

> The **LEGO** brand has been around for many decades and its appeal has spread to children (and adults) across the world. A non-stop programme of range enhancement and new product development has incorporated themes from the latest blockbuster movies, kept pace with the boom in video and PC games, and adopted the LEGO positioning to incorporate theme parks and merchandising. There is much more to LEGO than the familiar plastic building bricks. Such global expansion and continued popularity have been achieved in the face of increasing competition from other toy producers as well as a plethora of products and activities targeted at LEGO's core target market, children.

> The **CityBee** was developed by a Norwegian company whose executives were aware of the impact of traditional petrol and diesel engines on the natural environment. For consumers, such a solution – an EV – was unfamiliar and the Norwegian company unknown. Researching consumer attitudes under such circumstances is problematic, but nevertheless such marketing intelligence is essential. The CityBee is now marketed as the Ford **Think**.

> Creating a differential advantage or competitive edge is never simple; packaging is often an option neglected. The retailers who test marketed **Stepcan** quickly realized the container's benefits, but not so everyone at Metal Box. The case also illustrates the role of the marketing environment, the problems

of marketing across international frontiers and of controlling the supply chain.

Kodak Norge, in common with many companies, believed it had an incomplete marketing information system and inadequate marketing intelligence. The company was highly successful but faced strong international and local competition. It was particularly important for Kodak Norge to understand its market segments and to control effectively its marketing channels.

The mergers in the ***forecourt sector*** are reducing the number of competitors but have increased the intensity of rivalry. The various partnerships between fuel businesses and grocery retailers have broadened the scope of the intense rivalry in the forecourt sector. For these businesses, such changes pose opportunities but also the need to develop clear branding strategies and trading propositions. A principal prong of attack has been the introduction of loyalty schemes to persuade customers to select forecourts based not only on the price of petrol or diesel.

Waterford has had a long and successful history, but risked devaluing its premium branding with the introduction of its Marquis range. Far from causing difficulties, this new range inspired further innovations from the Irish crystal producer. The new lines reflect the findings from customer research and adhere to a shrewd target market strategy. It was important for Waterford to venture into new lines, but only having first established the target markets' buying behaviour and brand perceptions.

The marketing of services is different from the marketing of consumer goods, partly because of the intangibility of the product, the extended marketing mix and the integral role of personnel. It is also, for these reasons, more difficult to create and sustain a competitive advantage. These services marketing issues are well illustrated with this discussion of Whitbread's roll-out of ***TGI Friday's***.

Ahold has expanded around the globe. The company's focus is on successful expansion but not at the expense of society or the natural environment. The company's mission and operating ethos are strongly driven by a desire to behave responsibly socially. Trends in Ahold's marketing environment have encouraged this positioning, but so has a carefully devised corporate vision.

As a company, ***Heineken*** is active throughout the world. As a brand, Heineken is familiar to consumers in North and South America, Africa, Asia-Pacific and most of Europe. The company, though, takes account of the needs of local consumers and has a portfolio containing local brands alongside leading international brands. The company's fortunes have frequently been affected by the forces of the marketing environment.

The ***Games Workshop*** phenomenon has won over many 'fans', from young children playing make-believe battles, to teenagers developing gaming strategies, to adults hooked on the Games Workshop worlds, figures, games, events and modelling opportunities. Recent international expansion implies the concept has more widespread appeal than perhaps even its founders first envisaged.

The marketing environment in the **Turkish ice-cream** market has given many international manufacturers cause for concern over the years, but the leading players have now all established operations in this growing market. The influx of international brands has created problems for existing domestic ice-cream producers, but for some it has provided an opportunity of forging alliances with the global ice-cream giants. For Nestlé, the leading position of arch-rival Unilever has caused additional problems as it attempts to build market share in the Turkish ice-cream market.

The **hotel** sector has witnessed significant growth in recent years and a proliferation of well-defined brands, notably in the **budget** sector. In the marketing of any service, branding and shrewd targeting are known to be important. The operators of the leading budget chains have adhered to these principles as they have expanded their hotel networks. For leading hotelier Whitbread, branding and the development of tightly defined trading concepts have been central to the company's rapid expansion. As with most large hotel operators, Whitbread has more than one brand and chain of hotels, opting to target different brands and concepts at separate target market segments.

ABN AMRO recognizes, with its *internal* and *interactive marketing*, the importance of personnel and the interaction with customers in a service business. The bank has global ambitions, but has not lost sight of local needs and the importance of establishing an operating hierarchy that enables national managers to fully understand their markets.

Chester Zoo has overcome social disquiet about animal captivity owing to its enlightened breeding programmes and animal enclosures. More than a zoo, this popular leisure attraction has developed a sophisticated new marketing strategy designed to bolster its income, uphold its charitable status and fend-off the threats of major neighbouring new leisure attractions.

Carrefour is one of the most successful retailers in the world, now active in Asia Pacific, South America, much of Europe and is even competing in Wal-Mart's home market of North America. Through organic growth and acquisition, Carrefour has grown to become one of the world's leading retailers, but such international expansion has not always been trouble-free.

Theory Notes

The themes in the cases relate to the marketing concepts and frameworks discussed in the accompanying theory note overviews:

T1   Marketing Defined
T2   The Marketing Environment
T3   Buying Behaviour
T4   Marketing Research
T5   Forecasting
T6   Market Segmentation
T7   Competition
T8   The Marketing Mix: Products and People
T9   The Marketing Mix: Place and Channels
T10   The Marketing Mix: Pricing
T11   The Marketing Mix: Promotion – Marketing Communications
T12   Direct Marketing
T13   The Marketing of Services
T14   Industrial, Business-to-Business Marketing
T15   Marketing Planning
T16   International Marketing
T17   Ethics and Social Responsibility

Each theory note summarizes in around 7 or 8 pages the concepts presented in the leading textbooks in 40 to 50 pages. As such, they are usefully concise overviews and have provided examination revision summaries for many students since the first edition of *The Marketing Casebook: Cases and Concepts* was published. The end-of-case cross-referencing of relevant theory notes is intended to prompt students tackling the cases in syndicate groups and seminar conditions to utilize pertinent marketing concepts.

How to Use this Book

Part I   How to Tackle Case Study Analysis and Presentations
Part II   Short Cases for Discussion
Part III   Full Cases
Part IV   Theory Notes
Part V   Glossary of Key Terms
Part VI   Further Readings

Part I: How to Tackle Case Study Analysis and Presentations

Part I's set of guidelines is aimed to assist students new to the world of case study teaching. There are basic rules designed to aid your assimilation of material in the cases, your analyses and the presentation of your solutions or responses. The presentation may be in front of a live audience or in a written report, but either way, there are tips offered on how best to perform. These guidelines cannot be definitive as each tutor has personal expectations, but these notes will enhance your approach and use of these cases.

Part II: Short Cases for Discussion

The one-page 'caselets' of Part II are narrowly focused and are intended for instant seminar discussion or examination case study question revision assistance.

Part III: Full Cases

There are 17 full-length cases in Part III exploring most facets of marketing, as outlined in the preceding matrix of case issues. These are factual cases intended to highlight marketing issues while providing the opportunity to apply marketing concepts and frameworks. Each case is cross-referenced with the most pertinent theory notes. At the end of each case is a summary section and set of issues – questions – to consider. The *Instructor's Manual* addresses these issues, suggesting solutions.

Part IV: Theory Notes

The 17 theory notes in Part IV overview the fundamental concepts and frameworks of modern marketing. Each theory note chapter introduces the subject, explains its main features and summarizes its core concepts. These overviews are included in this casebook to reduce the annoyance experienced by those students desiring 'one-stop' reading and to offer concise guidance for examination revision. Additional texts will only need to be consulted to follow up certain topics if a deeper understanding is required for a term-time assessment paper or report. Each theory note concludes with our suggestions for further reading: UK, US and practitioner texts. Each theory note is cited at the conclusion of the cases that relate to the specific concepts highlighted in the theory note chapter. The theory notes are used by many tutors as lecture handouts, subject to ALCS copyright permissions.

Parts V and VI: Glossary and Further Readings

Part V of *The Marketing Casebook: Cases and Concepts* presents a glossary explaining over 100 key marketing terms, with full cross-referencing for their appearance – and more comprehensive discussion – in the associated theory notes. Part VI summarizes the key recommended further readings from each theory note.

And Finally ....!

If you are a student or marketing practitioner, we hope you find at least some of these cases to be of interest and of assistance in enhancing your understanding of the role and techniques of marketing. If you are a lecturer or in-company trainer, we hope we have made your tutoring a little easier to undertake. Good luck!

Sally Dibb
Lyndon Simkin
University of Warwick

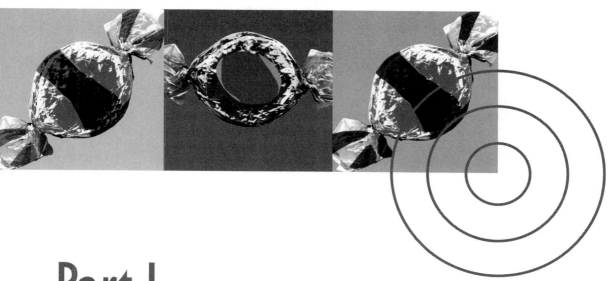

Part I

How to tackle case study analysis

This section contains a set of guidlines aimed at assisting students new to the world of case study teaching.

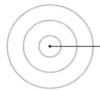

Case Study Analysis

At undergraduate, postgraduate and practitioner levels, the case study is a well-accepted and widely used learning tool. The popularity of case studies in marketing management education is primarily linked to the technique's ability to bridge the gap between marketing theory and practical situations, thus allowing students to apply the concepts which they have learnt. Success in providing case study solutions, as in real life, is largely determined by the nature and quality of the analysis carried out. Learning how to make decisions about case studies in a logical, objective and structured way, is essential. Such decisions must take into consideration all relevant aspects of the marketing and competitive environment, together with an appreciation of the company's resources. In developing the necessary decision-making and analytical skills an understanding of different corporate structures and philosophies and of the implementation of a range of marketing tools is achieved. In addition, the learning process allows the risks and problems associated with managerial decision-making to be experienced at first hand.

Working in seminar or syndicate groups is a popular approach to case study learning. This helps develop group as well as individual skills; a very positive contribution given the extent to which managers in real business situations must work in teams. Developing group skills takes time as individuals learn to cope with the differing opinions and views of colleagues. However, this closely emulates real work situations where a working consensus must be reached. Although preparing cases on an individual basis may appear simpler than taking a range of disparate group views into consideration, a more limited range of alternatives may be developed. Nevertheless, tackling cases individually also builds up analytical and decision-making skills. If a written solution to the case is required, the opportunity to develop report writing skills also arises.

This chapter is divided into three parts. The first considers the fundamentals of situation analysis, which should be undertaken to give a general overview of the key case issues. The second part reviews the five stages of case study analysis which follow the situation analysis, while the third examines the presentation of case findings.

1. Situation Analysis

A thorough understanding of the situation in which a business operates helps to put the problems in the case into context. The areas requiring attention are:

■ Company position (financial, structure, marketing).

- Market analysis.
- External environment, threats and opportunities.
- Competitor situation.

Company's internal position

An appreciation of the company's internal position, drawing attention to particular capabilities and resources, is vital. This analysis should take into consideration company structure, the financial situation and marketing.

COMPANY STRUCTURE

The structure of organizations impacts upon the operational and managerial decisions that are made. By answering the following questions an appropriate overview of company characteristics can be developed. This understanding should be used as a basis for assessing how realistic are the various case solutions eventually recommended:

- Is the organizational structure hierarchical or flat?
- Where does the balance of power lie?
- What is the company's mission statement?
- Does the company have particular philosophies?
- What are the key characteristics of the company?
- Is managerial activity delineated by function?
- Who are the key decision-makers for each functional area?
- How do the lines of communication operate?
- What formal and informal decision-making structures operate?

COMPANY FINANCIAL SITUATION

Various techniques can be used to assess the financial position of the company. An overview of the financial health of the company can be achieved from the business's balance sheet and income statement. Comparing current year figures with those from earlier trading periods is especially informative because it allows changes over time to be mapped.

Financial ratios are calculated using information from the basic balance sheet and income statement (see Table I.1 below). These ratios can be used to achieve greater financial insight into an organization and can be compared with ratios from competing organizations to allow a better understanding of the company's relative position. It can also be useful to carry out a break-even analysis and to try and build a better understanding of the relationship between supply and demand.

| **Table 1.1** | *Key Financial Ratios* |

- *Profitability Ratios*
These ratios measure financial and operating efficiency by assessing the organization's ability to generate profit from revenue and money invested.

Name of Ratio	*Calculated*
i) Gross profit margin	$\dfrac{\text{Sales} - \text{Cost of goods sold}}{\text{Sales}}$

This shows the total margin available to meet operating expenses and generate a profit

| ii) Net profit margin | $\dfrac{\text{Profit after taxes}}{\text{Sales}}$ |

Sometimes called return on sales, this ratio shows after tax profit per £ (pound) spent

| iii) Return on assets | $\dfrac{\text{Profit after taxes}}{\text{Total assets}}$ |

This ratio measures the company's return on total investment

| iv) Return on net worth | $\dfrac{\text{Profit after taxes}}{\text{Total shareholders' equity}}$ |

Also referred to as return on stockholders' equity, this ratio gives a measure of the rate of return on shareholders' equity

- *Liquidity Ratios*
These ratios are used to demonstrate the company's ability to meet current liabilities and to ensure solvency.

Name of Ratio	*Calculated*
i) Current ratio	$\dfrac{\text{Current assets}}{\text{Current liabilities}}$

This demonstrates the company's ability to satisfy short-term liabilities

| ii) Quick ratio | $\dfrac{\text{Current assets} - \text{Inventory}}{\text{Current liabilities}}$ |

Also referred to as the acid-test ratio, this demonstrates the company's ability to meet current liabilities, in the period in which they are due, without resorting to the sale of stock

| iii) Inventory to net working capital | $\dfrac{\text{Inventory}}{\text{Current assets} - \text{Current liabilities}}$ |

Indicates the degree to which company working capital is tied up in stock

- *Leverage Ratios*
This group of ratios helps in the assessment of the company's responsiveness to debt and ability to meet repayments as scheduled.

Name of Ratio	*Calculated*
i) Debt to assets ratio	$\dfrac{\text{Total liabilities}}{\text{Total assets}}$

Indicates the extent to which borrowed funds have been employed to finance the company's operations

ii) Debt to equity ratio

$$\frac{\text{Total liabilities}}{\text{Total shareholders' equity}}$$

This shows the balance of equity provided by the owners, and funds provided by creditors

iii) Long-term debt to equity ratio

$$\frac{\text{Long-term liabilities}}{\text{Total shareholders' equity}}$$

This ratio allows the balance between owners' equity and liabilities to be viewed in context of the company's overall capital structure

-Activity Ratios

These ratios can show how effectively the company generates sales and profit from assets.

Name of Ratio	Calculated
i) Total assets turnover	$\dfrac{\text{Sales}}{\text{Total assets}}$

This ratio, which signals the level of sales productivity and utilization of total assets, can be compared with the industry average to show whether the volume of business generated justifies the level of asset investment

ii) Fixed assets turnover	$\dfrac{\text{Sales}}{\text{Fixed assets}}$

Measures both sales productivity and utilization of equipment and plant

iii) Inventory turnover	$\dfrac{\text{Sales}}{\text{Inventory}}$

This measure of inventory turnover can be compared with the industry norm to show whether the company carries too large or small an inventory

---

When using financial ratios it is important to be aware of the following points. First, ratios represent a snapshot of a company's financial state at a particular point in time. When comparing the results from more than one ratio, it is therefore necessary to ensure that the figures applied are from the same time period and calculated according to similar accounting conventions. Second, how ratios are interpreted and used is more important than the figures in isolation. To understand the significance of a particular ratio, it is essential to understand all of the internal and external factors that have caused the financial position reflected in the figures.

Once the financial analysis has been completed, it is necessary to pull together the different strands of the overall financial picture and identify which issues are likely to impact upon the case solutions which are recommended.

COMPANY MARKETING ORGANIZATION

Evaluating how the company handles its marketing should systematically cover all aspects of the marketing strategy and programmes. This will include marketing research processes and marketing information systems, maintenance of the product portfolio including new product development, pricing strategies, distribution policy including the policing and management of distributors, all aspects of marketing communications, personnel, customer and after sales service.

Market analysis

Understanding market structure and customer requirements is a fundamental stage in any case analysis. The following key questions should be addressed:

MARKET STRUCTURE

- What is the market size?
- What are the trends in market size – is it increasing or decreasing? How quickly?
- How is the market structured? What evidence is there of segments?
- Which segment(s) or customer group(s) is the company targeting?

CUSTOMERS

- Who are the customers?
- What are the customers like?
- For what purpose do they buy the product/service? What are their needs?
- What features do they look for in the product/service?
- What is the buying process?
- What factors impact upon and who influences them as they buy?
- How do they feel about the product/service?
- How do they feel about alternative suppliers?

Clear insight into the customers who make up a particular market is essential to organizational success (see T3, in Part IV). Having conducted the *market analysis*, it is necessary to assess how effectively the company is reaching its target customers and whether it is geared for expected changes in customer needs and/or market structure. This analysis will impact on the solution(s) that are selected.

External environment

A wide range of factors from the external marketing environment impact upon the well being of an organization (see T2, in Part IV). These include economic, political, social, cultural, technological, legal and regulatory issues. Monitoring these factors is important because changes can have a major impact on an organization's business dealings. Recognizing the significance of such changes early on can help companies to maximize the positive benefits and minimize the detrimental effects.

Early warning of the effects of environmental factors can be achieved by assessing the potential opportunities/threats presented by changes. In case study analysis, as in real life, it is often necessary to extrapolate trends and make predictions regarding the level of future change. It is helpful to remember that most potential threats can also be viewed as opportunities should an organization have the resources and interest to pursue them.

Competition

Understanding the competitive structure of markets helps companies put their marketing options into perspective (see T2 and T7, in Part IV). From the customer's viewpoint, buying decisions are based on the strengths and weaknesses of a particular player relative to other available choices. There are a number of key questions that should be considered in relation to an organization's competitive situation:

■ Who are the key players?

■ How is market share divided amongst competing organizations?

■ What competitive positions do the players occupy, who is market leader, which companies are challengers, followers and nichers?

■ How aggressive are the competing organizations and what are the trends? Is it possible to identify fast movers?

■ On what basis are key competitors competing? What are their differential advantages, are these sustainable and how are they supported with marketing programmes?

Understanding the answers to these questions allows the case analyst to fully appreciate the relative competitive strengths and weaknesses of the company and to assess whether or not different case solutions are realistic. It may also be possible to use this information to predict how key competitors are likely to respond to different case solutions.

2. The Case Study Process

Many attempts have been made to summarize the case study approach into a process. The following five stages are often cited:

1. Understand and analyse the problem.
2. Derive alternative solutions.
3. Analyse alternative solutions.
4. Recommend the 'best' alternative.
5. Implement the chosen solution.

Understand and analyse case problem areas

After the situational analysis has been conducted, a clear view of the problems/ key issues set out in the case study must be developed. Although the use of specific case questions will impact upon exactly where the key areas lie, the company and other analyses undertaken will usually have revealed a range of problem areas which need to be addressed. Formally listing these issues helps ensure that no omissions are made when alternative scenarios are considered. Any specific questions can be tackled once these problem areas have been identified.

One way to make this assessment of the case material and the core issues is to carry out a *marketing audit* (see Kotler, 2000). The marketing audit offers a systematic way of considering all aspects of the company's marketing set-up, within a pre-determined structure (see Table I.2). Carrying out a marketing audit should aid the analysis by:

- describing current activities and results: sales, costs, profits, prices, etc;
- gathering data about customers, competitors and relevant environmental developments;
- exploring opportunities for improving marketing strategies;
- providing an overall database to be used in developing marketing strategies and programmes for implementation.

Table I.2	The Marketing Audit

Part1: **The Marketing Environment Audit**

Economic-Demographic	Markets
Technological	Customers
Political	Competitors
Legal-Regulatory	Distributors and Dealers
Cultural-Social	Suppliers
Ecological	Facilitators in the Channel
	Publics

Part II: **Marketing Strategy Audit**
Business Mission
Marketing Objectives and Goals
Strategy

Part III: **Marketing Organization Audit**
Formal Structure
Functional Efficiency
Interface Efficiency

Part IV: **Marketing Systems Audit**
Marketing Information System (MIS)
Marketing Planning System
Marketing Control System
New Product Development System

Part V: **Marketing Productivity Audit**
Profitability Analysis
Cost-Effective Analysis

Part VI: **Marketing Functions Audit**
Products
Price
Distribution
Promotion
Personnel

Not all cases require or have sufficient information for a formal audit nor do they necessarily present sufficient information for such as an audit. The initial *situational analysis* may well give adequate focus and understanding. In more complex cases covering dynamic and competitive markets, the marketing audit can assist in sifting through the market and company data to identify more thoroughly the most pertinent issues.

When developing a list of problem areas, it is necessary to distinguish clearly between symptoms of problems and the problems themselves. Symptoms are defined as the outward signs of an underlying problem or problems. For instance, symptoms might include falling sales, declining profits and reducing market share. The problem may be poor understanding of customers, signalling a need for closer links with customers and regular feedback from the marketplace.

The identification of symptoms and problems should start with the most major problem(s). The associated symptoms can then be pinpointed and listed. Minor difficulties, whether or not related to the major problems, should be kept until after the main problem(s) have been signalled. It is helpful to signal whether the problems are impacting on the company's position in the short, medium or long term. This makes it easier to predict the likely effect of the problems on the company's objectives and plans.

Derive alternative solutions

Selecting an appropriate case solution is an iterative process that should start by generating a number of alternatives. Each potential solution must relate to the case's key problem area(s) and offer a realistic way of solving it. Make sure that the alternatives suggested are distinct and different. Spending time reviewing many similar solutions can be counter-productive. Detailed fine-tuning can be carried out at a later stage, once a selection has been made. In some circumstances it is helpful to frame the generation of alternatives around the following questions:

- Where is the company now?
- How did it get to its current position?
- Where does it want to go/what does it want to achieve?
- How can it achieve what it wants, and head to where it wants to go?

The understanding of the organization's current position should have been achieved through the *situational analysis*, but explicitly framing the first two questions helps ensure that these issues from the earlier analysis are not overlooked. At this stage it ought to be possible to exclude the more unrealistic solutions, so that the more likely options can be analysed further.

Analyse alternative solutions

The next step is to critically evaluate the suitability of the solutions identified. This should involve a formal assessment of the advantages and disadvantages of every alternative. Each proposal should be considered within the context of the company, market, competitor and environmental analyses that have already been carried out. Conducting 'What if…?' analysis – where attempts are made to predict the likely outcome(s) of alternative solutions – can be a useful input. It is helpful to formally list each advantage and disadvantage with, if possible, a ranking of the relative importance of each. This ranking should help identify the best solution.

Recommend the 'best' alternative

Providing that the case analysis has been thorough, selecting the best solution should not be too complex. Whichever option is chosen, the environmental, competitor and market analyses must be double-checked to ensure that the solution is consistent with prevailing market conditions. It is rarely possible to identify a course of action that is ideal in all respects, so it is helpful to consider both the acceptability of the various options and the associated risks. Limited data availability and/or ambiguous market conditions may create problems. However, it should be remembered that managers must often make decisive decisions when only limited information is available.

Once a decision has been made, arguments should be prepared supporting the choice(s). In some circumstances, part of the recommendations may be based on the success of initial actions. Some flexibility will be required in responding to the differing circumstances that may arise. It may be helpful to develop *decision trees* that show different routes to the final objectives, depending on the short-term reactions to the recommendations.

Implement the chosen solution

Ensuring the recommended plans and marketing programmes can be implemented is as fundamental to case study learning as the analyses and choice of the 'best' solution.

- At which target groups is the solution aimed?
- How will the company's offering be positioned?
- Exactly how will the solution be implemented?
  - Marketing mix proposals (product, people, price, promotion and distribution)
  - What processes will need to be set up to ensure that implementation occurs?
- Which departments/individuals will take responsibility for the day-to-day implementation?
- When will the solution be implemented?
- What will be the likely cost implications of implementing the solution?
- What are the expected benefits of implementing the solution – revenues, cash flow, competitive position, customer perceptions, etc.?
- What will be the relevant performance measures and success criteria?

In real situations, implementation may be affected by a range of interacting factors and unforeseen circumstances. For this reason, it is helpful to recommend a *contingency plan*, to be followed in the event of the initial recommendations being unsuccessful. These back-up suggestions should be limited to the key recommendations and should not go into too much detail.

3. Presenting the Case Study Findings

There are various formats that can be used to report the findings of case study analysis, including an informal discussion, a structured presentation, or a written report. Learning how to present case solutions, like the analysis itself, takes time. While there is a strong personal element in presentational style, the following guidelines are intended to help develop effectiveness in this area. After all, marketers must be able to make professional presentations and write good reports!

Formal presentations

Case study presentations can become turgid, clumsy and monotonous. With care and imagination such sessions can be easily transformed into a lively and interesting forum for debate. The following simple suggestions should assist in this process:

- Keep repetition of the basic case facts to a minimum. After all, other students will probably have read the case study anyway. There is nothing worse than hearing group after group present the same basic material over and over.

- Try to maintain eye contact with the audience. This can be achieved by not 'talking to' the overhead screen/overhead projector/computer/board.

- Avoid the use of fully scripted notes. Prompt cards inserted between overhead transparencies or 'key word' notes can be helpful. Using these kinds of prompts become easier with practice.

- Keep visual material as simple as possible. An audience will have difficulty taking in highly complex tables or visual aids that are covered in text. Clever use of colour and diagrams can make such visual aids easier to follow. Presentation slides, whether on computer or transparencies must *never* be too 'wordy' or detailed.

- Use lively material, add the occasional touch of humour and try to involve the audience. Attempt to vary the presentation format: do not always opt for the formal approach with the stand-up and 'lecture' style.

- Avoid using too much material for the presentation time allocated.

- Do not use too many presenters: hand-over time is wasteful and boring for the audience.

- Rehearse! Never be surprised by your own material. Think through, in advance, the points that need making at each stage of the presentation. Also check equipment and computer links — making sure you know how to use them.

- Introduce the presentation, its aims and presenters. Conclude with a brief summary of key points.

Writing reports

The most appropriate structure for writing up case analysis will depend on the student's or tutor's objectives as well as on individual style and any organization constraints regarding format. Report writing is a skill developed through practice, which offers considerable rewards when mastered. The purpose of the case study report is to present analyses and recommendations, demonstrating that a full and thorough understanding of the situation has been achieved. The emphasis should be on reasoned argument to support the key recommendations and should not merely reproduce the information presented in the case. Students often get caught in the trap of quoting verbatim from the source material and presenting raw material without offering an interpretation.

Much has been written about report structure. This should be an area of concern for student and tutor alike. Too often reports are submitted with imperceptible structure, verbose paragraphs and no sense of direction or clear recommendations. While it is impossible to present a standard report format for all circumstances, certain generalizations are possible. Essentially, the report is presenting the following:

- *Background to the case study:* This should give a simple overview of the company/industry and may include an indication of the nature of the market.

- *Understanding of the underlying problem(s):* This will probably focus on the areas highlighted by the tutor or in case questions. The problem should be briefly stated at this stage.

- *Analysis of case study material:* The analysis part of the case study will involve the most extensive and detailed discussion. This is where the student reports back on the company and market analyses undertaken. The length of this part of the report will probably mean that a series of sub-headings is used to add structure and clarity to the discussion.

- *Recommendations with justifications:* The recommendations represent the outcomes of the case study analysis and should fall naturally out of the discussion in the report. The report itself should have '*told a story*', so there are no surprises about the recommended course of action.

Every report is different but the following simple checklist of section headings may be helpful to consider when structuring the final report document.

- I.   Executive/management summary
- II.   Contents
- III. Introduction (including objectives)
- IV.   Background to the problem
- V.   Analysis (divided into relevant sections)
- VI.   Conclusions and recommendations
- VII. Bibliography/references
- VIII. Appendices (supporting data and facts)

POINTS TO REMEMBER:

1. The executive summary should provide a succinct, one or two page account of the entire report. It should explain the background to the case, discuss the key issues and themes, report on the analysis and list the recommendations.

2. Make the report as user-friendly as possible, with numbered sections and pages, a contents list and sub-headings. References should be sourced within the main body of the report and then listed in full in the bibliography. Diagrams and tables should also be properly numbered, labelled and referenced.

3. Make the writing style as clear as possible. Avoid long sentences and jargon. If jargon is unavoidable, use a glossary to explain terms that are not in common usage.

4. Support arguments with appropriate sources (references, statistics, quotes, examples, comparisons, etc.), as available. This considerably adds credibility to the discussion.

5. Use data from the case with care. If possible interpret the information: this may involve extrapolating trends or making predictions regarding the likely outcome of certain activities. Only use data that are relevant to the point being made.

6. Appendices should include any relevant material that would clutter the main body of the document. Each appendix should be referred to from within the main body of the report and listed in the contents section of the report.

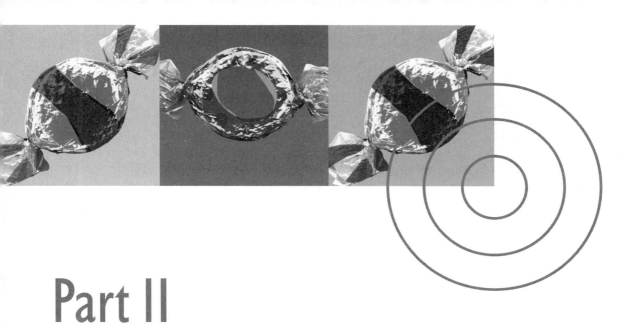

Part II

Short cases for discussion

This section contains narrowly focused 'caselets' intended for instant seminar discussion or examination case study question revision assistance

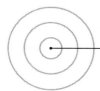

Short Case 1: Ethical Marketing GM Foods: Supermarkets versus the Regulators

In 1999 there was yet another food scare, but this time with implications for retailers, producers, consumers and regulators. Leading agrochemicals businesses such as Monsanto and Zeneca had produced strains of soya, tomatoes and even tobacco, genetically modified to exaggerate their proliferation and ability to ward off disease and pests. So soon after the BSE scare in beef production, this further instance of natural farming techniques being artificially aided caused great concern. Despite government assurances, a NOP opinion poll claimed over half of the general public was concerned about eating genetically modified food, 88 per cent was aware of GM foods while 60 per cent worried about eating them.

The reaction from the major supermarket groups was swift. They promised to seek assurances from suppliers about the content of GM ingredients in products delivered to them. With this clarification, the retailers intended providing better labelling to enable their customers to make their own choice about whether to buy GM-modified foods. While seeking to improve labelling, the supermarkets' initial responses were varied:

- Iceland: 'We are unsure of the long-term effects of GM foods'.
- Somerfield: 'Until the EU addresses the issue there is not a lot we can do'.
- Sainsbury's: 'We are looking hard to find alternatives but have to look at the long term'.
- Tesco: 'Customer calls peak every time there is media interest'.
- Asda: 'The food has been passed as safe by the government … we are taking a responsible approach'.

Although a diverse set of views, the implication was that those with political control had deemed GM food safe to consume, so until they altered their stance, it was to be stocked by the retailers. Politicians joined the debate, with many MPs calling for a moratorium on the sale of GM foods pending further safety testing. While Prime Minister Tony Blair stated he was happy to eat GM foods, the government did promise additional research funding. The difficulty for the supermarkets was that government passed the GM products as safe for consumption, despite growing consumer fears.

Tesco and Safeway had already clearly labelled GM modified lines. Their rivals followed suit. Sainsbury's set up a dedicated hot-line to help address consumers' queries and fears. A third of all customer enquiries to Sainsbury's related to the GM food issue. Iceland was more proactive, immediately banning GM ingredients from its own label lines, but still stocking manufacturer brands containing GM ingredients, notably soya-based lines. The remaining supermarkets in conjunction with the British Retail Consortium put pressure on the government to make the decisions about GM foods. Somerfield had lobbied the US government since 1997 and in 1999 switched to pressurizing the British government and EU regulators. Ultimately, most supermarket managements were forced, by consumer pressure, to remove GM-modified ingredients from their own label lines and de-stock manufacturer proprietary brands which failed to remove GM-modified ingredients.

Discussion themes

1. What would an ethical marketing policy have been under these circumstances?
2. How could supermarketers have behaved in a socially responsible manner?

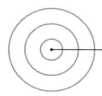

Short Case 2: The Marketing Environment Formula 1 and Tobacco

Throughout the 1980s and 1990s, the anti-smoking lobby had grown in stature. Governments banned TV tobacco advertising and most employers created no smoking areas in offices, canteens and on the shop floor. Some even prohibit smoking totally. Restaurants and bars are increasingly encouraged by the government to provide no smoking areas and air purification equipment, public transport is largely a no smoking zone and commercial carriers such as British Airways ban in-flight smoking. Nevertheless, statistics indicate that the majority of youths smoke, particularly teenage girls. Most forecourt shops, CTN newsagents, supermarkets and convenience stores stock the leading brands of cigarettes. Even with billion dollar lawsuits and the US Federal Government's aggressive stance against the major cigarette manufacturers, the industry is very much alive.

As in any industry, for the manufacturers there is the need to promote their brands against rivals' products. Advertising in any form has been ruled against by EU legislators. An alternative was sports sponsorship: football competitions, tennis tournaments, horse racing all received lucrative sponsorship from the major cigarette producers. Perhaps the sponsorship arrangement with the highest profile, though, was the tobacco industry's involvement with Formula 1 (F1) grand prix motor racing. The famous black cars carrying the John Player Special design led the way in the 1970s, followed by many years of success on the track for the Marlborough-sponsored McLaren team. Winfield now supports once-dominant Williams. Half of Jordan's sponsorship of £38m comes from Gallaher's Benson & Hedges. Although F1 receives sponsorship from many other businesses, including car manufacturers and clothing producers, to management consultants, the tobacco industry has for 30 years provided the bulk of the sport's income excluding television rights.

The world audience tuning in to live coverage of F1 races is the primary reason for the huge amounts of sponsorship poured into this sport. Gallaher openly states that F1 is seen as a major advertising opportunity with the Benson & Hedges brand on television, in the press, in magazines and all over the media, aggressively putting the brand in front of a world-wide audience.

At the start of the 1999 season the newest team to join the F1 roadshow, British American Racing, revealed its two cars, which were very different in appearance to each other. Jacques Villeneuve's car was red and white, matching Lucky Strike cigarette's – a leading brand in Latin America – pack design, while Ricardo Zonta's car promoted Far East cigarette brand 555. British American Racing, owned by British American Tobacco (BAT), was clearly promoting the tobacco industry and the Lucky Strike and 555 brands specifically. Some onlookers felt the cars resembled cigarette packets with wheels! Here was a case of a sponsor truly attempting to maximize the brand exposure gained from its financial outlay. Not all teams are quite so blatant with their tobacco links. Japanese brand Mild 7 supports the Benetton team, but the Italian clothing giant's own colours dominate its cars.

For BAT, ownership directly of its own team has stemmed from the impending ban of tobacco sponsorship of F1 motor racing. There are few prominent places for tobacco advertising and promotion. F1 is one. The EU and the British government are banning tobacco sponsorship in an attempt to reduce teenage smoking and the health risks in general associated with this market. BAT hopes that by owning a team and naming its cars and racing team after its products, it might get around some of the impending regulation changes for tobacco companies sponsoring motor racing.

The European ban will come into effect in 2006 but the F1 'circus' visits Australia, Japan, North America and a growing number of non-EU countries. China, South Korea, Malaysia, Indonesia and South Africa have shown interest in staging F1 races as the industry seeks to attract the huge sums of sponsorship required to keep a leading team going: between £30m and £60m annually. Most Asian countries are much more relaxed about smoking than the EU. The economic collapse of these *Tiger* economies has put a question mark over these new entrants staging events. China's scheduled 1999 race was cancelled after it failed to meet financial commitments. While the F1 managers hoped to work around the EU's ban on tobacco advertising and sponsorship by seeking new territories, this unexpected collapse of the Pacific Rim economy placed any hope of attracting new venues in doubt. As a result, it is possible FIA may well have to comply with the EU's desire for a world-wide ban on F1 tobacco sponsorship.

Discussion themes

1. How has the marketing environment impacted on Formula 1 racing?
2. How else could the cigarette producers promote their brands?

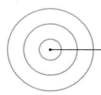

Short Case 3: Non-Business Marketing
Marketing the NSPCC

The National Society for the Prevention of Cruelty to Children (NSPCC) pledged to raise £300m in just 12 months through a multimedia campaign. This was 6 times more than the charity's usual target of £50m. Through its *Full Stop* campaign, the NSPCC hopes to bring an end to child cruelty within a generation. Following the trend for provocative charity advertising, the NSPCC campaign utilized an unsettling series of television advertisements, depicting various toys and other children's icons, such as Action Man, Rupert Bear and the Spice Girls, covering their eyes against a soundtrack of shouting parents and crying children. Some 3,500 posters carrying the same message appeared, with the NSPCC web site offering support. There was also a mailing of leaflets to every UK household bearing the message, *Together we can stop cruelty to children once and for all.* The intention was to capitalize on the awareness created by the advertising campaign. At the centre of the campaign was a pledge document, through which the public and businesses were invited to donate funds to the charity.

The Campaign Timescale

- *Early March*: PR campaign, which continued through to Easter. Public address systems at airports and railway stations broadcast reminders.
- *March 9*: 'Early warning' letter to the NSPCC's 160,000 'best donors', alerting them to the campaign and seeking their support.
- *March 15*: Updated web site went 'live', encouraging people to sign the NSPCC pledge on-line.
- *March 16*: Three-week TV and poster campaign began. Sixty-second adverts in the first week were followed by thirty and ten second versions. 48-sheet posters on 3,500 sites delivered 55% national coverage with 21 opportunities per person to be seen. 4,000 sites for 6-sheet posters were also used.
- *March 22*: Personalized letters to just under one million existing donors went out. Delivery of door-drop letter and pledge document to 23 million homes began. Press advertisements appeared, offering an alternative vehicle for signing the pledge.
- *March 27–28*: 'Call to action weekend', with volunteers manning 2,000 sites.

Source: Adapted from 'NSPCC aims to convert abuse anger into cash', *Marketing*, 25 March 1999, pp. 37–38.

The NSPCC hoped that 20 per cent of its donations would come from businesses. There were many ways in which businesses could become involved. The NSPCC developed a special toolkit that explained some of the sponsorship opportunities and cause-related marketing possibilities. Microsoft, which sponsors NSPCC advertising and holds fundraisers for the charity, is one company that already had links with the charity. The software business was happy to be associated with a cause that supports child welfare. The NSPCC campaign's scale and use of the promotional mix ingredients were certainly impressive and award winning.

Discussion themes

1. Why is it more difficult to promote a charity or a service than a consumer good such as a Sony Walkman?

2. Which ingredient(s) of the promotional mix might be most appropriate in promoting a charitable cause? Why?

Short Case 4: Marketing Mix
Private Health Care

For many employees a benefit offered by their employers is private health insurance. Until the 1980s, BUPA dominated this market with health insurance policies and a network of private hospitals and clinics. The primary benefits to customers were claimed to be speedy consultations and treatment – avoiding state hospital queues – and hotel-like facilities in hospitals for patients and their relatives. However, in recent years demand has levelled off with only around 12 per cent of the population buying private health cover. Competitors to BUPA have been far from inactive. Private hospital operators have proliferated and many new sites have opened. Many mainstream insurance companies have launched their own private health insurance schemes: Norwich Union, Legal & General, Royal and Sun Alliance, and Abbey National's *Abbey Healthcare* have combined to erode BUPA's market share from 60 per cent to 40 per cent. Market challenger PPP has really made in-roads, taking 30 per cent of the £2 billion market.

For all companies operating in this market, the fundamental problem is the complexity of the 'product' being offered. BUPA's group marketing director Pat Stafford believes that consumers – as with all financial services – are not sure what they have bought. The product needs simplifying and its benefits stressing. Accordingly, BUPA invested £50 million in developing *Call BUPA First*, its paperless system of claims. Customer service became a priority with better training of personnel, new procedures and a responsive attitude to customer requirements. A brand building initiative was launched to explain policy benefits. The strapline *You're Amazing* was at the centre of this brand building, emphasizing the importance of customers being able quickly to deal with any ailments or medical concerns without undue inconvenience or delay. To ensure BUPA is fully customer oriented, the business was divided into five distinct divisions: healthcare, nursing homes, hospitals, the Spanish subsidiary Sanitas, plus dental/travel insurance. Each SBU was allocated top-level marketers from consumer goods and services backgrounds.

Research identified the general public to be largely cynical about health insurance, creating a significant challenge for BUPA's expanding team of marketers. The situation was further complicated for BUPA because it targeted both consumer and business-to-business market segments. A growing number of householders are being enticed into the private healthcare market by seductive television advertising, direct mail and offers 'piggy-backing' on existing contents, motor or home insurance schemes. The core market remains, though, the corporate sector with large and small businesses providing policies for their employees along with pension schemes and company cars. The marketing packages required to entice a private consumer at home into protecting his or her family and the proposition necessary to persuade ICI or JCB to buy into a scheme for thousands of their employees, are both quite different. BUPA intends not only to effectively defend its position against the growing band of competitors, but to successfully attract new category users into the private health sector.

Discussion themes

1. Why is customer service so important to BUPA's product offer?
2. Why must BUPA develop separate marketing mix executions for its consumer and business target markets? How might these marketing mixes differ?

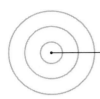

Short Case 5: New Product Development Smelly Fabrics

Exotic flavours and names ...

> Ambrosia, Apple, Bouquet, Coffee, Cola, Eau de Cologne, Fidji, Forest, Lavender, Lemon, Lime, Orange, Peppermint, Pineapple, Pizza, Rose, Strawberry, Tropical Paradise, Vanilla, Wild Flowers, Floral Bouquet, Jasmine and Banana.

The connection? Foods? Paint colours? Brand names?

The link is they are all odours. Smells! Courtaulds Textiles – now part of Sara Lee – has developed an innovative range of *Fragrance Fabrics*. The 'micro-encapsulated' scent is added to the fabric through an acrylic polymer and applied in solution to the fabric during its final production process, the stenter run. The fragrance is released via rubbing of the fabric, which breaks the scent 'capsules'. After over 30 washes at 40°C, the fragrance is still evident.

The Japanese producers of the micro-capsules carried out extensive skin sensitivity tests at the Japanese Laboratory for Cutaneous (Skin) Health. Courtaulds Textiles' subsidiary Jersey Underwear Ltd has now found ways of adhering the fragrances to 150g cotton single Jersey and to 150g cotton Lycra fabrics. The core fragrances in demand include:

- *Lemon*. A refreshing scent characteristic for its uplifting properties, associated with cleansing and ability to revive the skin.
- *Orange*. Slightly sweet scent known for calming qualities.
- *Rose*. The 'queen' of essential oils, associated with beauty, femininity and purity, and a relaxed state of mind.
- *Vanilla*. Commonly linked with taste, vanilla has a distinctive smell which is obtained from the pods of a beautiful tropical orchid.
- *Lavender*. A beautiful scent with endearing qualities, peaceful sleep and balancing properties. Widely used in perfumery and with an oil base to ease away muscular aches and pains.
- *Apple and Strawberry*. These fresh and fruity fragrances are the essence of a sunny summer.
- *Forest and Wild Flowers*. Mirroring the scents of woodland, these two fragrances combine tranquillity and freshness.

So why the excitement? In fabric development, innovations tend to be based around texture and durability: for example, the stretchy Lycra phenomenon. New product development rarely has been so innovative in this market and for Courtaulds Textiles the result has been a competitive edge over rivals. The main target market is sportswear: clothing which with this new technology emits a pleasant odour when the wearer becomes hot and sweaty on the squash court or in the gym. However, it is not only overly hot sports enthusiasts for whom this new product technology has appeal. The technology also exists for intelligent fabrics which can detect, for example, when a women is menstrual, releasing lavender or soothing rose fragrances.

It would seem that in the next few years, many clothing applications will be found to combine with the micro-encapsulated scents. The task for the fabric manufacturers' marketers is to promote these attributes to the garment makers, whose marketers will need to entice retailers to stock these new lines and consumers to trial these fragrant products.

Discussion themes

1. Discuss the stages of the new product development process and how they might be applied to these 'smelly' fabrics?

2. For such an innovative product, why is it important for marketers to understand the product adoption process?

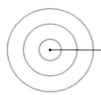

Short Case 6: Promotion
Surprising Advertising

Advertising is no longer confined to the press, magazines, television, radio and cinema. Advertising increasingly appears in unusual locations: Volkswagen promotion on the handle of a petrol pump, an advert on a bus ticket or even the promotion of clean air in Wales on the back of a dirty van. The industry refers to the use of such media as ambient advertising. According to outdoor advertising specialist Concord, 'ambient advertising is non-traditional out-of-home advertising'. At the Atlanta Olympic Games, sprinter Linford Christie promoted Puma by wearing contact lenses featuring the sportswear brand. Devotees of the new approach believe that ambient advertising has huge potential.

Companies commissioning promotional work involving ambient media have been pleased to discover that free press coverage can result. Ben and Jerry's, the American ice-cream brand, attracted considerable publicity when it hired cows to act as mobile advertising hoardings. The animals, which were grazing alongside a major motorway, were fitted with coats sporting an ice-cream advertisement. Beck's beer was promoted using an advertisement grown (mown) in a 30-acre field sited alongside a heavily used railway line. In addition to identifying new surfaces as replacement billboards, ambient advertising makes use of existing objects as promotional sites. Elida Faberge advertised its Vaseline Intensive Care deodorant by attaching fake roll-on containers to the hanging grab-straps on the London Underground. The aim was to draw attention to the product at a time when commuters might be particularly amenable to considering its benefits. Unilever targeted consumers' sense of smell by impregnating the scent of Radion washing powder onto the reverse of bus tickets.

Views about the effectiveness of ambient advertising vary. One observer criticized the Beck's beer field:

> Ambient campaigns don't always target a specific audience. The Beck's advert was successful because of the press coverage it generated but as an advertisement it didn't target the correct demographic spread. It targeted a whole commuter train of people, only a small number of whom like to drink Beck's.

The Media Initiatives agency believes that ambient is fine in certain circumstances, but must be linked to an appropriate medium for the brand, as in the example of the Vaseline Intensive Care deodorant. The decision to advertise breath mints Clorets on the lids of curry takeaway boxes was clearly an appropriate one. With just 12 per cent of outdoor spend devoted to ambient advertising, it remains a relatively small part of the industry. Growth of this novel area, though, is considerable.

Discussion themes

1. Why must the media selection for ambient advertising reflect the characteristics of the advertised brand?

2. Think of other uses for ambient advertising: brands and media executions.

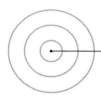

Short Case 7: Direct Marketing
Boxman on the Internet

Marketers all over the world are turning to the Internet. American investment bank Morgan Stanley has suggested that in the next 5 years or so, approximately 5 per cent of world retail trade and 11 per cent of business-to-business transactions will be conducted on the Internet. The best Internet selling opportunities look to be in the areas of financial services, travel, books and software, but sales of video and music products also have considerable potential. Globally, the sector is already buoyant, with thousands of different sites selling on-line CDs.

Boxman is one of the music companies which plans to capitalize on Internet selling opportunities. According to its web site, Boxman is a music retail company which aims, 'to sell more music to more people, faster, cheaper and more conveniently through the new possibility provided by the Internet'. Boxman sees the Internet as a means for reaching a mass market, through mass communications to sell mass products. The company hopes that it will be able to satisfy the needs of consumers with a diverse mix of musical tastes, whether or not they are currently familiar with the Internet. Boxman offers six key values:

- *Simplicity.* The web site is easy to navigate and simple to use, so consumers can find, pay for and receive their requirements with ease.

- *Speed.* Boxman is sympathetic to the relatively high costs of Internet connections in Europe, so use of the site and receipt of the music is high speed.

- *Ease of use.* Through its technical collaboration with IBM, Boxman has provided a site which is easily accessible and which communicates effectively with even the most inexperienced Internet user.

- *Value.* Savings achieved by avoiding the usual distribution costs associated with the sale of music are shared with Boxman customers. For example, a chart product sold in the high street for £14.00, is available for just £10.00 from Boxman.

- *Security.* Boxman is aware of consumer concerns about security, particularly in relation to Internet sites and the transmission of credit card details. Boxman offers consumers security in the sophisticated payment system it uses and by ensuring delivery in a short time.

- *Real added value.* Boxman has a clearly stated intention of offering the consumer access to a diverse mix of music at competitive prices from the comfort of home.

'Boxman is an attitude, a clever way of life, which is simple, practical and current'.

Discussion themes

1. What is direct marketing? How can it be used to sell products such as those supplied by Boxman?

2. How is the Internet altering the sales and marketing approaches of many businesses?

Short Case 8: Marketing Operations McDonald's Controls

Mighty McDonald's was established in 1940 when Dick and Mac McDonald opened up in San Bernadino in California. Ray Kroc, credited with the chain's global ambitions, bought the rights to develop the brand in 1955 and created McDonald's Corporation and the famous golden arches. Every day, from Moscow to Hong Kong, McDonald's serves over 38 million people, including a million in the UK where the company enjoys a 75 per cent share of the hamburger market. Nearest rival Burger King, despite massive recent expansion, can manage only 15 per cent. There are 23,000 McDonald's restaurants in 110 countries producing sales of close to £25 billion. Leading branding consultancy Interbrand ranked McDonald's as the most recognized brand in the world, beating even Coca-Cola.

Whether in Lisbon, Chicago or Manchester, a McDonald's restaurant is instantly evident, with its familiar layout, ambience, design and 'feel' the envy of most services marketers. The menus change slightly to reflect local tastes, but overall there is consistency in the product the world over. Alcohol is available in Lousanne, while incredible ice-cream desserts are on offer in Porto, but everywhere the core dishes are the same: the Big Mac, chicken nuggets and Filet-O-Fish. McDonald's is available as eat-in or as a drive-through take-away. McDonald's caters for a wide range of customers: single adults snacking, sales reps lunching, children partying or teenagers dining before going to a movie.

When McDonald's first came to the UK, it had to educate its customers to expect unbuttered rolls, no knives or forks and no table service. This may seem strange to a generation that has grown up in fast-food restaurants, but it was a major marketing task. Staff, too, had to be trained and managed to perform effectively their duties. Behind the scenes, internal marketing programmes still ensure staff grasp the fundamentals of the McDonald's trading concept and ideals.

Controls are central to the trading practices of the company. Every customer ordering a Big Mac must receive a similar meal every time: cooked identically, with similar relish, wrapping, pricing and a smile. With 70 per cent of McDonald's restaurants franchised to independently owned companies and operators, such uniformity does not occur by accident. McDonald's promotes the whole restaurant experience and establishes performance standards to maintain a consistent customer offer. As the company continues to grow, with innovative outlets on ferries, at football grounds and even in hospitals, internal operational controls are crucial. McDonald's understands the importance of maintaining high standards and of integrating the brand, people, design, ambience, technology and food to create a winning experience.

Discussion themes

1. Why is it important for McDonald's to have tight operational and marketing controls?

2. Why is internal marketing so important to McDonald's?

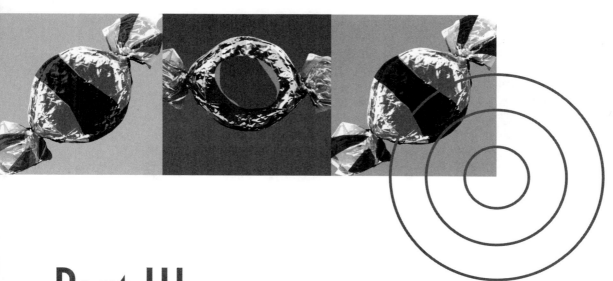

Part III
Full cases

This section contains full-length factual cases intended to highlight marketing issues while providing the opportunity to apply marketing concepts and frameworks.

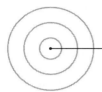

Full Case 1: Aer Lingus Beyond Face Value

Since the 1930s Aer Lingus has carried the flag as Ireland's state airline. In the early 1990s, the business faced financial crisis. Now privatized and an independent company, Aer Lingus has gone from strength to strength, winning countless awards for its business and tourist class services to and from Ireland. The buoyant Irish economy of the 1990s – 6–7 per cent annual growth – supported the airline's turnaround, in conjunction with shrewd marketing and an eye for customer service. By 1996, the business had a new strategy, livery and realization that in reality, the brand metamorphosed as its people – notably at their 'point of interaction' with Aer Lingus customers. Towards the end of the 1990s, turnover (over £800 million p.a.) and operating profits (£47 million in 1997) rose, as carefully honed business strategies were implemented. Aer Lingus strove to put people first in its marketing programmes – customers but also the airline's own personnel. Aer Lingus had for many years been perceived as a 'friendly airline'. The challenge was also to be viewed as professional, efficient and friendly.

Intense Rivalry

Aer Lingus competes in four distinct markets: the transatlantic long-haul sector against such giants as American Airlines, Delta and British Airways; within the European Union against a plethora of national carriers such as Lufthansa, Air France, Air Italia; in the London/provincial UK market, against British Airways, British Midland, Ryan Air and a host of smaller airlines; and domestically within Ireland, where Aer Lingus competes with small Irish airlines, road and rail. Even before the arrival of low-cost, no-frills operators GO (BA's discount brand) and easyJet, Aer Lingus considered entering the fray with a low-price operation. With Irish rival Ryan Air's strong position in this segment – and Aer Lingus's heritage of friendly service – the company opted instead to compete in the full service segment, prioritizing premium business class.

The same customer may fly with both Aer Lingus and Ryan Air, but on different occasions. The manager travelling on expenses will invariably opt for the reassurance and service of Aer Lingus when flying on business, but might choose Ryan Air for a low-cost family leisure trip to the UK. Aer Lingus's marketing programmes must reflect the nuances and requirements of its international and national markets, while acknowledging that as a service provider, its marketing mix is complex and difficult to control. Aer Lingus is a 'people business', and as such believes its future depends on its ability to satisfy its target customers in a way which gives it an edge over its competitors.

A People Business

The Aer Lingus Board is on record as stating that 'Aer Lingus is in the service business, not a supplier of seats on aircraft — a traditional international organizational focus of many airlines – but as a supplier of a total travel experience'. To compete successfully, the airline knows it must increase its already strong emphasis on service and quality. The Aer Lingus brand is successful in its core markets and can only be strengthened by the company's desire to be ever more customer-focused. This emphasis inevitably leads to the airline's personnel; their recruitment, training, attitudes, ability and motivation, to ensure they give 'good service'. It also extends to any environment – terminal, aircraft or booking point – in which customers encounter Aer Lingus, as well as the ease with which customers can book seats, travel and experience the airline's service product.

Business Class and Margin Management

A core target market for Aer Lingus is business travel. For such customers, price *per se* has not tended to be an overriding decision variable in selecting an airline. Concerns such as frequency and times of flights, punctuality, ease of airport access, route destinations and speed of boarding/disembarkation have been core factors. There have been few innovations in business class travel in recent years: most rivals offer e-ticketing, large seats, free newspapers and drinks. The move increasingly is to provide ever more 'seamless travel', reducing waiting times in airport lounges and speeding up ticketing. It is anticipated that more and more business users will utilize web sites for booking and pricing information, with expense account financiers increasingly wising-up to alternative price options. This may lead to keener prices being offered by competing airlines to business users. In an industry plagued with heavy uncontrollable costs – aircraft purchase/leasing, airport handling charges, labour costs – any move to reduce ticket prices poses significant commercial challenges. For a business, such as Aer Lingus, promoting itself on the basis of customer service – which requires many well-trained and motivated personnel – reducing costs is even more problematic.

Margin management is a key task for Aer Lingus, which recently joined the global airline alliance *One World*, including Quantas and British Airways. Richard Branson of Virgin Atlantic is on record as stating that while he would prefer to go it alone, such global alliances are increasingly fundamental to gaining access to global markets, routes and airports, while offering loyal customers seamless ticketing and transfers to innumerable destinations. For Aer Lingus, it is hoped the *One World* alliance will provide access to the huge North American market and the extensive demand via New York for flights to Ireland. There are now nine million active American flyers aware of the Aer Lingus brand and schedule because of the *One World* alliance.

Aer Lingus argues its success stems from the considerable effort it has put into analysing its markets and tightly defining its business proposition, 'developing necessary new skills and brand values to meet the ever changing needs of customers, while retaining an emphasis on core strengths, such as friendliness and Irish identity, which have been important factors in our success in the past.'

Aer Lingus's current strategy centres on increased differentiation in the market-place with the right package of service and product at competitive prices.

The market is becoming polarized between low priced, no frills, point-to-point service providers and, at the other extreme, full service, added value airlines such as Aer Lingus. It is likely the low-price sector is now over-served with impending rationalization and withdrawal by some operators anticipated by market observers. The full service operators seek to provide comprehensive service levels and flexible travel options throughout the business and leisure markets at all price points. While there has to be low pricing 'down the back of the plane' for economy tourist travel, Aer Lingus still provides good and 'dignified' in-flight service to its standard class customers. The full service market remains the mainstream, despite the in-roads of Go or easyJet, and comprises customers who wish to travel with an airline offering a top quality, reliable product and service at competitive prices. It is, according to Aer Lingus, 'not intrinsically price sensitive, but is highly "value sensitive"'.

A Programme for a Better Airline

Recently, Aer Lingus internally launched its *Programme for a Better Airline*. This aims to ensure it effectively continues to identify and meet its customers' needs. Marketing analysis revealed where the company was positioned within its chosen target markets and on-going contact with customers ensures they assist in developing a customer-oriented culture. Regular customer feedback and focus group discussions had provided management with a shrewd insight into passengers' perceptions and expectations. The company added to this marketing intelligence, using a 'break through' technique involving 50 passengers and 50 staff from various functions to 'bring the brand to life'. This research and brainstorming identified the essential needs of Aer Lingus customers, plus the inherent essence of the Aer Lingus brand and proposition. Now an on-going qualitative research activity, the staff and customer participants regularly up-date and inform the airline's marketers.

The *Programme for a Better Airline* is an articulation of how the airline is focussing on its customers, with clear structures, priorities and empowered actions. It also has led to specific improvements for customers based on feedback revealing their key concerns, which are:

- Punctuality
- Queuing
- In-flight experience
- Baggage delivery
- Airport facilities.

Aer Lingus established minimum performance standards in each of these prime areas. These were then communicated to customers. The airline is now one of the most punctual in Europe and is consistently more punctual than its rivals on every route it flies. To reduce the length of queues, dedicated check-in facilities have been created at Dublin and London Stanstead. At London Heathrow a new fast-track security channel saves passengers time between check-in and departure points, while new baggage delivery systems and airport lounges have improved the passenger experience at most airports used by the airline. More customer service staff have been deployed and in-flight cabin crew have been encouraged to build on the airline's perceived friendliness and helpfulness. In order to achieve the company's over-riding objective – to remain the preferred choice for customers flying into and out of Ireland – Aer Lingus continues to build alliances with other airlines through code sharing agreements, joint marketing programmes and alliances such as *One World*. More than half a dozen times in recent years, these initiatives have resulted in Aer Lingus being voted the best airline on transatlantic and London routes by business commuters and tourists travelling to and from Ireland. Market share and profitability have risen accordingly.

The over-riding emphasis on customer satisfaction and enhancing the image of the airline is summed up by the company:

> Behind every strategic and tactical decision – including aircraft acquisition – there must be a single, unwavering commitment to enhancing customer value. We live in an age when customer demand and awareness are growing rapidly. Paying lip service to the concept of putting the customer first is easy. The real work is ensuring that it is more than an attractive business theory and that we make it a practical, every day objective of everyone in the airline in everything they do.

The results have been impressive:

- Transatlantic routes into Dublin and Shannon airports saw an increase of 14 per cent in flights and 16 per cent in passenger numbers to close to three quarters of a million people each year.

- Traffic on London routes increased by eight per cent.

- Continental Europe witnessed new, larger aircraft, extra destinations and greater frequency of departures, notably serving Finland (with Finnair), Spain, Italy, France and Germany.

- Over one and a half million passengers use *Aer Lingus Commuter* each year, with the sub-brand's eight destinations in Britain and five Irish airports feeding into Dublin. Despite fierce price competition on these routes, passenger numbers rose by eight per cent, supported by cost-saving ticket books for frequent flyers, up-graded ground services, a new bespoke *Aer Lingus Commuter* check-in facility at Dublin Airport and the introduction of the business-oriented *Premier* service.

- Cargo has risen by 10 per cent to 42,000 tonnes, with the load factor improving 2 per cent to 72 per cent of capacity. This has been supported with the introduction of an interactive tracking and schedule information service via the Internet.

Professionalism, Intuition, Intimacy

Aer Lingus is seeking to build a reputation for being 'world class' in managing customer relationships with special emphasis on three core values: professionalism, intuition and intimacy. These three core brand values (see Figure III.1) build on the company's reputation for friendliness and strive to enhance on-going relationships with customers to provide passengers with peace of mind and a well serviced experience.

Figure III.1	*Aer Lingus's Brand Values*

Intuition

Meeting unexpected
Proactive
Anticipating
Sensitive
Perception
Little touches

Professionalism

Adult/Equal
Dependable
Reassuring
Committed
Consistent
Switched on
Calm
Confident
Respectful

Intimacy

Friendly
Involved
Comforting
Caring
Listening
Giving
Treating as individual
Empathetic

Standards of *professionalism* are rising throughout the business community and this is being reflected in Aer Lingus's activities. The airline insists its staff recognize the importance of 'designing a product or delivering a service to reflect these rising standards'. *Intuition* is the utilization of staff experience, 'to see beyond first appearances' and to understand the customer. As the airline's senior marketers explain, 'as it becomes more difficult to establish tangible product advantages over competitors, intangible skills, such as our ability to understand customers, become increasingly important'. *Intimacy* involves 'establishing a genuine empathy' with customers, to see situations from the customer's view and to strengthen customer relationships.

While other airlines can emulate these brand values, Aer Lingus has an 'ace up its sleeve' to help create a competitive edge – its *Irishness*. The company's Irish identity is an important facet of its trading image and branding, providing a reassuring mix of emotions bound to appeal to its customers, many of whom are Irish or of Irish descent:

- Genuineness
- Naturalness
- Friendliness
- Sense of humour

If only more service providers could incorporate such traits in their marketing propositions! Coupled with Ireland's resurgent characteristics – youthful, dynamic, proud, and confident – Aer Lingus's *Irishness* is a formidable marketing asset. The core brand values of professionalism, intuition and intimacy, along with the *Programme for a Better Airline*, provide a well-honed marketing proposition and business strategy in a highly competitive marketplace.

Acknowledgement

This case and its inherent enthusiastic energy stem from the much appreciated help of former Aer Lingus Marketing Director David Bunworth.

Issues

Aer Lingus is a service business that has utilized marketing to rejuvenate its fortunes, researching customers' expectations and their perceptions of competitors, customizing its marketing mix programmes to reflect the needs of its principal target markets, while enhancing the standing of its brand in an increasingly competitive marketplace.

Buying behaviour and target marketing

How has Aer Lingus attempted to put its customers at the forefront of its business development? To what extent has the airline built up an understanding of its customers' perceptions and expectations?

The extended services marketing mix

In what way is the role of personnel central to the airline's operations and marketing strategy?
Why must the airline's marketing mix focus on more than the traditional 4Ps?

Creating a competitive advantage

How has the airline defined its differential advantage? To what extent is this sustainable? Why is it difficult for a service business such as Aer Lingus to identify a differential advantage over its rivals?

Marketing research

Aer Lingus has undertaken extensive marketing research of its customer base. Did it opt for the best selection of survey tools?

Relevant Theory Notes

T3:   Buying Behaviour, pp. 199–204
T6:   Market Segmentation, pp. 229–236
T13: The Marketing of Services, pp. 280–284
T14: Industrial, Business-to-Business Marketing, pp. 285–290
T8:   The Marketing Mix: Products and Product Management, pp. 246–254
T7:   Competitive Strategy, pp. 237–245
T4:   Marketing Research, pp. 213–220

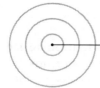

Full Case 2:   JCB Backhoe Loader Internationally into the Dictionary

A small lock-up garage in rural Staffordshire producing farm vehicles from wartime scrap metal has grown into what is today a manufacturing and marketing success on a global scale. JCB's award winning, fully landscaped modern production facilities continually set industry standards – as do the company's products. There are now seven UK factory sites, a newly constructed manufacturing plant in North America, a joint venture manufacturing facility in India, eight subsidiary sales companies and eleven regional offices around the world. JCB is the fifth largest construction equipment manufacturer in the world and market leader in Europe. The company is now making significant in-roads in the 'back yard' of key American rivals Caterpillar and Case. Of JCB products 76 per cent are exported to over 140 countries.

Pursuit of new ideas has characterized this success story. JCB created the backhoe loader – the digger seen on most construction sites and at many road-works – and is world leader in this core product category. The JCB Loadall was the world's first telescopic handler, a product found on construction sites, in warehouses, on farms and even at Grand Prix racing circuits. The JCB Robot is the world's safest skid steer, with operators able to climb out without encountering the lifting arms. The JCB Fastrac is the world's first high-speed tractor, much sought after by macho-farmers! A recent move away from construction equipment has built on the company's knowledge of vehicle construction and hydraulics, with the innovative Teletruk forklift truck. JCB brought the first four-wheel steer, four-wheel drive backhoe loader to the market and its Nephron oil filter system means that in JCB tracked excavators, the oil is cleaner when it is drained from the machine than when it was first poured in.

The company's founder is still at the forefront of product development and technical innovation, and the Bamford family controls one of the UK's main privately owned companies. Continued growth is typified by the story of the backhoe digger and the reputation of a brand name now part of everyday language. As humorist Miles Kington of *The Independent* newspaper has written:

> I don't suppose the marketing managers of the Roman Empire ever sat down one day and worked out a snappy set of initials, then did some market research on it to see if it was going down well with the people they had just conquered. They just had SPQR on their plates and used it. A bit like JCB. If the man behind JCB had not been called Joseph Cyril Bamford, but something like Patrick James Walker, we would now be saying: 'Look at all those PJWs – they must be building a new road', or, 'Sorry I'm late – I was stuck behind a bloody PJW for five miles down a B road', or, 'Pardon, mais ma voiture fut attrapée derrière un sacré PJW pendant des heures'.

JCB, the UK construction and agricultural equipment manufacturer, breaks several rules. In the dictionary, 'JCB' is virtually defined as the generic term for the backhoe digger, irrespective of the manufacturer. As a middle-sized player in a highly competitive market dominated by US giants Caterpillar and Case, plus Japanese challengers Komatsu, the Staffordshire company bucked the economic recession of the early 1990s. Profits dipped from 1989's record £50 million on turnover of £460 million, but the company remained profitable in a period when US rivals reported losses ranging from $200 million to $800 million. By 2000, turnover was close to £800 million, with profits touching £90 million. JCB is the market leader in Europe, and for several core products dominates markets from Israel to India, from North America to Nigeria.

According to management writer Robert Heller,

> JC Bamford, a very British company, is also devotedly international in two powerful senses. In the worldwide spread of its bright yellow machines to 140 different countries, and in its methods. Design-led, aggressively innovative, progressive in its manufacturing and European in its thinking. JCB has consistently raised its global market share in the teeth of world-class competition, while averaging high profitability over a sustained period.

Table III.1	*Milestones in the History of JCB*

- 1945 – JCB founded by Joseph Cyril Bamford in a lock-up garage in Uttoxeter, producing farm machinery from wartime scrap metal.
- 1953 – First JCB Mark 1 backhoe loader launched onto the UK market.
- 1970 – First of seven Queen's Awards, five of which were for export achievement.
- 1973 – First of four Design Council Awards for technological design.
- 1977 – The trend-setting JCB 520 telescopic handler introduced.
- 1979 – Royal Society of Arts, Presidential Award for consistently distinguished design.
- 1979 – Joint venture with Escorts in Delhi, India.
- 1980 – 3CX backhoe loader launched, taking JCB's world market share from 12% to 25%.
- 1985 – British Quality Award for product design and quality assurance.
- 1988 – JCB 801 mini-excavator launched, achieving 10% market share in its first year.
- 1990 – JCB 2CX compact backhoe loader launched, creating a significant new market.
- 1991 – JCB Fastrac high mobility vehicle introduced, yet again setting new standards in performance and operator comfort.
- 1991 – 4CX 4x4x4 high productivity backhoe loader launched, bringing innovative four-wheel steer to add to market supremacy.
- 1991 – 3CX 4x4 backhoe loader introduced, described by many as *the formula for the 1990s*.
- 1991 – The fruits of a joint venture with Japan's Sumitomo led to the 1992 successful launch of a new generation of crawler excavators, catapulting JCB into joint UK market leadership.
- 1993 – Further range extensions enabled JCB to more comprehensively enter the compact equipment market with a single-arm range of skid steers.

- 1993 – Europe's leading range of telescopic handlers extended and re-launched.
- 1993 – JCB's Compact Division created, specializing in smaller pieces of equipment with expert dealer staff and support.
- 1994 – launch of the 1CX 'baby' backhoe to support the Compact Division.
- 1995 – *Keep It Genuine* led to an improved aftermarket provision, with guaranteed spares and service boosting residual values for traded-in JCB equipment.
- 1995 – A joint venture for backhoe production in India opened up significant sales opportunities.
- 1996 – The new JS range of tracked excavators launched.
- 1996 – The JCB clothing range was successfully piloted in Debenhams department stores.
- 1998 – JCB committed itself to an extensive $64 million investment in production plant in North America at Savannah, Georgia.
- 1998 – JCB entered the forklift truck market with its novel Teletruk.
- 1999 – New JCB Earthmover 250,000 square foot factory at Cheadle for wheeled loading shovels.
- 1999 – JCB acquired the controlling interest in the Escorts joint venture in Delhi: 70 depots across India.
- 1999 – The 1000th JS tracked excavator produced.
- 1999 – The 240,000th export machine shipped, to a customer in France.
- 1999 – New range of hand-held tools and portable power packs launched.
- 2000 – Creation of a 33 tonne tracked excavator for the demolition industry.

Source: The JCB Experience

Huge Market

World-wide the construction equipment industry is huge, with sales close to $60 billion. The US giant Caterpillar tends to concentrate on the very large earth-moving and construction equipment. Similarly, the Japanese players such as Komatsu (number two world-wide to Caterpillar) and Hitachi compete for sales of the larger machines. JCB, however, dominates the middle ground, avoiding many small tools and much really heavy earthmoving equipment. The backhoe common to most construction sites, road works, many farms and traffic jams, is the company's staple product.

The company has over 25 per cent of the world's and close to 40 per cent of Europe's backhoe market, led by constant mechanical innovation and improved driver comfort: Case, Ford and Massey Ferguson all trail behind JCB. The JCB brand name is synonymous with this product, often being used as a generic term for the backhoe digger in the industry. Nevertheless, JCB is very much a growing company and the backhoe is only one of eight core product areas. More are being added, such as the Teletruk forklift, based on thorough market opportunity analysis, comprehensive marketing planning and product innovation (see Figure III.2).

Figure III.2 | *Major Product Group – Construction Equipment*

Articulated dump trucks
*Backhoe loaders***
*Crawler excavators**
*Fork lifts
Motor graders
Rigid dump trucks
*Skid steer loaders**
*Telescopic handlers***
*Wheeled loading shovels

Asphalt finishers
Crawler dozers
Crawler loaders
*Mini-excavators**
Motor scrapers
*Rough terrain fork lift trucks
Tractors
*Wheeled crawler excavators

* = JCB's product entries   ** = UK leadership for JCB   *** = World leadership for JCB

Marketing Ethos

The company has six bespoke dealers with 49 outlets in the UK, with an extensive array of franchised dealers throughout the world. In addition, core overseas markets have JCB-owned subsidiaries – locally formed companies which oversee local product enhancements, supervise dealers and run marketing programmes oriented to their markets' needs; all carefully orchestrated from the company's Staffordshire (UK) base. Here there are five core operations: *JCB Sales* handling marketing, planning, sales, dealer strategies; *JCB Service* orientated to product support and dealer control; *JCB Finance* offering credit and tax-saving financing packages; *JCB Insurance Services* tailoring policies for construction and plant businesses; plus the various production units.

From once being product or technical innovation led, to becoming sales led, the company now benefits from a carefully integrated sales and marketing function which liaises closely with the production, finance and service functions. The air of 'entrepreneurial flair' still exists, but now is supported with a host of management skills which have together allowed a family-run business to more than adequately compete with the world's major construction and agricultural equipment manufacturers.

Marketing Planning

Planning and analysis have enabled JCB's marketers to better understand their marketplace. The company has invested heavily in researching its core customer groups throughout Europe, carefully utilizing the strengths of its subsidiaries' personnel in the field. Extensive evaluations of competitors' strengths and weaknesses, their competitive positions and likely strategies have led JCB to successfully pre-empt competitors' thrusts and to quickly establish new product launches in target markets.

For backhoes, too, there have been lessons from this strategic marketing planning. For example, the indigenous Italian manufacturer FAI (partly owned by Japan's Komatsu) is strong only in its home market and poses a genuine threat in Italy, requiring a different set of tactics to those employed in the UK. The German construction industry has never really used backhoes, preferring instead larger excavators or smaller compact equipment. The opportunities presented by the united Germany and beckoning Eastern European markets, however, led JCB to develop this market. For backhoes the Scandinavian market is small and sluggish, reflecting local cultural and competitive characteristics not common to the rest of Europe, but presenting a different set of marketing challenges. JCB's sales and marketing personnel are well aware of these nuances, modifying their product specifications and tactical marketing mix programmes accordingly.

Varied Customers in a Turbulent Environment

The market is highly competitive, and often the victim of economic recession. Whenever there is a dip in spending, economic 'belt-tightening' or a hefty rise in interest rates, the construction industry suffers. This contraction is reasonably regular and must be combated by shrewd planning and effective marketing programmes. In such economic troughs, civil engineering projects fail to find adequate financial backing, governments suspend capital expenditure and halt infrastructure improvements, and house building declines. For example, in the UK 50,000 construction workers lost their jobs in the 1992 recession.

Lower numbers of new housing starts have a significant, harmful impact on the market. The purchase of equipment costing anything from £5,000 to £150,000 leads to prudent spending by purchasers, particularly in an economic recession. Product reliability, length of service, aftermarket servicing and parts costs, versatility in operation, residual operating values when re-sold/replaced, all become crucial issues to the operators of such equipment. These customers range from owner-operator 'one-man' companies, to multi-depot plant/tool hirers, to large construction and extractive companies/contractors (Tarmac, ARC or Wimpy, for example) which own/hire and operate dozens of machines sourced typically from a variety of manufacturers and plant hirers/contractors.

Selling to the one-person owner-operator is not easy. A high retail price is a real obstacle; access is difficult as generally these customers are out on a job, rather than conveniently in an office awaiting a 'phone call or cold-call visit; and their business acumen and sophistication are often limited. Potential per unit profit rewards, though, are very good from sales of construction equipment to these customers. The plant and tool hirers, on the other hand, do not use the equipment themselves, but their customers do. These renters/hirers often have little direct experience of the product or the different manufacturers' offerings – they are steered by the plant hire depot personnel's recommendations and the fleet stocked by a particular hire depot. At the other extreme, the large construction companies such as Tarmac or Wimpy both own and hire-in equipment. They purchase from various dealers and manufacturers. These large construction companies may have well-defined purchasing routines and even specialist purchasing managers. The driver or operator is unlikely to be the purchase decision-maker or the budget holder in such organizations.

| **Figure III.3** | *Key Customer Sectors – Construction Equipment* |

Plant hire
Extraction (mining/quarrying)
Civil engineering
Contractors
Landscaping
Public utilities
Manufacturing

Tool hire
House building
Agriculture
Earthmoving
Waste disposal
Local authorities
Industrial services

The Backhoe Loader (Digger)

JCB's first backhoe was launched by Joe Bamford in 1953. Since the 1950s, most rivals in the manufacture of construction or agricultural equipment have produced copycat machines. Companies from Ford (5 per cent of the market) to Case, from Massey Ferguson (9 per cent) to Volvo have attempted to feed from a market created by JCB, now estimated to be worth £1,750 million world-wide, and £800 million within Europe. Despite this competition, JCB accounts for nearly 60 per cent of the near 2,500 annual backhoe sales in the UK, and for approximately 40 per cent of sales within Europe. Even the giant Caterpillar's share has declined, to 7 per cent. JCB now also competes in most sectors of the market: backhoe loaders, telescopic handlers, wheeled loaders, mini excavators, skid steer loaders, rough terrain forklifts, tracked and wheeled excavators, high speed tractors and forklift tucks. The company is constantly evaluating other product categories, such as hydraulic lift ramps and platforms, military products and emergency vehicle applications. Although successful in other product areas, the bulk of the company's success stems from its domination of the backhoe market.

JCB's key backhoe strengths are:

- the JCB brand name;
- product awareness;
- media domination within the category;
- technology leadership;
- product design and innovation;
- coverage with distributor outlets/salesforce.

Such market domination has not encouraged the company to sit back. The 3CX (the traditional digger common to most building sites) had been the staple product. By the end of 1991, JCB had a range including the smaller, more manoeuvrable and versatile 2CX, supported by the larger and more powerful

4CX. The company had introduced the concept of four-wheel drive years earlier with great success. In 1991 it caught the competition napping by bringing on stream the 4x4x4 version of the 4CX model range: four equally sized wheels, four-wheel drive, plus four-wheel steering. With the promotional strapline of '*JCB: The formula for the '90s*', the company had moved the backhoe into a new generation. One major competitor pulled out of backhoe production, while the others could only look on with resentful admiration.

Simultaneously, work continued to boost performance levels across the range, to enter unrealized markets, develop derivatives for specialist applications – particularly in the undeveloped German market – improve driver comfort and safety with air conditioning, greater sound proofing and stronger, more durable cabs. JCB is highly aware of the growing concern for the environment. Biodegradable oils, lower noise levels, recyclable components (similar to BMW's actions in the car market), plus training literature and videos for operators, are all integral to the overall product offering.

Backhoe Launches in the 1990s

The backhoe loader is JCB's core product. The 3CX used to account for 60 per cent of the company's volume sales. As the *Financial Times* pointed out at the 1991 launch of the replacement 3CX, the event was in earth-moving circles as important as an innovative new product launch from a German or Japanese car manufacturer. As creator and brand leader of the world's backhoe market, the whole industry was primed with a sense of expectancy.

JCB had extended the versatility of its backhoe digger range with the introduction in 1990 of the smaller and more manoeuvrable 2CX. The competition thought that was the only newcomer for a while: after all, JCB had not introduced new backhoe models since 1980. In the summer of 1991, 300 dealers from around the world were flown into JCB's trend-setting headquarters. Along with representatives of the world's press, they were wowed first with the new, high-powered, technologically advanced 3CX. This was no model re-vamp: the new 3CX was a totally new design, extending the generic parameters for the whole industry. Audiences at the launch shows were visibly impressed. The revised 2CX then appeared, emphasizing the newly extended range. To steal the show, and to truly dazzle the audiences, however, JCB had an ace still to play. On to the dry-iced and laser-decked stage came a third model: the 4CX. To complete the demolition of the competition, the company added 4x4x4 (four-wheel drive and steer) as its differential advantage – a technological breakthrough few other competitors had the resources to match for several years.

The launch was carefully planned. Catching competitors unaware because of 1990's 2CX launch, JCB's marketing director employed a well-orchestrated selection of promotional tools to gain maximum impact. As indicated in Table III.2, the trade press was used for an extensive advertising campaign, running over five months in the key titles. This UK campaign was replicated by JCB's subsidiaries world-wide. Public relations, though, was the key tactic employed. The launch attracted terrific media attention, ranging from TV and radio interviews with Chairman Sir Anthony Bamford to in-depth features running over several pages in all of the specialist publications. National newspapers and local press were equally keen to give coverage to such a spectacular launch for such an important UK manufacturer. Press days were held at the Rocester headquarters, main dealers, and at the main construction and agricultural trade shows such as England's SED construction fair, the Royal Agricultural Society of England's Royal Show, and Germany's massive Bauma festival.

Table III.2	*UK Backhoe Launch Media Schedule 1991*							
Journal	*No. of Insertions*	*Size*	*Position*	*Aug*	*Sept*	*Oct*	*Nov*	*Dec*
	1	5 × A4 teaser	Consecutive R.H. pages	29				
Construction News	2	6-page Insert	Centre Spread		5,12			
	9	Double-page spread	Centre Spread		19	3,17 31	7,14 28	5,19
	1	5 × A4 teaser	Consecutive R.H. Pages	29				
Contract Journal	2	6-page insert	Early		5,19			
	7	Double-page spread	Early		26	3,10 24	14,21	19
	1	6-page	Early					
Plant Managers Journal	3	Double-page spread	Early					

Source: JCB

The attention devoted to external target audiences did not detract from the effort intended to inform and encourage JCB's own personnel. Dealer training was fundamental given the technical enhancements to the backhoe product, but it became part of the morale-boosting fanfare surrounding the launch. Every few days for two weeks, international dealers and their personnel were flown in on chartered aircraft to London and East Midlands airports; over 1,000 visitors. They witnessed stage shows with simultaneous multi-lingual translation, lighting rigs and stage effects to shame many pop stars, plus fact-finding sessions and full product training. A huge investment, but anyone witnessing the buzz and excitement, the belief in the new models and JCB, would have found the expense difficult to fault. The show was also staged for the company's shop floor workers, creating equal excitement and commitment for the products and company. The result was that in certain countries, JCB's market share doubled.

The company more than dominated the bulk of its European markets, gaining the majority of sales in core markets in the UK and northern Europe. Sales of backhoes rose sharply, too, in North America, Africa, India, Israel and South East Asia. The new range had cost JCB £25 million in development and engineering costs, with nearly £5 million for new production lines, and £0.5 million on marketing launch expenses. With the company's overall market share in Europe climbing by close to 5 per cent and nearing 40 per cent, the company's investment in backhoe developments and the introduction of other new ranges had paid off. There were short-term rewards, but also the creation of an enviable competitive positioning as market leader in Europe, posing a significant threat to the US and Japanese construction equipment giants.

1992's launch of the new crawler excavators, the result of a joint venture with Sumitomo of Japan, built on the success of 1991's backhoe launches. The venue for the equally slick and sensational launch this time around was Faro in southern Portugal, with dealers and press flying in from around the globe. This new range increased JCB's crawler excavator market share by over 100 per cent, causing the market leaders Komatsu and Hitachi to take evasive action. In 1993 it was the turn of the more compact end of the construction equipment market. Joining JCB's mini-excavator range came the innovative range of single arm skid steers – the safest and most environmentally friendly on the market – to create JCB's new Compact Division. In 1994 it was the turn of Malaga in Spain, for more high profile product launches, including the baby 1CX backhoe loader. More derivatives of leading models were unveiled with similar flair at La Manga in 1996.

Compact Equipment and JCB Service

The Compact Division was treated by JCB like Toyota's *Lexus* operation, with bespoke sales and service personnel in dealers, separate marketing campaigns and focused product development. Centred initially around the 800 series of mini excavators and the single arm Robot skid steer, in recent years the Compact Division has enjoyed range extension of these two product categories, and the addition to the product portfolio of smaller backhoe loaders, wheeled loading shovels and the Teletruk forklift truck. A multi-million pound factory extension at JCB's Hydrapower operation in Staffordshire was required to support the rapid growth of this smaller equipment range and the impact in the marketplace of JCB's Compact Division. Recently, portable powerpacks and a range of hand-held power tools for drilling, cutting, lifting and pumping, have been added to the product portfolio.

Underlying the success of JCB's machines is a commitment to customer service. With over 90 products, long-life quality to support, sales in 140 countries and a brand identity inextricably linked with quality and innovation, JCB's after-market operation has to be effective and reliable. Dealer engineers are trained to very high standards. JCB's parts – promoted through the *Keep it Genuine* campaign – are well branded and marketed, offering peace of mind to a growing number of users and customers, who in turn find the residual value of their machines is maintained when the time comes to sell the product or trade it in against a new replacement. Downtime caused by product failure is costly and annoying for customers. JCB's UK dealers all stock the core 300 spare parts most commonly required; 250 vans offer rapid and mobile response to customer problems, and the company guarantees a response within four working hours. Dealer personnel elsewhere in the world are similarly committed to solving user difficulties. The company's helicopters and corporate jet have been known to airlift spares for customers in emergencies. Fixed price menu servicing, pleasant customer areas and facilities in dealer depots, plus friendly and proficient service personnel, have added to the impressive customer service provided by JCB. Indeed, the service business is a major profit contributor for JCB and is branded as strongly as the machines.

What Next?

JCB has been one of the UK's most successful privately owned companies. Despite its relatively limited resource base, the company has given its multinational US and Japanese rivals severe problems. During the recession in the early 1990s, JCB was virtually alone in its industry in trading profitably. A marketing ethos has helped the company to stay ahead in its core markets: new product development which has innovated and grown markets, prudent target marketing to identify lucrative core customer sectors, and a commitment to dealer and customer service. The brand is in the dictionary. It and the famous yellow paintwork are synonymous with technical expertise, design and effective marketing. The company's success has, however, brought it increasingly to the attention of its global rivals, many of which dwarf JCB. JCB's first half century has been an unqualified success. The future is a little more uncertain. JCB is a highly successful middle-sized player in a recession-prone market with brooding competing giants. Continued growth and success will be harder to maintain.

Table III.3	*Shows and Exhibitions*

Days	*January 2000* *Dates*	*Event*
Tue/Wed/Thur/Fri/Sat	18/19/20/21/22	Bouwvakbeurs Zuidlaren
Mon/Tue/Wed/Thur/Fri/Sat/Sun	24/25/26/27/28/29/30	Superbowl

Days	*February 2000* *Dates*	*Event*
Tue/Wed/Thur/Fri/Sat/Sun	8/9/10/11/12/13	Agribex – Brussels
Wed/Thur/Fri/Sat/Sun	16/17/18/19/20	SMOPYC
Tue/Wed/Thur	22/23/24	Hirex 2000
Mon/Tue	28/29	Lanbouwwerktuigenbeurs

Days	*March 2000* *Dates*	*Event*
Thur/Fri	2/3	Lanbouwwerktuigenbeurs
Wed/Thur/Fri/Sat/Sun/Mon	20/21/22/23/24/25	Hanover Exhibition
Sun/Mon	31	Aquaculture Int 2000

Days	*April 2000* *Dates*	*Event*
Sat	1	Aquaculture Int 2000

Days	*May 2000* Dates	Event
Sun	14	Essex Show
Tue/Wed/Thur/Fri/Sat/Sun	16/17/18/19/20/21	Intermat
Fri/Sat	19/20	Shropshire and West Midlands Show
Thur/Fri/Sat	25/26/27	TKD
Mon	29	Northumberland Show
Wed	31	Stafford Show

Days	*June 2000* Dates	Event
Thur	1	Stafford Show
Tue/Wed/Thur	6/7/8	SED
Thur/Fri/Sat	8/9/10	Royal Cornwall
Tue/Wed/Thur	13/14/15	IWM
Wed/Thur	14/15	Cereals 2000
Thur/Fri/Sat	15/16/17	Three Counties Show
Sun	**18**	**JCB OPEN DAY**
Wed/Thur	21/22	Lincoln Show
Fri/Sat/Sun	23/24/25	Royal Highland Show
Sat/Sun/Mon/Tue	24/25/26/27	Royal Welsh
Tue/Wed	27/28	Sprays and Sprayers
Wed/Thur	28/29	ADA

Days	*July 2000* Dates	Events
Mon/Tue/Wed/Thur	3/4/5/6	Royal Show
Tue/Wed/Thur	11/12/13	Yorkshire Show
Sat	15	Cumberland Show
Mon/Tue/Wed/Thur	24/25/26/27	Royal Welsh
Fri/Sat/Sun/Mon	28/29/30/31	Libramont – Wallonie

Days	*August 2000* Dates	Event
Tue	1	Turiff Show
Wed/Thur	2/3	Black Isle Show
Thur	3	Burwaton Show
Sat	5	Dumfries Show
Sat	12	Orkney Show
Tue/Wed/Thur	15/16/17	Pembrokeshire Show
Thur/Fri/Sat	17/18/19	Scot Plant 2000
Sat	19	Skelton Show

Days	*September 2000* Dates	Event
Tue/Wed/Thur	5/6/7	Saltex
Thur	7	Bucks Show
Sat/Sun	16/17	Newbury and Berks Show
Wed/Thur	20/21	Euro Dairy Event
Wed/Thur/Fri/Sat	20/21/22/23	Galabu Show
Wed/Thur/Fri	27/28/29	APF

Days	*October 2000* Dates	Event
Wed	4	Brailsford Plough Match
Wed	4	South West Dairy
Sat/Sun	14/15	Northumberland Show

Days	*November 2000* Dates	Event
Tue/Wed/Thur	14/15/16	Scotbuild

Days	*December 2000* Dates	Event
Mon/Tue/Wed/Thur/Fri/Sat	11/12/13/14/15/16	Landbouw Rai

Source: JCB

Issues

The JCB story is one of success for a large, privately owned UK engineering company. The case highlights reasons for this success on an international scale, featuring JCB's branding, positioning, marketing planning and promotional strategies. JCB's product innovation and attention to customer service are also explained. The difficulties of selling and marketing in industrial business-to-business markets are more than evident.

Organizational/industrial buyer behaviour

Which are the main market segments? What are their buying characteristics, processes and influences? How can these be harnessed by JCB's sales and marketing activities?

How is the purchase decision for a jobbing builder different to that for a large construction business such as Tarmac?

Branding, product management and positioning

How important to JCB is the strength of its brand? How does the brand assist the company's marketing programmes? What is the positioning of the brand? How can this be maintained?

Why are product and service innovations important to JCB's brand positioning?

Promotional strategy

What are the principal promotional tools in industrial marketing? Which form the basis for JCB's work? What could be done additionally or differently?

Marketing planning

What is the main focus of effective marketing planning? How does JCB use the marketing planning process? What are likely to be the benefits of marketing planning to JCB? What problems in planning are to be encountered?

International marketing

How has JCB coped in its international markets? How has its growing presence outside of the UK altered its strategy and marketing programmes? What are the main considerations when adopting an international marketing strategy?

Relevant Theory Notes

T3: Buying Behaviour, pp. 205–212
T8: The Marketing Mix: Products and Product Management, pp. 246–254

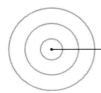

Full Case 3:   LEGO
Building for the Future

Buying a Gift for a Child

Somewhere in the world a child is searching for a birthday gift. Perhaps the gift is for the child's brother, sister or best friend. Maybe the child is searching for the gift in a local toyshop, hypermarket, toy superstore or even on the Internet. The choices available to the child may be extremely diverse or quite constrained. However, whatever the circumstances of the child and no matter where they are located, sooner or later they are likely to encounter the world famous LEGO brand. Perhaps this enormous range of building bricks and other play materials is already one of the child's favourites? If not, it is likely that their parents will be able to tell them about the world-renowned brand.

For many of today's parents, each new LEGO experience brings back memories of their childhood. Although the format of the product and extent of the range used to be very much simpler, the creative imagination it was designed to capture was exactly the same. So as they wander through the aisles of Toys 'R' Us or delve among the shelves of a local independent toyshop, many adults are re-living their own LEGO moments:

> I remember my brother had a biscuit tin full of red and white LEGO bricks. One of my clearest childhood memories is the sound of him rummaging through the contents of the tin for a vital piece to complete his latest masterpiece.

Today, this family-run enterprise has more than 10,000 employees in 30 different countries and is among the world's largest toy manufacturers. Indeed, LEGO is the only European company to occupy a place in the world's Top Ten toy manufacturers. LEGO products are produced in Denmark, the US, Switzerland and Korea and retailed through some 60,000 outlets in more than 130 countries. It is estimated that in the 50 years following its inception, some 203 billion LEGO elements have been produced.

Although the size of the LEGO enterprise has mushroomed, the company philosophy has not changed. The desire to stimulate children's creativity is an enduring theme for the LEGO group. The company's website describes this fundamental philosophy and explains the continual search for new ideas and opportunities which ensures it can maintain its product offer and live up to its positioning statement, 'Creativity unlimited … Just imagine'.

> Our vision is for people all over the world to experience positive, happy associations every time they see a LEGO logo, see a LEGO element or hold it in their hands. Imagination, exuberance, spontaneity, self-expression, quality – these are some of the words we wish to link with the LEGO name, together with values like development, concern for others and innovation.

> Source: www.lego.com.

The History of LEGO

The LEGO story began more than 60 years ago, with a carpenter called Ole Kirk Christiansen. In 1932, Ole and a few employees started making wooden toys in his small workshop in Billund, Denmark. Before very long, he was selling his wooden animals, yo-yos and toy vehicles right across Denmark. Little could he have suspected that these early creations were laying the foundations for a global toy brand which is known and loved by billions. The inspiration for the LEGO name, which was first used in 1934, came from combining the Danish words 'Leg Godt'. This can be translated as 'play well'. Even at this early stage, Ole was keen to establish a reputation for quality, adopting the slogan 'Only the best is good enough'. By the 1940s the workshop had expanded considerably and the robust and rugged range had been extended to include around 150 different products.

Towards the end of the 1940s, Ole Kirk Christiansen was beginning to realize the huge potential of plastic as a new and exciting medium and seized the opportunity to add to the existing wooden range. Most significantly, in 1949, Ole's son, Godtfred Kirk Christiansen used the new material to create simple four and eight stud building bricks. These 'Automatic Binding Bricks' were the forerunner of the LEGO brick we know today. Five years later the 'LEGO System of Play', with the LEGO brick as its basis, was created. This consisted of a range of boxed construction sets containing the kinds of building elements – including people and vehicles – with which LEGO has become synonymous. By 1956 the company was already selling the products outside its domestic market, but it was later, in 1958, that Godtfred made the most important discovery, that tubes positioned inside hollow bricks dramatically improved their ability to join together. International patents were soon sought and before long the new LEGO brick was being sold in a number of European countries. Following this, a number of important steps were taken: first, the company discontinued production of its wooden toy range; second, improvements were made in the technical qualities of the bricks and third, resources were concentrated on developing the LEGO System of Play.

New Developments for the LEGO Range

The LEGO group organizes its business into four main categories: the core business of play materials, family attractions, lifestyle products and media.

Play materials

At the heart of the company's core business – play materials – remains the ever-popular ubiquitous little brick. However, remaining competitive in the fast-moving world of children's toys means that the company must stay in tune with tastes and be ready to respond to the latest fads and fashions. After all, LEGO competes with a plethora of toys, ranging from Action Man and Barbie dolls to

Furbies and computer games. With a target age range of 0 to 16+, catering for so diverse a mix of children's needs is no easy task. The company has tackled this challenge by dividing its core business into four main groups: 'play materials 0–5', 'play materials 4–9', and 'play materials 7–16+' are available to consumers through retailer outlets. For educational establishments there is also a category of 'learning materials 7–16+'. LEGO products aimed at the consumer are then split into eight different product programmes: LEGO PRIMO, LEGO DUPLO, LEGO SCALA, LEGO Belville, LEGO SYSTEM, LEGO TECHNIC, LEGO MINDSTORMS and ZNAP. The company has also developed a range called LEGO DACTA which consists of products for kindergartens and schools.

Play Materials 0–5

LEGO PRIMO: The 37 different sets of toys, which include rattles, animal characters, aeroplanes and boats, are for children from birth to 36 months. They include baby toys, stacking toys and mobility toys which have been designed to develop motor skills and senses.

LEGO DUPLO: There are two groups of these products for the 18 months to six-year age range: Basic and Theme. Basic LEGO DUPLO is a system which allows different products to be combined with each other. Children can experiment with many different ways to assemble the bricks, people and other components. The theme sets are intended to encourage role-play and develop imagination. Each set consists of a variety of basic figures and animals. These elements can be used by children to simulate everything from a visit to the zoo to a favourite Winnie the Pooh story.

Play Materials 4–9

LEGO BASIC: This system has a range of basic bricks and supplementary additional sets. The aim is to encourage the over threes to build a diverse mix of free form items. There are no rules for what they should build or how they should go about it.

ZNAP: This recently launched construction system features vehicles which once built, can be transformed into something else, such as a monster.

GIRLS: The LEGO SCALA and LEGO SYSTEM Belville sets are especially designed for the needs of girls. Research demonstrates that girls particularly enjoy role-play situations, but may be less interested in construction. The LEGO SYSTEM Belville sets encourage girls to enjoy a range of horse riding, fairy tale, beach and other themes using quickly constructed components. Meanwhile, the LEGO SCALA doll's house also provides plenty of opportunity for imaginative play.

LEGO SYSTEM: The wide-ranging product lines, which include 157 different sets, have a variety of themes. Many of the products are designed with the specific needs of boys in mind. Each set can be combined with a diverse mix of others to provide a limitless range of themes and playing opportunities. Themes include: City, Action, Ninja, Adventurers, Space, Star Wars, Trains, Model Team and Radio Control.

Play Materials 7–16+

The ever-popular LEGO TECHNIC products and the new LEGO MINDSTORMS range combine to provide older children with a host of play opportunities. The LEGO TECHNIC products use a technical design and construction system. The Starter, Advanced and CyberMaster options allow children to choose the level and theme of interest. The technical components within the sets encourage the design and building of models using a wide range of axles, motors cogs, pneumatic and other elements. CyberMaster, a new addition to the range, links the traditional LEGO TECHNIC with robots and computer software, to allow the construction of programmable toys.

LEGO MINDSTORMS is a revolutionary new system based on the LEGO RCX microchip. Using the system it is possible to design and build robots which can move and act on their own. Owners of the system use a special programming language known as RCX code to program a microcomputer which then acts as the robot's brain.

Family attractions

The constant revitalizing of products is just one way in which the LEGO group has developed its business. Indeed, the company is continually searching for innovative and exciting ways to move forward. The development of LEGO theme parks, which are profit centres in their own right, is an example of this approach. There are now three LEGOLAND parks, with plans for two more in Germany and Japan early in the new Millennium. The original LEGOLAND is located close to the company's home in Billund. Now more than 30 years since it opened, the park attracts each year around 1.4 million visitors and is one of Denmark's most popular attractions. Some 45 million LEGO bricks are used in the models and rides on display.

In 1999 LEGO opened a new 128 acre-theme park in Carlsbad, just north of San Diego in California. Open throughout the year, the park aims to attract around 1.9 million visitors per annum. LEGOLAND Carlsbad combines retailing, restaurants, live entertainment, rides, sightseeing and construction opportunities. There are four retail shops selling LEGO bricks, LEGO clothing, LEGO games and software as well as LEGO watches and other souvenirs. The management aims to ensure that at least one of every product LEGO sells is on offer in one of the outlets. The park is organized around six themed areas which offer a diverse selection of rides and attractions. Those visiting Fun Town are invited to enjoy a variety of role-playing experiences. The chance to learn to drive an electrically powered car is on offer — but only to the children. Waterworks is a water play area featuring water cannons and fountains. The Adventurers' Club consists of a mix of exciting attractions including polar caves and Egyptian tombs. Although LEGOLAND Carlsbad encourages the whole family to visit, all aspects of the park, its building and rides are designed with children in mind. Windows, counters, toilets and washbasins are all low enough for children to reach. With four different live entertainment shows, it is not just children who are enjoying the LEGOLAND experience. Analysis of the visitor profile at LEGOLAND Carlsbad suggests that senior citizens make up nine per cent of the 15,000 daily visitors. Although many initially attend the park with their grandchildren, they enjoy the experience so much they are buying season tickets so that they can visit again and again.

There are already good reasons to be optimistic about the prospects for LEGOLAND Carlsbad. The 150-acre LEGOLAND built on the site of Windsor Safari Park in the UK has demonstrated the affection which consumers have for the brand. Following its opening in 1996 the park, which attracts 1.5 million visitors annually, was voted Great Britain's most popular new attraction. The emphasis is on combining family entertainment and the use of LEGO bricks in interesting and innovative ways. The aim is to nurture children's innocence by establishing a peaceful oasis far from the tensions and problems of society. Thus the park's buildings and rides are enveloped in LEGO camouflage and there are opportunities for all the family to engage in imaginative play. By using giant LEGO bricks it has been possible to recreate famous buildings such as London's Big Ben and events and personalities from stage and screen. These form a centrepiece for the park.

Lifestyle products

One of the key aims of LEGO Lifestyle is to raise awareness of the LEGO brand. The business believes that becoming involved in a variety of co-operative agreements to supply licensed products will enhance sales of LEGO's other lines. Thus the company actively promotes a wide range of licensed items for children including children's wear, bed linen, games, shampoo, towels and other accessories. In selecting its partners, LEGO management points out that only products of specific interest to children which match up to the company's stringent quality and safety standards are allowed to bear the LEGO brand.

LEGO Kids Wear, which is brightly coloured and functional clothing, is one of the best-known lifestyle ranges. Launched in 1993, the range is the result of a licensing agreement with the Danish Brandtex Group. Initially available through only a small number of outlets in certain parts of Europe, LEGO Kids Wear is being rolled-out around the world. Customers in the USA, Canada, Australia and New Zealand are now able to buy everything from socks and underwear through to T-shirts and outerwear for their under-tens. Indeed, LEGO has ambitions for its Kids Wear to become one of the biggest global children's clothing brands.

LEGO Lifestyle products are available through a number of different types of outlets. In addition to the usual department stores and other shops which specialise in children's apparel, the company is launching its own retail outlets. LEGO Lifestyle shops, to be run on a franchise arrangement, will stock all kinds of LEGO products. Customers will be able to purchase items from the various LEGO play materials and LEGO Media ranges as well as LEGO Lifestyle lines. This is not the company's only retailing development. By the end of 1999, LEGO opened 15 shops selling LEGO Kids Wear alone. These are operated by the company which manufactures the clothing.

Media

LEGO interest in innovation and new ventures is demonstrated by its move into media products. The LEGO Media Products initiative offers consumers a range of children's software, videos, books and music. Initial successful forays into computer games, with the launch of LEGO CREATOR, LEGO LOCO and LEGO Chess, were quickly followed by new titles. Now enthusiasts of the LEGO SYSTEM Rock Raiders range will be able to enjoy a new format for games with their favourite characters. This gang of tough, hard working rock drillers who research alien planets in their hunt for energy crystals and have their hands full dealing with boiling hot lava, rapid rivers and rock monsters, now have their own discovery adventure game.

Links with technology are further exploited in interactive centres at the company's theme parks. In view of this interest in new technology, LEGO's use of the Internet should be no surprise. The company's user-friendly website provides extensive information about its product range and theme parks. Customers can use the Internet to peruse descriptions of the latest LEGO product launches, book tickets and plan their visits to the LEGOLAND theme parks or even buy items from the company's on-line shop. Launched in 1999, the cyberspace LEGO World Shop (www.LEGO.com/LEGOWORLDSHOP), is accessible to consumers in the EU, Norway, Canada, the USA, Australia, New Zealand, Iceland and Israel. Consumers use an electronic 'shopping basket' to collect the items they wish to buy. Payment is by credit card, with a guaranteed high level of security. The system even provides the shopper with an electronic receipt. The initial range of LEGO MINDSTORMS and LEGO TECHNIC products available through this route will quickly be extended.

Poor Results

Following a disappointing set of results in 1998, the senior management team realized that it must focus on increasing the efficiency of the business. The company recorded a before-tax loss of DKK 282 million, its worst ever set of figures. According to the company's annual report a variety of factors contributed to the group's difficulties:

- Financial problems in Russia and Asia substantively affected the results. In Russia, there was a 40 per cent fall in sales to the retail trade and distributors, while in Asia the economic crisis in Korea resulted in a 52 per cent reduction in sales to the retail trade and distributors. Some estimates suggest that as much as DKK 150 million were wiped off the bottom line from this factor alone.

- Stock reductions by the retail trade, with sales to retailers and distributors increasing by a mere 0.8 per cent. This strategy of stock reduction may have accounted for a DKK 150–200 million dip in sales. This was particularly disappointing in view of the substantial growth in sales achieved in America and Japan.

- Product recall of a rattle design cost the business DKK 35 million.

- Difficulties in co-ordinating production with demand for the most popular LEGO lines.

Figures for Europe suggest that in the company's heartland there was actually a 1 per cent fall in sales to the retail trade. Although these figures are somewhat distorted by the particular difficulties in Russia, results were also disappointing in Italy (20 per cent fall in sales to the retail trade), Germany and France. Much more optimism was evident in the Polish, Portuguese, British and Norwegian markets, which all enjoyed retail trade increases. Even though Europe continues to represent the heartland of LEGO sales, the significance of the American market, which has become the company's largest single market, cannot be over-looked. Here sales to the retail trade were up by 13 per cent, while consumer sales rose by 20 per cent. Other positive figures were recorded in the Japanese market, where LEGO turned around a two-year sales decline, increasing sales to the retail trade by 30 per cent (up 40 per cent to consumers).

Region	Sales to retail/distributors (% change)	Sales to consumers (% change)
The Americas	+ 13%	+ 20%
Asia/Pacific & S. Africa	– 38%	– 14%
Europe	–	–
Japan	+ 30%	+ 40%

LEGO hopes that it will be able to overcome its financial difficulties by maintaining close controls over costs. This includes an expected ten per cent reduction in the company's workforce. The management team is also committed to its aptly named 'Fitness Programme' which it believes will put the organization in good shape to improve profitability and further develop its global brand. The aim of this programme is to improve customer focus and establish clearer individual responsibility within the business by reducing the number of organizational levels and cutting overlap between functions. In the words of the company's president and chief executive: 'The distance from the top to bottom within our organization is still too complex and impenetrable. We have to acknowledge that growth and innovation are not enough. We also have to be a profitable business ... '.

High Technology Innovation

The financial difficulties which LEGO has faced have been partly caused by the changing expectations of children and a shift in what they want from the toys with which they play. It seems that the low-tech construction sets on which LEGO built its business have lost ground to computer and video games. The company's approach to innovation is now increasingly rooted in the notion that it must supplement its traditional lines with a wide variety of high technology play offerings.

There is little doubt that a characteristic of LEGO's past success has been the business's willingness to pursue new ideas and stretch the LEGO concept into hitherto unexplored areas. LEGO knows that if it is to reverse its changing financial fortunes, its continued commitment to innovation is essential. This commitment is evident in the various licensing deals with which it has become associated. In LEGO's first licensing arrangement of this type, the company linked up with Lucasfilm Ltd, to offer older children a range of LEGO Star Wars products. LEGO, which was just one of many businesses to set up Star Wars licensing deals, timed the launch of 25 different sets of Star Wars toys to coincide with the opening of the movie. In some stores, the toys were an immediate sell out. Following the marketing hype accompanying its launch and subsequent success of the new Star Wars movie, *The Phantom Menace*, it seemed that the popularity of merchandise for the film was assured. LEGO has subsequently used the licensing route to incorporate a number of Disney film characters into the Play Materials range. Two-to-five year olds are targeted with LEGO sets based on their favourite Winnie the Pooh, Tigger, Piglet and Eeyore characters.

Whatever the future holds for LEGO, the company's focus on children and their needs will continue to dominate its strategic thinking. The company's concern for children has already provided the impetus for its involvement in setting up a new global institution – Next Generation Forum – which aims to encourage children's creativity, imagination and learning. These are the basic principles on which LEGO's success has been based, and whatever changes the market may bring, they will remain at the fore of the company's strategy.

Issues

The LEGO brand has been around for many decades and its appeal has spread to children (and adults) across the world. A non-stop programme of range enhancement and new product development has incorporated themes from the latest blockbuster movies, kept pace with the boom in video and PC games, and adopted the LEGO positioning to incorporate theme parks and merchandising. There is much more to LEGO than the familiar plastic building bricks. Such global expansion and continued popularity have been achieved in the face of increasing competition from other toy producers as well as a plethora of products and activities targeted at LEGO's core target market, children.

Buying behaviour

LEGO has kept pace with evolving needs and expectations of its core target market. What must the company do to ensure it continues to develop products that appeal to the increasingly sophisticated demands of children? Who else must the company strive to satisfy with its products and play-time solutions? How best can LEGO monitor the evolving requirements of its customers?

Product development

LEGO has added a wide variety of products to supplement its core building brick ranges, from clothing, to software to theme parks. To what extent do these additional ranges and products enhance the core LEGO product and brand positioning? Why must LEGO strive to continually innovate and launch new lines?

International marketing

To what extent must LEGO understand the international marketing environment as it expands its operations? Why might social and cultural issues impact on the extent to which the brand can truly become a global leader in the toy industry?

Forecasting

Which techniques should LEGO consider deploying to predict future demand for its products? As it targets new geographical territories, why might the company find insufficient information to be a problem in producing accurate sales forecasts?

Relevant Theory Notes

T3:   Buying Behaviour, pp. 205–212
T8:   The Marketing Mix: Products and Product Management, pp. 246–254
T4:   Marketing Research, pp. 213–220
T5:   Forecasting, pp. 221–228
T16: International Marketing, pp. 297–301

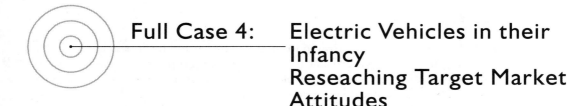

Full Case 4: Electric Vehicles in their Infancy
Reseaching Target Market Attitudes

The UK Government's Green Paper *Transport: The Way Ahead*, indicated a projected growth in traffic of up to 80 per cent by the year 2025. With increasing use of vehicles and journey length, there are congestion and environmental problems. A combination of rising levels of carbon dioxide, nitrogen dioxide and sulphur dioxide have already caused acid rain, global warming problems and an increase in respiratory disease. A variety of UK and EU legislation has drawn attention to the environmental difficulties associated with road usage trends. The European Commission's *Auto Oil Package* has focused attention on air quality standards, demanding considerable reductions in vehicle emissions. The expectation is that the future will bring increasingly stringent national and EU legislation.

It is possible that European moves to reduce vehicle emissions will follow a similar pattern to that seen in California. There, strict environmental legislation required that by 2003, 10 per cent of all new vehicles (some 800,000) should be zero emission. Not surprisingly, car manufacturers have invested heavily in developing a range of alternative fuel technologies in their drive towards more environmentally friendly vehicles. Currently, only battery-powered electric vehicles (EVs) are able to achieve zero emissions. Other fuels under investigation include the use of alcohol, compressed natural gas, hydrogen, liquefied petroleum gas (LPG), coal derived liquid fuels and fuels derived from biological materials such as soya beans. Some manufacturers are developing 'hybrids': cars and vans powered by combinations of petrol with batteries or petrol with LPG. Chrysler, Ford, General Motors, Honda, Nissan and Toyota are just some of the manufacturers that have actively developed EVs for the Californian market.

Pivco's CityBee

Norwegian plastics specialist Pivco produced a revolutionary one-piece car body shell which evolved into the CityBee electrically powered prototype car. This was a two-seater, three-door urban run-around/'second family car'. In appearance, it was similar to the Daewoo *Matiz*, Fiat *Seicento*, Hyundai *Atoz* or Mercedes *A-Class*. At the time of the marketing research study, it was innovative, unique and very much at the forefront of technology. In order to successfully bring the CityBee or its derivative to market, Pivco had to identify the correct niche for this vehicle in a marketplace where (a) consumer views were relatively unknown, (b) the concept of electrically powered vehicles was far from accepted in consumers' minds, (c) indications were that major car manufacturers were also targeting this niche of the car market, and (d) Pivco's reputation was not high in the vehicle buying market.

Pivco identified a set of questions it anticipated would be addressed in a programme of marketing research: What do consumers expect of electrically powered vehicles (EVs)? Which consumers will prove more receptive? What are the barriers to overcome if there is to be a successful market entry? What are the principal competitive threats and perceptual concerns in the market? For the CityBee prototype, what do consumers view positively and negatively?

Generator PowerGen for several years had been monitoring the growing market for electrically powered vehicles. Early studies revealed the slow 'milk float' image to be overly dominant in the consumers' mind and thinking of the large motor manufacturers. Today, with the rapidly 'greening' consumer, households are more environment-conscious, businesses are having to become increasingly socially aware and the major vehicle manufacturers are all developing car and van models oriented to electricity, liquid petroleum gas (LPG) or hybrid combinations with petrol, as power sources. Together, PowerGen and Pivco decided to research UK consumer attitudes to EVs and Pivco's CityBee prototype. The CityBee eventually came to market as the Ford Think.

Market Background

There is a real trend towards 'the greening consumer'. Whether it is BMW building recycling plants for its cars, P&G modifying packaging, refuse collections taking paper separately for recycling, industrial conglomerates such as ICI or Monsanto stating publicly their emissions and waste disposal policies, pressure groups warning about global warming and waste levels, or school children receiving lessons featuring environmental concerns. The rapid take-off, in new product development terms, of unleaded petrol reflected how quickly consumer attitudes can be altered by manufacturers' and regulators' policies. Such manufacturers, however, are only reflecting the marketplace and wishes of their target customers. In the vehicle industry, most leading manufacturers are developing models designed to use electricity. Increasingly these vehicles look like their petrol-powered cousins and match their performance capabilities. While giving these manufacturers good opportunities for publicity in the light of consumer trends, this move clearly reflects the dramatic changes in consumer attitudes and awareness of pollution, the environment, safety and the long-term impact on society of today's marketers.

For most of the twentieth century, mass produced vehicles – cars, public transport and haulage – were powered by oil-based fuels: petrol and diesel. There were various attempts to break this stranglehold, notably with gas-powered vehicles. These early trials came to little. Electric power is not new to vehicles and various programmes in Europe, North America and Asia-Pacific have attempted to popularize this form of auto-motion, but with relatively little mass market commercial success. To most consumers, the slow-moving milk float is the real face of electric vehicles. As the major car manufacturers experiment with adapted versions of their standard petrol powered model ranges, more familiar car designs are on the streets but powered by electricity. Currently Peugeot has electric variants of its *106* 'mini' on trial with local authorities, police forces and the MoD in at least four countries. These vehicles require charging every 50 miles or so and cannot exceed 60 mph.

At the other extreme, GM in the States has a family saloon which is capable of matching its conventionally powered models and such prestigious names as Mercedes and BMW are fine-tuning electrically powered concept cars with executive car performance levels. Most Vauxhall models in the UK are now available as petrol/LPG hybrids. There is no doubt that the marketplace is changing and most car producers are seriously examining the options provided by including LPG or electrically powered vehicles in their ranges. Technology enhancements are leading to the development of electrically powered vehicles which genuinely are able to match the performance of existing models. Re-charging infrastructure exists to slow-charge at home over-night or fast-charge at the curb, at the garage forecourt or in a suitably cabled car park, while shopping, sitting in a restaurant or watching a movie at a multiplex. Legislation in the EU and the States is an important force, too, with regulators and legislators aiming for zero emission vehicles and reduced pollution levels. The UK Government, is also now encouraging lower emissions from vehicles and putting pressure on the major vehicle manufacturers.

Marketing Research Aims

PowerGen and Pivco specified a programme of consumer – and subsequently business-to-business – marketing research to assist in their understanding of the market's dynamics and to help steer their on-going planning. The project objectives were:

1. To understand the marketplace better and determine the segments of the market most prone to purchase an electrically powered vehicle.
2. To be able to produce a marketing strategy, with an understanding of the required marketing proposition and incentives to stimulate buyer interest.
3. To identify 'hooks' and messages which will convince customers to purchase electric vehicles in preference to petrol or diesel powered vehicles.

The marketing research had to examine:

■ Consumer views of the CityBee prototype.
■ Consumer versus organizational (fleet) buying needs and preferences.
■ The 'fit' between the vehicle, the possible energy sources and re-charging options.
■ Re-charging infrastructure options and potential site/billing/purchasing partners.
■ UK versus Norwegian versus Asia Pacific branding.

Marketing Research Programme

The research was designed to examine the views of potential specifiers, owners and users of electric vehicles. Specifically, attitudes towards:

- the concept
- family run-around or commuter vehicles
- the prototype CityBee and existing competitors
- two-seater, two plus two, or larger cars
- the power source
- a possible launch strategy.

Table III.4 summarizes the specific research issues examined during this marketing research project. These were suggested by Pivco, PowerGen, the marketing research specialists recruited to undertake the research project and the findings from preliminary desk research into the electric vehicle (EV) market.

Table III.4	*Specific Research Issues*

Concept
  Understanding/beliefs
  Questions
  Strengths/weaknesses of concept
  Degree of interest
  Barriers to interest

Possible motivations and their rankings
  Ecology/environment
  Social
  Novelty/'being first'
  Cost/value
  Low noise levels
  Emotion

Prototype product
  Opinions of prototype
  Comparisons with existing competitors
  (e.g.: Peugeot's *106* electric)
  Standing versus 'conventional' vehicles
  Branding
  Country of origin

Reliability versus cost
  Will it be reliable
  Servicing
  Running costs
  Depreciation
  Lifetime costs

Social issues
  Deter or stimulate ownership/interest
  Fit with the 'greening consumer'
  'Green' in mind or overt behaviour

Price
  Perceptions of price
  Positioning versus 'conventional' vehicles
  If there is a premium, what is the basis

Relationship with existing products
  A first car
  A second car
  A short trip commercial vehicle
  Vans for on-site use only
  Longer distance running
  A young person's or older person's car
  Private use or commercial

Distribution
  Where should it be sold:
    Motor dealers
    Halford's
    Lex
    Innovative/straight through
    (supermarkets, Daewoo-style or
    other)
    In to rental businesses such as
    Hertz and Avis, or in to leasing
    businesses
    Others?
  Used car/second-hand dealerships

Source/type of re-charging/billing
Preferred type/format/timing of billing
Value placed on fast/slow re-charging
Viable re-charging locations/'partners':
Tesco, Sainsbury, Safeway, Asda
Curry's or Comet
Direct Line
Virgin
Regional Electricity Companies
(RECs) – e.g.: Eastern or Scottish
Power
PowerGen or National Power
Shell or Esso
Vehicle dealers
National Car Parks (NCP)
Others?

Potential re-charge sites
Home
Office/work
Pub/fast food
Restaurant/cinema/bowling/leisure/social
clubs
Supermarket
Motorway service area
Vehicle dealer
Shell/Esso forecourt
NCP/town centre
Short-stay car park
Long-stay car park
Transport termini/station/airport
Council/local authority owned sites
Others?

Potential profile
Who is the likely specifier going to be
Profile skews by respondents/likely buyers:
Urban/rural
Class/education/career
Other brands bought/loyalties to other products, services
Existing vehicle ownership
Patterns of adoption (e.g.: what have they recently bought in innovative categories
such as direct financial services/mobile 'phones/CD/microwave/camcorder/satellite
TV/BT rivals/digital broadcast services)
Business versus private purchase/use
Likely users of self-service vehicles at pick-up/drop-off nodes
Value placed on leasing
Value placed on third-party sponsorship
Are consumers ready for the idea now or do they have to 'wait and see'

The research commenced with desk research: a trawl through secondary sources
in order to help fine-tune the issues outlined in Table III.4. Then there was a series
of in-depth discussions to probe consumers' feelings and attitudes towards EVs
and the CityBee. This qualitative research was based on focus groups – discussion
groups lasting around two hours, each with eight consumers present. Finally, the
findings from the focus groups were validated through a programme of telephone
and omnibus interviews. This quantitative research solicited the views of several
hundred respondents. Throughout all stages, the research examined the concept,
CityBee prototype and power source issues.

The research targets were two sets of potential specifiers/consumers of the
electric car:

- Male and female
- ABC1
- 20–64

- Male and female
- ABC1
- 20–64

- New car owners/second car owners
- Who may already own a new small car
- Are environmentally concerned enough to consider electricity as a power source/do not reject the concept 'within the next five years'
- Relatively early adopters of technology.

- Already own or would consider owning a small car or MPV
- Not budget conscious
- Early adopters

Specifically, the focus groups were intended to determine the response of potential consumers to the concept of the electric car, their existing awareness and knowledge, perceived potential benefits, plus any probable queries or problems.

The research needed to determine how consumers regarded their current conventional cars and in particular new small concepts such as Ford's *Ka*, and how these products compared with the electric car concept:

- relative strengths;
- relative weaknesses/concerns/questions;
- what would it take to convert a 'conventional' car to an electric product;
- what are the characteristics of the consumer most likely to transfer;
- what process will that consumer have to go through in order to transfer.

The specific issues included:

- Response to concept
- Imagery of concept (who for, perceived motivations)
- Response to product design
- Response to refuelling
- Locations for refuelling
- Payment for refuelling
- Price
- Channel choices
- Motivations for purchase – practical versus emotional versus ecological

Two forms of qualitative focus groups were available for use:

1. focus groups without product
2. focus groups with product – *clinics*

Focus groups – without product – had the advantages of being able to focus on the concept, taking less time and costing less. *Clinics* – with product – had the advantages of being able to cover the real product, but required more time and used up more budget.

This research opted for six clinics with the CityBee and other manufacturers' cars (eg: Peugeot *106* electric and the – at the time – wacky Ford *Ka*) present. Table III.5 details the clinic composition.

Table III.5	*Clinic Composition*					
Group	**Sex**	**Age**	**Class**	**Life Stage**	**Car**	**Location**
1	f	20 – 29	BC1	Pre-family	Small	SE
2	m	20 – 29	BC1	Pre-family	Small	North
3	f	30 – 44	ABC1	Family	2 car	North
4	m	30 – 44	ABC1	Family	2 car	SE
5	f	45 – 64	AB	Empty nester	Small/2 car	SE
6	m	45 – 64	AB	Empty nester	Small/2 car	North

Two locations were used to obtain a geographic spread, while avoiding having to set up costly clinics at too many sites. The discussion flow was based on the research issues detailed in Table III.4 and the desk research. All discussions were taped, observed by client personnel and transcribed for verbal and written debriefs.

The findings and associated recommendations from the qualitative marketing research were followed up in the final phase of research. This confirmatory research also quantified key conclusions. The quantitative research was tackled by (a) buying into a consumer omnibus survey, whereby a small selection of core issues/hypotheses was addressed as part of one of the many continuous, on-going omnibus studies taking place throughout the UK; and (b) a series of telephone interviews. This phase of the research programme provided several hundred sets of responses to a reasonably lengthy and detailed questionnaire. These results were quantified and formally analysed using appropriate multivariate techniques and significance tests.

The Outcomes

The marketing research moved into a second stage, with an examination of fleet car buying: potential trade users who controlled/influenced the purchase of cars and light vans. This marketing research emulated the consumer research undertaken in the clinics, examining:

- cars: fleets/hire/leasing;
- light vans: companies/public sector/non-profit organizations
- relatively early adopters.

In addition, 'pockets' of other consumers were researched in order to further identify the innovators and early adopters likely to consider being one of the first to own or lease an EV. As with most marketing research, budgets rarely provide for a census of opinion. Small samples of selected parts of the buying public must be hypothesized by the client and marketing researcher to be the most attractive for questioning. Perhaps other segments of the car buying public should have been included in the marketing research for CityBee? Nevertheless, through the composition and mix of the research clinics and the sample design for the confirmatory quantitative research, the bulk of the car buying market likely to be interested in EVs and the CityBee was included in this marketing research programme.

The perceptions of the CityBee and of EVs were far removed from the milk float or *Dr Who* car jibes anticipated by some of the researchers. The CityBee was well received. Apart from a few stylistic changes, Pivco was told by a sizeable minority of those included in the research that an EV and the CityBee would be considered as their next car purchase, were both available in the marketplace. Young men particularly cited the novel design and dent-proof plastic body as major plus points. Middle-aged parents thought the CityBee to be an attractive proposition for a second family car low daily mileage urban run-around, which also would be an environmentally responsible purchase. Young ladies were not so keen: apparently the CityBee lacked 'pulling power' – not of horse power, but in terms of the opposite sex! For Pivco, the solution was taken out of its hand by Ford, who took over the CityBee concept and EV development in 1999. Ford launched the CityBee as its Think model.

Ford's interest reflects the rapid increase in alternative fuel car designs, prototypes and adaptations of existing models by the major vehicle manufacturers, which all have models already on the market or in preparation. For EVs, the future is not so certain, however. Recently, liquid petroleum gas (LPG) has made the headlines. This alternative fuel has been selected by Vauxhall and Volvo. Many manufacturers are experimenting with hybrid designs which integrate petrol engines with LPG energy, enabling the driver to extend distances between refuelling and adopt a driving pattern of behaviour similar to driving a conventional petrol powered car. The mighty petroleum companies such as Shell and BP are encouraging this move to LPG, as their refineries produce both petrol and LPG, while their forecourts are still required for LPG refuelling. A switch to electricity, with at-home re-charging or re-charging in car parks while at work, shopping centre or entertainment venue, poses a significant competitive threat to such petroleum producers and their expensive, extensive garage forecourt networks. This marketing research programme identified significant interest in alternative energies and particularly EVs. It is still unclear, however, how this marketplace will evolve.

Issues

The CityBee was developed by a Norwegian company whose executives were aware of the impact of traditional petrol and diesel engines on the natural environment. For consumers, such a solution – an EV – was unfamiliar and the Norwegian company unknown. Researching consumer attitudes under such circumstances is problematic, but nevertheless such marketing intelligence is essential.

Marketing research

Were there additional target audiences for the marketing research? How else could the marketing researchers have specified the desired respondent profile? Of the many surveying tools, which techniques could best be deployed to examine an innovative and unfamiliar product?

Why would marketing researchers wish to mix qualitative and quantitative marketing research in a marketing research programme? Why was desk (secondary) research insufficient in the case of the CityBee? In what situations might secondary research be adequate without the addition of any primary data collection?

The marketing environment

What were the forces of the marketing environment driving the development of the CityBee? Are the major car manufacturers correct in their approach to alternative fuels?

Buying behaviour

Why must consumer attitudes be researched before an innovative product is launched? What difficulties are likely to be encountered in properly gaining an impression of such consumer views?

Why is the buying decision process likely to be more extensive for an EV than for a conventional vehicle? What are the implications for EV marketing programmes?

Relevant Theory Notes

T4: Marketing Research, pp. 213–220
T2: The Marketing Environment and Competition, pp. 199–204
T3: Buying Behaviour, pp. 205–212

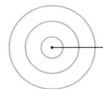

Full Case 5: Stepcan Differential Advantage Through Packaging

For several decades, fruit products had been tinned by canning companies or fruit producers for sale as predominantly manufacturer brands such as Del Monte, or as voluntary group brands such as Spar or VG. With the success of retailer own-label brands, fruit producers and canning companies had to satisfy the merchandisers of the large retailers with their own-label packaging requirements. In the mid-1980s, retailers such as Tesco, Sainsbury's and Marks and Spencer (M&S) in the UK, Carrefour in France and Ahold in the Netherlands, were seeking to differentiate their products not purely through quality, value or taste, but increasingly with the packaging and appearance of merchandise. Visual appeal of items on shelves was perceived to increase purchase rates, and potentially unit ticket prices, too. For the suppliers of cans and packaging materials, however, it was still very much a price-driven commodity business: high volumes, low prices, and small returns. But then came Stepcan.

The Introduction of Stepcan

'M&S adopts clear plastics STEPCAN for premium fruit pack presentation', screamed the news headline in *Packaging News.* According to Metal Box (MB), the developer of Stepcan, this form of food packaging benefited from numerous advantages:

- Clarity
- High quality image
- Long ambient shelf life
- Lightweight
- Shatterproof
- Easy open ends
- Stackable
- Re-usable
- Interchangeable on canning lines.

The feature in *Packaging News* elaborated:

> Marks and Spencer has nationally launched satsumas, grapefruit and red grapefruit in clear plastic cans following successful test markets last year. A particular advantage of the can is that the shopper can see the contents at a glance and the clarity of the pack enhances the eye appeal of the fruit. M&S has further enhanced this high quality image by including a gold colour ldpe overcap on top of the metal ends.

Metal Box has developed this patented style of container – Stepcan – over a number of years, and it is manufactured by the *stretch tube extrusion process* in pet. The metal ends are conventionally double seamed on, but importantly they feature an easy ring pull. Additional benefits include less rusting, no shattering and of course distinction on shelf. It is also lighter and easier to handle and the ring pull makes it a highly convenient pack to use. 'Stepcans present the ideal image for premium products in the quality sector of the convenience foods market,' says Steve Thomas, business development manager at MB.

In fact, Marks and Spencer had test marketed Stepcan-contained products in several stores, examining price points ranging, for example, from 60 pence to £1.30 for a 330 gramme 'can' of peach slices. It was found that even where Stepcans were placed on shelves immediately adjacent to tin cans of similar weight and content, the Stepcans heavily outsold the tin cans. Even where the price differential between the two types of containers differed by three to one, Stepcan still outsold the cheaper tin cans, often by up to four times!

Consumers Preferred the Visual Appeal

Tracking research revealed the visual impact of the peaches or fruit cocktail, plus the shatterproof container, outweighed higher prices. The packaging enhanced the product's appeal and gave a genuine competitive advantage in a previously unexciting commodity-based market for containers. The consumers interested in Stepcan wanted high quality products: the visibility of the fruit implied safety in the purchase; quality was taken for granted. They were reasonably affluent, 'up-market', educated shoppers, making purchases not out of necessity but by choice and they were not too constrained by price.

The result was heavy demand for MB's Stepcan, with several major retail groups – including Waitrose, Sainsbury's and M&S – adopting Stepcan and wanting exclusivity of supply.

An Unknown Commodity within MB

For Metal Box, Stepcan's success was something of a problem. Initially developed on a sideline as 'a whim' of certain engineers and a couple of middle managers, the product was 'too successful' too quickly in that production could not be geared to meet demand immediately. There was a lead over competitors of approximately two years, but the company had many difficult decisions to make.

Stepcan, unlike the company's staple packaging products, was not a cheap, easily discounted commodity item. Retailers were charging premium prices because of the perceived quality and safety expectations of their customers. Unfortunately, the MB salesforce, used to selling tin cans at so many pence per thousand, found it difficult to grasp that they should be seeking higher returns from the Stepcan product. This was a problem inherent in MB; many senior managers seemingly were unaware of Stepcan's potential for higher unit prices and profit margins. Although a slight price advantage was gained from Stepcan over tin cans for the company, the bulk of the price premium gain was going to the retailers. There was, perhaps, a need to set Stepcan up as a self-contained operation within MB, with a product champion senior executive, bespoke production and separate distribution. The real risk was that MB would fail to recognize the potential of the product, allowing only the retailers to gain from the higher retail prices.

Difficult Decisions

Retailers were seeking Stepcan supplies, but so were the fruit growers. MB needed to have clear priorities. Stepcan's positioning – '*The Choice is Clear*' – was based on a quality image and the opportunity presented to retailers to premium price previously low-margin commodity foodstuffs. Were distribution coverage to be too diluted, this quality, high price base would quickly be eroded. MB needed to concentrate either on retailers or on growers, but probably not both. The company had limited production capacity and needed to maximize returns. Particularly in countries dominated by the large grocery retail chains, MB had to tie in retailers before competitors' products appeared. Partners needed to be selected with caution. Various avenues were explored, ranging from the existing structure and approach, to the establishment of a separate operating company within MB, to a joint venture with a grower or major retail group. Ultimately, with a few minor changes, the existing situation was allowed to continue: there was no joint venture or separate operating division within MB. The company slowly rolled out production of Stepcan.

The European Dimension

Outside the UK, Stepcan was gaining a following, but not with the enthusiasm as demonstrated by the UK retail groups. MB subsidiaries outside the UK had mixed feelings, with some seeking the right to produce and sell Stepcans, but with others more reluctant, instead desiring to focus on metal-based containers and other plastics. Opinion within the industry was also divided; some rivals were envious, but there were those that were cautious, believing that Stepcan would find general acceptance difficult. However, certain competitors were known to be researching and developing similar products. The general consensus was that Metal Box had a winning product in Stepcan, but not on the scale implied from the UK market.

Consumer reaction differed between countries. The company commissioned marketing research that, through personal interviews and focus group discussions, sought consumer reactions in several countries. Interviews with supermarket managers and merchandisers (buyers) gained the retailers' views. In most of Europe, particularly France and Scandinavia, the consumers perceived the shatterproof containers to be a real advantage, which when coupled with their liking of the transparency of the Stepcan, seemed to auger well for Stepcan.

However, in certain areas of Scandinavia and particularly in Germany, the raw material – plastic – was a significant drawback. The recyclability of glass was preferred over any container made from plastics. At the time (1988), however, there was no indication that the strength of the German 'green consumer' would spread to France, Britain or the Mediterranean countries. The ring pull lid was perceived, during the European research, to be more of a disadvantage than a product benefit, often proving difficult to remove from the container.

Table III.6	The Canned Fruit Market – Brand Shares in the Canned Fruit Market, UK

	% of volume	
Manufacturer	*1987*	*1990*
Del Monte	16	17
Princes	12	9
John West	3	3
Gerber Pride	4	3
Dole	-	2
S & B	-	2
Australian/Premier Gold	4	1
Own label (retailer)	32	47
Others	29	16
Total	100	100

Source: Retail Business

Table III.7	UK Retail Distribution of Canned Foods, 1988

	% of volume
All grocery multiples	73
Co-operatives	15
Independent grocers	12

Source: Euromonitor

Table III.8	Major Grocery Retailers, UK, Denmark, France and West Germany

UK: major grocery retailers	*% market shares*	
	1987	*1989*
Sainsbury's	10.7	13.0
Tesco	11.1	12.3
Argyll	7.6	9.0
Asda	5.9	8.6
Gateway	8.8	6.7
Others	55.9	50.4

Denmark: major integrated food retailing groups, 1987–8

	Net turnover (DK m)	No. stores
Co-op Group:		
FDB	8,457	442
Independent Societies	7,863	865
Fakta (discount)	1,237	76
Bonus (discount)	392	20
Irma	3,979	190
Dansk Supermarket Group:		
Salling	85	2
Bilk (hypermarkets)	2,025	5
Foetex	3,052	39
Netto (discount)	1,733	76
Aldi (discount)	1,742	88
Jaco Group:	317	5
Alta Discount	300	15
ABC Laupris (discount)	100	5
Loevbjerg:		
Loevbjerg (incl. Normann)	832	22
Prisa Discount	305	22

France: leading groups of supermarkets and hypermarkets, ranked by sales area, 1989–92

	'000m
ITM Enterprises	1,829
Leclerc	1,279
Promodès (excl. co-ops)	1,094
Carrefour	671
Casino	592

West Germany: Top 10 food retailers, 1988

	Retail sales DM bn
Aldi	19.7
Rewe Leibbrand	16.3
Tengelmann	14.6
Co-op AG	11.4
Asko-Schraper	9.4
Spar AG	7.9
Edeka	7.6
AllKauf	4.5
Massa	4.0
Lidl & Schwarz	3.9
Market share of Top 10	58.8%

West Germany: food sales by organization type, 1987–8

	1987	1988
	%	
Multiples	23.5	23.2
Co-operatives	11.4	13.9
Edeka	17.0	16.7
Rewe	15.7	15.6
Spar AG	7.6	8.1
Others	24.8	22.5

Sources:
UK: Retail Business; Denmark: Euromonitor; France: Euromonitor; West Germany (food retailers): Euromonitor, company reports, Statistisches Bundesamt; West Germany (food sales): Gesellschaft für Konsum, Markt und Absatzforschung, Euromonitor

Where Next?

Stepcan had many inherent product benefits. Consumers, on the whole, were favourably inclined and so were the large retail groups. There were problems, however. The positive response to the test market was not uniform across all countries. Costs of producing the Stepcan were higher than for rival tin cans. The ring pull was not functioning correctly and in certain territories plastics were certainly not *de rigueur*. In addition, within the Metal Box company, Stepcan posed some fundamental questions. How should MB have proceeded with the development of the Stepcan and its market? The choice was not clear.

Issues

Creating a differential advantage or competitive edge is never simple; packaging is often an option neglected. The retailers that test marketed Stepcan quickly realised the container's benefits, but not so everyone at Metal Box. The case also illustrates the role of the marketing environment, the problems of marketing across international frontiers and of controlling the supply chain.

Creating a differential advantage

Why is a differential advantage important? How can one be achieved? Did Stepcan give MB a competitive edge? Could Stepcan's apparent advantages be defended?

International marketing

Stepcan was researched in various countries. Reaction was mostly favourable, but not totally so. Why were there some warning signs in the negative reactions? Were these unusual in marketing a product across national borders? Could they be addressed with the marketing mix?

The marketing environment

Social, cultural and regulatory changes may mean that had MB test marketed Stepcan today the product would receive the thumbs down from the European consumer. Why? Is this change of heart surprising?

Pricing

The retailers tested Stepcan at various prices: it was successful at all levels, including the highest. Why was this so? What should have been the implications to MB and its sales force?

Product management

Metal Box had problems defining a role for Stepcan in its product portfolio. What were the options available? Which could have given the company the best rewards? Were there any obvious problems with this 'best' approach?

Product development and packaging

How should MB have persuaded its retailer customers that Stepcan offered an innovative packaging solution with the potential to create product differentiation?

Relevant Theory Notes

Full Case 6: Kodak Norge
The Search for Information

Kodak Norge AS (Kodak Norway Ltd) represents the face of the US Eastman Kodak Corporation in Norway: it is a wholly owned subsidiary of the large multinational. Established in 1969, Kodak Norge splits its sales effort into six divisions: business imaging systems, health imaging, digital and applied imaging, professional motion imaging, Kodak professional, plus consumer imaging. Imaging technology and technical innovation for image capture and reproduction are the core activities. Through the divisions, the company offers many Kodak branded lines including photographic film for slides, prints and films through to cameras, copy products, business imaging services, health screening equipment and film processing.

In consumer photo-products Kodak Norge is dominant, with just over 40 per cent share of the market. However, since the 1960s the company's market share has declined from an overwhelming 90 per cent, with Swedish companies taking more than a quarter of the processing market. During this period, key competitor Fuji was successful in entering the Norwegian film market. Today, Fuji is Kodak Norge's most aggressive competitor, accounting for around a third of the film market. Kodak management now believes that relatively sluggish reactions to changes in customer needs, particularly in the industrial and commercial sector, were partly to blame for this dramatic downturn in Kodak's fortunes. As well as Fuji, Kodak Norge faces keen competition for graphic arts materials and professional films from Agfa. The Norwegian photo-processing market, attracting prices that are around 15 per cent higher than the rest of Europe, is highly competitive. Local companies capitalize on the multi-nationals' premium prices by offering heavy discounts.

Customers and Market Segments

For Kodak Norge, the *retailers* of film and cheap cameras are key customers. The average consumer of photographic products, the 'snap-shooter', is seen as a relatively unsophisticated buyer, purchasing film products on impulse from petrol stations, hotel shops and a variety of leisure attractions. Kodak executives believe that these consumers do not differentiate much between brands, instead buying the most readily available product. The key for Kodak Norge is to achieve as much shelf space as possible in a multitude of retail outlets.

In the photographic products market, segmentation has evolved at two levels: consumers and distributors. Perhaps most importantly, Eastman Kodak and its subsidiaries must thoroughly understand the requirements of consumers who use photographic products, enabling the company to consider the value of various segmentation schemes. For instance, Eastman Kodak groups consumers according to patterns of product usage: snapshooters, keen amateurs and professionals. These consumer groups are served by ranges of different quality and specification film and imaging products. In addition to segmentation at the consumer level, players in this market need to decide how best to segment and service the needs of distributors: retailers, wholesalers and buying groups.

In the early 1990s, managers at Kodak Norge found that segmenting according to distribution channel had been an effective approach to follow in the Norwegian market. This had involved servicing photo-dealer shops directly while supplying Kodak's distributors through wholesalers. This gave Kodak Norge an edge over arch rival Fuji, which had only 20 employees in Norway and lacked distribution outside of the photo-dealers.

Marketing Research

Each Kodak sales division is required to estimate its share of key markets and also highlight those areas where sales performance is weak. Management at Kodak Norge obtained market and customer information from both internal and external sources. Individuals within the company had responsibility for tracking aspects of the marketing environment, for example checking on the likely impact of any legislative changes. External information came from government statistics, distributors and marketing research agencies, such as Nielsen. The focus for these external data was on market trends – such as ownership patterns of photographic equipment or consumer leisure activities – rather than individual consumer requirements.

Despite such marketing research information, there was concern in the company – a concern echoed by most 'tuned in' companies – that efforts had to be maintained to understand consumer needs and attitudes. For instance:

■ How did consumers select their film products and what factors influenced the choices that they made?

■ How did consumers spend their leisure time and what role did photography play in it?

■ What were consumers' perceptions of competing brands?

■ What was the buying process like for company (business-to-business) purchasers and what particular needs did they have?

■ From where were growth opportunities to come for Kodak Norge?

■ How could key rivals be kept at bay?

Quality information on these and a host of related issues was seen as vital to the development of effective marketing programmes. Competitor research also had to be continually updated for Kodak Norge to make informed judgements about targeting and its product positioning. How else could a clear and sustainable competitive advantage be ensured in its key markets? Kodak's position had been eroded, partly perhaps because insufficient information meant that management did not totally keep abreast of consumer expectations and behaviour or competitors' activities and trends.

In order to plan future marketing research efforts, management at Kodak Norge needed to consider its information requirements and priorities. These priorities had then to be satisfied using appropriate research techniques and data collection methods. Kodak's executives acknowledged that any survey – sample base, issues, techniques and material – had to be carefully designed, with specific targets in mind and the most suitable method for conducting the research selected. Probable analysis of resulting data and implementation of findings had also to be considered in advance of any survey work to ensure the results were actionable and constructive.

The challenges for Kodak Norge were to fend-off Fuji, steal market share from local Scandinavian businesses, while building up its customer base. Innovative products and a strong brand helped, but there was a need for a better under-standing of consumer and business customer perceptions and expectations. There was an urgent need to better grasp competitors' strategies and likely plans. A core requirement was to bolster Kodak Norge's marketing intelligence.

Issues

Kodak Norge, in common with many companies, believed it had an incomplete marketing information system and inadequate marketing intelligence. The company was highly successful but faced strong international and local competition. It was particularly important for Kodak Norge to understand its market segments and to control effectively its marketing channels.

Marketing research

What were Kodak Norge's marketing research needs? Which were the most appropriate research tools? Why?

Buying behaviour

What did Kodak Norge need to know about its customers and target markets? Knowledge of which aspects of their buying behaviour would most assist in the company's decision-making?

Segmentation

What were the key market segments available to Kodak Norge? On what basis were these segments identified? Could a different approach to segmenting this market have been adopted? How and why?

Channels

Kodak world-wide comprehended the importance of choosing effective marketing channels, and the need to control and assist its intermediaries. What were the main marketing channels in this market? How could Kodak Norge have exerted influence over them? Why was it important for such a major branded manufacturer to control its marketing channels?

Relevant Theory Notes

T4: Marketing Research, pp. 213–220
T3: Buying Behaviour, pp. 205–212
T6: Market Segmentation, pp. 229–236
T9: The Marketing Mix: Place – Distribution and Marketing Channels, pp. 255–260

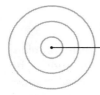

Full Case 7: Petrol Retailing Supermarket Giants take on the Oil Companies

Few markets are higher pressure or more cut-throat than petrol retailing. Consolidation amongst the large petroleum brands has increased competitive rivalry. Concerns about the environmental impact of petrol engines have pressurized governments to increase fuel-related taxation. Forecourts are having to adopt environmentally responsible systems for waste disposal and oil storage. Consumers are also being encouraged to make greater use of public transport. The UK government has already taken steps to reduce the road-building programme and is committed to a range of other measures designed to reduce car usage. The result? Retail fuel margins are being squeezed even further.

Petrol forecourt retailing faces two major problems. First, fuel sales are growing very slowly. Despite the increasing size of the UK vehicle park and a marked increase in the number of vehicles on the road, the increase in fuel sales has been small. Households acquiring a second or third car account for much of the vehicle park increase. These additional vehicles are often low mileage. Second, there has been a rapid contraction of the forecourt sector. Between 1990 and 1996, there was a 25 per cent decline in the sector, with an estimated 750 outlets closing each year. The balance of power among those remaining is shifting as the larger oil companies seek to increase control over their portfolio of forecourts, closing those which are least profitable.

| Table III.9 | UK Petrol Sites |

| | Total UK Petrol Sites | | Self-Service Petrol Sites | | Average |
	Total Number	Percentage Change	Total Number	Percentage of Total	Throughput (Million Litres)
1988	20,016	–0.90	8,841	44.17	1.50
1989	19,756	–1.30	10,836	54.85	1.56
1990	19,465	–1.47	11,043	56.73	1.62
1991	19,247	–1.12	11,886	61.76	1.62
1992	18,549	–3.63	12,249	66.04	1.67
1993	17,969	–3.13	12,873	71.64	1.72
1994	16,971	–5.55	12,549	73.94	1.76
1995	16,244	–4.28	12,574	77.41	1.76
1996	14,748	–9.21	11,600	78.65	1.97
1997	13,953	–5.39	10,302	73.83	2.18

Source: Petroleum Review: Retail Marketing Survey 1998.

The large petrol companies have also found themselves under attack from a surprising source. In the UK, the large supermarket chains have invested in developing their own forecourts. In 1998, only around 50 new petrol forecourts opened in the UK, the majority of which were operated by the supermarket companies. Tesco alone accounted for over half of these new openings. As these new entrants have increased their grip on the market, they are increasingly dictating pricing levels for the industry. Their cut-price petrol, often sold as a loss leader to attract customers to the main store, has taken the market by storm. By 1997, supermarket forecourts accounted for a staggering 23.3 per cent of the market, an increase of nearly 5 per cent on the previous year. In a market estimated in excess of £2.8 billion, this represents a substantial amount.

Table III.10	*Petrol Sales Share*

Company	1996	1997
Supermarkets	18.8%	23%
(includes Sainsbury's and Tesco)		
Esso	20.3%	18.7%
Shell	17%	16.7%
BP/Mobil	14.8%	13%
Texaco	4.4%	4.5%
Total	4.3%	4.3%
Elf	3.1%	4%
Others	14.8%	15%
(includes Jet and Fina)		

Source: Datamonitor

Table III.11	*Principal Petrol and Diesel Suppliers to the Retail Market*[1]

Brand	Retail Outlets Selling Petrol	Retail Outlets Selling Diesel	Brand	Retail Outlets Selling Petrol	Retail Outlets Selling Diesel
Esso	1,874	1,855	British Fuels	195	180
BP	1,831	1,811	Butler	190	177
Shell	1,459	1,451	Anglo/Repsol	188	154
Texaco	1,147	1,147	Safeway	156	156
UK	726	605	Rix	148	148
Jet	670	670	WCF/BJ/Texaco/Gulf	135	132
Total	568	550	ASDA	129	129
Save	524	512	Maxol	128	125
Elf	499	497	Proteus[1]	113	113
Q8	439	417	Bayford Thrust	109	106
Fina	424	422	Flare	97	93
Murco	401	390	Spot Petroleum	81	80

Gulf	382	377	Morrisons	64	62
Tesco	288	286	Heltor/Gulf	43	39
Power/3D/Phoenix	215	205	Snax 24	40	40
J Sainsbury/Savacentre	205	205	Globe	35	35
Total[2]				**13,953**	**13,566**

Notes: [1] As at 31.12.97.

[2] Total includes unlisted smaller suppliers. These figures include shared sites, e.g. on motorways, and are therefore higher than the actual number of petrol/diesel stations. 10,302 sites are self-service; 6,317 are company owned. On motorways, 123 outlets sell petrol and 141 sell diesel. At hypermarkets and supermarkets, 934 outlets sell petrol and 928 sell diesel.

Source: Petroleum Review: Retail Marketing Survey 1998.

In this environment, the biggest victims are the independent wholesalers that buy their fuel on the spot market for supply to small, lower volume operations. These operations, many of which are one-site businesses or small regional chains, claim that it is virtually impossible to make money from selling petrol, are finding it increasingly difficult to survive.

Attempts to differentiate the product itself have met with an unenthusiastic response from customers. Shell's now famous attempt to brand its petrol with the Formula Shell label became an embarrassing flop. The problem was that the additives that were meant to lead to improved engine performance actually damaged some vehicles. Petrol, it seems, is a standard commodity-type offering and little can be done to excite customers about it or make one brand stand out from another. The majority of customers still view their regular trips to their local forecourt as an inconvenience – a begrudged purchase. For many the primary concern is to make the experience as simple as possible, visiting the most conveniently located forecourt at a time when they know it will not be too busy. In a recent survey nearly 80 per cent of customers questioned about their reasons for selecting the petrol station they visited most often claimed that it was because it was close to home or on a route they regularly travelled.

Merger Activity

In a market so firmly driven by price, merging operations with competitors has become a logical response for some operators. This bringing together of rivals allows the companies to take advantage of scale economies and cut their running costs. Any savings can then be invested in adding value to the petrol forecourt experience. Such was the logic behind the merger of Exxon and Mobil. In a £60 billion deal, the new petrol giant became the world's leading oil business ahead of Royal Dutch Shell and BP Amoco. The size of the company will make it easier to compete on price with key supermarket rivals. Meanwhile the earlier trading agreement between BP and Mobil resulted in a combined operation of 1600 sites. An extensive programme followed to re-brand the Mobil forecourts to BP's modern green and yellow livery, with Mobil handling the combined lubricants business. The French business Total also became involved in merger activity, with the take-over of Belgian company PetroFina.

Bringing the Supermarket onto the Forecourt

Since the mid-1990s the petrol companies have been diversifying into retailing in order to lure customers onto the forecourts and increase exposure of their brands. With some service stations making 60 per cent of their sales from non-fuel purchases, the attractions of this trend are clear. Margins in non-petrol retailing are much higher and motorists can be persuaded that there is so much more to their forecourt visit than the purchase of fuel. Forecourt stores are providing the customer with a much needed added service, a convenient location to stock up on groceries they have run out of or to buy the snacks, newspapers, gifts and cards they need for their business trip or family visiting. In general, the mix of products available is increasing and forecourt outlets are becoming the new 'corner shop'. Although the petrol companies have no illusions about their ability to compete with the floor space and variety of the large supermarkets, by being more customer focused they believe that they can become the venue of choice for top-up purchases.

Initially it seemed that the petrol companies were using forecourt stores purely as a means to encourage customers to buy their petrol. Now it seems as if a more substantive transformation is under way, with the realization of the importance of the non-petrol component of sales. Following on from its link up with Mobil, BP Oil UK decided to reposition itself as a multiple convenience retailer. This meant the company promoted its role as a convenience retailer over and above its more traditional positioning as a petrol provider. In the words of BP UK marketing manager Sally Bye, 'We are building on the existing strengths of our brand and the extensive network gained through the joint venture with Mobil to position BP as the convenience retailer of choice'. According to Shell UK trading manager Jim Rands, BP is not alone in its changing focus, stating, 'Convenience shopping is becoming our whole reason for being'.

The convenience shopping trend has also resulted in a new type of merger activity, with some of the petrol companies linking up with their supermarket rivals. The idea is simple: join forces with a leading supermarket, then build forecourt shops around the brand. Tesco and Esso are co-operating. BP and Safeway became involved in an unlikely alliance, aimed at sharing their respective expertise. A successful trial in seven towns of a joint 'mini-supermarket and forecourt' concept was rolled out to one hundred sites around the UK. The costs of the initiative were shared on a 50: 50 basis by the partners and led to the development of sites carefully chosen from among BP's 900 company-owned petrol stations. With over 3,000 product lines including everything from fresh produce and dairy products to bread and breakfast cereals, the mini-supermarkets are much more substantial than the traditional forecourt shop. Safeway's Chief Executive, Colin Smith commented:

> The combination of superstore quality and pricing with extended opening
> hours has been a real hit with customers, and the strength of both BP and

Safeway brands has been instrumental in the success of the trial. I am excited by the potential of our mini-supermarket and forecourt concept and we are confident that the BP and Safeway partnership will be a major force in the UK convenience market within three years.

Price versus Loyalty

For many years loyalty schemes were a fundamental part of petrol retailing. From the free mugs and football card collections of the 1970s and 1980s to the loyalty cards and tokens of the 1990s. In recent years, in a direct response to the threat posed by the supermarket forecourts, the emphasis has shifted to price-cutting. This shift was epitomized by market leader Esso's decision to ditch the Tiger Tokens loyalty scheme in 1986. Instead, Esso launched Price Watch, a programme designed to make Esso the cheapest brand of petrol available.

Not all petrol retailers have moved away from loyalty-driven promotions. The Shell Smart Card has been rolled out around the UK, and the scheme has been extended to include non-petrol items. The supermarket forecourts have also brought back a version of loyalty programmes by extending their retail schemes to the petrol part of their business. Tesco acted to extend its Clubcard scheme to include petrol purchases early in 1996. This was seen as one way to combat the price-cutting which had accompanied Esso's Price Watch. Since introducing Clubcard to its forecourts, Tesco has also run 'double points' promotions on fuel purchases. The other supermarket operators have also been dynamic in seeking repeat purchases from fuel customers. Sainsbury's has pursued a combined approach of matching prices of local competitors and including petrol in its Reward card loyalty programme. Meanwhile Asda's stance on petrol sales is designed to match its lowest price marketing strategy. As a result, the retailer has consistently offered most competitive fuel prices. This low price is backed up with Fill 'n' Save petrol loyalty card for consumers and a business fuel card for corporate customers.

It is difficult to predict the precise role of price cutting and loyalty programmes in petrol retailing in the future. However, increasing environmental and economic pressures suggest little prospect for recovery in petrol margins and further contraction in the number of petrol forecourts seems inevitable. This means that the ongoing tussle between traditional and new forecourt operators looks set to continue.

Issues

The mergers in the forecourt sector are reducing the number of competitors but have increased the intensity of rivalry. The various partnerships between fuel businesses and grocery retailers have broadened the scope of the intense rivalry in the forecourt sector. For these businesses, such changes pose opportunities but also the need to develop clear branding strategies and trading propositions. A principal prong of attack has been the introduction of loyalty schemes to persuade customers to select forecourts based not only on the price of petrol or diesel.

Competition

To what extent do the alliances between fuel companies and supermarket retailers provide the opportunity for the creation of a differential advantage? Do such relationships provide companies preferring to 'go it alone' with opportunities or threats?

The marketing environment

The trading environment has changed dramatically for forecourt operators in the last decade, with fewer outlets, rationalization of the number of fuel brands, alliances with grocery retailers, the move to alternative fuels and legislative pressures on vehicle use. How should a business such as Shell assess the likely impact of these forces? Will such marketing environment forces affect all forecourt operators similarly?

Buying behaviour

The consumer is now expected additionally to treat many forecourts as mini-supermarkets. Will this change in the forecourt proposition have any impact on consumers' buying decision processes? Will the joint branding of BP and Safeway forecourt sites have any impact on consumers' perceptions and expectations?

Pricing

Petrol is viewed by many motorists as a commodity product. How are the fuel companies striving to persuade consumers to consider value rather than raw price? Why are the major petroleum companies attempting to move away from head-to-head price competition? In what ways are the strategies of the forecourt operators designed to instil brand loyalty?

Relevant Theory Notes

T7: Competitive Strategy, pp. 237–245
T2: The Marketing Environment and Competition, pp. 199–204

Full Case 8: Waterford Crystal Targeting Youth

Irish crystal manufacturer Waterford Crystal Ltd is renowned for its superior design and craftsmanship, unique clarity and brilliance of its crystal products: stemware, giftware, sports trophies, lighting, corporate gifts, customized chandeliers and special commissions, engraved pieces and sculpted pieces. Waterford's glass crystal products are exported to more than 106 countries. Of sales, 70 per cent are in North America, where it now captures a market leading 40 per cent of the premium crystal market.

Businessmen George and William Penrose founded the Waterford Glass House in the busy port of Waterford in 1783, producing crystal 'as fine a quality as any in Europe ... in the most elegant style'. The Penroses mingled minerals and glass to create crystal with beauty and mystery, a sweet chime when tapped and a sheer brilliance. At the 1851 Great Exhibition in London, Waterford Crystal won several gold medals and much acclaim. Then came recession and closure of the factory. After a gap of close to a century, in the 1940s a group of Irish businessmen resolved to revive the Waterford legacy. Waterford commenced full-scale production of handmade full lead crystal in 1947 and now is world leader and the largest producer of hand-cut crystal. The Waterford Visitor Centre at its Waterford base attracts over 300,000 visitors per annum and is one of the most popular tourist venues in Ireland.

Waterford acquired the famous Staffordshire chinaware manufacturer Josiah Wedgwood in 1986 in an agreed bid of £265 million. The china division has since become profitable, but the crystal operation suffered an immediate 73 per cent drop in profits and has only recently recovered. Nevertheless, Waterford-Wedgwood is the world's leading manufacturer of high quality china and glassware. The Waterford-Wedgwood Group now includes the well known brands Stuart Crystal; Johnson Brothers, Coalport and Jasper china; Germany's Rosenthal, plus financial interests in Royal Doulton. The company is particularly strong in North America, with expanding markets in Japan and Europe. Its premium-priced giftware is bought for special occasions or as notable gifts – emotional purchases supported by its strong, reputable deluxe brand names: Waterford, Wedgwood and Coalport.

Crystal in Recession

Expensive giftware items are anything but recession proof. The deepening recession in the early 1990s led the company to lay-off 750 of its 3,000 crystal workers, primarily at its Waterford base in Ireland. Crystal sales were hard hit, failing from IR£43.lm to IR£30.6m in 1991. Sales in the USA and Ireland (a large proportion of which are to American tourists), fell by 29 per cent to IR£25.9m. Sales outside the USA and Ireland, handled by Wedgwood's distribution, fell by 30 per cent to IR£4.7m. Sales of Wedgwood's ceramics held up better, with only a 4.5 per cent decline to IR£4.7m. In 1992's recession, there were total group sales of IR£130.6 million and a record loss of IR£1.762 million.

The marriage of the two famous names – Waterford and Wedgwood – significantly benefited distribution and brand awareness, although the two companies still independently manufacture and design. Wedgwood's presence in Japan and Waterford's in the USA gave a springboard for each other in Australia and Canada. However, in the early to mid-1990s, all profits stemmed from the UK, mainly through Wedgwood's china tableware. The distribution strengths and brand awareness of the Waterford-Wedgwood combination were not enough to bring growth or better financial returns. Shrewd target marketing, branding and product development were to be at the heart of Waterford's recovery and its on-going development.

Table III.12	Financial Summary, Waterford-Wedgwood			
		1987 IR£m	1990 IR£m	1996 IR£m
Sales	Waterford	76.4	87.0	153.0
	Wedgwood	169.9	204.1	223.3
	Total:	246.3	291.1	376.3
Operating Profit	Waterford	–18.3	–5.0	21.2
	Wedgwood	25.1	17.3	18.0
	Total:	6.8	12.3	39.2

Sources: Fitzwilton, Ireland and Waterford Ltd

Product Innovation

To grow their markets, major crystal manufacturers have introduced new products to take advantage of the growing popularity of crystal giftware. Some have moved away from conventional bowls and platters with lines as diverse as salt and pepper mills to individual designer pieces – a new wave in crystal: candle-sticks, animal figurines, personalized items. Crystal giftware, according to the US consumer magazines, now outshines traditional stemware.

Waterford's success and revival of its financial fortunes resulted from product innovation and new brands. In 1991 it launched Marquis, the first new Waterford brand in over 200 years. Now Marquis rates as the most successful ever new entry in the tabletop market. Marquis includes contemporary and traditional designs, produced by crystal makers throughout Europe, notably in Eastern Europe. Marquis is targeted at a younger, more price-sensitive consumer, at a lower entry point to provide the opportunity for appreciating crystal en route to 'moving up' to pristine classic Waterford crystal. In the core North American market, Marquis has become one of the consumer's favourite brands in its own right.

In addition to Marquis, following extensive consumer research, Waterford launched a range of less formal, modern designs aimed to appeal to a younger and more fashion-conscious target market. This move was epitomized by John Rocha's wonderful designs for Waterford. John Rocha, the Hong Kong born, Irish-based fashion designer has tackled many projects since being named British Designer of the Year, from interior designs for chic hotels to new uniforms for Virgin Atlantic. A range of crystal ware for Waterford, mixing oriental influences, Celtic flair and the traditions of Waterford, has proved a major commercial success for Waterford. Wine glasses, goblets, flutes, tumblers, vases, bowls, centrepieces and unique crystal sculptures have created a new market for Waterford – designer crystal ware.

Devaluing a Brand?

With its Marquis line, the venerable Irish crystal maker adopted a new approach to manufacturing and marketing. Waterford moved its production into Europe and scaled down its price points in the USA, which started at less than $30 for smaller pieces, on average 30 per cent cheaper than traditional Waterford lines. This was seen by some US observers as risky: introducing a line for 'the less well-heeled', manufactured in Germany, Portugal and the former Yugoslavia, and leading to labour unease at Waterford's Irish plants.

In America, where Waterford has 40 per cent of the luxury crystal market, '*Marquis* by Waterford Crystal' was launched in the $30 to $40 niche – although larger platters and bowls retailed at $135 – in order to compete more directly with crystal suppliers Mikasa, Lenox, Miller Rogasks and Gorham. The 1991 launch into 30 stores immediately proved profitable. Nevertheless, Marquis was a huge gamble, moving away from the 'finest hand-crafted Irish' traditions, and away from the Waterford brand heritage; a brand reputation which in the USA and Japan put it alongside names such as Rolls Royce and Rolex.

Consumer and retailer response has been highly positive, making Marquis the fourth largest tabletop brand in the world. Its *Millennium Celebration Collection* included a $99 champagne bucket, $49 flutes, $29 votive with candle and a $29 bell ornament. In other designs such as *Caprice* or *Trillium*, Marquis is available as wine goblets, vases, bowls, pen holder, golf tee clock or desk set, and Christmas ornaments. Most smaller items are priced around $29, with larger items rarely exceeding the $99 mark. By branding this range as Marquis, Waterford Crystal has cleverly avoided damaging its premium Waterford brand, while successfully broadening the appeal of its products to a new target market. Sales indicate this younger and more price-conscious target market has been appreciative of the Marquis range. With both *John Rocha at Waterford* and Marquis, the company has successfully added to the appeal of crystal without damaging the reputation held by its core Waterford brand of crystal.

Customer Targets

The Wedgwood and Waterford ranges are not, on the whole, designed to be day-to-day functional lines. They are premium priced and intended to be special, lasting purchases. This is an image well cultivated by the company's advertising and public relations, plus Waterford's refusal to become involved with discounting and retailer promotions. Carefully controlled distribution through only leading china/crystal showrooms and department stores further enhances the exclusive branding. In recent years, combined Waterford-Wedgwood shops have opened in selected cities and tourist locations, presenting the crystalware and tableware in perfect surroundings.

The core market is the giftware sector, in which its ceramics and glassware vie with cutlery, jewellery – by far the dominant gift category – toys, games and leather goods (see Table III.13). Within crystal giftware there are five distinct segments:

- *General giftware.* Formal, informal and special occasions: anniversaries, retirements, birthdays, romantic interludes, public holidays and festivals.
- *Weddings.* A distinct market where young couples often gain entry into the market for expensive 'home adornments', particularly in America where the *wedding chest* (registry) at specific stores is so popular.
- *Investment giftware.* Items bought both for their intrinsic beauty and for their latent, accruing value. A market exploited to great effect by Lalique's range of glass sculptures and more recently by Waterford's designer pieces.
- *Business gifts and incentives.* £30 million is now spent annually in the UK on china and glass for promotional purposes.
- *Specials.* Such as the growing market for glass and crystal sporting trophies; particularly important in Europe and Canada.

Emotional Appeal

The continuing success of crystal, even through any economic recession, is due in part to the manufacturers' broadening ranges and innovative designs, as well as their marketing and image-building activities. The emotional appeal of giftware – especially of crystal – is the dominant force. Once the domain of weddings and female consumers, the appeal of crystal has grown. One-off special purchases have become recognized as family heirlooms, collectors buy for longer-term investment, married couples add piecemeal to growing collections, while companies – for promotions and special gifts – have recognized the longevity and appeal of crystal, china and silver *fine giftware.*

| Table III.13 | *UK Retail Gift Market* |

Retail market size (£m)	1987	1988	1989	1990
Glassware	120.7	132.0	151.3	151.1
Ceramics	391.1	435.3	490.9	439.7
Cutlery	30.1	33.3	34.4	26.1
Jewellery	–	789.5	928.2	931.5
Toys and games	821.8	831.6	1,007.4	1,012.9
Leather goods	41.4	45.4	51.9	52.1
Total	–	2,267.1	2,664.1	2,613.4

Source: Key Note, 1992

The giftware market hinges around emotions. The selection of a gift, no matter the occasion, is a personal, subjective and often risky action. Nowhere are individual consumer tastes and social influences more to the fore. Innovative, individually crafted, expensive crystal is a difficult, agonized-over purchase. High unit prices and the very 'personal' nature of the merchandise often extend the buying process as family and friends' opinions are sought. Will the choice be liked? Is it right for the intended home? Is it correct for the occasion? Is it value for money? Waterford's various brands, designs and pieces hope to help address these queries.

Waterford has an enviable reputation world-wide, built on a heritage of hand-crafted superior workmanship at its Irish birthplace. The company has been able to command premium prices in expanding international markets. The giftware market is idiosyncratic and very much consumer driven. In an economic recession, premium-price crystal is not top of every consumer's shopping list. Waterford is striving to build on its roots, while taking its wares into more countries and to a wider audience with its new ranges, brands and lower price points. This has risked alienating its traditional target customers but is a strategy that appears to have paid dividends for the Irish crystal maker.

Issues

Waterford has had a long and successful history, but risked devaluing its premium branding with the introduction of its Marquis range. Far from causing difficultites, this new range inspired further innovations from the Irish crystal producer. The new lines reflect the findings from customer research and adhere to a shrewd target market strategy. It was important for Waterford to venture into new lines, but only having first established the target markets' buying behaviour and brand perceptions.

Product management and branding

Why was the introduction of the Marquis brand risky for Waterford Crystal Ltd? In what ways has the proliferation of Waterford's sub-brands and ranges strengthened the company's standing in the crystal market?

Market segmentation and targeting

In what ways has target marketing been important to the change in Waterford's fortunes? How must Waterford vary its marketing of its traditional lines, Marquis range and modern John Rocha designs to reflect the separate targeted customer expectations?

Buying behaviour

How might the buying decision process differ for a purchase of John Rocha designer crystalware, a Marquis set of wine goblets and a traditional Waterford-branded set of crystal glasses? Will these differences force Waterford to consider varying its channels of distribution more in the future?

Marketing research

How should Waterford have deployed marketing research to address such considerations? Which survey tools would be most useful?

Relevant Theory Notes

T8: The Marketing Mix: Products and Product Management, pp. 246–254
T6: Market Segmentation, pp. 229–236
T3: Buying Behaviour, pp. 205–212
T4: Marketing Research, pp. 213–220

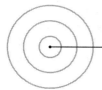

Full Case 9: TGI Friday's Themed Restaurants Compete

As living standards have risen, the UK, as in much of Europe, has seen tremendous growth in the hotel and restaurant sector. In the latter half of the 1980s and throughout the 1990s, in real terms, expenditure on eating out rose by over 50 per cent. Now, over 50 per cent of the population regularly dines out. This growth has been accompanied by the opening and development of thousands of hotels, restaurants, pubs (bars), and fast food outlets. The figures in Table III.14 illustrate the scale of the catering outlet industry within the UK. The numbers of outlets in the particular categories to some extent disguise the near 25 per cent share of the market held by hotel restaurants, restaurants and public houses. For the last three decades, the brewery-run steak house and pub-restaurant chains, led by Beefeater, Berni, Harvester and Porterhouse, have dominated the middle, mass market. Currently, the Beefeater chain (which acquired the bulk of the Berni Inns estate) leads with close to 300 outlets, followed by Toby (120), Porterhouse (90), Harvester (80) and Aberdeen Steak Houses (30). Whitbread is the market leader, operating a host of restaurant brands, including Beefeater, Bella Pasta, Pizza Hut, Dragon Inns, Café Rouge, Dome, Mamma Amalfi, Costa, Tascaria Maredo, Churrasco and TGI Friday's.

For many years the UK consumer who did not wish to eat at home was faced with simple choices: a fast food take-away such as a fish and chip shop or a burger bar, a snack bar café, a steakhouse, ethnic restaurant, upmarket restaurant, or hotel restaurant. The introduction to the UK of McDonald's, which now has close to 800 outlets, and the aggressive retaliation from Burger King, added a new dimension to the market during the 1980s and 1990s. Within the restaurant sector, however, the steakhouse and pub-restaurant concepts reigned supreme throughout the 1990s, attracting the bulk of middle-spending consumers and families. Here, Whitbread's Beefeater chain led the way. Introduced in 1974, by 1981 there were 50 outlets. The company has coverage throughout the UK. Eighty per cent of the population lives within 10 miles of a Beefeater. The brand also operates in Germany. Beefeater serves 18 million meals per annum, more than any other full service restaurant brand. 'Beefeater: first choice for value and quality.'

Beefeater's success historically was attributed mainly to its staff training, its ability to target specific groups of customers and to update its trading concept to keep a fresh appeal to its well-honed target market. The company realized that such success was not guaranteed and placed a great deal of emphasis on staff training and customer care – the *Beefeater Care Programme* – with the aim of establishing a caring culture within the whole of the company. As Beefeater enters the new millennium its promotional activity – mainly direct mail and sales promotions – is working hard to shed any staid steakhouse image. The chain now has a softer 'look' with informal, friendly interiors, less focus on red meat dishes and full scope for vegetarians. Spicy dishes, more fish, regional specialities and more frequently changing menus greet customers. Beefeater is no longer a steak-house, as Whitbread's marketers have kept pace with changing customer expectations and behaviour.

Table III.14	*Catering Outlets and Eating Out in the UK*

Meals consumed outside the home

			Million meals
Profit sector, (total)	**5,758**	**Cost sector, (total)**	**3,078**
Pubs	1,404	Staff catering	1,326
Leisure	1,135	Education	862
Cafés/take aways	1,038	Health care	750
Hotels	636	Services/welfare	140
Fast food	631		
Restaurants	461		
Travel	453	**Total**	**8,836**

Note: Meals served to UK residents and overseas visitors while working, shopping, travelling, studying, in hospital, etc., as well as enjoying their leisure time.

Restaurants: frequency of visits

				Percentage of GB adults	
	Daytime	Evening		Daytime	Evening
More than once a week	1.2	0.8	Once a month	10.0	13.2
Once a week	3.6	2.5	Less than once a month	20.1	30.5
2 or 3 times a month	7.8	8.1	**Ever**	**50.8**	**63.0**

Take-away/fast food restaurants: visits in the last 3 months

				Percentage of GB adults	
	Take-Away	Eat-in		Take-Away	Eat-in
Burger King	9.7	11.2	Other burger bars	1.9	0.8
Deep Pan Pizza	2.0	2.6	Other pizza bars	7.7	1.6
KFC	13.1	4.4	Fish & chip shop	47.1	4.5
McDonald's	26.6	26.3	Chinese take-away	44.3	–
Pizza Express	1.6	1.9	Indian take-away	23.3	–
Pizza Hut	6.7	8.9	Others	5.9	4.7
Wimpy	1.5	2.4	**Ever**	**74.8**	**47.2**

Sources: Foodservice Intelligence, Target Group Index and *The Marketing Pocket Book* from NTC Publications and The Advertising Association

And Then Came Friday's

In the mid-1980s, the UK restaurant scene was altered beyond recognition when Whitbread followed up its strong presence in the restaurant sector with the introduction of the American-originated TGI Friday's restaurant brand. Operators within this sector, customers and media had experienced nothing to equal or compare with the sheer vitality and enthusiasm, supported with quality control and excellent standards, of TGI Friday's.

US in origin

The first TGI Friday's was opened on New York's First Avenue and 63rd Street in 1965. The restaurant boasted the same red and white striped awnings, wooden flooring, Tiffany lamp shades, bent-wood chairs and striped tablecloths retained in today's restaurants. An immediate success – with sales of over one million dollars in the first year – TGI Friday's was an instant hit with young New Yorkers, quickly becoming *the* place to meet. By the early 1970s, the concept was being franchised and extended into Dallas. With this opening, the 'elegant clutter' which remains one of Friday's most famous features first appeared. The Dallas restaurant in its first year achieved sales of over two million dollars. By 1975 there were ten restaurants in eight States, at which point the company was acquired by the massive Carlson Hospitality Group. Following the take-over, Friday's success was comprehensively analysed and a number of key philosophies were crystallized to form the basic principles by which Friday's operates today. Central to Friday's success was its ability to *care* for its guests, anticipating and supplying their needs more effectively, offering more enjoyment than competitors could match.

TGI Friday's is an American diner operating from 3,500 square metre sites (including parking), offering a full cocktail bar and restaurant service. Whether it is a simple coffee, an unpronounceable cocktail, a bowl of chips or a five-course meal, TGI Friday's will provide every customer or 'guest' with a truly memorable experience. In the UK, food accounts for 60 per cent of turnover and beverages 40 per cent.

From its original New York origins in 1965, the concept has become one of America's most famous eating places. There are now close to 175 TGI Friday's restaurants in 37 States. Whitbread brought it, unaltered, to Britain in 1986. TGI Friday's continues to reign the undisputed UK market leader of themed restaurants, despite a host of subsequent imitations. Friday's London Covent Garden restaurant quickly became the busiest TGI Friday's in the world with average weekly sales of over £150,000.

The concept

The Friday's concept centres on a simple layout: a raised bar in the centre with dining area around the periphery of the one-storey building. All the artefacts/atmospherics are genuinely American, shipped from the American host company to European franchisees. In the UK, the brewer Whitbread now operates 30 sites with a target of 50.

The restaurants' red and white striped awnings herald a theme that continues inside with striped tablecloths and the staff's striped shirts. The focal point in every Friday's is a large ornate wooden bar with brass rails, which complements the polished wood floors, bent-wood chairs and Tiffany lamps. But perhaps the most striking feature of the restaurants is what Friday's terms 'elegant clutter'. Half an eight-man rowing scull, an antique wooden aeroplane propeller, a pair of old skating boots and a rocking horse are all at home at Friday's; as is the rest of the clutter of items, each with a story to tell.

Staff are encouraged to express their personalities through wearing their own hats, braces and badges. They are trained to help guests relax and every member of staff provides the willing, professional service that is a keynote of the successful American restaurants. Whitbread's stated ethical policy is for staff and company to have a basis of honesty, integrity and fair dealing. This is more than echoed within Friday's. At TGI's, guest satisfaction is of ultimate importance. To help recruit approximately 100 staff (150 in the larger branches) for each new restaurant, Friday's holds two days of auditions that act as an applicant screening process. Candidates tackle challenging tasks that test their manual dexterity, communications skills, determination and ability to deal with unusual situations and people.

The menu is culturally diverse, offering more than 70 American, Tex-Mex, Cajun and Italian dishes, plus over 500 cocktails. Dishes range from New England Clam Chowder, San Francisco Chicken Skewers, Jack Daniels Glazed Pork Chops, West Coast Snapper Fettuccini, Pumpkin Cheesecake to Cookie Madness. Cafe latté, thick ice-cream shakes, alcohol-free frozen cocktails, a Lynchburg Lemonade, New York Martini or a simple beer; there is a drink to suit all tastes.

Training

Staff training and selection are a fundamental priority, with staff being selected for personality and dedication to looking after guests. The company has its own full-time training function, but for new store openings brings over experienced US trainers. With their experience of 20 or 30 new store openings, these US trainers are able to set the urgency and pace needed to get the job done. At the same time, the UK trainers learn the tricks of the trade from their US counterparts. The importance of the US tradition of service to TGI's is explained by Patti Hoban-Simpson, the UK's training manager: 'In the US there is not the tradition that service equals servile. In the UK we have actively to teach the American attitude to service and focus on the employer and the guests'. Having the US team working closely with the UK trainers also adds to the fun and cultural experience of the whole TGI's phenomenon.

'We may all speak English,' says US trainer Cheryl Domitrovic from Pittsburgh, 'but the words mean different things. It's been really amusing working out what means what – you have to be quite careful or you can cause hilarity without knowing why. It's suspenders and braces that really confuse me. In the US, suspenders hold your pants (trousers) up and braces run metal tracks around your teeth. In the UK, suspenders hold your panty hose (stockings) up and braces hold your trousers up. It's confusing!'. The US training team has had to do more than adjust to the UK English language, having to develop new methods to get the best out of the UK trainees.

We have to adjust our training methods to the British personality. In the UK we have to teach Friday's staff to make people feel comfortable and to treat customers as real guests – as real people. We also have to encourage new staff to show their personalities at work – this does not come spontaneously to the more reticent British. But once we show how, employees quickly catch on – suddenly work can be tremendous fun, rewarding and enjoyable! In a way, training in the UK is more rewarding than in the US because a transformation is so much greater.'

Attention to detail

The focus on all facets of staff training is echoed by the management's control and expertise in running the successful US concept within the UK. Restaurant menus are carefully thought through to offer variety and 'mix and match' dining. Despite the elegant clutter and artefacts, hygiene and cleanliness standards are high. Rigorous cleaning and maintenance programmes, and tight management controls result in few problems for customers to worry about.

The attention to detail goes far. Once recruited, before working in a TGI's restaurant, staff members learn in the classroom and from numerous manuals how to look after all parts of the business. Although the button-badged adorned striped shirts and trousers with braces may look haphazard, there *is* a uniform and dress guide stringently enforced which specifies everything from the suitability of button badges, to length of hair and finger nails, use of plasters for cuts and grazes, etc. Once selected to work in the restaurant, new recruits must pass step-by-step tests, immediately leaving the payroll if they fail to progress satisfactorily. For a new restaurant opening, the whole team comes together several weeks before the first paying guest visits the premises, working flat out for several days on volunteer customers and friends of the company so that the first paying customers are not the guinea pigs. This level of training, financial commitment, and attention to detail are all somewhat unusual in what is often a cost-focused industry.

The 'feel'

'If all the world's a stage, then Friday's must compare to a first night on Broadway,' remarked Dave Donnelly, Friday's MD. In the UK, research shows that 25 per cent of customers return once a month. It is seen as a narcotic experience for customers: 'You will have a good time, but it won't be yours, it will be ours'. The vibrant buzz in the atmosphere is deliberate and well orchestrated. The buzz and vitality are the essence of the service product offered by Friday's.

The Friday's experience and atmosphere are difficult to communicate to non-users of the Friday's themed restaurants. The company has utilized a trend-setting campaign of three-dimensional advertisements. Friday's has proved that it is well ahead of the competition with an exciting communicative and totally 'off the wall' advertising campaign that did not aim just to get people talking, but also hoped to make 'their mouths water and their hands reach out to pick a cocktail right off the page'. 3D photos showing the fun and enjoyment for both guests and staff within the Covent Garden restaurant appeared, along with 3D spectacles, in the up-market magazines *GQ, Tatler, Vanity Fair, Punch* and *Arena*. With only 30 restaurants, the use of television as a medium is prohibited by cost. The written word and printed page of a normal press advertisement do little justice to the fun and excitement to be found in a Friday's restaurant. The 3D campaign went a long way to bring into the homes of the magazine readers the TGI Friday's experience.

Customers – The Guests

The typical customer is in *her* thirties, intellectually secure, confident enough to dress down (be informally clothed) to go out in an evening; someone who can relax, sit, watch and enjoy the experience. However, the customer profile switches throughout the day: business lunches, families in the afternoon and early evening, couples and young adults in the later evening. Typical weekday guests are professional people between 25 and 49 years old. At weekends, Friday's is particularly popular among families with children. High chairs for babies, helium-filled balloons and a special kids' menu take the pain away from eating out with young children.

Customer and staff loyalty is phenomenally high for the catering and restaurant industry. The whole themed concept is very much a carousel (a merry-go-round) which goes faster and faster as the night goes on, with both staff and customers living on adrenalin and the TGI brand of excitement. Regular visitors to Friday's talk about the Friday's experience – a mix of buzzing atmosphere, flamboyant decor and friendly staff, with a real will to please. Central to the Friday's concept is its emphasis on guest satisfaction. The staff are meant to treat guests as if they were valued visitors to their own homes. Customers are met at the door with a warm welcome and accompanied to their table in a true Friday's frenetic, good humoured style.

The media has not been slow to recognize the unique proposition offered by Friday's. From BBC television's *The Generation Game* and the Dutch equivalent, to a BBC 2 *Business Matters* feature on staff training, to Children's TV *Motormouth* and to *Daytime UK*, most facets of the Friday's experience and company philosophy have been dissected, analysed, shown to the public for inspection, and passed with flying colours. The expert bar staff were employed to train Tom Cruise for his exploits behind the bar in the film *Cocktail*. The company now sponsors a regular National Bar Tender of the Year competition, which featured prominently on the BBC *The Wogan Show*.

What Next?

Friday's has its critics. Not everyone wants to eat in the middle of a circus. No matter how good the management and quality control, sometimes the guests may be disappointed. Not every meal is cooked to perfection or 'dub-tub' waiter right on the ball. Success and popularity also bring the occasional queue and delay. However, the management philosophy is unbending, believing that there is an equal partnership at stake between the three components or elements of business success: the guest (the customer), the employee, and the company. This, Friday's coins the *Triangle Theory* – there must be an equal balance between guests, employees and the company, and if the balance and status quo are disturbed, the success of the company will be put in jeopardy. No single element must become dominant, nor must one component weaken.

The company is aware of the need to move forward. New openings are planned in order to take the concept to new geographical markets. Whitbread holds the franchise for countries outside of the UK and is considering developing these options further. There is a regular programme of customer analysis and collection of customer thoughts and perceptions, all of which are fed into the on-going and evolving development of the TGI Friday's concept and business strategy. There is constant change and tweaking of the concept and branding, but it is carefully controlled and it is 'Friday's change'!

But then Came the Imitators …

As with any good product or service concept, in any market, if it is seen to be successful it will be copied. The financial investment in developing the brand, the product proposition, in attaining and developing sites, in training and motivating staff, in promoting and controlling the brand concept, is costly. Trade name and identity can be legally protected. There are, though, relatively no barriers to entry – except financial and human resources – for potential copycat competitors. In the UK there is already a host of direct rivals, ranging from the US-sourced Calendars and Old Orleans, to Fatty Arbuckles, Mamma Bell's Mexican restaurants and various one-off locally focused rivals.

In many ways, Friday's has been a victim of its own success. Because of its commitments to training and authentically sourced artefacts for its restaurants, plus its desire for carefully selected sites, it has not been able to expand nationally perhaps as quickly as Whitbread may have desired. Where branches have opened, the impact on the local customer base has been dramatic with high footfall and terrific brand loyalty. However, this clear success has inspired many national and local rival restaurant operators to target this new market, which in many ways has been created by Friday's: a market which no longer is associated with the traditional steakhouse offering, pub grub, or fast-food snack.

So where does Friday's go from here? How can it maintain its quality, continue to motivate its staff, keep fresh its ideas both within its own organization and with its exterior face as presented to its target audience? How can it successfully fend-off the burgeoning number of direct rivals? The restaurant sector is much more competitive and cut-throat than in the buoyant late 1980s when Friday's first entered the UK market. As a concept, Friday's has been highly successful. Financially, for Whitbread, the company has contributed significantly right from its first year of operation to the parent company's fortunes. There is little doubt that Friday's in the UK has been a success. As with any service business, though, it is difficult to expand and develop on success that is people and 'experience' based, while simultaneously maintaining costs, controlling standards and staying ahead of the competition.

Issues

The marketing of services is different from the marketing of consumer goods, partly because of the intangibility of the product, the extended marketing mix and the integral role of personnel. It is also, for these reasons, more difficult to create and sustain a competitive advantage. These services marketing issues are well illustrated with this discussion of Whitbread's roll-out of TGI Friday's.

The marketing of services and the intangibility of the product

For TGI Friday's what is the product: the drinks, the food, the atmosphere, the people or simply the overall experience? Why must TGI Friday's devote so much resource to recruiting the 'right' personnel?

A competitive edge

How difficult is it for Whitbread to create a differential advantage? Can this differential advantage be sustained'?

Customer targets

TGI Friday's is a carefully honed concept, targeted at specific groups of customers. Who are they? What influences their choice of restaurant?

Promotional strategy

There are only a few TGI Friday's in the UK. Promotional budgets are relatively limited. What is the promotional strategy adopted by management? Which are the main elements of the promotional mix? Should these priorities be any different? Against whom or what is Friday's competing?

Relevant Theory Notes

T13:   The Marketing of Services, pp. 280–284
T8:   The Marketing Mix: Products and Product Management, pp. 246–254
T7:   Competitive Strategy, pp. 237–245
T6:   Market Segmentation, pp. 229–236
T3:   Buying Behaviour, pp. 205–212
T11:   The Marketing Mix: Promotion, pp. 266–274

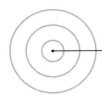

Full Case 10: Royal Ahold
Socially Responsible Global Expansion

Retail group Royal Ahold has, from humble beginnings, become a leading global competitor. From its base in the Netherlands, the company has spread across Europe, the US, Latin America and into the Asia Pacific region. Much of this expansion has taken place since the 1970s, with Ahold taking advantage of a range of acquisition and investment opportunities. There are many reasons why retailers such as Ahold seek opportunities away from their domestic market. Most moves are triggered by the need for growth, but there is considerable variety in how this comes about. For one retailer growth may happen almost by accident – simply because the business has outgrown its existing situation. For another, the acquisition of a business with interests in a different market may bring with it a ready-made portfolio of outlets. Or, for a retailer, commitment to new situations and markets might be part of an ambitious, carefully planned internationalization strategy.

Whatever the motive for expansion, retailers have to ensure that they have the resources and local understanding to develop in new markets. Businesses must also give due consideration to their stance on ethics and social responsibility issues. There are many recent examples of companies that have failed to appreciate the impact which careless handling of such issues can have upon business prospects, especially in a new location. Consumers increasingly expect the companies with which they do business to behave in an ethical and responsible manner. For companies such as Ahold, which are trading in so many different parts of the world, the problem is even more complex, as consumers in different cultures have different views on these issues.

The Ahold Story

The Royal Ahold story began in 1887 when a man called Albert Heijn opened his first shop. Nearly 25 years later, Albert began baking his own cookies. These were the first products to be sold using the Albert Heijn brand and were soon followed by others. These simple beginnings mark the early chapters in the story of Royal Ahold, an enterprise that was to become one of the world's leading grocery outlets. The Ahold grocery offer today is driven by consumer requirements for variety, convenience and quality.

Ahold's Key Landmarks include:

- 1951: Company becomes listed on the Amsterdam Stock Exchange
- 1955: First self-service supermarket opened in Rotterdam
- 1959: 100th Albert Heijn supermarket opened

- 1971: Ahold NV founded to prepare the business for domestic and international expansion.
- 1977: Ahold moves into the US market.
- 1987: Queen Beatrix of the Netherlands grants the designation 'Royal' to commemorate the company's 100th birthday.
- 1990: Fall of communism allows Ahold to establish a holding company in Czechoslovakia, where it was later to develop a major presence.
- 1996: Acquisition of US-based Stop & Shop, the market leader in New England with annual sales of US$ 5 billion.
- 1997: US market generates more than 55 per cent of Ahold's sales and 61 per cent of profits. In conjunction with local partners Ahold also opens the first TOPS supermarket in Shanghai and a further 15 TOPS outlets in Bangkok.
- 1998: Major new investments in the US and Latin America, with the acquisition of Giant Food Inc. (173 stores and sales of US$ 4.2 billion).
- 1999: Ahold announces it intends to acquire US Pathmark Stores Inc. (132 stores and sales of US$ 3.7 billion). A total of 150 supermarkets are also acquired from four companies in Southern Spain.

Table III.15	Sales and Operating Results				
AREA	**SALES**		**PROFITS**		
	1998	**1997**	**1998**	**1997**	
United States	US$ 16,182	US$ 14,299	US$ 714	US$ 574	
The Netherlands	16,995	15,930	671	607	
Other European countries	3,828	3,198	215	179	
Latin America	4,664	2,622	138	81	
Asia Pacific	903	925	(103)	(79)	
Corporate costs			(88)	(71)	
Total	**58,364**	**50,568**	**2,242**	**1,837**	

Source: Ahold Annual Report 1998

In its domestic market Ahold is strongly represented with the Albert Heijn supermarkets, the Gall & Gall liquor stores and the Ethos health and beauty chain. With more than 1700 outlets, Ahold has more than a third share of the retail market in the Netherlands. The company also owns a large interest in a wholesale supplier that services independent stores and operates various food supply and production facilities. The company's sales figures in 1998 showed a 15.5 per cent increase on 1997, with profits up by 22 per cent (see Table III.15). Internationally, the Ahold presence is growing fast. With growing representation in the US, Asia, Latin America and Southern and Central Europe, the company is building an impressive profile. Table III.16 breaks down the Ahold's results by region.

Table III.16	*Breakdown of 1998 Retail Figures*

AREA	SALES (millions)		GROWTH	LOCATIONS		ANNUAL SALES/AV. SQUARE FOOT	
	1998 US$	1997 US$	%	**1998**	1997	**1998** (xUS$)	1997 (xUS$)
United States							
Supermarkets							
Stop & Shop	**6,187**	5,492	12.6	**193**	187	**830**	770
Giant-Carlisle	**3,417**	3,156	8.3	**149**	144	**720**	750
Tops*	**3,061**	3,034	0.9	**250**	236	**590**	600
BI-LO	**2,887**	2,826	2.1	**266**	263	**440**	450
Giant-Landover**	**837**	–	–	**173**	–	**810**	–
The Netherlands	**NLG**	NLG				**(xNLG)**	(xNLG)
Supermarkets							
Albert Heijn	**9,506**	8,981	5.9	**517**	512	**1,520**	1,510
Albert Heijn Franchising*	**2,014**	1,900	6.0	**169**	168	**1,320**	1,300
Schuitema*	**4,542**	4,142	9.6	**464**	485	**1,480**	1,380
Speciality stores							
Etos*	**598**	509	17.4	**395**	350	**930**	1,180
Gall & Gall*	**507**	486	4.3	**485**	471	**1,190**	1,240
*Other**	**266**	304	–	**185**	249	–	–
Other Europe	**NLG**	NLG				**(xNLG)**	(xNLG)
Supermarkets							
Pingo Doce (Portugal)	**1,551**	1,364	13.7	**147**	131	**1,200**	1,170
Mana (Czech Republic)	**372**	295	26.0	**84**	76	**630**	620
Sesam (Poland)	**158**	94	67.5	**61**	45	**530**	510
Hypermarkets							
Feira Nova (Portugal)	**1,019**	935	9.0	**17**	15	**1,380**	1,410
Other	**720**	429	–	**109**	81	–	–
Latin America	**NLG**	NLG				**(xNLG)**	(xNLG)
Supermarkets							
Bompreco (Brazil)	**1,398**	1,059	32.0	**56**	58	**1,110**	850
Disco (Argentina)**	**777**	–	–	**111**	–	**1,980**	–
Santa Isabel (Chile)**	**380**	–	–	**90**	–	**990**	–
Hypermarkets							
Bompreco (Brazil)	**1,827**	1,311	39.3	**14**	14	**1,860**	1,490
Other	**308**	246	–	**21**	21	–	–
Asia Pacific	**NLG**	NLG				**(xNLG)**	(xNLG)
Supermarkets							
TOPS (Singapore/Malaysia)	**239**	128	86.7	**59**	18	**560**	800
TOPS (Thailand)	**550**	703	(21.7)	**39**	39	**500**	830
TOPS (China)	**96**	43	123.8	**40**	21	**360**	440

*Net consumer sales
**Sales since consolidation date

Source: Ahold Annual Report 1998

Motives for International Expansion

To understand Ahold's commitment to grow its business in this way, it is necessary to consider the underlying rationale for international expansion. Often this is caused by limited growth opportunities in maturing domestic markets. For many Dutch companies the particularly constrained characteristics of the domestic market have played a major role in their attempts to pursue growth elsewhere. As new competitors continue to enter the market, pressure on the existing incumbents increases and even established players face a squeeze on market share. These problems are commonly accompanied by increasingly restrictive regulation. At such times internationalization opportunities, particularly those involving underdeveloped, high growth markets, can help fulfil corporate expansion goals which could not be achieved domestically. When an organization has an internationally appealing and innovative retail concept, the possibilities for growth are substantially enhanced.

Ahold's motives for international expansion have primarily been linked with the declining opportunities for growth in its domestic market, the Dutch national culture of foreign expansion and the attractions of new, immature, international markets. Some of Ahold's key competitors in the international retail business have different reasons for following the same route (see Table III.17).

Table III.17	*International Retailer Motives for Expansion*

Retailer	Motives for Internationalization
Ahold	■ Pushed by poor domestic growth potential, proven retail experience and national culture of foreign expansion. ■ Pulled by growth potential of consolidating and emerging economies, accumulation of best practice experiences from operations in different markets.
Carrefour	■ Pushed by restrictive government regulations in its domestic market, a proven retail format and considerable international experience from the Latin American market. ■ Pulled by growth opportunities in emerging economies, geographical and cultural proximity (Spain) with other markets, assets in other markets gained through acquisition in the domestic market (Portugal).
Tesco	■ Pushed by heavy domestic competition and 'me-too' strategy following key competitor Sainsbury's US expansion. ■ Pulled by growth opportunities in emerging markets, underdevelopment of retail industry in some markets, opportunities in consolidating economies (France), geographical and cultural proximity with other markets (Scotland and Ireland).
Wal-Mart	■ Pushed by corporate culture seeking to establish Wal-Mart as a global brand, expansion experience from the domestic market and internationally (Mexico and Canada), proven retail formula, low-cost base from efficient operating system. ■ Pulled by reducing political and economic barriers (NAFTA – Canada & Mexico), opportunities in emerging economies, efficiencies generated from experience of global operations.

Senior management attributes Ahold's successful expansion to its commitment to a highly efficient and flexible distribution system, which puts customers at the top of the supply chain. In particular, the organization believes in the power of scale economies and knowledge-sharing among sister companies. The retailer is pursuing two routes to continued growth. In the mature Netherlands and US markets, the aim is to improve efficiency and exploit synergies in whatever ways it can. In developing markets Ahold will combine acquisition, joint ventures and the development of Greenfield sites to grow its business.

Different Routes to Internationalization

There are various internationalization approaches open to a retailer such as Ahold. The chosen route depends on how the retailer balances the degree of control required with the flexibility it wishes to exert over its international interests and the level of resource it is prepared to commit to the venture. In general, there is a positive relationship between the control required and costs of internationalization. Thus a retailer wishing to retain total control over a retail format which has been transplanted from another market will find that this is achieved at substantial financial cost. In addition, the company will probably have less flexibility to exit the market than if a joint venture agreement is entered into.

- *Organic growth*. A retailer adopting this type of entry strategy is attempting to establish and build an international retail proposition. The intention is to establish a position and influence retail development in the chosen market. Common trading formats, fascias and displays are adopted across different markets. Speciality retailer Body Shop and grocery retailer Aldi are examples of this method.

- *Joint venture and alliances*. Businesses choosing to pursue joint ventures and alliances are aware of the advantages of access to local experience. By joining forces with a locally based partner, the retailer can draw upon a wealth of local expertise. This approach potentially allows relatively straightforward access to markets with which the retailer is unfamiliar.

- *Take-overs*. This approach allows the retailer to gain an instant presence in a new market. By taking over an existing player, it is not necessary for the business to familiarize local customers with an unfamiliar brand and product proposition. Wal-Mart's takeover of UK supermarket company Asda, is an example of this particular route.

- *Franchising*. Speciality retailers, including Benetton and Body Shop, sometimes use franchising to enter new markets. Franchise agreements vary but, in general, a franchisee pays a fee that allows them to use the retail brand and trading concept. The costs of entering new markets are therefore kept to a minimum, with much of the risk borne by the franchisee.

Instilling a Sense of Social Responsibility

In the new Millennium marketing ethics and social responsibility are at the forefront of the thinking of many businesses. Fast-growing organizations such as

Ahold must pay close attention to their responsibilities to society and the environment. For Ahold, this involves a detailed and carefully constructed strategy around *what* they sell, *how* they sell and *where* they sell (see Table III.18).

Table III.18	*Ahold's Approach to Ethics and Social Responsibility*		
	PRODUCTS: *(what we sell)*	**FACILITIES/OPERATIONS:** *(how we sell)*	**COMMUNITIES:** *(where we sell)*
Business Strategy and Focus	Provide superior service to our customers	Increase productivity and efficiency, control costs	Expand operations in mature and new markets
Environmental Objective	QUALITY CHOICES Respond to and anticipate customer needs for quality choices that reflect care for the environment	EFFICIENCY Eliminate waste and increase the efficiency of natural resource use	CARE Maintain and build on our reputation as a good neighbour and a source of vitality in our communities
Underlying Actions	▪ Integrate environmental performance as an element of quality ▪ Provide choices and information ▪ Ensure consumer health and safety are top priorities ▪ Innovate in partnership with suppliers to reduce environmental impact of products and packaging	▪ Improve energy efficiency ▪ Eliminate waste throughout operations ▪ Maintain and upgrade facilities ▪ Apply state-of-the-art technology to new facilities ▪ Innovate in partnership with manufacturers and service providers ▪ Share expertise and experiences among Ahold companies	▪ Care for quality of life in our communities ▪ Deal responsibly with new site development ▪ Provide options for customer access ▪ Be involved in the community ▪ Communicate openly and transparently

The Products Ahold Sells

Ahold is quick to recognize that the manufacture, use and disposal of the products it sells impact upon the environment. The company also realises that customers are increasingly concerned about the safety, quality and environmental friendliness of the products they buy. In order to deal with these concerns the company endeavours to reflect care for the environment in the areas of product choice, product packaging and product policy.

To provide better product choice, Ahold is increasing its commitment to organic goods and those produced under *Integrated Crop Management* (ICM). In Tops stores in the US, the banner 'More Good Choices Naturally' identifies organic and natural products with three characteristics: (a) no artificial flavours, preservatives or colours, (b) environmentally friendly and (c) organic if possible. The ICM approach reduces impact on the environment by combining natural and technical approaches to plant nutrition and pest reduction. This means that the use of chemical herbicides and pesticides is kept to a minimum. The release of beneficial insects, such as ladybirds and Japanese beetles, helps to control pests, while special irrigation techniques reduce the need for fertilizer. Of course, the decisions Ahold makes about which products to sell are not solely governed by environmental consideration. Customers are not always prepared to pay extra for organic or ICM produce, so the company must consider carefully the products it offers. Ahold is particularly interested in being able to offer environmental benefits at no additional cost to the customer.

Pressures to reduce packaging waste and cut the costs of recycling are increasing. As EU countries strive to hit tough environmental targets, the variety of initiatives is also rising. Ahold has pursued its own version of these initiatives in a number of areas. For instance, the company is deeply committed to the Dutch covenant process, which was set up to cut landfill waste. This is a system of agreement among all supply chain members for implementing packaging reductions. The current covenant in operation commits Dutch companies to recycling 65 per cent of all packaging by 2001 and to have cut packaging materials by 10 per cent from 1986 figures. This has encouraged the company to implement a range of consumer packaging measures. At Albert Heijn relationships with suppliers are used to identify irritating and hard to handle packaging. Known as the 'Top Irritations' initiative, this approach has already resulted in many packaging improvements. In addition, many Albert Heijn own-label products, including detergents, now use less packaging. Other products have had their packaging simplified or improved to make recycling easier.

Ahold has also addressed the need for reusable transport packaging. The vast majority of such plastic/carton transport packaging is now recycled. In Albert Heijn stores agreements with suppliers allow standard sized, reusable containers to be used. American chain Tops packs local produce in reusable plastic containers that can be placed directly onto store shelves. As well as cutting labour costs, this packaging saves energy because it is easier to cool than other materials. The emphasis in cutting transport packaging has been on lowering costs and increasing operating efficiency. Thus reusable packaging and cost-neutral or revenue-generating recycling have been the focus. Customers are also encouraged to recycle, with many Ahold outlets offering recycling facilities. In general, packaging innovations are designed to make appropriate environmental concessions while ensuring that effectiveness is maintained, so that customer confidence is not affected.

Product policies are guided by the principle of safe, good quality merchandise, with appropriate food safety and hygiene programmes in place. Ahold is not opposed to the use of biotechnology and genetic modification. However, there must be clear customer benefits and stringent environmental safety controls are essential.

The Facilities Ahold Operates

A number of energy efficiency and waste elimination themes underlie the environmental performance of Ahold facilities and operations. As the company upgrades its existing facilities and develops new ones, it is keen to carefully control these themes so that productivity and operational efficiency can be improved and costs reduced.

■ *Energy management*. Energy, whether used for lighting, heating, cooling or operating equipment, is one of the company's largest variable costs. Continual efforts are made to improve energy conservation. Just a few of the initiatives include the use of high efficiency lighting, investments in next generation refrigeration and the installation of energy management systems which control and monitor energy use. Energy management expertise is shared in a number of ways. Experienced managers are moved around the company to pass on their skills. The International Construction and Maintenance Synergy group meets regularly to share ideas.

■ *Refrigerant management*. Refrigeration is a necessary but environmentally costly challenge for any organization that needs to maintain the quality of fresh and frozen foods. Common refrigerant gases CFCs (chlorofluorocarbons) and HCFCs (hydro chlorofluorocarbons) both deplete the ozone layer. Though kind to ozone, HFCs (hydrofluorocarbons) promote global warming. In the spirit of various environmental conventions, Ahold has a policy to limit the impact of existing refrigerants (including dealing with leaks), phase out CFCs and HCFCs while innovating to develop better alternatives for the future.

■ *Waste management*. The reduction of waste leads to improvements in efficiency and reduces pressure on staff who can then spend more time with customers. The initiatives already described to reduce packaging and encourage customers to recycle are part of Ahold's waste management strategy. The company also has a series of positive measures to deal with waste food trimmings. For example, local pig farmers collect food waste from many Stop & Shop stores.

■ *Store design*. Traditional store design does not lend itself to easy remodelling. A joint study between Ahold USA Construction and Maintenance departments has resulted in a new flexible store design with a range of innovative features. For example, the careful selection of building materials, such as hard ceramic floor tiles that can be easily cleaned, can impact upon efficiency. High insulation levels reduce heat loss and cables fitted inside ceiling cavities mean that future remodelling of stores can be achieved without digging up the floor.

■ *Transport and distribution*. The environmental impact of transportation is considerable. Trucks add to already congested roads, increase air pollution and noise. Refrigerated trucks also cause problems for the ozone layer and build up greenhouse gases. Ahold has designed its distribution system to optimize truck utilization. This improves cost effectiveness and reduces negative environmental effects. By replacing older parts of the trucking fleet with new vehicles and installing on-board computers, fuel efficiency is increased.

■ *Production companies*. The environmental principles adopted by Ahold's retailing chains are also in evidence in the company's production facilities. For example, Albert Heijn's meat packing centres have instigated an environmental management system designed according to ISO 14000 standards. (The International Organisation for Standardisation (ISO) has devised an internationally acknowledged approach for environmental management systems.)

The Communities in Which Ahold Operates

For Ahold, commitment to the communities in which it operates is demonstrated by its ability to be a good neighbour and to bring something positive to the local area. When the company develops new stores it is keen that they are sited close to where they are needed most. In Poland through a joint venture between Ahold and Allkauf Polska, stores are being built between the apartment blocks of Krakow. Being close to the customer is crucial there, because locals still do their shopping several times each week. Here, as in other locations, a new store can help revitalize the economic fortunes of an area. The siting of a Stop & Shop on abandoned warehouse land in Dorchester, Massachusetts, helped bring better quality, lower priced food to an economically disadvantaged area.

Elsewhere Ahold is taking on environmentally contaminated sites that need cleaning up. The company also takes care that its stores are accessible to customers, whether or not they have their own transport. Sometimes this means that stores need to be integrated into existing public transport systems. Other ways in which Ahold tries to be a good neighbour are by protecting sensitive natural or significant sites which border its own and taking initiatives to minimize disruption for its neighbours.

Like many other large companies, Ahold seeks ways to become involved in and show concern about its local communities. This takes the form of charitable activities and voluntary community deeds. In addition, to its usual charitable donations, Ahold is committed to food donation programmes, where edible goods which it cannot sell (such as bruised fruit and dented cans) are donated to local community causes. Interest in local communities is also shown by Ahold's commitment for purchasing locally grown goods. Such initiatives are popular with customers who like to support their local suppliers and many of the goods are fresher and in better condition than those shipped from elsewhere.

Businesses such as Ahold are under increasing pressure from a variety of sources to behave in an ethical and socially responsible fashion. This has far-reaching implications for all aspects of an organization's operations. For Ahold, with so diverse a mix of markets, the complexity of managing these issues is increased. As a result, the company has developed a structured and co-ordinated approach that guides its decisions about what it sells, how it sells and where it sells.

Issues

Ahold has expanded around the globe. The company's focus is on successful expansion but not at the expense of society or the natural environment. The company's mission and operating ethos are strongly driven by a desire to behave socially responsibly. Trends in Ahold's marketing environment have encouraged this positioning, but so has a carefully devised corporate vision.

Social responsibility

Why is it important for businesses to behave in a socially responsible manner? Critically appraise Ahold's approach to managing social responsibility issues.

International marketing

How has Ahold expanded from its domestic market? What kinds of social responsibilities must be considered by an international retailer as it expands into new markets?

The marketing environment

Is Ahold's socially responsible approach at odds with the driving forces in the marketing environment for such a retailer? How are the forces of the marketing environment impacting on Ahold's business strategy?

Relevant Theory Notes

T17: Ethics and Social Responsibility in Marketing, pp. 302–306
T1: What is Marketing?, pp. 191–198
T16: International Marketing, pp. 297–301
T2: The Marketing Environment and Competition, pp. 199–204

Full Case 11: Heineken Global Expansion, Local Branding

Heineken is the second largest brewery group in the world, operating in more than 170 countries and brewing in 50. Core beer brands include Heineken, Amstel, Murphy's and Buckler's, supported by a host of regional and local brands. Although Heineken's activities were once centred predominantly in Europe, world-wide sales have grown and the company ranks behind only US-based leader Anheuser Busch. Today, Heineken the beer brand is enjoyed by more consumers world-wide than any other beer. Heineken Export, the original full strength Heineken brewed to an 1873 recipe, is the number one international premium beer and the world's top imported beer. The *How Refreshing How Heineken* promotional theme is known to consumers around the world.

Financially, the Heineken group is successful and well established, with good sales and profit growth in recent years (see Table III.19). The company has taken care not to become over-extended, ensuring solid return on assets and on equity ratios for its shareholders. Heineken adopts a pragmatic view to growth, balancing the need to expand with the need for caution when entering new markets. Growth takes place organically, as well as through acquisitions, joint ventures and alliances, depending on management's view of the appropriate route. Table III.20 illustrates how Heineken's beer sales can be broken down geographically, including export and licensed operations.

Table III.19	*Heineken Financial Summary, 1996–1999*

Full Year Results in ECUs, million

	1997	1996	% Change
Net Turnover (exc. Excise duties):	6,066	5,627	7.8%
Operating Profit:	540	467	15.7%
Net Profit:	342	303	12.8%
Dividend:	79	81	-2.8%
Cash Flow (from operating activities):	745	548	35.9%
Balance sheet in millions of ECUs			
Total Capital Employed:	5,054	4,919	2.8%
Group Funds:	2,471	2,273	8.7%
Net Equity:	2,291	2,084	9.9%
Issued Capital:	563	579	-2.8%

For six months, January 1st to June 30th, euros million:
(1 Euro = NLG 2.20371)

	1999	1998
Net Turnover:	3,390	3,103
Operating Profit:	353	307
Net Profit:	210	190

Source: Heineken Annual Report

Table III.20	*Geographic Breakdown of Heineken's Sales*	

	1997 Sales *millions of ECUs*	% Sales in 1999
The Netherlands	1,023	N/A
Rest of Europe	3,092	73.16 (inc The Netherlands)
Western Hemisphere	686	12.9
Africa	429	5.0
Asia Pacific	711	8.96

ECU Rate: 1 Euro = NLG 2.20371

Source: Heineken Annual Report

Changing Patterns of Consumption

Europe is a major part of the beer industry, providing around 40 per cent of beer production globally. Changing patterns of consumption over the last decade have seen falling volumes in high-consuming Germany, Belgium, Denmark and the UK, with rapid growth of consumption in Spain, Italy, Portugal and Greece. Tourism is seen as a key contributing factor in these traditionally lower-consuming countries. Sales in Asia Pacific were static, in North America up 15 per cent, while the French and African markets saw a slight decline. In 1999, sales of the Heineken brand rose 2 per cent and for Amstel 5 per cent, while overall beer sales rose by 13 per cent. Overall sales benefited from the integration of the Polish brewer Zywiec.

Overall, despite certain regional differences, there is evidence that tastes within Europe are gradually converging. Analysts predict that the growth seen in part of southern Europe will continue, joined by rapid increases in consumption in former USSR countries. In the mature markets, the decline may be exacerbated by increasing social pressures, as consumers become more health-conscious. Pressure on the brewing industry from governments is also set to increase, with interest focusing on a number of key areas:

- Efforts to reduce levels of alcohol consumption. Associated with this are limits on the nature and style of advertising. For example, beer advertising is banned in Austria, Denmark, Finland, Norway and Sweden. France brought in restrictions in 1993. The EU is reviewing the ethical issues of promoting alcoholic beverages, including beers.

- More stringent drink-driving legislation is expected, reducing permitted consumption of alcohol when driving. There is significant variation within the EU, with the UK one of the more lenient member states. Harmonization of legislation is likely to settle on the lowest drink-drive permitted levels.

- The drive for legislation regarding environmentally friendly packaging. In Germany and Denmark, the importing of non-returnable bottles is prohibited. In addition, manufacturers must ensure that at least 65 per cent of packaging is reusable.

Heineken World-Wide

As the largest brewery group in Europe, Heineken generates 73 per cent from this region, an increase of 39 per cent in the last decade thanks to significant expansion in eastern Europe where political regimes had previously prohibited Heineken's activities. The Netherlands, France and Spain are particularly large contributors, accounting for just under half of all European sales. Heineken's geographic coverage is related to the company's historical development. Early involvement in, and domination of, the European market can be traced to the company's expansion from The Netherlands into countries close by.

As Heineken increases its coverage of world markets, the company adapts its entry method to suit local conditions: direct investment, joint ventures or other alliances. A typical entry strategy would be to begin exporting via intermediaries, move into direct export, look at licensing and joint ventures with local brewers, with finally direct local production either through acquisition or organic investment. Whatever the approach selected, Heineken has a reputation for making careful, well-considered decisions.

With the addition of Poland's Zywiec, Heineken has controlling interests in eight Polish brewers and two Slovakian businesses: Karsay SRO and Zlaty Brazant AS, providing 20 per cent market share in Slovakia. Heineken's share of leading Spanish brewer Cruzcampo is up to 98.7 per cent. In 1999, the company acquired a 35 per cent stake in the Israeli Beer/Bornstein Group which controls the Tempo company responsible for Israel's two leading beer brands: Maccabee and Goldstar. Tempo has 70 per cent market share and Heineken's stake in its new owners gives the Dutch giant immediate access to yet another rapidly growing market.

The Netherlands

With a market share of 52 per cent, the company is a strong market leader in The Netherlands. These figures far exceed the shares of rivals Grolsch (15 per cent) and Verenigde Brouwerijen (15 per cent). The Heineken brand's 45 per cent market share in 1980 dropped to only 30 per cent in 1991. This decline was halted, and lager fought back against the rise of amber and white beers. The introduction of an innovative Heineken can in the shape of a beer glass rejuvenated sales in the late 1990s, supported by the introduction of Cooltap systems for bars. A customer service strategy bolstered the brand's share in the hotel, restaurant and café sectors. Amstel maintained market share and Buckler's, the first non-alcoholic beer available on draft, successfully defended its niche.

France

The Heineken interest in France was developed when, in 1982, the company acquired Albra, which had an 8 per cent market share and owned two breweries. Heineken continued along the acquisition route when in 1984 it merged Albra with Brasseries et Glacieres International to form the Sogebra group. Sogebra has a 30 per cent market share, challenging the first-placed BSN Kronenbourg (50 per cent). St Arnould and Fischer were acquired in 1996. Since the formation and successful reorganization of the Sogebra group, Heineken's fortunes continued to improve until the late 1990s when the premium beer sector suffered a slight decline, with some consumers switching to lower priced brands. Lower priced popular brand Desperados maintained sales growth for Heineken, '33' Export improved sales and Amstel established leadership in the keg beer sector, but premium brands like Heineken suffered a moderate set-back.

Italy

Heineken's presence in Italy started in 1960 when the company acquired a minority stake in a small brewing company. This minority stake was extended in 1974 when Heineken and Whitbread each bought a 42 per cent holding in the company, renamed Birra Dreher. By 1980, having acquired the Whitbread 42 per cent, Heineken was the sole owner of Dreher. As it moved towards its current one-quarter share of the Italian market (market leader Peroni takes around 40 per cent), Dreher was further strengthened by mergers with two former Henniger breweries. The decline in the Italian beer market in the early 1990s was more marked than in some other European markets. Fierce price competition meant that by maintaining its margins, Dreher saw an overall cut in market share. Despite this gloomy scenario, the Heineken brand has retained its position while Buckler's beer has benefited from the increasing growth of the non-alcoholic segment. Here, as in other European countries, Heineken, through Dreher, has increased its control on distribution by purchasing a number of drinks wholesalers. Furthermore, efforts to cater more effectively for the premium lager segment resulted in 1991 in the importing of other Heineken brands. Overall, Dreher's slide has been stemmed, while local 'strategic brand' Moretti has grown significantly. New bottle designs and sponsorship of jazz and sporting events enabled the Heineken brand to grow moderately.

Spain

Heineken's entry into the Spanish market took place in 1984, much later than in other parts of Europe. At this time, the company was able to purchase a 37 per cent stake in the local El Aguila company. This stake has since been increased to 71 per cent, giving Heineken a controlling interest. In order to make a success of its Spanish interests, Heineken had to instigate major changes at El Aguila, which suffered from outdated production techniques and poor branding. Heineken was forced to re-structure production, with inevitable redundancies and short-term losses. Branding strategy changes involved positioning the Aguila Pilsener brand in the standard beer segment, while introducing the new Adlerbrau brand for the premium segment. The Heineken brand is marketed in the top, premium segment. Further change occurred in 1991, when Aguila Master was introduced to replace the badly performing Adlerbrau in the premium segment. Despite the problems with El Aguila, the Spanish market was a particularly attractive one for Heineken, with beer consumption the third highest in the EU. Not surprisingly, other companies were also keen to compete for a slice of this market. Now, the Heineken brand is the undisputed brand leader in the premium sector. Aguila-Amstel has maintained its minority position since its introduction a few years ago and Murphy's Irish stout, launched in 1996, is growing a loyal following.

Greece

Greece is dominated by the Athenian brewery, which is owned by Heineken and Henniger Heblos. Heineken's involvement began with the acquisition of Amstel in 1965. Today, with a market share of approximately 70 per cent, Heineken has three production sites in Greece. This strong position has allowed the company to strengthen the Heineken brand, while importing Dreher and Coors beers. Amstel is the overall market leader, while in the premium sector, Heineken dominates.

Ireland

Ale consumption is declining, but lager and stout are growing strongly, which fits with Heineken's brands, notably Heineken and Guinness-rival Murphy's. The Heineken brand is the market leading lager, growing its share of the market year-on-year, supported by strong sponsorship of Irish cultural and music events. Murphy's growth has been quite phenomenal, even in the home market of the market leading stout, Guinness. Heineken has been producing the Heineken brand under licence in Ireland since the 1970s, acquiring its own production site in 1983. Murphy's stout has been a particular success story, becoming the number two brand of stout in both Ireland and the UK. The brand is also now being sold in some 65 countries and has gained significant market share in the US.

The UK

In the UK, Amstel production began in 1997. While a small brand in a highly crowded marketplace, growth is solid. Sales of Heineken Export outstripped the sales growth for the premium lager sector, while Heineken Cold Filtered maintained market share in the face of heavy promotional spending by rival brands.

The UK, which is the second largest market for beer in Europe, warrants special attention. Here, the pattern of beer consumption is different from the rest of Europe with more than 80 per cent being drunk in pubs, many of which are still linked or tied to breweries. Heineken's route to the market was through its connections with Whitbread, which allowed the company access to Whitbread's distribution network with a licensing agreement. In the 1960s, when Heineken entered the UK market, the beer-drinking public was not familiar with the strong lager beer being drunk in other European countries. Instead, Whitbread brewed a weaker version of the Heineken brand that proved very popular with lager drinkers. In 1990 it was estimated that 10 per cent of all lager drunk in the UK carried the Heineken brand. In the early 1990s, as beer drinkers become increasingly familiar with the continental brands, the company introduced Heineken Export to the UK market. This brand is also brewed under licence by Whitbread.

Germany

Heineken began its entry into the German market in 1993. In consumption terms this is the largest beer market in the world. On average, each year Germans consume 142.8 litres of beer per head. Heineken's late entry to this market can be explained by historic German beer purity laws, only recently relaxed. Today, the attractions of the market are limited by very strong loyalty to the 1,200 local German breweries. The regional variations that result make it difficult for Heineken to achieve distribution on a national scale. One possible route identified by Heineken's marketers was to seek distribution through top restaurants, hotels and cafés. Over 2,000 bars and restaurants in Germany now serve the Heineken brand.

The rest of Europe

In Switzerland, Heineken is the number one premium lager. The acquisition of Calanda Haldengut has finally proved profitable. Regional brands Calanda BraY and Haldengut increased margins and brand loyalty. Amstel is now brewed locally, doubling sales since its 1996 launch. The French speciality beer brands Desperados, Kingston and Adelscott have proved popular in strong Swiss niche markets. Opportunities for Heineken in the eastern European market are potentially large. Beer is already accepted and enjoyed in these parts of Europe, although shortages due to production and distribution problems deprived consumers of the product until the 1990s.

The Hungarian operation is progressing well, maintaining market leadership and increasing sales of Amstel and Buckler's, although low-priced brand Talleros has seen falling sales in recent years. The Zlaty Bazant brewery in Slovakia increased market share to achieve market leadership. Amstel has been launched as a higher-priced brand. Recession in Bulgaria has caused beer sales to fall, but Heineken's Zagorka brewery traded profitably. With a view to a future up-turn in the Bulgarian market, Heineken – with joint venture partner the Hellenic Bottling Company – acquired a 60 per cent interest in Sofia's Ariana brewery. Sales have risen in Kazakhstan and the Ukraine; Heineken has maintained its position in Russia, although import restrictions are restricting any growth; and Amstel has been launched in seven eastern European countries.

The rest of the Heineken world

Outside Europe, sales are progressing well in North America, home of arch rivals Miller and Budweiser. Heineken's growth is sure and steady, while Amstel has made significant in-roads, supported by new launches for Amstel Light, Amstel Bier and Amstel 1870. Murphy's growth has been significant in the stout market. In the Caribbean, Heineken is the largest imported beer brand and a well-known sponsor of local jazz festivals. Bahamian-based Kalik lager has sold well. Investment is under way to boost Heineken's brand presence in Central and South America. Heineken has a 10 per cent stake in Cervejarias Kaiser of Brazil, while in Argentina, Heineken's partner Quilmes is producing the Heineken brand under licence.

Economic and political tensions in Africa have hindered market growth, but Heineken's operations are continuing to expand, in Sierra Leone, Angola, Ghana, Nigeria and notably in South Africa, with particular growth of Amstel. Breweries in the Democratic Republic of Congo (formerly Zaire) and Rwanda had to be closed owing to political unrest. In Asia Pacific sales have risen by around 10 per cent per annum, with China now accounting for half of the region's beer consumption. Heineken has breweries in many countries in the region, including Singapore, Papua New Guinea, Cambodia, Thailand, New Caledonia, East Java and naturally, China. There are partnerships in Vietnam and Indonesia, with strong export markets in Hong Kong and Taiwan. The company's leading brands in Asia Pacific include Heineken, Amstel, Anchor and Tiger.

Brand strategy

Flexibility is a key characteristic of Heineken's approach to market segmentation and branding. Company philosophy suggests that it should be possible to target segments in each market with the company's own core brands: Heineken, Amstel, Murphy's and Buckler's. This, it is argued, is because there are customer segments and tastes which cross both national and regional boundaries.

Despite its interest in pursuing general, cross-boundary segments, Heineken is also realistic about the need to cater for the tastes of local, smaller segments. Each country is catered for by combining the use of global core brands with those which are indigenous to the local market; 'strategic' or 'regional' brands. This allows local brands, differing in taste, packaging and image, to be offered in conjunction with Heineken's core international brands. This is usually achieved by targeting three segments in each market:

- A local, 'standard brand' for the high volume market segment: Dreher in Italy, '33' in France, and Tiger in Singapore.

- A brand to occupy the higher middle segment of the market. This may be a local brand such as the Spanish Aguila Master, or the Amstel brand.

- The Heineken brand in the top premium lager segment in the market. This may be brewed locally or exported directly. The image and quality of this brand are always carefully controlled by the Dutch head office. Only in the UK do the recipe and taste vary significantly from the original Heineken.

Heineken has successfully promoted its core brand names throughout the world. The company recognizes the differing expectations and tastes of each national and even regional market. The international brands are distributed in each territory, but alongside locally produced and sold beers. However, wherever they are produced, Heineken, Amstel, Murphy's and Buckler's are marketed with common brand identities and positioning strategies. For example, the Heineken experience is branded similarly throughout the world and the company's marketers strongly utilize sponsorship of cultural and music events to create brand awareness and a positive brand attitude amongst target market consumers.

Heineken's strategy of giving autonomy to local operating companies in the markets it enters has resulted in the production of beers that appeal closely to local tastes and preferences. It has also enabled the company to use its foothold in the marketplace to understand and anticipate market trends. The use of a stratified segmentation approach, by offering brands to the lower, mid- and premium lager segments in each market has prevented the company becoming trapped as a niche player, or vulnerable to a decline in any single sector of the beer market. With the stated aim of becoming the world's number one beer company, Heineken is continually seeking ways to spread into new markets while moving towards domination in those it already occupies. The company has a global philosophy and internationally known brands, but also an understanding and commitment to local markets and production.

Issues

As a company, Heineken is active throughout the world. As a brand, Heineken is familiar to consumers in North and South America, Africa, Asia Pacific and most of Europe. The company, though, takes account of the needs of local consumers and has a portfolio containing local brands alongside leading international brands. The company's fortunes have frequently been affected by the forces of the marketing environment.

Branding

Heineken as a brand is available throughout the world. In most countries, differing competitive positions and consumer tastes have led the company to offer locally produced brands alongside its mainstay Heineken. Why is this approach to branding necessary? How does it gain market share for the company's portfolio? What are the disadvantages with this multi-branding strategy?

International marketing

There are few genuinely global brands. Perhaps Heineken is one. How does Heineken deal with its different market territories? Why? Does the company have one standard product offer, branded as Heineken, for the whole world? How would you tackle such a complex international branding problem?

The marketing environment

Cultural, political and economic forces, amongst others, have benefited Heineken on certain occasions and hampered the company's plans on others. Why must the company take account of its marketing environment? How best should it monitor and assess these forces?

Relevant Theory Notes

T8: The Marketing Mix: Products and Product Management, pp. 246–254
T16: International Marketing, pp. 297–301
T2: The Marketing Environment and Competition, pp. 199–204

Full Case 12:   Games Workshop
Warfare in the Crèche

As the name suggests, Games Workshop manufactures and sells games. But these are no ordinary games and this is no ordinary business. With a turnover of £70 million, this fast-growing company employs more than 2,000 people and has over 200 retail outlets world-wide. In recent years the company has spread its operation to take in a number of countries away from the UK domestic market. Representative offices are now open in Australia, Canada, Germany, Hong Kong, Spain and the USA, with the growing Italian market still being serviced from the UK. In 1999 the company opened its 200th store, in Amsterdam.

The fantasy games produced by Games Workshop take place in one of two settings. The first is a fantasy world filled with Dwarfs, Elves, rat-like Scaven, green Orcs and Goblins. The second is in the future: a war-torn universe in the 41st Millennium. This setting is occupied by the enigmatic Eldar, genetically enhanced Space Marines and an alien race called the Tyranids, who are all battling for survival. Games Workshop enthusiasts can buy from a range of boxed games (see Figure III.4). These games contain the rulebook, charts and templates, dice and miniature figures needed to begin their fantasy battle. The basics can then be added to from the extensive range of Games Workshop troops, special

| **Figure III.4** | *Games Workshop Fantasy Games* |

Warhammer 40,000: **40,000 years into the nightmare world of the far future, there is only war! Humanity stands at the final and bloody crossroads between survival and utter destruction.**

Warhammer: **Vast armies, led by mighty heroes, clash in mortal combat. Terrifying monsters and deadly war machines wreak havoc as Wizards and Sorcerers conjure up arcane and destructive spells.**

Battlefleet Gothic: **Massive fleets of enormous starships clash in battles of incomprehensible destruction. In the dark future of the 41st Millennium there is no peace among the stars, there is only war!**

Epic 40,000 – War on a Whole New Scale: **In the 41st Millennium, war rages across the universe as the battle for supremacy and survival continues never-ending. Complete victory lies across a thousand fronts on a hundred planets throughout the galaxy.**

Necromunda – Battle for Survival in the Nightmare Undercity: **In the subterranean depths of Necromunda's dark underworld, the hard-bitten survivors stalk through crumbling domes and ancient machines, fighting for the spoils of a derelict civilization.**

Source: www.games-workshop.co.uk

squads and war machines. As enthusiasts develop their armies and paint them in colours of their choice, they begin to build their own personalized version of their game of choice.

Head Office

Visitors to the Games Workshop head office in Nottingham in the Midlands of the UK quickly begin to understand the ethos underlying the business. Outwardly, this is a modern, stylish, purpose-built office block, manufacturing and warehouse facility on a typical edge-of-town industrial park. A giant Space Marine statue adjacent to the car park and a huge Imperial Eagle emblem above the main entrance give some clue, though, as to the building's purpose. Upon entering the facility, perceptions are altered as visitors encounter the gothic mouldings in reception and are struck by the all-encompassing enthusiastic buzz and creative energy. The usual suits, ties and briefcases of office life are not in evidence. Instead, dress is informal, office spaces are highly personalized and managers are likely to be found clutching paintbrushes and modelling knives or to be clustered around a gaming table battling each other's miniature armies. For most, a childhood obsession with fantasy games and models has developed into an occupation, leading to a kind of infectious enthusiasm for the Games Workshop brand.

This sense of excitement and anticipation accompanies each stage of new product development. The central feature of the main modelling area is the gaming table. Here, at every conceivable opportunity, new games and figures are tested out, often in long-running battles lasting many lunch times. Such 'research' has become an integral part of the business's success.

Visitors find that the head office site has a number of distinctive features:

- Publications area, where highly skilled staff handle the full range of Games Workshop magazines. The sheer international scope of the story and artwork contributions for these publications is in evidence. Here there is a high-level of planning, with editorial staff keeping track of both current and future issues.

- Upstairs in the modelling area, visitors can witness the entire process of creating a new character or gaming concept. Often this begins with a series of simple sketches that are later converted into more detailed and colourful drawings. Half-completed mock-ups cover the desks, constructed from the mundane (such as paper clips and coffee cups) as well as the more usual modelling materials.

- The gaming table, so much a part of the Games Workshop ethos, is also in evidence in the modelling area. Here staff spend every spare moment in experiments with new models, games and strategic moves.

- A bank of rooms with model mould makers, showing the painstaking detail and weeks or months taken to create a new character or gaming concept.

- The company's painters of its miniatures – highly skilled artists – can be found concentrating hard on every small detail of the figures in front of them. Most have their own personal stereos to help maintain concentration!

- Re-assuringly, production and warehouse facilities are like those to be found in most modern plastics manufacturers, with the usual picking and storage logistical support.
- Exhibition Centre, a sports hall-like complex with plenty of space for large and small gaming events for staff and adoring fans.
- The Games Workshop Museum, offering low-priced tours on most days. Visitors can enjoy the life-size Warhammer 40,000 characters sited in realistic settings or view the superbly painted miniatures set in massive gaming displays.
- Bar and leisure area for the workforce. This simulated 'dungeon', a replica of a bar in Warhammer World, provides a popular out-of-hours focal point for the workforce to share new ideas.
- An on-site shop provides a location for staff training, in-store layout experimentation as well as a central point for bringing the finished product together. Staff and visitors can enjoy discounts in the store.
- Mail-order dispatch point. Here the Games Workshop Mail Order Trolls send out everything from individual figures to large boxed sets. The company claims to be able to supply any component or miniature the company has ever made.

Much of the company's ethos hinges on the people who are employed. In the modelling area, personnel do not appear to suffer from executive stress. Life at Games Workshop HQ for many is a vocation: an extension of how they would like to spend their spare time. Indeed, for many, leisure activities mirror their working days! A better insight into the policy behind this can be seen in the company's recruitment literature. Here the required characteristics of potential applicants are clearly laid out. In a recent advertisement for recruits to the Games Workshop Mail Order business, key attributes were listed:

The Skills

- Huge passion for the Games Workshop hobby
- Enjoy talking to people of all age groups
- Excellent communication skills
- A good telephone manner
- Previous telesales experience would be useful but not essential.

The Person

- Loads of energy and enthusiasm
- Able to use your own initiative
- Confident
- Good sense of humour
- Customer service orientated – you will know the need for excellent customer service.

The Shops

For those unfamiliar with the fantasy game concept, the uncharted territory of the retail outlets can feel like alien territory. Wall space stacked high with numerous games, figures, paints, magazines, books and t-shirts. In the centre is a gaming table, which is usually covered with the remains of an ongoing battle. At other times, the shops are full of teenagers and children, conducting a closely fought *Warhammer* contest. On some days the outlets resemble a crèche for big kids, with staff carefully orchestrating activities. The battles organized in-store are an important part of the weekly itinerary. The featured game varies on different days, so that enthusiasts of *Warhammer*, *Warhammer 40,000*, *Necromunda* and the other Games Workshop products can all get their turn. These games induct newcomers into the gaming experience, while for 'old hands', they showcase new product launches.

Games Workshop managers are mindful that they must cater for the varying needs and skill levels of different hobbyists. Many stores devote Sunday opening to those who are relatively new to the hobby. The emphasis is on learning the basics of how to collect, paint and play. Saturday is a gaming day, with a different game each week. Hobbyists of all levels can come along and take part in the battle. With one night each week devoted to *Warhammer* and another to *Warhammer 40,000*, the needs of the more experienced hobbyists are also catered for. These evening sessions provide the opportunity to learn advanced painting techniques and to build up experience of more complex gaming tactics.

In addition, to the regular itinerary of gaming days and evenings, the stores run special events. The following is a description of one such event that was run to coincide with the launch of the company's biggest ever model – Asdrubael Vect, Supreme Lord of the Kabal of the Black Heart.

> Imperious Rex: On Saturday 18th December you can take part in an awesome battle every store is running to celebrate the arrival of two of the most infamous individuals the galaxy has every seen. *Solar Lord Macharius* and *Asdrubael Vect* fight it out across the country, so make sure that you pop down to your local store to take part in the action. You can either bring your own troops, or fight it out with store miniatures. The choice is yours, and all you have to do to take part is turn up.

(Games Workshop Newsletter — December 1999)

Visitors can stay in the stores for as long as they like, comparing gaming ideas and joining in with the battle if they choose. They are even encouraged to bring along their own figures, especially those which have been painted in new and exciting ways. It is common to see shop staff and half a dozen youngsters clustered around a new arrival, making admiring comments about a series of tiny, carefully painted miniatures.

The shop staff, always Games Workshop enthusiasts, are vital to the success of the retail outlets. They must be able maintain an enthusiasm for the brand, keeping up to date with all of the latest new product launches. The ability to handle customers of all ages and backgrounds is also essential. From the young teenagers who regularly 'hang out' at the stores to the uninitiated visiting the outlets for the first time. Nonplussed parents clutching 'Christmas lists' or birthday present suggestions have so often experienced a friendly welcome from staff who will happily search among the reams of Games Workshop packaging to retrieve some unlikely named item.

Access to the Games Workshop Mail Order facility is also available through the outlets (as well as direct by telephone). This £3 million+ operation has 40 staff and a database of 150,000 contacts. The aim is to provide a fast and efficient service, despatching all orders within 24 hours. This facility handles up to 1,000 calls daily and can deal with enquiries in a range of languages.

The Customers

The company is quick to observe that Games Workshop enthusiasts generally remain committed to their hobby for many years. Once captivated by their new interest, many enthusiasts make weekly visits to the Games Workshop stores, spend hours pouring over the latest hobby magazines and dedicate all of their spare time to painting miniatures and developing new battle strategies. As they become increasingly involved in the Games Workshop world, many enthusiasts develop their own creative slant on their hobby. They build their own mix of miniatures, preferred battle strategies and convert or modify the component they use. Such 'conversions' take the hobby into a different stage, as blades and glue fashion fantastic creations utilising in part Games Workshop models in conjunction with any suitable household object or throw-away item. The perspective in Figure III.5 provides an insight into the psyche of these hobbyists. Unlike most children's hobbies and toys, the Games Workshop experience tends to have longevity.

The continuing interest and commitment of Games Workshop hobbyists is fundamental to the success of the brand. Not surprisingly, the business has devised many ways of satisfying the needs of these customers. In addition to the diverse mix of games, models and miniatures, the devoted enthusiast is offered a wide range of reading material, including:

- *White Dwarf*: highly popular magazine with many subscribers that keeps hobbyists up to date with new releases and information about existing lines.
- *The Citadel Journal*: the magazine for the Games Workshop hobby, written by hobbyists and filled with rules, strategies and ideas for converting miniatures and figures.
- *Warhammer Monthly*: an all-adventure comic, packed with carefully scripted and illustrated fantasy adventures.
- *Inferno!*: this is a selection of short stories, comic strips, diagrams and features from the gothic Warhammer and Warhammer 40,000 worlds.

There now are ranges of fantasy novels based on favourite armies and battles, plus annuals.

Regular Games Workshop events are staged at the Nottingham head office and other locations. In a typical year these might include Open Days, Grand Tournaments and full-scale wars. In addition, there is an annual Games Day. In 1999, as in previous years, this took place in the large and well-equipped Birmingham National Indoor Arena. This UK version of the company's largest event – with retail stands, displays and participation gaming – allows more than 8,500 Games Workshop fans to share all aspects of their mutual interest. Such

Figure III.5	*The Games Workshop Enthusiast's Perspective*

An Enthusiast's Perspective

Huge armies fighting across battle worn fields, deadly beasts bigger than houses, mile-long cruisers battling it out in the void and, a rather annoyed ex-Dwarf barber who decides to give the troll who destroyed his shop (and his honour) more than a haircut. This is what makes me like Games Workshop so much, the sheer scope of it all. You can fight battles to represent the destruction of an entire city one day, and yet have just as much fun playing small skirmishes representing the hit and run raids of the survivors afterwards.

The great thing about Games Workshop is not all the details it includes about the places of the Warhammer world, or the many planets in the 41st Millennium, but the gaps it leaves for your imagination. You start to think about what you are doing, what you are playing for. You could be fighting to take an enemy stronghold or to protect an entire world. Sure you can play without thinking about this, but it's a lot more fun if you do!

You could, if you were a player who likes historic games, still get a lot out of Games Workshop. By taking a human army, (especially Bretonians) not including any Wizards, magic items or monsters and only fighting other so-equipped human armies, you could get the desired effect. You could play out historic battles, such as the Welsh longbow beating the crossbow (not to mention the French knights) in the Hundred Year War.

Of course, probably the biggest reason for Games Workshop's popularity is the complete hands-on approach to the whole hobby. You choose, collect, assemble convert and finally paint your chosen force. And even then you can go back to it, adding new models or adding more to the ones you already have.

But before even that, you have to choose which Games system you want to play. The choice is huge, with Warhammer 40,000, Warhammer, Epic 40,000, Space Hulk, Necromunda, Battle Fleet Gothic, Gorka Morka, Middenheim, Talisman, Blood Bowl, Space Crusade and Man O War. Although several of these are now redundant, I expect there are still people playing them somewhere. Then you have to choose the race. In Warhammer alone there are two human, two Dwarf, three Elf, three Chaos, two Undead, one Mercenary, one Orc, one Scaven and one Lizardmen army! That's six races, (Undead and Daemons – one of the Chaos armies – not included) and sixteen armies to chose from, whoa!

This huge variety of races and games means there's a force out there to suit every taste, hence Games Workshop's popularity. Even inside the armies there is lots of choice. An Empire army could consist of mainly cavalry (charge), infantry or archers and war machines (splat). Whereas an Imperial guard army could be a huge force of infantry or a company of tanks (kaboom!).

The models themselves are excellent, especially the new plastic kits, which are better value than most of the other models. Most of the models are quite easily converted (though I would love to know how Paul Swayer removed the guns from those Redemptionist Gangers!). The plastic kits especially seem designed for conversions. The fact that most of them are inter-changeable is a masterstroke and shows why Games Workshop is so successful.

The actual stores themselves are the cream on the cake. You can go in to play battles, ask questions (or just to bug the staff), learn new rules or (shock, horror) actually buy something! The staff are friendly, not to mention insane and most of them deserve medals. The atmosphere is friendly and you can quite happily play a game against someone you wouldn't go near at school.

James Dibb-Simkin, aged 13 years, 1999

| **Figure III.6** | *Scyla: Games Workshop Character* |

events generate tremendous enthusiasm from devoted customers but also amongst staff from head office and the stores.

Financials and the Future

Figures for the Games Workshop business show strong growth and future prospects for the business are encouraging. In order to retain the flexibility to deal with the growth ahead, the Games Workshop Board of directors has been restructured. The company has also taken steps to cater for the increasingly international dimension of the business by formalizing its global operating structure and creating an international operating Board. In the words of Chairman Tom Kirby, 'The hobby continues to grow strongly. The test is whether Games Workshop can continue to serve it – and it seems to me that the prospects for the business with its strengthened senior management structure and the boundless energy to succeed are as gloriously rich as ever'.

The key points from the financial results for the year ended 30 May 1999, included:

- Operating profit before royalty income at £12.6m (1998: £11.2m).
- Turnover at £72.6m (1998: £64.8m).
- Pre-tax profit at £12.5m (1998: £11.5m).
- Earnings per ordinary share at £0.26 (1998: £0.241).
- Dividend of £0.097 (1998: £0.09).
- Strong like-for-like growth restored to the retail operations.
- 25 new stores opened (including 200th store) – 19 of these outside the UK.
- Successfully launched major games system – Warhammer 40,000.
- Acquired and integrated plastic injection moulding and tool-making operations.
- Made first sales into Japan.
- Management strengthened and international management board established.

The Board of Games Workshop has ambitious future plans. The company aims to build markets in each of the world's major economies. With 60 per cent of sales already from outside the UK market, it seems as if the business is well on its way to achieving this objective. Sales to the Americas have increased through independent retailers and an accelerated store opening programme. The figures for Continental Europe are also up, with seven new stores opening in France, Spain, Germany and Italy. This brings the tally for Continental Europe to 44. In the Asia Pacific region, sales showed a slight decline, but this was accounted for by a downturn in Australia and New Zealand, with increases in the Philippines, Taiwan and Korea. The changes that have been made to the company's international operations, allowing senior managers from other markets to become involved in strategic decision-making, will help ensure overseas sales continue to grow. The fanatical enthusiasm of Games Workshop's staff and increasing band of loyal customers seems destined to maintain the incredible growth of this brand.

Issues

The Games Workshop phenomenon has won over many 'fans', from young children playing make-believe battles, to teenagers developing gaming strategies, to adults hooked on the Games Workshop worlds, figures, games, events and modelling opportunities. Recent international expansion implies the concept has more widespread appeal than perhaps even its founders first envisaged.

Services marketing

To many customers, Games Workshop is an experience, notably in the shops and at the major events hosted at head office and suitable venues. How important to the Games Workshop ethos are staff training, selection and motivation?

Buying behaviour

Why has Games Workshop created 'crèche-style' shops? How has an understanding of its customers' buying behaviour led to this development?

Marketing channels

Why has Games Workshop adopted more than one marketing channel? Are additional channels, such as mail order or the Internet, likely to threaten the Games Workshop 'experience'?

Relevant Theory Notes

T13: The Marketing of Services, pp. 280–284
T8: The Marketing Mix: Products and Product Management, pp. 246–254
T3: Buying Behaviour, pp. 205–212
T9: The Marketing Mix: Place – Distribution and Marketing Channels, pp. 255–260
T12: Direct Marketing and the Internet, pp. 275–279

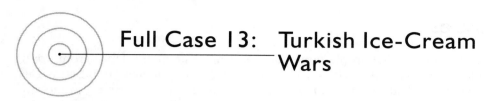

Full Case 13: Turkish Ice-Cream Wars

The Freezer Wars

Close to £10 billion is spent each year by Europeans on ice-cream. Half of this goes on impulse buys – products bought to be eaten immediately. Market leader Unilever – Wall's and Ola in the ice-cream market – has been accused by new-comers Haagen-Dazs, Ben & Jerry's and Mars of sharp practice. Unilever has a Europe-wide strategy of lending freezers to retailers on condition they are used only to sell Unilever brands. As most small shops cannot accommodate more than one cabinet, this effectively excludes rival brands. In addition, Unilever's network of wholesalers offers discounts to retailers who only stock Unilever products. The 'freezer wars' has led EU and UK competition regulators to investigate this highly competitive marketplace. The EU used Ireland as a test case, ruling that the freezer restrictions imposed by Unilever were anti-competitive. Unilever's defence is simple: only retailers requesting its freezers are offered them and a growing number of retailers are purchasing their own cabinets.

The intensity of competition must not be under-estimated. Confectionery giant Mars introduced its Dove ice-cream lolly in 1989. Dove struggled to survive for three years before being killed off. However, Unilever's Magnum, virtually identical to Mars' Dove was launched in 1990 and attained blanket coverage, making it the world's number one ice-cream brand. According to Mars, consumers loved Dove, but found access to it restricted to only a few retail outlets. Mars fought back, launching its highly popular range of countline bars in ice-cream format: Mars, Snickers, Twix and Milky Way. To compete effectively, however, it had to offer retailers its own range of freezer cabinets. Unlike Unilever, it asked retailers to fill only 40 per cent of space with Mars products.

Diageo's premium Haagen-Dazs brand has attacked Unilever's market lead-ership by targeting adults, rather than children, with deluxe flavours and ingredients and 'sexy advertising'. Indeed, the brand was launched with press advertising depicting a naked couple entwined while enjoying Haagen-Dazs ice-cream. Ice-cream was transformed from a children's product to a self-indulgent adult oriented product with the launch of Haagen-Dazs. Diageo (Grand Metropolitan at the time) targeted delicatessens, bistros and premium super-markets for Haagen-Dazs distribution, rather than CTN newsagents or corner shops. One in four consumers now opts for Haagen-Dazs in the premium ice-cream sector. Unilever retaliated with its own luxury brand, Carte D'or, which takes around a third of the premium sector's sales. Zany, ethical, environmentally aware Ben Cohen and Jerry Greenfield are making significant in-roads in Europe with their Chunky Monkey or Coffee Coffee BuzzBuzzBuzz flavoured Ben & Jerry's ice-cream. (Note: Unilever recently acquired Ben & Jerry's, reflecting the impact made by this innovative US brand.)

All of this is a far cry from a few decades ago, when only children sought ice-cream, and then predominantly in the summer months or while on excursions to the theatre or cinema. The bulk of the market was accounted for by just two rivals: Wall's and Lyons Maid. What happened to Lyons Maid? It became Nestlé. In Europe as a whole, Nestlé is number two, but in most countries it is a long way behind the mighty Unilever Ola/Wall's empire. This creates significant challenges for Nestlé's marketers. This is particularly so when entering a new territory of operation, such as Turkey.

Turkey: a Challenging Environment

The Turkish army is very much in control, but is striving to bring about the unification of centre-right political forces. The Government has struggled to create an economic revival and continually has fallen short of IMF demands. Recently, the situation has improved slightly. GNP has risen by between 3 per cent and 5 per cent per annum. Private consumption has been buoyant since the mid-1990s, although the Government is pledged to slow this down to a more manageable level. While job creation has been on the increase, wage awards have been generous, with inflationary impact. Inflation ranged between 60 per cent and 90 per cent for much of the 1990s, with the Government setting an overly optimistic target of 50 per cent! This was despite various enforced price freezes, including a six-month holding of petrol prices.

Interest rates have led to appreciation of the lira: lower interest rates are only likely if a new reformist Government comes to power. The currency is also volatile, with the country struggling to maintain adequate foreign exchange to service its large external debt payments. Exports have been hit by Asian rivals, while imports are growing, led by the upsurge in consumer demand. Nevertheless, the growth of the private sector and strong trading links with the EU have stalled a bleak economic outlook. Indeed, many EU businesses are seeking expansion inside Turkey. The country's 62 million people, rising incomes and growing receptiveness to foreign brands have encouraged businesses such as Nestlé to establish a more substantial presence. Table III.21 demonstrates the attractiveness of Turkey's consumers. The horrendous earthquakes in 1999 severely impacted on daily life and commerce, but for pan-European businesses, Turkey remained a viable and potentially lucrative market.

Table III.21	*The Attractiveness of Turkey's Consumers*
Population	62.6 million
Population in the four key cities	17.2 million
Population in A, B and C1 social groups	20.3 million
Proportion under the age of 20	46%
GDP per capita	$5,691
Export GDP growth	5%

The Growth of Nestlé

Major acquisitions of leading manufacturers and brands, such as Rowntree in the UK or Perrier in France, has continued unabated for the truly global business of Nestlé. Based in Vevey on Lake Geneva in Switzerland, Nestlé has close to a quarter of a million employees and 500 factories in 80 countries. The world's number one food producer, Nestlé manufacturers beverages (Nescafé, Nestea, Perrier); milk, dietetic and ice-cream products (Carnation, Fitness, Frisco); prepared dishes and cooking aids (Stouffer's, Ortega, Alpo); plus chocolate and confectionery (Butterfinger, Crunch, KitKat, Polo). Nestlé is also Europe's number two petfood producer, behind Mars. In addition, the company manufactures pharmaceutical products (Opti-Free contact lens solution and ophthalmic drug Ciloxan), and it owns 49 per cent of cosmetics giant L'Oreal.

With a portfolio of over 8,500 products and marketing operations in 100 countries, Nestlé has a strategy of promoting global brands while reflecting the nuances of local markets. Brands are important to Nestlé's trading philosophy, but so too is the need to reflect local tastes. A quality product image is integral to the Nestlé mission. The world-wide food market is static, while the global ice-cream market is growing at 5 per cent per annum. This prompted Nestlé to establish ice-cream as an SBU (strategic business unit), which now accounts for 4 per cent of the company's overall sales: three billion Swiss Francs. In the early 1990s, Nestlé had less than 1 per cent of the world-wide ice-cream market, but now has an impressive 10 per cent, and climbing! Against this backdrop, the recent expansion into Turkey's ice-cream market was not too surprising. Nestlé first established an office in Turkey as far back as 1909 and its first factory in 1927. Most Turkish children and young adults are very familiar with the Nestlé logo, particularly in the chocolate (Nestlé Damak) and confectionery market. The treat of Nestlé chocolate has become well entrenched in Turkish culture. The challenge is to extend this desire to Nestlé ice-cream. Until the new millennium, Turks did not associate the Nestlé name with ice-cream.

The Competitive Arena in Turkey

While ice-cream is long established, it would seem from international comparisons and the per capita consumption of ice-cream in Turkey (see Table III.22), that there is much scope for growth. Compared with Turkey's 50 million litres in the mid-1990s, Portugal consumed 15 million litres, Ireland 33, Greece 39, Switzerland 62, The Netherlands 132, Spain 203 and Italy a staggering 225 million litres. Figure III.6 plots ice cream consumption against gross domestic product (GDP), again demonstrating the growth potential for the Turkish market.

By 2000, it was estimated the Turkish market had reached 60 million litres, with the impulse market accounting for 17 million litres. The challenge for Nestlé was to reach a critical mass in terms of distribution coverage to warrant the promotional spend required to achieve the brand awareness likely to effectively rival leading competitors. While the overall ice-cream market is destined to grow, Nestlé had to devise a strategy capable of creating a sizeable presence at the

Table III.22	*Turkey's Ice-Cream Market*
1999 ice cream sales	50 million litres
1991 sales	42 million litres
Five-year volume increase	20.23%
US$ value five-year increase	68.82%
Per capita volume	0.8 litres
Total value US$	164 million

expense, inevitably, of established competing brands. Perhaps unsurprisingly, Unilever had already successfully entered the Turkish market.

Unilever, with 20 per cent of the global ice cream market, created an operation in Turkey in 1990. Until then, the market was managed by local brands Panda and Alaska. These two players are still active and have greatly improved their product, branding and marketing programmes in an attempt to co-exist with their international rivals. Mars, too, is in the Turkish market, but presently only as a very minor supplier. Unilever is the principal rival to Nestlé, particularly as it has specifically targeted expansion in developing markets. Unilever has made acquisitions in Argentina, Brazil, Colombia and Mexico, while establishing ice-cream operations in Vietnam and most cities in China. Now active in 100 countries, the biggest threat to the Wall's/Ola ice-cream business of Unilever stems from the EU's anticompetitive probes of the company's freezer distribution to retailers.

Trading as Algida in Turkey, Unilever has been market leader since its 1990 entry, holding 65 per cent of the market. Algida offers impulse, take-home tubs/packs, catering and dessert-type ice-cream products. The business has striven to create its own marketplace, so enlarging the overall market. For example, it offers a range of 35 impulse-oriented lollies and ice-cream bars. It operates a purpose-built factory near Istanbul and is the largest industrial ice-cream producer.

Figure III.7	*Ice-Cream Consumption versus GDP per Capita: an International Comparison*

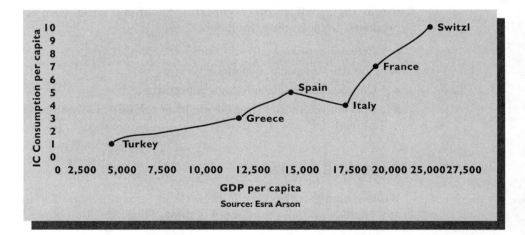

Mars is one of the world's leading chocolate and confectionery producers and is quickly developing its ice-cream business. After several false starts, this has now been achieved by brand extension of popular countline brands into ice-cream products: Mars, Snickers, Twix and Milky Way. In Turkey, Mars confectionery is distributed by Sezginler AS, while ice-cream lines are distributed by local company Efemex Memo. Ice-cream distribution is weak by comparison with other Mars products. Mars ice-cream lines are sold at a 25 per cent price premium over Unilever Algida brands. Without extensive promotion and brand building, sales are accordingly weak.

Turkish private company Panda is the principal competitor to Unilever's Algida, although Nestlé is quickly making in-roads. Panda was the first to introduce factory-produced ice-cream in Turkey and had the market – much smaller then – to itself until Unilever's 1990 entry. Panda fought back against Algida, building new production facilities and investing in promoting a strong brand identity. The product range and pricing are similar to Algida's, but distribution outlets are being squeezed by Unilever's retailer and wholesaler incentives. A second domestic rival is Memo, which now also distributes Mars's ice-cream products. Memo is a more traditional company which focuses on an ice-cream choc bar sold in theatres and cinemas. Memo is primarily strong around its Aegean base.

The existing ice-cream rivals are faced with new entrant rivals. In addition to a growing attack from Nestlé, Germany's Scholler has identified Turkey as a growth opportunity. Although only small globally with 2 per cent of the ice-cream market, Scholler has some well-known brands: Scholler, Fischer and Movenpick. It is particularly active in Germany, Austria, the Netherlands, Belgium, Britain, France, Poland, Hungary, Slovakia and the Czech Republic. Scholler chose not to develop its own Turkish operation, but instead created a joint venture with Turkish frozen foods company Kerevitas. The frozen foods market is very small in Turkey, but Kerevitas's Superfresh operation commands 65 per cent market share. The joint venture with Scholler and Kerevitas is a $30 million investment. The production plant will supply take-home and impulse ice-cream lines to Turkey and also for export to neighbouring emerging countries. Scholler knows that to be successful, it must create brand awareness and establish point-of-sale freezer cabinet distribution in retailers. Many of these retailers currently are 'signed up' to Unilever's Algida or are being targeted by Nestlé.

Owing to the lack of an ice-cream heritage in Turkey, a major competitive threat facing all of the competing ice-cream producers is from substitute products. Notably, these include:

- Artesian ice-cream (traditional soft scoop).
- Soft drinks (easily available).
- Confectionery (already high penetration).
- Non-food activities a child might purchase (entertainment, toys, computer games).

Nestlé's Options

While strong globally, Nestlé has little ice-cream penetration in Turkey. As with any business, it has a number of options. These are summarized in Table III.23.

Table III.23	*Entry Mode Options*

- *Exporting* The lowest level of commitment and the most flexible approach to international marketing. A channel intermediary such as an agent could handle the task. Minor changes to packaging, labelling style or colour will be the extent of any product adaptation.

- *Licensing* When production, technical assistance and marketing know-how are required across national boundaries, licensing is an alternative to direct investment. The licensee pays commissions or royalties on sales or supplies.

- *Franchising* A form of licensing, franchising also avoids direct overseas investment by granting the right to use trade names, brand names, designs, patents, copyright, production and marketing processes to locally based third-party businesses.

- *Joint Ventures* A partnership between a domestic company and a foreign business or government is a joint venture in international marketing. This is very popular when hefty investment is required or extensive resources are needed in production.

- *Strategic Alliances* An extension of the joint venture concept, where partnerships are formed to create competitive advantage on a world-wide basis. The partners retain their own identities, but each brings a unique set of competencies to the combined operation.

- *Trading Companies* These provide a link between buyers and sellers in different countries. A trading company is not involved in manufacturing nor does it own production-based assets. Instead it buys in one country and sells to buyers in another country.

- *Foreign Direct Investment* Once a business is committed to an overseas country or market which it views as stable and offering longer term potential, direct ownership of a foreign subsidiary or division becomes a viable option.

Unilever opted for direct investment in Turkey. Scholler chose a joint venture. Nestlé initially opted for direct export until its local production facilities could be developed. It has not the scale economies to be cost focused, so its competitive strategy is one of differentiation. This requires the development of quality and distinctive products with strong brand identities. However, this will require service, quality, style, technology, distribution, promotion or price leadership. Against the mighty Algida (Unilever), which currently lays claim to many of these traits, Nestlé's task is far from straight forward. Nevertheless, the Swiss company's world-wide ice-cream ambitions have led to impressive growth and the number two position in the global marketplace. It is unlikely Nestlé will fail in its Turkish quest.

Acknowledgement

With thanks to journalist Claire Murphy and former MBA student Esra Arson.

Issues

The marketing environment in the Turkish ice-cream market has given many international manufacturers cause for concern over the years, but the leading players have now all established operations in this growing market. The influx of international brands has created problems for existing domestic ice-cream producers, but for some it has provided an opportunity of forging alliances with the global ice-cream giants. For Nestlé, the leading position of arch-rival Unilever has caused additional problems as it attempts to build market share in the Turkish ice-cream market.

The marketing environment

What marketing environment forces are likely to impact on the ice-cream market in Turkey? What is the nature of the competitive arena in the Turkish ice-cream market? Why are substitute products such a competitive threat to the leading ice-cream brands?

International marketing

Why have global businesses such as Unilever and Nestlé targeted the Turkish market? What approach could Nestlé best adopt to quickly establish a strong presence in the Turkish ice-cream market?

Relevant Theory Notes

T2:   The Marketing Environment and Competition, pp. 199–204
T7:   Competitive Strategy, pp. 237–245
T16:   International Marketing, pp. 297–301
T14:   Industrial, Business-to-Business Marketing, pp. 285–289

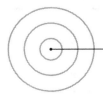

Full Case 14: Sleeping on a Budget
Lodge Hotels Lead the Way

Every-Day Low Prices

In the late 1990s a popular marketing angle was for companies to stress every-day low prices or value-for-money. Businesses have attracted customer interest with low pricing for decades, but in recent years the message has not centred on a 'no frills' approach or 'pile it high and sell it cheaply'. Major grocery retailers such as Tesco, Sainsbury's and Asda had spent many years building brand positionings based on quality merchandise, extensive selections, pleasant shopping environments, helpful personnel, in-store specialist fresh produce departments and customer services such as free parking, long opening hours, in-store cafés and crèche facilities. For such companies, an Aldi-style price-led 'cheap 'n' cheerful' approach was not desirable. Instead, every-day low pricing was an expedient way of enhancing their reputations with loyal customers. It was not a move away from years of emphasizing customer service and quality merchandise in their brand positioning.

A similar trend emerged in the hotel sector. There had always been cheap bed and breakfast (B&B) accommodation on offer. Then, throughout the 1990s, the European hotel sector witnessed a tremendous growth of low price hotel brands from the major hotel groups. These hotels offered many of the amenities of larger three and four star hotels, but were targeted at the budget conscious business user or leisure traveller.

Budget Chains

Whitbread Hotels, the UK's second largest hotelier, trades as Marriott for its selection of four-star deluxe hotels. Its great expansion, though, stemmed from its network of budget-oriented Travel Inns. The giant French group Accor – Novotel to Sofitel – has invested in no less than four budget chains, including Ibis and the very basic Formule1. Forte Hotels, now part of the Granada entertainments group, has a selection of hotel brands ranging from the prestigious Le Meridien chain, Posthouse, Forte Heritage to the budget priced Travelodge brand. All three of these major hoteliers – Accor, Granada and Whitbread – have a portfolio of brands targeted at different segments of the hotel market, but they all have included a value-for-money lodge-style proposition.

These lodges are far-removed from the small family-run private hotels or bed and breakfast houses which until relatively recently provided the only low price alternative to staying in expensive mainstream hotels. Campanile, now to be found throughout Europe, is perhaps typical of the genre. Table III.24 summarizes the Campanile offer, which is much more than just a cheap place to sleep.

Table III.24	*The Campanile Budget Priced Proposition*

Campanile
Good night!

- Spacious and comfortable, each room is equipped with:
- Bathroom with bath and shower
- Worktop
- Colour TV with satellite
- Automatic alarm clock
- Direct-dial telephone

- Free bed for the under-12s in their parents' room.
- Single or double rooms, communicating rooms and rooms for disabled people.
- In most Campanile Hotels, the room block is separated from the reception/restaurant, allowing more independence.

■ *Service 'Extras'*
- Courtesy tray for a light snack: kettle, coffee, tea and biscuits.
- Telephone connection for your personal computer.
- A minitel (computerized directory) may be borrowed from reception.

Bon appetit!
- Family-style and regional cuisine
- The majority of our host couples have been trained at hotel and catering schools and prepare for you regional specialities, included in fixed menus or à la carte. You will appreciate the famous Campanile buffets of starters, cheeses and desserts.

■ Breakfast buffet
- All you can eat … Coffee, tea, chocolate, boiled eggs, delicatessen, cheese, yoghurt, varied breads, cereals, pastries, fruit salads … .

■ Service 'Extras':
- If you plan to arrive after 10:00pm, you may order in advance a cold meal to be enjoyed in the comfort of your room.
- For those late wakers, a Continental breakfast may be served in your room on Sundays and bank holidays from 9:30 to 11:00 am.
- Happy birthday! Book your table two days in advance and Campanile will offer you the birthday cake and candles.

Source: Campanile promotional literature

Travel Inn Overtakes Travelodge

In the UK, the leading budget hotel rivals are Whitbread's Travel Inn chain, with 225 hotels (doubling by 2005 to over four hundred hotels and 20,000 bedrooms) and Granada's Travelodge. Granada's acquisition of the giant Forte empire enabled it to merge its Granada Lodges with Forte's Travelodge. Table III.25 summarizes the leading UK hotel groups. There are over 200 Travelodges in the UK, with a growing presence in Europe, notably via alliances with Bastion Hotels in the Netherlands and Climat de France. The US-branded Travelodge chain is now a separately owned and managed operation, although there are joint booking arrangements.

Travelodge was the first major budget-oriented chain and its proposition is one of the most carefully honed:

> For Britain's business people, Travelodge is the ideal place to stay. As well as excellent in-room facilities, you'll have access to a telephone and fax machine to help you keep in touch with the office. A comfortable bed for the night, a good breakfast (starting from as little as £4.25) and, because you pay on arrival, just drop your key at reception and you're on your way.

Table III.25	*The Leading UK Hoteliers*		
		Hotels	*Bedrooms*
	Granada, incl. TraveLodge (170/7,450); Forte Hotels (London Hotels; Forte Posthouse; Forte Heritage) (158/22,200)	328	29,650
	Whitbread Hotel Company, incl. Travel Inns (200/8,900); Marriott/Courtyard by Marriott (35/5,300)	235	ca. 14,200
	Intercontinental (6/2,421); Crowne Plaza (6/1,462); Holiday Inn (17/3,014); Holiday Inn Garden Court (12/1,153); Holiday Inn Express (22/1,584)	63	9,634
	Thistle Hotels	70	8,900
	Stakis Hotels & Inns	54	8,000
	Hilton International[1] (9/3,360); Hilton National (24/4,124); Associate Hotels (4/459) (Ladbroke Group)	37	7,943
	Queens Moat Houses	50	7,091
	De Vere Hotels (16/2,423); Premier Lodge (51/2,293); Village Leisure Hotels (10/792) (The Greenalls Group)	77	5,508
	Accor S.A. (incl. Ibis 15; Formule 1 4; Novotel 18)	37	ca. 5,500
	Jarvis Hotels	64	5,400
	Regal Hotels (incl. White Hart)	90	ca. 5,000
	Friendly Hotels	62	4,500
	Swallow Hotels (Vaux Group)	38	4,430
	Millennium & Copthorne Hotels (CDL Hotels International) (Millennium 4/1,365; Copthorne 15/2,564)	19	3,929
	Macdonald Hotels	35	ca. 2,000
	Intercontinental Hotels (Seibu Saison)	3	1,600
	Warners (The Rank Group)	8	1,571

Notes: Figures in brackets: (hotels/bedrooms). [1] UK Hotels only.

In late 1999 Whitbread took over the 38 Swallow hotels.
Source: *The Marketing Pocket Book*, NTC Publications

This also makes us the perfect choice when visiting family or friends, or for a short stop-over on a long journey. Whenever you travel, you'll find a Travelodge offering superb facilities and unbeatable value. We have lodges nation-wide, on motorways and A roads, in town and city centres, near tourist attractions and areas of outstanding natural beauty.

At Travelodge you can enjoy all the comfort of a quality hotel for less.

Source: Travelodge

One Room: One Price

Travelodge was one of the first operators to bring to the UK the US notion of one room: one price. Previously, quoted prices had been per person at most hotels, rather than per room. Most Travelodge rooms can comfortably sleep two adults and two children, all for under £50. The lodges brought another 'novelty' for the hotel market: hotels without restaurants. Previously, to be considered as a hotel or classed in the leading guides, full in-house restaurant meal services had to be provided by the hotel facility. For Forte, with its chains of Little Chef and Happy Eater diners and its Welcome Break motorway service areas, it was cost effective to build lodges adjacent to existing catering facilities. Travel Inn emulated this approach. For operator Whitbread, this was also straightforward. The brewer owned extensive chains of pubs, diners and restaurants, including well-known brands such as Beefeater, Brewers Fayre and TGI Friday's. More recently, other hoteliers have incorporated this innovation in their hotel concepts. Holiday Inn Express – a 'three and a half star' spin-off by Bass from its mainstream four-star Holiday Inn chain – provides well-appointed bedrooms in purpose-built blocks adjacent to Bass-run pubs and restaurants, such as Harvester or The Porridge Pot.

The principal rival to Travelodge, Travel Inn – 'the UK's favourite place to stay' – operates as *Travel Inn* (£39 per night) along major trunk roads and near principal tourist attractions, airports and urban areas; as *Travel Inn Metro* (£49 per night) in major conurbations, and for London as *Travel Inn Capital* (£59 per night). These three sub-brands were created in 1999 as part of a new brand expansion strategy 'to maintain Travel Inn's market leadership in the budget hotel sector'. This followed marketing research of over 5,500 consumers, which led specifically to the creation of Travel Inn Metro. The aim with this new brand was to provide affordable, quality accommodation in the key business and tourist areas in the heart of cities and top regional airports. Travel Inn Metro planned to challenge mid-market and upper-market hotels that traditionally had dominated such locations. For London, this notion was taken further with the introduction of the Travel Inn Capital brand. Each sub-brand had new logo, signage, website, stationery, literature, uniform, customer services and price points, reflecting the views of surveyed consumers.

Whitbread has every intention of maintaining its leadership in the budget hotel sector. It is clear that with maturity, this sector is witnessing more sophisticated branding and marketing propositions such as Travel Inn's new derivatives, and that within the sector there is increasing diversity of offer. However, as Table III.26 illustrates, the two leading rivals are matching each other very closely.

The budget hotel sector's growth has not only provided value-for-money alternatives for existing hotel users. According to Whitbread, three-quarters of the UK population have never stayed in a hotel before. The Travel Inn Metro brand is in over 30 towns and cities, offering accommodation for 'a special weekend break in the heart of the city at half the price of any other hotel'. Certainly Travelodge owes much of its success to its value-based, easy-to-use proposition attracting former clients of bed and breakfast private hotels. Many of these consumers, exposed to the pleasures of well-appointed bedrooms with modern amenities, vowed never to return to B&Bs.

The sector's growth has also stemmed from the leading operators' shrewd specification of the room/meal/service offer. As Table III.26 demonstrates, these hotels are intended to serve leisure users and private travellers alongside business users and company expense account holders. The figures in Table III.27 reveal the business traveller to be a key target market in the hotel industry.

| **Table III.26** | *The Leading Rivals' Propositions* |

The Travelodge Offer

- Spacious en-suite rooms
- Satellite TV with a choice of cartoons, sports and films
- Tea & coffee making facilities
- Free newspaper
- Free car parking*
- Friendly restaurants*
- Luxury Hypnos beds*
- Easy check-in & check-out
- Easy booking (reserve up to a year in advance!)
- One price per room
- All major credit cards accepted
- Business account:
- Guaranteed bookings
- Bill-back facility to your company.

* At most sites

Source: Travelodge and Travel Inn web sites

The Travel Inn Offer

For a single price per room per night, every Travel Inn provides:

- En suite bedroom with shower and bath
- Double bed with duvet
- Family room that sleeps up to 2 adults and 2 children under 16
- Remote control TV and radio alarm
- Tea and coffee making facilities
- Spacious desk area
- Licensed restaurant and bar (integral or next door)
- In-room phone and data port in Travel Inn Metro and Travel Inn Capital

'Great food from breakfast to dinner!':

- Every Travel Inn has a high quality licensed restaurant either inside or right next door:

Beefeater Brewers Fayre TGI Friday's
David Lloyd Slice Potters

| **Table III.27** | *The Nature of Travel and Hotel Usage* |

OVERSEAS TRAVEL, TOURISM AND EXPENDITURE
Number of visits and expenditure by country of permanent residence

| | Visits Abroad by UK Residents | | | | Overseas Visits to UK | | | |
| | No. of Visits | | Expenditure | | No. of Visits | | Expenditure | |
	'000s	%	£m	%	'000s	%	£m	%
Total all visits	42,569	100.0	16,310	100.0	25,293	100.0	12,369	100.0
Area visited (outward)/Area of residence (inward)								
Europe (EU)	31,054	73.0	8,855	54.3	15,508	61.3	5,363	43.4
Europe (non-EU)	3,641	8.6	1,462	9.0	2,189	8.7	1,162	9.4
N. America	3,597	8.5	2,710	16.6	3,688	14.6	2,287	18.5
Other countries	4,276	10.0	3,284	20.1	3,908	15.5	3,557	28.8
Mode of travel								
Air	28,017	65.8	12,984	79.6	16,395	64.8	9,998	80.8
Sea	11,094	26.1	2,539	15.6	6,179	24.4	1,603	13.0
Channel Tunnel	3,458	8.1	788	4.8	2,719	10.8	768	6.2
Purpose of visit[1]								
Holiday	27,057	63.6	10,651	65.3	11,041	43.7	4,876	39.4
Business	6,941	16.3	3,387	20.8	6,133	24.2	3,244	26.2
Visiting friends/relatives	5,534	13.0	1,541	9.4	4,921	19.5	1,851	15.0
Miscellaneous	3,037	7.1	732	4.5	3,199	12.6	2,374	19.2

Note: [1] Expenditure figures refer to average expenditure during visit in £ sterling.
Source: ONS
Source: *The Marketing Pocket Book*, NTC Publications

Managing a Portfolio of Brands

All of the principal budget-oriented chains – Ibis, Campanile, Travelodge or Travel Inn – are part of much larger hotel groups. France's Accor operates over 15 hotel brands around the world, ranging from the Sofitel, Novotel and Parthenon business and leisure chains, to the Ibis, Formule1, Motel6 and Etap economy hotel chains. Accor has acquired some of its portfolio of brands, but continues to trade under so many guises in order to cater for many varied target markets and loyal groups of existing clients. Whitbread has two principal hotel brands, and three chains: four-star Marriott hotels, through which Marriott is the UK's leading golf operator; the three-star Courtyard by Marriott business-focused value-based hotels, and the leading budget hotel brand Travel Inn. Any hotels not fitting this two-pronged brand strategy, such as the market town-focused Lansbury chain, were sold-off. The 1999 purchase of the Swallow chain was fully incorporated into the Marriott brand. This ruthless branding and service proposition conformity has enabled Whitbread to overtake long established hotel rivals. It has also allowed the business to address a mix of core target markets: leisure and business users, conferences and seminars, domestic and overseas visitors, service-led and value-based consumers, single travellers and touring groups.

Long-established market leader Forte – formerly Trust House Forte – once operated close to 400 hotels. These ranged from the deluxe five-star Grosvenor House or Hyde Park hotels in London, Le Meredien hotels, the business-oriented chains Crest and Posthouse, quaint village inns and market town hotels, to motorway Welcome Break lodges and the Travelodge brand. New owners Granada merged its lodges and hotels into the network and devised a more tightly controlled set of hotel brands for its extensive portfolio. This estate includes the Travelodge chain, Forte Agip, close to 100 deluxe Le Meridien hotels around the world, plus a further 160 UK hotels trading as Posthouse, Heritage or London Signature hotels. Each brand is distinct from its cousins in the Granada portfolio, with separate management teams, service standards, branding and marketing programmes. For example, Le Meridien hotels, formerly owned by Air France, are predominantly in capital or large cities and tourist resorts, offering five-star amenities, service levels and comforts. The Posthouse brand is a collection of over 80 modern hotels with informal bars and restaurants, extensive business meeting facilities and leisure amenities, appealing to families and business users. The Heritage brand encompasses a more diverse estate of former coaching inns and grand Victorian properties, but all offering an 'old world' charm. Travelodge is the market challenger to Whitbread's Travel Inn.

As for Accor or Whitbread, this portfolio of brands enables Granada to target a variety of customer segments and combat a wealth of rival hotel brands. Each Granada hotel brand has its own business plan, budgets, target market strategy, marketing programmes, performance measures, management teams and investment programmes. Each brand has a unique identity and promotional mix designed to stress the brand's positioning and marketing proposition. Financially and in terms of brand standing, there is little doubt that Accor, Granada and Whitbread are highly successful businesses. Although not the exclusive reason, the growth of the budget hotel sector has played a major role in this success.

Issues

The hotel sector has witnessed significant growth in recent years and a proliferation of well-defined brands, notably in the budget sector. In the marketing of any service, branding and shrewd targeting are known to be important. The operators of the leading budget chains have adhered to these principles as they have expanded their hotel networks. For leading hotelier Whitbread, branding and the development of tightly defined trading concepts have been central to the company's rapid expansion. As with most large hotel operators, Whitbread has more than one brand and chain of hotels, opting to target different brands and concepts at separate target market segments.

Branding

Why do the major hotel groups such as Whitbread, Accor or Granada operate a portfolio of hotel brands?

How important is branding in the budget hotel sector? Whitbread's Travel Inn has devised a set of sub-brands. How are these intended to cement Travel Inn's market leadership?

Target marketing

Whitbread's Marriott and Travel Inn operations are targeted at different market segments. Why has the company adopted this strategy? How and why are the respective marketing mixes of these separate hotel brands different?

Services marketing

Why has the product/service mix been so important in the development of budget hotels? Which ingredients of the marketing mix are most important in the budget sector?

Relevant Theory Notes

T8: The Marketing Mix: Products and Product Management, pp. 246–254
T6: Market Segmentation, pp. 229–236
T3: Buying Behaviour, pp. 205–212
T13: The Marketing of Services, pp. 280–284

Full Case 15: ABN AMRO
Global Strengths, Regional Necessities

ABN AMRO Bank is a long-established, solid, multi-faceted and prominent bank of international reputation and standing.

We will strive to fulfil the bank's ambition in being a frontrunner in value added banking, both on a local and worldwide level.

The aspiration is based upon the preservation of ABN AMRO's reputation and tradition of high quality, and upon the expertise of our highly motivated and qualified professional staff.

Our fundamental motivation is the ongoing desire to maintain as well as strengthen the trust of our customers, financial investors, supervisory authorities, staff and the general public.

Source: ABN AMRO Corporate

The Merger

On 22 September 1991 the merger between Algemene Bank Nederland NV (ABN) and Amsterdam-Rotterdam Bank NV (AMRO) was finalized, creating ABN AMRO Bank NV. The merger of these two largest Dutch banks created the dominant financial institution in the Netherlands, with a total market share of 50 per cent in the corporate sector and 33 per cent in the Dutch securities market. With assets of over Dfl 430 billion, the new bank was the seventh largest in Europe and the eighteenth in world-wide rankings. The leading financial magazine *Institutional Investor* believed each bank had core business strengths that complemented the other's. ABN was a solid, well-organized retail bank with a prestigious network of branches world-wide. AMRO had a smaller international presence but controlled 40 per cent of the Dutch corporate market, and was known to be a pre-eminent merchant bank, with a strong marketing division. AMRO's bankers were described as aggressive, 'street fighters', whereas ABN was seen to be more of a 'gentlemen's club'.

Any merger of such large, established companies with differing management styles would lead to some resentment from the senior managers and employees. This merger was no different: many senior managers left the company as they jockeyed for positions in the new organization. Theodorus Meys, a senior director, explained: 'Everyone expected the AMRO people to dominate but that hasn't happened. ABN got a lot more out of the deal, perhaps because ABN was more organized'. Nevertheless, despite early teething problems, the merger was voted a success by the Dutch business press. The new bank developed a unified front in a relatively short space of time. This easy transition was helped by the two senior chairmen of the original banks; colleagues sharing a common goal.

Discussions about a possible merger started between Robertus Hazelhoff, ABN's chairman, and Roelof Nelissen, AMRO's chairman, shortly after AMRO's plans to merge with Generale de Banque failed in 1990. Talks between these two men were kept a tightly guarded secret, often taking place at each other's homes. 'In a couple of nights, we had decided everything – including who would be chairman for the first two years and who would take over for the next two years,' stated Hazelhoff. Nelissen became the first chairman of ABN AMRO Bank, concentrating on the internal restructuring necessary with the merger, leaving Hazelhoff to consider the more strategic aspects of the new bank's position in its marketplace. Hazelhoff's priority was to show ABN AMRO to be a genuinely global concern, with a world-wide standing.

As Table III.28 reveals, the two chairmen's aspirations have led to even more success. In terms of tier 1 capital, ABN AMRO a decade after its creation is ranked fifteenth world-wide and sixth in Europe. In terms of total assets, the bank is an impressive sixth world-wide and third in Europe behind only Deutsche Bank and Swiss-based UBS. Total revenue rose from 4,554 million euros in 1990 to 12,538 million euros in 1998. Net profit rose accordingly, from 601 million euros in 1990 to 1,828 million euros in 1998 – see Table III.29. This growth has been based on the structure, ethos and marketing strategies deployed by Hazelhoff and Nelissen.

| **Table III.28** | *World Rankings — Leading Banks* |

■ **Ranking world-wide**
Based on total assets

1999	1998	
1.	2.	Deutsche Bank (Germany)
2.	13.	UBS (Switzerland)
3.	22.	Citigroup (United States)
4.	30.	BankAmerica Corp. (United States)
5.	1.	Bank of Tokyo-Mitsubishi (Japan)
6.	**11.**	**ABN AMRO Bank (the Netherlands)**
7.	5.	HSBC Holdings (United Kingdom)
8.	4.	Credit Suisse Group (Switzerland)
9.	8.	Crédit Agricole Groupe (France)
10.	7.	Société Générale (France)
11.	6.	Sumitomo Bank (Japan)
12.	17.	Dresdner Bank (Germany)
13.	10.	Sanwa Bank (Japan)
14.	21.	Westdeutsche Landesbank Girozentrale (Germany)
15.	14.	Norinchukin Bank (Japan)
16.	9.	Dai-Ichi Kangyo Bank (Japan)
17.	3.	Industrial & Commercial Bank of China (China)
18.	16.	Sakura Bank (Japan)
19.	26.	Commerzbank (Germany)
20.	20.	Banque Nationale de Paris (France)

■ **Ranking world-wide**
Based on tier 1 capital

1999	1998	
1.	4.	Citigroup (United States)
2.	7.	BankAmerica Corp. (United States)
3.	1.	HSBC Holdings (United Kingdom)
4.	3.	Crédit Agricole Groupe (France)
5.	2.	Chase Manhattan Corp. (United States)
6.	22.	Industrial & Commercial Bank of China (China)
7.	5.	Bank of Tokyo-Mitsubishi (Japan)
8.	14	UBS (Switzerland)
9.	17.	Sakura Bank (Japan)
10.	–	Bank One Corp. (United States)
11.	11.	Fuji Bank (Japan)
12.	6.	Deutsche Bank (Germany)
13.	12.	Sanwa Bank (Japan)
14.	16.	Credit Suisse Group (Switzerland)
15.	**8.**	**ABN AMRO Bank (the Netherlands)**
16.	10.	Dai-Ichi Kangyo Bank (Japan)
17.	9.	Sumitomo Bank (Japan)
18.	27.	Bank of China (China)
19.	18.	Rabobank Nederland (the Netherlands)
20.	26.	Industrial Bank of Japan (Japan)

Source: *The Banker/FT*

| Table III.29 | *ABN AMRO's Financial Record* |

ABN AMRO from 1990 in euros

Income statement (in millions)

	1998	1997	1996	1995	1994	1993	1992	1991	1990
Net interest revenue	7,198	6,294	5,230	4,645	4,442	4,013	3,726	3,329	2,883
Total non-interest revenue	5,340	4,491	3,433	2,708	2,353	2,405	1,932	1,823	1,670
Total revenue	12,538	10,785	8,663	7,354	6,795	6,418	5,658	5,152	4,554
Operating expenses	8,704	7,450	5,867	4,962	4,595	4,256	3,797	3,494	3,156
Provision for loan losses	941	547	569	328	681	681	635	599	545
Fund for general banking risks	(101)	179	66	308					
Pre-tax profit	2,897	2,626	2,175	1,743	1,526	1,437	1,164	1,059	854
Group profit	1,989	1,872	1,563	1,233	1,081	955	780	708	632
Net profit	1,828	1,748	1,499	1,187	1,037	918	764	697	601
Net profit attributable to ordinary shareholders	1,747	1,667	1,414	1,075	925	835	686	619	584
Dividends	906	844	733	623	550	486	439	421	353

Balance sheet (in billions)

	1998	1997	1996	1995	1994	1993	1992	1991	1990
Shareholders' equity	10.7	11.7	11.3	9.2	8.8	8.7	7.3	6.9	6.5
Group capital	24.4	24.1	20.1	15.2	14.2	13.8	12.3	11.3	10.5
Total customers' account and debt securities	243.5	221.1	159.3	147.3	138.5	136.3	128.2	117.7	112.5
Loans	220.5	201.1	150.5	132.8	122.8	121.7	110.7	102.6	95.7
Total assets	432.1	379.5	272.0	248.0	229.0	222.8	203.5	186.8	176.9
Contingent liabilities and committed facilities	124.0	102.8	80.9	63.8	51.0	45.3	44.1	41.5	41.3
Risk-weighted total assets	215.8	208.7	176.7	149.6	136.9	130.5	128.1	120.4	

Ordinary share figures

Net earnings per share	1.23	1.20	1.05	0.87	0.78	0.73	0.63	0.59	0.58
Fully diluted net earnings per share	1.22	1.19	1.03	0.83	0.74	0.71	0.62	0.59	
Dividend per share (rounded)	0.58	0.54	0.48	0.41	0.36	0.34	0.33	0.33	0.33
Net asset value per share (year-end)	6.85	7.71	7.62	6.21	6.08	6.21	5.80	5.78	5.68

1 On 31 December 1998 the rate of the euro was fixed at EUR1=NLG 2.20371.

Source: ABN AMRO

Structure of the New Bank

The two banks, now joined as ABN AMRO, had to consolidate their systems, customer databases, market segments, management and organizations. Figure III.8 illustrates the management structure devised by Hazelhoff and Nelissen. The new structure principally had three core divisions: domestic, investment banking and global clients, and international.

Over a decade since the merger and creation of ABN AMRO, the structure devised by Hazelhoff and Nelissen is still more or less in place. The three core

Figure III.8 | *Divisional Structure of ABN AMRO after the Merger*

Domestic Division	International Division	Investment Banking and Global Clients Division
Wholesale banking Electronic banking Payment services Domestic branch network Consumer banking	International branch network: – Europe – N. America, Central and South America Middle and Far East, Africa	Trading Sales New issues, corporate finance and venture capital Global clients Asset management and trusts

Credit Division	Personnel Division	Automation Division	Central Services and Policy Support Division
Domestic credit Foreign credit			Application systems Computers and networks

Source: ABN AMRO Bank Annual Report and Accounts, 1991

divisions remain – Netherlands (Domestic), International and Investment Banking – supported by Risk Management, Resource Management and Policy Support divisions.

Domestic division

This core division which focused on the home market in the Netherlands was organized on the basis of different key customer groups, enabling the bank's specialist staff to target each group separately with different products and services. Primarily there were seven core groups of customers, which were in two operating divisions:

1. *Wholesale banking,* focusing on small and medium-sized businesses, corporations, global clients and public authorities.
2. *Consumer banking,* concentrating on personal customers, affluent personal customers, and private banking.

Within these different categories, operational managers further segment each customer group, classifying for example personal customers as students, senior citizens, homeowners, or by affluence.

In the domestic division ABN AMRO had, immediately upon its formation, market domination with a 50 per cent market share, due partly to its extensive branch network. However, other banks were targeting these customer groups. Rabobank, the number two bank in the Netherlands, broke from its traditional agricultural basis and expanded into the very profitable wholesale banking market. Wouter Kolff, an ABN career banker who had left during the merger period, headed the newly restructured corporate finance division at Rabobank. His stated aims were to compete in the capital markets, mergers and acquisitions businesses and to be active all over Europe in the corporate sector, competing with ABN AMRO head-on.

ABN AMRO's share of personal customers – the retail market – lagged behind both Rabobank and NMB-Postbank which had extensive domestic networks, but lacked the international presence. ABN AMRO, therefore, embarked on an extensive opening programme of new branches, introducing more ATMs – automated teller machines – with a newly developed corporate image making the bank seem more accessible to personal banking customers. Restructured marketing activity, with new databases, gave more attention to better targeting of specific groups, such as students, the medical sector, and the private affluent (very wealthy) customer segments.

The aim today is no different for ABN AMRO:

> To supply a comprehensive and high quality range of banking and insurance products using advanced technology. The focus is on the individual client with his/her unique financial situation, wishes and requirements.

There are now around 920 branches organized into 225 districts and 11 regions covering the Dutch market. Clients are also serviced through innovative distribution channels including electronic banking, the Internet and the ABN AMRO *24x7* call centre which provides around-the-clock banking.

Investment banking and global clients division

Prior to the merger AMRO had developed a *global clients* approach, which after the merger was adopted by the unified bank. This co-ordinated relationships with clients all over the world from ABN AMRO's central base at Amsterdam. A key function was to act as an intermediary between global clients and more specialist divisions within the bank. The organization was structured on regional lines, with the exception of groups specializing in particular industries. The bank fostered these global relationships primarily by providing an extensive and superior range of products and services, such as project finance, export finance, aerospace finance and syndication departments.

Investment banking in the newly formed ABN AMRO covered a wide range of customer groups and products, but the focus offered specific corporate finance facilities such as:

- New issues (shares, bonds).
- Trading (currencies).
- Corporate finance (mergers and acquisitions).
- Venture capital (equity and debt financing).
- Emerging capital markets (e.g. Far East, Eastern Europe).
- International private banking.
- Global custody (dividends, safe-keeping of securities).
- Asset management.

International division

The international arena was one of ABN AMRO's core areas of interest, with distinct advantages over many European rivals. There were immediately 400 branches in 51 countries outside the Netherlands, allowing ABN AMRO to provide clients with a finely meshed banking network unrivalled by most competitors. The global network was of strategic importance to the newly merged bank, enabling it to provide the highest standard of service direct to local and international customers alike. The international service, though, was targeted mainly at business customers and affluent personal customers. The geographic spread of the network was directly related to the historical development of the bank, being strong in Europe and Asia. Hazelhoff and Nelissen made acquisitions in North America, such as LaSalle National Corporation of Illinois.

With the view to EC deregulation in 1992, every effort was made to simplify and hasten cross-border payments within the Community, to give advice on business practices in neighbouring countries and advice to clients on the establishment of foreign subsidiaries. ABN AMRO combined had a strong presence in Eire and the UK. ABN Deutschland and AMRO Handeisbank were merged to form one operation in Germany, but in France the existing trading entities were kept separate because of strong customer loyalty: Banque NSM and ABN AMRO. The unified ABN AMRO retained its market leadership in diamond financing with a market share world-wide of 30 per cent, focused principally on its Antwerp operation. The newly merged group was one of the largest foreign banks in

Switzerland, specializing in asset management. A subsidiary based in Vienna concentrated on the newly emerging markets in Eastern Europe, offering advice on financing for the privatization of state operations and joint-venture activities. Operations in South America continued under the name Banco Holandes Unido, mainly in Brazil and Argentina. Activities in the Middle East were severely hit by the Gulf War, although, with the end of the war, the Middle East became an area for expansion, along with the Far East and Australia.

Today, this international perspective is still to the fore. ABN AMRO presents itself as *The Network Bank* owing to its impressive network of over 2,600 branches in 75 countries. In Europe, over 200 branches serve 27 countries. There is even a branch in Azerbaijan. The 1997 acquisition of Magyar Hitel Bank in Hungary and its national network of 85 branches gave a significant foothold in the Hungarian market. In North America, 400 branches and 18,000 employees make ABN AMRO one of the largest foreign-owned banks active in Canada, Mexico and the USA. To add to its Chicago-based LaSalle Group, ABN AMRO has acquired Standard Federal Bancorporation and Long Island-based the European American Bank. In Latin America, ABN AMRO operates in 17 countries, controlled from Sao Paulo in Brazil. Helped by the recent takeover of Banco Real SA and of Banco de Estado de Pernambuco, ABN AMRO has 1,400 branches throughout Brazil. In Asia Pacific, ABN AMRO has been operational for over one and a half centuries. It now has operations in 15 countries, supported by the recent acquisition of the Australian investment banking activities of Barclays de Zoete Wedde. Elsewhere, there are branches in 10 Middle Eastern countries and stakes in Saudi Hollandi Bank in Saudi Arabia and Delta EAB in Egypt. ABN AMRO has even successfully established units for Islamic banking in Bahrain and bond loans in the Lebanon. The South African operation is growing particularly quickly.

At the turn of the century, expansion was continuing, with ABN AMRO taking a majority interest in Thailand's Bank of Asia, with assets of NLG 8 billion and 2,500 staff. The French privatization of the mighty banking group CIC-Union Européenne de CIC caught ABN AMRO's eye. Total assets of FRF 639 billion, profits of FRF 1,123 million and 21,000 staff and significant market share in France formed an attractive proposition. There were many other rivals, though, bidding for CIC.

The New Strategy

By 1992 the integration process following the merger was over, with branches, administration and systems consolidated. The bank's senior managers genuinely believed they were part of a global bank, simply enhanced by the merger. They did not see themselves as a Dutch-based bank, or even a multinational bank, but felt they operated on a truly global scale with no single ties to one nation or region. English had been established as the corporate language in the bank so that management in all countries could share information opportunities. The style of the bank was to the fore: a strong sense of direction coming from the corporate headquarters in Amsterdam, with each division and each national network having a strong degree of autonomy, led primarily by 'home-grown' senior managers who progressed through the ranks. This created a strong corporate culture and sense of belonging, but with little resentment of head office directives.

Although the chairman and senior directors perceived the bank to be a global player, some analysts and investors believed ABN AMRO was merely a large bank based in the Netherlands rather than a world bank. ABN AMRO needed to change perceptions held by certain sectors of the business community and journalists.

The bank chose not to enter new financial centres or areas of operation without a clear expectation of long-term benefit. Short termism was not part of the bank's philosophy. There was a stated belief that there had to be the opportunity to utilize its international strengths with a strong local understanding for ABN AMRO to build a presence in a particular country or industrial sector, taking into account the specific cultural needs and operations of the market. This was in direct contrast to the majority of international banks whose aims were to 'cherry-pick' markets and customers, providing unlimited services to limited numbers of key, highly profitable customers. ABN AMRO's commitment to the long term was perhaps unusual. It necessitated the establishment of strong local banking capabilities and networks, and heavy capital outlay.

Within this semi-autonomous system was *global relationship management,* designed to identify 'global' customers – servicing their needs from head office, but linking various networks and branches as relevant. At a local level, though, branches were given autonomy to try to identify those market segments for which their history and capabilities were best suited. In Switzerland, for instance, the bank's private banking customers were of key importance to the branch; whereas in Germany the corporate customer base was the priority. This, by necessity, meant that each country's branch network developed its own ranges of tailored products and services designed for its own local market needs. This philosophy is still practised, led by the bank's International Relationship Management Directorate General.

Marketing Strategy – the Direction

ABN AMRO offers clients a range of quite varied services in many different locations across the world. Its strategy has been one of cautious expansion using the tried and tested formula of a strong local network, international capabilities, with a loose senior management structure and a great deal of autonomy for local managers. There has always been the ultimate belief that the bank is a global operation. This has been a successful strategy, with profits rising steadily ever since the creation of ABN AMRO – see Table III.29. World-wide standing has also grown and most observers would now agree that the bank is genuinely international in its operations and thinking.

The fundamental feature of the bank's business is its understanding that it is a service provider. As such, successful marketing strategy has to take account of the very different nature of a service organization. *Internal marketing* and *interactive marketing* are central themes for ABN AMRO. Internal marketing describes the work done by the company to motivate its staff to deliver a consistent and superior service. The bank believes it is only as good as its people – those individuals who, to many customers, represent the service being provided. Interactive marketing highlights the employees' skill in handling this customer contact. There is the belief that the bank is international, but the provision of local autonomy helps to motivate staff and enable them to perform and feel rewarded for their work. Managers, tending to be home-grown, perceive there to be career opportunities and reasons for performing well. Head office control is kept to a minimum; only 80 staff handle the thousands of employees in the international division, keeping demotivating and irritating corporate rigidity to a minimum. At times, however, this means there is a lack of information and knowledge at head office of specific local operating characteristics and market trends.

The bank has identified four corporate values which, it believes, underpin its activities and provide the 'fundamental cornerstones' for its success. They also reflect its people-oriented approach to the bank's provision of high quality service:

- Integrity
- Teamwork
- Respect
- Professionalism.

ABN AMRO Bank – with its incremental, cautious development, long-term aims, federal structure and marketing strategy centred on service provision – has succeeded in fulfilling fundamental services marketing prerequisites. It is truly people-oriented and service-led. The bank has established itself in most international markets and emerged as one of the major financial organizations of the twenty-first century.

Much has happened in a short space of time since the merger of Algemene Bank Nederland NV (ABN) and Amsterdam-Rotterdam Bank NV (AMRO), that created ABN AMRO Bank NV. Two already large, successful organizations have been fully integrated and harmonized. Within the strong international corporate identity and ethos, a great deal of attention has been given to allowing local managers discretion to focus on key market opportunities and customer segments. This has brought its own problems, but has proved very successful in terms of profit generation for ABN AMRO. The bank has not lost sight of the importance of its people – they must be motivated to succeed and do well. Similarly they must impart a professional and caring impression to their customers, be they local, private account holders or international corporations. Whether or not this approach – thinking internationally but acting locally – can be the basis for a longer-term competitive advantage remains to be seen. The international banking arena has been characterized by mergers and acquisitions, creating ever larger global financial organizations and stronger competitive challenges for ABN AMRO.

Issues

ABN AMRO recognizes, with its *internal* and *interactive marketing*, the importance of personnel and the interaction with customers in a service business. The bank has global ambitions, but has not lost sight of local needs and the importance of establishing an operating hierarchy that enables national managers to fully understand their markets.

Services marketing

What are the core aspects of ABN AMRO's marketing mix? How do these reflect the bank's provision of customer service and financial services? To what extent are people and processes key ingredients of ABN AMRO's marketing mix?

International marketing and branding

ABN AMRO's federal structure is intended to encourage national managers to target local customers and their requirements more successfully than most global banking operations. Is this approach to international marketing likely to succeed? What are the advantages and possible pitfalls?

Market targeting and segmentation

The bank is prudent in its selection of customer groups to target. Which are the core market segmentation bases used? How effective is this categorization? How adaptive is this approach to local needs? How could ABN AMRO improve its approach to target marketing?

Relevant Theory Notes

T13: The Marketing of Services, pp. 280–284
T8: The Marketing Mix: Products and Product Management, pp. 246–254
T16: International Marketing, pp. 297–301
T6: Market Segmentation, pp. 229–236
T1: What is Marketing?, pp. 191–198
T14: Industrial, Business-to-Business Marketing, pp. 285–289

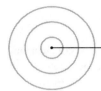

Full Case 16:   Chester Zoo Combining Marketing and Conservation

As it enters the new Millennium, Chester Zoo is completely transformed from the small Zoological Gardens that opened in June 1934. Operating in the highly competitive tourist market, the zoo of today faces the same pressures as other big businesses. The ever-increasing array of attractions with which the zoo competes are all seeking a greater share of consumer leisure spend. The recent opening of rival local attraction The Blue Planet Aquarium is just one of the recent challenges which Chester Zoo has faced. Responding effectively to such threats has required a combination of managerial flexibility and innovative marketing. This has helped the zoo to begin the new Millennium with a yearly visitor total in excess of one million.

Driven by the zoo's own strategy document – *2020 Vision* – a range of initiatives is in place to ensure a bright future for the attraction. The Small Mammal House has been replaced with The Twilight Zone, an exciting new bat cave, while the new Islands in Danger building provides an innovative setting for the Komodo Dragons and Birds of Paradise. Management has also secured substantial new funding to help the zoo pursue its conservation aims. In particular, a massive sponsorship deal with Jaguar, designed to show the car company's continuing support for the environment, will result in the best jaguar cat exhibit in Europe.

The origins of this well-established and successful wildlife establishment go back to George Saul Mottershead and his family, who founded the Zoological Gardens in order to improve captive conditions for wild animals. As a boy, George Mottershead had been horrified by conditions in zoos he visited. His concern, which led to the development of a spacious environment in which animals could roam with minimal restraint, was to be instrumental in changing the way animals in captivity were kept. Initially he concentrated his efforts on developing a small animal collection that later was to form the basis of the Zoological Gardens outside Chester.

The North of England Zoological Society was founded in 1934 to manage the Zoo and Gardens. Following a split with a business partner, George Mottershead had to find a new and larger site for the Zoo. After several months of consideration, in 1931 he purchased Oakfield, a Victorian mansion in seven acres of grounds located in the village of Upton, two and a half miles from Chester city centre. The purchase price of £3,500 necessitated taking out a large mortgage. However, the well-maintained grounds and collection of large outbuildings meant the property was ideal for his zoological aspirations. In the zoo's early days it was Mottershead's family who undertook the day-to-day running. Mottershead's daughter recalls the division of labour:

> My mother, who was a farmer's daughter, loved animals. All her life she kept a
> sharp eye on their well-being in the zoo. However, it had been decided that to

add to our income my mother would run a café in the reception rooms of the Oakfield. Morning coffee, cold lunches and afternoon teas were served. The free-roaming peacocks and pheasants would beg titbits from the customers. My most vivid memory of those days is of the piles of washing-up that had to be done each evening.

My 75-year-old grandfather took over the garden. In the kitchen garden he grew vegetables and fruit for use in the cafe and as food for the animals. The main gardens consisted of rose beds in front of the house and herbaceous flower beds at the rear. The rest of the gardens were made up of lawns, Victorian shrubberies with clipped holly and yew trees. Amongst these, my father had built pens and enclosures. He also put up a wooden pay-box near to the black and white lodge where my grandparents lived. It was my grand-mother's job to collect the entrance fee of one shilling (5p) adults and six (old) pence children!

(June Williams, Chester Zoo Life, Summer 1991)

Growth and Objectives

Throughout the 1930s Mottershead continued to buy land around the zoo site. The zoo's success was cemented during World War II, as it remained open and vibrant throughout the war years proving popular with locally based servicemen and Merseyside families. In 1950 the scope of the North of England Zoological Society was broadened to become an educational and scientific trust. These themes, together with an emphasis on the need for conservation, remain today with 1999 membership exceeding 14,500, up 7 per cent on the previous year. Today, covering 110 acres, with the Zoological Society owning an additional 350 acres of land, Chester Zoo is the largest wildlife leisure attraction of its type in the UK.

On the scientific side the Society's aims are to continue to expand its programme of breeding endangered and vulnerable species – in co-operation with other zoos in the UK, Europe and further afield – and has already participated in a variety of re-introduction programmes. In addition, the Society seeks involvement in joint ventures with other wildlife establishments through its membership of the World Zoo Organisation, IUCN: The World Conservation Union, EAZA (European Association of Zoos and Aquaria), Joint Management of Species Programmes, European Union of Aquarium Curators and the Federation of Zoological Gardens of Great Britain and Ireland.

Establishing zoo breeding programmes is seen as an important route to ensure the conservation of threatened species. The success of these programmes is obvious with nearly all the zoo's mammals and over 90 per cent of the birds and reptiles being zoo bred. The positive impact of its endangered species programme has been instrumental in attracting support for future activities — sometimes from surprising sources! In 1998, to coincide with the launch of the 'Baby Jaguar', built nearby at Halewood, Jaguar Cars agreed a £1,800,000 sponsorship deal to create a world-class jaguar facility at the zoo. The Spirit of the Jaguar exhibit, to be completed in 2001, is based around the mythical status of the creature in Mayan and Aztec religion. Visitors will find themselves on expedition in a rainforest and will learn about the variety of environments in which the jaguar lives. Natural lighting, rock faces, waterfalls, pools and streams combined with lush planting will create an ideal habitat for the inhabitants. The zoo facility will be combined with an *in situ* conservation programme in Central America.

The zoo actively participates in conservation efforts and through its various links has an extensive and successful breeding programme. In the 1980s the Rodrigues Fruit Bat *(Pteropus Rodricensis)* was the focus of attention as the zoo co-operated with a rescue bid fronted by the Jersey Wildlife Preservation Trust, acting on behalf of the Government of Mauritius. This involved setting up a carefully controlled breeding programme, initially with 10 bats. In 1992 the colony had more than quadrupled to 41. Today, support for the Rodrigues Fruit Bat continues with financial backing for a number of studies on behaviour and nutrition. With the zoo's own Fruit Bats enjoying their move to the world's largest free-flight walk-through bat facility, the ongoing commitment to this curious creature is readily apparent. In 1998, the zoo also enjoyed successes in its elephant breeding programme. As a key player in the Joint Management of Species Group (JMSG) for elephants, the rearing of Chester's own female Asiatic elephant calf Sithami was especially pleasing. In addition, two female elephant calves – Tara and Karishma - were born at Twycross Zoo following matings at Chester. The recent opening of the new bull elephant extension, which will allow safer housing for resident Chang, is further evidence of the commitment to this conservation work.

Chester Zoo into the 21st Century

In 1998 the North of England Zoological Society looked after some 6,680 animals from 531 different species. These comprised 652 mammals, 958 birds, 268 reptiles, 232 amphibians, 3,163 fishes and 1,407 invertebrates. Almost 50 per cent of the species represented at the zoo are regarded as threatened in a conservation sense. The zoo regularly breeds from around three-quarters of the threatened species.

Site facilities include catering ranging from the formal Oakfield restaurant, to the relaxed Jubilee cafe, Oasis snack bar and kiosks selling a variety of ice creams, confectionery, crisps and drinks. In 2000, the café benefited from an £800,000 refit, which doubled its size. The souvenir hunter is also well catered for with a number of shops and kiosks that suit every pocket, selling postcards, books, pens and a wide range of gifts and toys. The zoo has its own CDs, selection of videos and many books in stock. The keen rose gardener can even purchase a bag of 'Zoo Poo' (courtesy of the elephants) with which to adorn his/her own garden. Commercial retailing and catering activities supplement the entry admissions, which in 2000 were adults £9, children £6.50, concessions (pensioners, etc.) £7, with family tickets (two adults and three children) at £32 and children under three, free.

The gardens, always a feature of the zoo, for many visitors form the focus of their visit rather than an additional benefit. Consistently successful in the Britain in Bloom and Chester in Bloom competitions, the gardens find popularity with young and old visitors alike. The gardeners are responsible for the raising and planting of 80,000 spring flowers and another 80,000 summer flowers. They tend everything from 15,000 roses in the gardens to banana plants, palms and rubber trees in the tropical house and buddleias, azaleas, honeysuckle and viburnum in the butterfly garden.

Education activities at the zoo are diverse. The education division, staffed by qualified teachers, works in conjunction with teachers from middle, secondary and tertiary establishments. Booklets aimed at Pre-School, Primary, Middle and Secondary levels cover a full range of practical and written activities, information and work sheets, fully tied into National Curriculum requirements (the UK's Department for Education guidelines for school exam syllabuses). In addition, a wide variety of information sheets about the zoo inhabitants is available.

As in any service organization the staff are an important feature of zoo life. Training is seen as an essential part of the zoo's activity. More than 55 keepers, 14 maintenance staff, 12 groundstaff, 10 education specialists, 12 marketing personnel and 23 in finance and administration, not to mention the many individuals involved in retail activities and a host of others, work together to ensure the enjoyment of the zoo visitor. During the summer months the number of retail, catering, gate cashier and ground staff more than doubles.

Leisure Trends

Surveys of leisure trends generally indicate a rise in the attendance at both free and paid-for popular leisure attractions (see Table III.30). This is not particularly surprising given that overall time for leisure is on the increase taking up between 31 per cent and 90 per cent of total hours per week for the average adult (see Table III.31).

Table III.30	*Attendances at Tourist Attractions*		

			Number of visitors
Attractions charging admission	1995	1996	1997
Madame Tussaud's	2,703,283	2,715,000	2,798,801
Alton Towers	2,707,000	2,749,000	2,701,945
Tower of London	2,536,680	2,539,272	2,615,170
Natural History Museum	1,442,591	1,607,255	1,793,400
Chessington World of Adv.	1,770,000	1,700,000	1,750,000
Canterbury Cathederal[1]	–	1,700,000	1,613,000
Science Museum	1,556,368	1,548,286	1,537,151
Legoland, Windsor[2]	–	1,420,511	1,297,818
Edinburgh Castle	1,037,788	1,165,132	1,238,140
Blackpool Tower	1,205,000	1,200,000	1,200,000
Windermere Lake Cruises	1,054,414	1,034,188	1,131,932
Windsor Castle	1,212,305	1,215,631	1,129,629
Flamingo Land Theme Park	–	1,161,000	1,103,000
London Zoo	1,042,701	1,002,104	1,097,637
Victoria & Albert Museum[3]	–	–	1,040,750
Drayton Manor Park	1,000,000	937,296	1,002,100

Notes: [1] Admission charge introduced in June 1995. [2] Opened in 1996 [3] Admission charge introduced in October 1996

Source: *Digest of Tourist Statistics No.22,* British Tourist Authority

Table III.31	*Use of Time per Week by Age and Sex*

	Paid Work	Comm-uting	House work[2]	Eating	Per. Hygiene	Shop-ping[3]	Sleep	Free Time
Total	**20.7**	**2.8**	**15.8**	**8.5**	**5.1**	**2.0**	**49.3**	**63.8**
Sex								
Male	28.4	3.9	10.1	8.5	4.9	1.7	48.6	61.9
Female	13.6	1.8	21.1	8.5	5.3	2.3	49.9	65.6
Age								
16–24	22.3	3.2	11.0	8.1	5.5	1.5	48.4	68.1
25–34	27.9	3.7	16.0	7.5	4.6	2.2	50.0	56.1
35–44	31.6	3.7	18.0	7.9	4.8	2.2	49.6	50.1
45–59	25.3	3.7	15.1	8.8	5.5	2.0	49.1	58.5
60+	2.5	0.4	18.2	9.7	5.0	2.2	49.3	80.7
Couples								
Both full-time	39.5	4.2	14.8	8.5	4.8	1.3	48.4	46.4
Male works[4]	24.0	3.8	15.1	8.7	4.8	2.6	50.8	58.2
Female PT, Male FT[5]	31.0	4.2	14.7	7.9	5.6	2.0	50.2	52.4
Other	4.4	0.8	17.7	9.7	5.0	2.2	49.8	78.4
Singles								
Working	36.3	5.1	12.7	8.3	5.1	2.1	47.7	50.6
Not working	1.3	0.5	18.1	8.3	5.2	2.1	49.3	83.3

Average hours per week[1]

Notes: [1] There are 168 hours in one week. [2] Includes house cleaning, everyday cooking, washing clothes, ironing and washing up. [3] Essential shopping only. [4] Male works, female does not. [5] Female part-time, male full-time.

Source: The Henley Centre, Leisure Tracking Survey, 1997/98

An overall upward trend in leisure activity (see Figure III.9) is reflected in Chester Zoo attendance figures. Despite an increase in local competition, annual attendance for 1998 exceeded one million visitors, reaching a 20-year high. These figures make the zoo the eighteenth most-visited attraction in the British Tourist Authority's ratings.

Performance Indicators

Customer research is given the highest priority by the zoo's management. Regular customer surveys and focus groups have been conducted both at the zoo and within major target conurbations, such as Greater Manchester. These aimed to properly understand visitors' views of the zoo, but also rival attractions and consumer choice criteria.

The customer surveys, often carried out by the zoo's marketing personnel, seek visitor information on demographics, plus the scope and impressions of their visit. Of particular interest to the marketing department is the information this survey yields on visitor home locations, which provides essential information about drive times and likely competitors. The competitive insight provided is especially helpful to the marketing department, which is at pains to point out that the zoo does not only compete with other wildlife attractions. Alton Towers,

Blackpool Pleasure Beach, the Blue Planet Aquarium, Trentham Gardens, historic Chester, the north Wales coast, Liverpool's Albert Dock, the nearby Cheshire Oaks designer shopping village, or even a picnic in the park, are just a few of the numerous alternative days out in which the leisure seeker can indulge.

The market surveys also provide an important indicator for television and press advertising spend. An understanding of where the visitors travel from and how long they are prepared to spend in transit highlights where advertising, publicity and promotional spend should be focused. With 1.8 per cent of sales revenues, a relatively small £350,000, allocated to advertising and promotions, it is essential to minimize waste and make every £ spent work as hard as possible. Membership of the Association of Leading Visitor Attractions, the North West Tourist Board, the Yorkshire Tourist Board, North Wales Tourism, the Cheshire Tourist Attractions Consortium and other local consortia, all helps to spread awareness at minimum cost. Through these links, member attractions actively promote the visiting of neighbouring sites.

| **Figure III.9** | *Chester Zoo Attendances* |

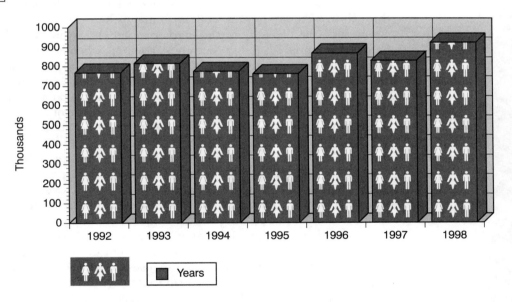

Note: If under 3s are included in our visitor total, we estimate that it now adds 11% taking it to more than 1,019,000 for 1998.
Source: Chester Zoo Annual Report, 1998

Towards the end of the 1990s the zoo became involved in a systematic programme of benchmarking research, commissioned by the Association of Leading Visitor Attractions. This research, which collects data on 32 different tourism sites, measures performance using a series of different indicators, including five-hour 'dwell time' and value for money. Chester Zoo has added to these measures and includes in its performance indicators:

1. Breeding of threatened species.
2. Growth in membership.
3. Growth in animal adoptions.
4. Five hour + high season 'dwell time' (number of visitors staying at the zoo for more than five hours).
5. 'Value for money' ratings.
6. 'Value for money' comparisons with other top UK tourist sites.
7. Recorded publicity — press cuttings.

Figure III.10 illustrates how the zoo has performed according to these measures. Performance on dwell time and value for money was especially pleasing, when compared with rival attractions.

Marketing Activities at the Zoo

From photographic competitions, animal adoption schemes and sponsorship, through to birthday parties, children's menus and the junior members' club for youngsters, the diversity of the marketing activity is obvious. Recent activities include an annual Disability Awareness Evening, when nearly 7,500 guests, many of whom would normally be unable to visit, enjoyed access to the full range of zoo facilities. Air and Sea Cadets were on hand to help with wheelchair pushing. Meanwhile BBC TV series *Vets to the Rescue*, featuring popular vet Trude Mostue, was filmed at the zoo. This was just one of a number of television programmes featuring the zoo, all of which help in raising public awareness of the attraction. A high profile visit by John Prescott to hand over an award was surpassed only by the arrival in December of Father Christmas in his bat-cave Grotto.

The zoo's animal adoption scheme continues to be a success bringing in more than £110,000 in 1998 (up 14 per cent on the previous year). This enables individuals, families and companies to contribute towards the upkeep of their favourite animal in exchange for a certificate of adoption, free tickets and their name on a plaque in the relevant enclosure (see Figure III.11).

Of all advertising 75 per cent is now spent on TV. Newspaper advertising, which is aimed coast-to-coast, often focuses on special offers timed to coincide with key bank holidays. Budgets mean that television advertising is concentrated in Granada, Central, and Harlech (HTV) regions with 10-second commercials. Slots are booked for immediately prior to and during peak visiting periods, supported by regional and local press advertisements, with some radio slots and PR activity. These always feature new arrivals to the zoo. In 1991 these concentrated on the recently opened Zoofari Monorail and the zoo's then current celebrity, a baby black rhino called Emma. Lion cubs, baby orang utans, baby elephants, bats in the Twilight Zone have all had their own advertisements.

Chester Zoo marketing staff believe that to be credible on television, advertising must exceed 600 TVRs in the target area. Television advertising was originally concentrated on the Granada and HTV ITV regions. As the zoo's marketing has become more sophisticated and its target catchment has grown as

Figure III.10 | Chester Zoo Performance Indicators

1. Threatened species: breeding

Just under half of the collection is considered 'threatened'. The proportion of these species that we have successfully bred remains similar to 1997.

531 species in the collection

278 'Safe'

253 'Threatened' 48%

177 bred to date

37 species with zoo community re-introduction plans

2. Membership growth

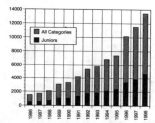

All Categories
Juniors

Total membership has continued the excellent upward trend, and now at 13.598 is our highest ever. There was a 14% growth in the year, on top of a 14% increase in the previous year. There has been a fourfold increase in the last ten years.

3. Animal Adoptions growth

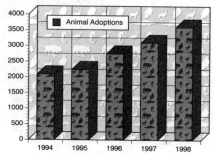

Animal Adoptions

The number of individual adoptions has risen to a record 3,600, our highest to date. We are very grateful for this generous help to the Society.

4. Five Hour + High Season 'Dwell Time'

1998 data shows a further encouraging continuation of the trend of growing *dwell time* in the zoo. Over two-thirds of visitors (69%) now stay over five hours in

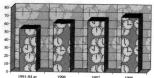

the high season, compared with just over half (54%) for the 1991-4 average. The average time spent by visitors in the zoo in Summer is now 5 hours 15 minutes.

5. Ratings for 'Value for Money'

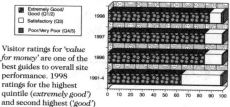

Extremely Good/ Good (Q1/2)
Satisfactory (Q3)
Poor/Very Poor (Q4/5)

Visitor ratings for *'value for money'* are one of the best guides to overall site performance. 1998 ratings for the highest quintile (*extremely good'*) and second highest ('*good'*) are similar to 1996-7 data, showing that we have maintained standards. Over five out of six visitors (88%) gave ratings in the first or second quintile categories.

6. 'Value for Money' - comparisons with top UK tourist sites

Independently conducted research showed that we were yet again, the best *value for money* family attraction of the 21 top *paid for* tourist sites in the British Tourism Authority listing, and the second best value overall (to the Victoria & Albert Museum in London). The figures show that our cost per hour

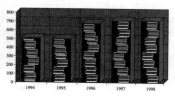

£1.42   £2.97

Chester Zoo   Top 21

is less than half the average of the top 21 sites.

These calculations divide standard adult admission by peak season *dwell time*, to obtain a *cost per hour*. In 1997, we achieved similar results, being only fractionally behind The Royal Botanic Gardens, Kew.

7. Recorded Publicity – Press Cuttings**

Cuttings for 1998 continued at the 1997 high level reflecting significant media interest in our baby elephant, baby rhinos and the bats in the *Twilight Zone*.

N.B. Percentages are rounded throughout.
**Publicity figures are based on a simple count (unduplicated), and do not include technical/specialist material. There is no attempt to weight by readership or to assess space 'value'.

Source: Chester Zoo Annual Report, 1998

motorways have improved, clever use of the ITV companies' different transmitters has meant an expansion into the Central (now Carlton) ITV region. The focus is still on the Granada (North West England) area, but now includes the north Midlands and some spots on HTV (Wales). The zoo also has a flourishing web site – www.demon.co.uk/chesterzoo – and is well established with e-commerce.

| **Figure III.11** | *Zoo Animal Adoption Leaflet* |

Source: Chester Zoo

The Story of the Blue Planet Aquarium

In addition to the regular marketing activity at the zoo, it is sometimes necessary to mount specific campaigns in response to a particular threat. Such was the case when management heard about plans to open a new aquarium, just three miles from the zoo site. This £13 million initiative, which had strong local authority support, was potentially the greatest threat the attraction had ever faced. The indoor deep-sea leisure experience was to feature more than 100 metres of walk-through and spiralling fish tanks. A travellator running through the giant tank would transport visitors around the attraction with ease. Divers would swim in the tanks and educational presentations would help explain the key features of the aquaria. There were to be shopping and eating facilities plus an underwater theatre. The focal point of the Blue Planet Aquarium would be a walk-through acrylic shark tunnel, allowing visitors to experience the thrills of moving among these feared predators.

Managers at Chester Zoo knew that the Blue Planet Aquarium would be a good quality leisure attraction. Furthermore, the company responsible had managed to attract £3 million of EU development money. An earlier incarnation of the aquarium in Scotland was attracting nearly half a million visitors per annum. Anxiety levels at the zoo were increased when research suggested that the zoo's attendance levels might drop by a quarter as a result of the new opening. This would have substantially affected the zoo's ability to maintain the conservation programmes to which it is so committed, and would probably have resulted in staff redundancies.

The challenge for the zoo's marketing team was to pre-empt the problems which might have arisen from this major competitive threat. In so doing, management was able to build on its experience of previous threats, such as the Liverpool Garden Festival (1984/1985). Following the opening of the Blue Planet in late summer 1997, the first step was to substantially increase marketing budgets for 1998. The marketing team particularly feared the impact of the competitor on figures for summer 1998, and so mounted a sustained *Operational Summer Sales* campaign designed to minimize the impact. Some of this activity centred on major animal developments at the zoo. For example, early in the summer of 1998 the Twilight Zone Bat Cave, an innovative and atmospheric new environment for these night-flying winged creatures, had been opened. The refitted penguin pool and the recent arrival of a baby elephant also provided a platform for the marketing activity.

It was expected that the Blue Planet Aquarium would price a little below the zoo and would mount an aggressive TV advertising campaign. The zoo's marketing team developed a series of tactics to counter the effects of this promotion. First, new versions of the zoo's advertising and leaflets were developed. These offered free child's admission (worth £6). Copies of the *Chester Zoo News* magazine that carried a similar coupon offer were also prepared. A press media schedule was then booked. This gave the zoo the option to switch to the free child admission copy at any time. To counter the effects of the Blue Planet's TV campaign the zoo's marketing team booked TV campaigns on Granada, HTV (Wales) and Central. These were designed to coincide with the start of the summer holiday. As soon as the Blue Planet opening date was confirmed, all press advertisements were switched to the 'save £6' copy. These advertisements also featured the most exciting new attractions at the zoo, including the *Twilight Zone Bat Cave* and various animal babies. This campaign was supported by distributing copies of the *Chester Zoo News* magazine (with coupon) at local events and shows.

All of this additional effort reaped considerable rewards. In 1998, the zoo recorded an 11 per cent increase in visitors in a year when the tourist attraction market was in decline. There was a 4.8 per cent rise in 1999 to 965,700 paying visitors (children aged under three are free) and the zoo's highest ever turnover. It would seem that the zoo has effectively countered the threat from its new neighbour, the Blue Planet.

Managing Publicity

Manyara, the zoo's sixth black rhino baby, was born in 1997. Her sister Emma, born in early 1991, was the first second-generation black rhino to be born and reared in a British zoo. At the time, Emma joined just 16 other black rhinos in British collections. Unfortunately Esther, her mother, did not produce sufficient milk for the underweight youngster, so Emma was keeper-reared. Keepers were delighted to find that second time around, Esther was able to rear her new baby. In addition to its contribution to the conservation aims of the zoo, the birth of endangered animals provides the publicity department with an important PR opportunity.

The zoo's black rhino breeding successes have attracted attention from local and national newspapers as well as being featured on radio and television. For an organization with so limited a marketing budget, this publicity has a particularly important marketing role to play. It seems that the public loves to hear about the birth of new and exotic animal babies and will respond to such news by planning a visit to the attraction. Not surprisingly, zoo management has gone to considerable lengths to ensure that other recent births attract similar attention. Thus elephant baby Sithami, the fourth new litter of Asiatic Lion cubs, the two Sumatran Orang utan new arrivals and the first parent-reared UK Andean Condor chick, are already becoming used to the glare of publicity. Zoo advertising material and the merchandising available on site carefully support the publicity that accompanies the arrival of these furred and feathered babies. The zoo has changed its core advertising strapline to, 'Chester Zoo — Always New'.

Keeping the Customers Happy

At Chester Zoo, careful focusing on customer needs and close attention to detail allow management to maintain high service standards. These standards are essential if the visitors are to be encouraged to return. Most of the zoo's visitors have been at least once before. Persuading new customers to visit and existing ones to return must be achieved without the assistance of the large advertising and promotions budgets on which organizations in other leisure sectors are able to rely. Alton Towers or DisneyWorld, Showcase multiplex cinemas or Manchester United football club can all out-spend Chester Zoo. The zoo's new Visitor Services operating division underlines the vital role of customer care and the need to ensure visitors want to return.

The marketing demands on any organization in this situation are considerable. Communications with the customer base, which is spread widely through the Midlands, North West, Wales and Yorkshire, must be conducted prudently, maximizing the use of limited resources. A variety of creative marketing schemes must be designed to support this effort and the use of free publicity must be managed to its maximum. All of this has to be achieved without damaging the zoo's charitable status or infringing its conservation aims. At a time when the competitive stakes are increasing, with the leisure consumer having access to more variety than ever before, the need to maintain this balance is crucial. Zoo management hopes that the guiding principles in its *2020 Vision* strategy document will secure the zoo's future by maintaining the interest of existing customers and attracting new visitors.

Table III.32	*Financial Data for the North of England Zoological Society*

FINANCIAL ACTIVITIES

CONSOLIDATED STATEMENT OF FINANCIAL ACTIVITIES FOR THE YEAR TO 31 DECEMBER 1998

	1998		1997	
	£000's	£000's	£000's	£000's
INCOMING RESOURCES				
Turnover of charitable trading activities		4,861		4,339
Other incoming resources				
Members' subscriptions	290		229	
Animal adoptions (restricted)	111		97	
Donations & legacies (see below)	124		96	
Contribution from Deep Sea Leisure Plc.	100		–	
Property rents received - external	42		39	
Property rents received - from trading subsidiary	297		297	
Net income of trading subsidiary	965		390	
		1,929		1,148
TOTAL INCOMING RESOURCES		6,790		5,487
RESOURCES EXPENDED				
Gross expenditure of charitable trading activities		988		986
Direct charitable expenditure				
Animal welfare	1,995		2,139	
Education	241		248	
Gardens	341		325	
Property maintenance	469		572	
		3,046		3,284

Other expenditure		
Fundraising and publicity	531	467
Management and administration	350	443
	881	910
TOTAL RESOURCES EXPENDED	4,915	5,180
NET INCOMING RESOURCES/ MOVEMENT IN FUNDS	1,875	307
Accumulated funds brought forward	2,862	2,555
ACCUMULATED FUNDS CARRIED FORWARD	4,737	2,862

All activities are continuing.

There is no material difference between the result disclosed above and that on an unmodified historical cost basis.

All the Society's income is unrestricted except for animal adoptions of £111,000 (1997 £97,000) and donations, grants and legacies of £80,000 (1997 £18,000) all held for, or expended on, specific projects.

The Society has no recognised gains or losses other than the net surpluses above and therefore no separate statement of total recognised gains and losses has been presented.

BALANCE SHEETS

BALANCE SHEETS AT 31 DECEMBER 1998

	CONSOLIDATED		SOCIETY	
	1998 £000's	1997 £000's	1998 £000's	1997 £000's
FIXED ASSETS				
Tangible assets	4,528	3,924	4,441	3,858
Investment in subsidiary company			0	0
	4,528	3,924	4,441	3,858
CURRENT ASSETS				
Stocks	276	268	42	52
Debtors	1,024	188	949	315
Cash at bank and in hand	322	51	301	40
	1,622	507	1,292	407
CREDITORS:				
AMOUNTS FALLING DUE WITHIN ONE YEAR	1,413	1,532	997	1,367
NET CURRENT ASSETS / (LIABILITIES)	209	(1,025)	295	(960)
TOTAL ASSETS LESS CURRENT LIABILITIES	4,737	2,899	4,736	2,898
CREDITORS:				
AMOUNTS FALLING DUE FROM TWO TO FIVE YEARS				
Corporation tax	–	37	–	37
NET ASSETS	4,737	2,862	4,736	2,861

FUNDS EMPLOYED

INCOME FUNDS - RESTRICTED	62	15	62	15
INCOME FUNDS - UNRESTRICTED				
Designated funds	2,858	1,393	2,858	1,393
Other charitable funds	1,817	1,454	1,816	1,453
	4,675	2,847	4,674	2,846
TOTAL FUNDS EMPLOYED	4,737	2,862	4,736	2,861

CASH FLOW

CONSOLIDATED CASH FLOW STATEMENT FOR THE YEAR TO 31 DECEMBER 1998

	1998		1997	
	£000's	£000's	£000's	£000's
CASH FLOW FROM OPERATING ACTIVITIES				
Net incoming resources	1,875		307	
Net interest payable	16		89	
(Profit) on sale of fixed assets	–		(2)	
Depreciation charges net of amortisation of capital grants	589		943	
(Increase) / Decrease in stocks	(8)		6	
(Increase) in debtors	(836)		(14)	
Increase / (Decrease) in creditors due within 1 year	578		(91)	
Net cash inflow from operating activities		2,214		1,238
RETURNS ON INVESTMENTS AND SERVICING OF FINANCE				
Interest received	26		7	
Interest paid - bank and other	(45)		(44)	
Interest paid - finance leases	–		(69)	
Net cash outflow from returns on investments and servicing of finance		(19)		(106)
TAXATION				
Net cash outflow from taxation		(37)		(38)
CAPITAL EXPENDITURE				
Receipts from diposal of tangible fixed assets	–		4	
Payments to acquire tangible fixed assets	(1,193)		(890)	
Net cash outflow from capital expenditure		(1,193)		(886)
NET CASH INFLOW BEFORE FINANCING		965		208
Less: FINANCING				
Repayments of capital element of finance leases	–		(168)	
Net cash outflow from financing		–		(168)
CASH				
Decrease in bank overdraft	694		57	
Increase / (Decrease) in cash at bank and in hand	271		(17)	
INCREASE IN CASH IN THE YEAR		965		40

In the 1990s, the financial standing of the zoo went through a transition. In the early 1990s, annual net income ranged from £361,000 to a loss of £362,000. Since 1995, financial fortunes improved, although there were large write-offs against net income in 1996 and 1997. Cash flow as a performance measure fails to take account of the impact of good or atrocious weather, a variable that has significant impact on the zoo's fortunes. The zoo has developed a ratio of cash flow per thousand visitors, which between 1995 and 1998 showed a 75 per cent improvement. Cash flow per thousand visitors:

Average 1990 to 1991   £671
1995   £898
1996   £1,399
1997   £1,105
1998   £1,574

The zoo cites reasons for this improvement as high profile births — notably the baby elephants and rhinos that generate great media interest, new exhibits and a new visitor entrance to lengthen visitors' 'dwell time', a series of special events and the Royal opening of *Monkey Islands*, together with excellent and caring marketing. In addition, ticket prices were raised to be in-line with direct competitors and extra funds allocated to promotional activity to increase both the awareness and desirability of the zoo. As a result, cash flow rose from an average of £800,000 per annum in the first half of the 1990s to over £1.2 million each year. The zoo's funds and Jaguar Car's sponsorship are earmarked principally for animal welfare initiatives, the replacement of the few remaining dilapidated buildings and new world class exhibits, such as the *Twilight Zone* – 'the largest and finest exhibit of bats in the world'. While prudent financial controls are pivotal to the zoo's operations, Chester Zoo does not intend to rest on its laurels.

Issues

Chester Zoo has overcome social disquiet about animal captivity owing to its enlightened breeding programmes and animal enclosures. More than a zoo, this popular leisure attraction has developed a sophisticated new marketing strategy designed to bolster its income, uphold its charitable status and fend-off the threats of major neighbouring new leisure attractions.

Services marketing

What is the essence of the 'product' being offered by Chester Zoo? Why is it important for the zoo to include more than the traditional 4Ps in its marketing mix programmes?

Marketing planning

The zoo's strategy vision has been developed to steer its future activities and marketing. Why is this important? How has the zoo utilized marketing planning to guide its activities?

Competitive strategy

The leisure sector is highly competitive with a wide selection of options battling with each other for consumers' time and spending power. The Blue Planet's arrival additionally threatened Chester Zoo's fortunes. How did competitor analysis help Chester Zoo? Why is it important to develop marketing strategies and programmes that thoroughly take account of competitors and their strategies?

Promotions management

Why must Chester Zoo frequently alter its television commercials and advertise in neighbouring ITV regions? How effectively does Chester Zoo utilize the ingredients of the promotional mix? What could be done in addition to promote the zoo?

Pricing

Why must Chester Zoo's prices be set in-line with rival attractions' prices? How might visitors gauge value for money? What impact on the zoo's business strategy has cash flow management?

Relevant Theory Notes

T13: The Marketing of Services, pp. 280–284
T15: Marketing Planning, pp. 290–296
T7: Competitive Strategy, pp. 237–245
T11: The Marketing Mix: Promotion, pp. 266–274
T10: The Marketing Mix: Pricing, pp. 261–265

Full Case 17: Carrefour
The Global Hypermarket

Developing the Hypermarket Concept

For many consumers the Carrefour brand is synonymous with France and yet the inspiration for the well-known hypermarket concept came originally from America. The story began in 1962, when three Frenchman attended a retailing conference in Dayton, Ohio. The principles of American supermarkets and discount stores quickly captured the imaginations of Marcel Fournier and Denis and Jacques Defforey. On returning to France, they decided to develop their own version of what they had seen. The new format was to be a vast one-stop outlet offering a combination of food and general merchandise. Prices were to be sufficiently low to encourage consumers to travel further to benefit from them. This was a major change for the French consumer, who was used to shopping in small, local stores. Despite its innovativeness, Carrefour's first outlet in Annecy was an instant success and the hypermarket concept was born. Consumers were strongly attracted to this clear and simple idea, and enthusiastic about being able to buy everything from food and other household items to clothing and appliances under one roof. This extensive array of products was also on offer at low prices, in a large, spacious self-service retail environment. Great car parking facilities helped ease the shopping experience. Carrefour capitalized on the success at Annecy by opening a new superstore in the Paris suburbs quickly followed three years later, in 1966, by Europe's biggest self-service hypermarket near Lyon.

According to most definitions, 'hypermarket' is the name used for superstores which exceed a certain size. In practice, the use of the different terms varies. In the UK, the term 'hypermarket' is more rarely used than in other parts of Europe, with retailers preferring to use the better-known 'superstore' tag. The more precise definition of the two terms is explained by the Unit for Retail Planning Information (URPI):

> Superstores are defined as single-level self-service stores selling a wide range of food, or food and non-food goods with at least 2,500 square metres trading floorspace and supported by car parking. Stores with 5,000 square metres or more are commonly referred to as hypermarkets.

So what is the Carrefour hypermarket really like? Huge shopping aisles in a 10,000m² format combined with free car parking. Most items are offered on a self-service basis, so customers are free to shop in their own way and at their own pace. However, by providing personal service in certain areas, such as the fishery and delicatessen sections, Carrefour ensures that customers have help when they need it. As they move around the store to fill their shopping baskets and trolleys, customers are offered three basic choices for most product lines: a branded line, a private label and a generic. Private (or own-label) products were only introduced in 1985, when Carrefour seized the opportunity to develop loyalty amongst its customers. The idea was simple. Carrefour own-label products would only be available at the retailer's stores. If customers were to develop a preference for these good quality and keenly priced brands, they would keep coming back to the hypermarket. The retailer was particularly keen to use this approach as a source of competitive advantage over its rivals. In addition to differentiating itself through its Carrefour product lines, the retailer sought to improve product margins by capitalizing on the higher margins which the private label commanded. Customer response to the new lines was excellent. Before long, typically one-fifth of the goods in store were Carrefour's own brand.

Unfortunately for Carrefour, it was not possible to sustain a competitive advantage built around an own-label brand. After all, there was nothing to stop its competitors adopting a similar strategy. New efforts were made to improve profit margins. Many of these emphasized judicious management of Carrefour's supply chain. To this end, management forged relationships with suppliers aimed at developing what were termed 'controlled supply chains'. The intention was simple: to keep margins as high as possible by keeping costs low and optimizing the supply chain. The retailer has also become involved in global buying groups. These links have allowed Carrefour to negotiate global supply contracts in certain product categories, thus helping the business to make the most of economies of scale. Access to detailed information about sales and stock flow has been a crucial strand of this strategy. The advent of new electronic stock control technologies helped the company by allowing stock levels to be reduced and future product requirements predicted.

Expanding into International Markets

As Carrefour's 35 years of experience have shown, this is a format with some of the necessary flexibility to transcend national boundaries. Indeed, the retailer showed its interest in international expansion at an early stage in the business's development. As early as 1969, Carrefour was looking for opportunities away from its domestic market. The result was the opening of hypermarket outlets in Belgium, Italy, Switzerland and the UK. This signalled the first phase of the retailer's international growth. Unfortunately, despite the retailer's enthusiasm for this kind of growth, these early forays into the international arena were problematic. In particular, it became evident that cultural similarity with France was not enough to guarantee Carrefour success.

To understand the difficulties Carrefour faced, it is necessary to examine the reasons which brought its initial success. Carrefour was launched in France at a time when French retailing was 'stuck in a rut'. Although consumers were comfortable with the French small shop culture, they were also receptive to new ideas and retail formats. Retailing in France was ripe for change and Carrefour was ready to seize the opportunity this presented. In later years the situation changed: rival operations established themselves in the retail environment, consumers became more sophisticated and the market much more developed. If Carrefour had attempted to enter French retailing at this stage in its development, the outcome might have been considerably different. This partly explains the difficulties which Carrefour faced with its early moves into the well-developed Belgian, Swiss and UK retail markets. The company's response to these problems was to abandon its expansion strategy to focus on its domestic development. As a result, many of the stores outside its domestic market were closed.

The second phase of international expansion began between 1973 and 1975, when Carrefour moved into the Spanish and Brazilian markets. At this stage, it seemed that two key forces were driving Carrefour's development. The first related to Carrefour's plans for the domestic market. At home, the retailer's expansion plans were being affected by a range of government initiatives designed to protect the same small shops which once dominated. France was waking up to the fact that these small businesses, previously at the heart of French retailing, were under threat from the new supermarket and hypermarket giants. The second key force related to Carrefour's international aspirations. The company had, following its initial forays into the international market, recognized that well-developed retail markets were not a particularly attractive opportunity. In such countries consumers were becoming increasingly sophisticated and selective, the competitive environment was often highly developed, usually featuring a number of powerful local operators and the regulatory environment often imposed a variety of restrictions. For Carrefour, the obvious response to these restrictions was to seek expansion in countries where retailing was less well developed.

Spain and Brazil, the first Carrefour locations outside Europe, satisfied the criteria which Carrefour had set for its next period of international growth. In both cases, good prospects for economic growth coupled with a total absence of hypermarket-type stores allowed the retailer to transplant the Carrefour concept into a new location. Because consumers were unfamiliar with the concept, relatively few changes were needed to effect the move. Although in Spain, it later proved necessary to modify the Carrefour banner to the more locally acceptable Pryca. As a bonus, as an early entrant to the Spanish and Brazilian markets, Carrefour was now ideally placed to shape the future of retailing in these countries. The retailer's expansion ambitions did not end with Spain and Brazil. A similar approach was behind Carrefour's moves into Argentina, China, Italy, Malaysia, Mexico and Taiwan. In many of these locations, the French hypermarket business was responsible for bringing new retail concepts and ideas to the local market. Carrefour has continued to grow its Brazilian interests. In a ten-month period from December 1998, the retailer made a series of acquisitions. Following these activities, Carrefour has control over 113 supermarkets and 74 hypermarkets in the Sao Paulo, Espirito Santo, Brasilia and Belo Horizonte areas.

Learning from Mistakes

Carrefour's experience of moving into new markets has not always been so successful. At times, the retailer has needed to respond quickly to rectify mistakes. Carrefour's 1988 move into the American market is an example of what can go wrong. The story began when managers decided that a logical expansion move would be to take the Carrefour concept to the country which had originally been its inspiration. The company's earlier successes in Europe and Latin

America during the 1960s and 1970s helped spur on its efforts. Before long, Philadelphia had been chosen as the location for the first store and a 30,000m² outlet had been built. Two years later a second, smaller store was located in New Jersey.

As in other parts of the world, the new Carrefour store provided a mix of food and general merchandise. Aisles were wide, offering plenty of room to manoeuvre and products were displayed using conventional supermarket fixtures at conventional heights. In-store signage was discrete, being confined to pricing and department information to guide consumers around the 10,000 SKUs of food and 30,000 SKUs of general merchandise. (SKU stands for 'store-keeping unit' and relates to the number of different lines a store holds.) The provision of 3,000 car parking spaces helped consumers gain ready access to the store. As management sought to establish Carrefour's position in the community, the key proposition was an offer of 'everyday low prices'. The retailer hoped to use the promise of competitive prices to encourage a weekly visit from consumers living within five miles of the store. This was combined with a number of 'We save – You save' in-store price promotions. Instead of planning a major promotional campaign to launch the new outlet, management decided to rely upon word-of-mouth communication, passing the Carrefour message from consumer to consumer.

Despite the optimism with which Carrefour set out on its own North American adventure, this particular foray into a new market was not a success. After an initial period of poor sales, a more proactive advertising approach was adopted. A long-running newspaper advertising campaign was launched to whip-up enthusiasm for the Carrefour concept. Changes were also made to the store itself, with different mixes of food-to-general merchandise being tried. A dramatic increase in the number of SKUs was instigated (up to 26,000 for food and 45,000 for general merchandise) and more vibrant display and in-store signage was used to emphasize the price-oriented focus. The result of all of this effort? The American dream was turning into an American nightmare for Carrefour. Problems persisted in adapting the French concept for American tastes. Even the launch of the retailer's second store was dogged by difficulties, despite considerable efforts to respond to the problems in Philadelphia. Management had hoped that this new foray into the market, with its discount store approach, smaller size and warehouse club layout, would appeal more strongly to local consumers. In reality, poor sales combined with the opening of a neighbouring Wal-Mart store resulted in a damaging price war between the competitors. At just the wrong time, Carrefour had to mount a rear-guard defence against the major television, newspaper and direct mail campaign that accompanied the opening of the Wal-Mart outlet. By September 1993, Carrefour had bowed to the inevitable when it announced that both of the stores would soon be closed.

Many industry experts suggested that a poor understanding of the American consumer lay at the heart of the failure. Others pointed to the retailer's inexperience of running a cost-efficient US store. There is no question that the considerable union opposition to the project, centring around a three-year picket of the store by the United Food and Commercial Workers' Union, was also unhelpful to trade. Whatever the exact mix of reasons behind the failure, the company admitted that it had made too many assumptions about the suitability of the French concept for the US market. In reality, the American consumer has a unique collection of needs and wants which were not being satisfied by the Carrefour concept, but which were very well served by the multitude of US super-store and hypermarket operators.

Carrefour Today

As competition in retailing rises, an increasing number of retail markets are becoming saturated. With the top 100 global retailers already responsible for 20 per cent of the world market, the power of leading players such as Carrefour and Wal-Mart is clear. The 1999 figures for Carrefour showed an 8.2 per cent increase in net sales, with 57 per cent generated outside the domestic market. Yet even the largest retailers must face the problems which market saturation causes.

In France, as in so many other countries with a well-developed retailing environment, Carrefour must operate within the constraints of a variety of local and national government restrictions. These are designed to control the limited amount of retail space available. For example, local government imposes regulations to limit the opening of new outlets and to restrict increases in selling space in others. Thus in 1996, the French government passed a law aimed at protecting small shopkeepers. The effects of this were to severely limit the opening of new hypermarkets. The result for Carrefour? In situations such as these, growth is only possible through the acquisition of a competitor based locally.

The retailer has followed this growth by acquisition route with some success. Early in the 1990s, Carrefour acquired the Euromarche Group and the Montlaur chain of outlets, allowing it to equal the sales volume of market leader Leclerc. Late in 1996, the retailer acquired more than 40 per cent of GMB, owner of Cora hypermarkets. More recently, Carrefour, which already owned a quarter of Comptoir Modernes, became involved in an agreed takeover bid for the remainder. The attractions of the link up for both parties are clear. Comptoirs Modernes, with 792 supermarkets in France, trading as Comod, Stock and March Plus and 76 outlets in Spain, would use the merger to radically increase sales outside the domestic market. For Carrefour, this further consolidation of the French retail sector would add a large number of additional outlets to the retailer's existing chains.

The Promodes Merger

In August 1999, in a deal worth 15.6 billion Euros, Carrefour joined forces with Promodes to create the second largest retail group in the world. The friendly merger, which was announced at a Paris press conference, reinforced the new retailing giant as a global force to be reckoned with. With a presence in 26 different countries and headquartered in France, the new group became the largest retailer in Europe. In addition, while still only half the size of key rival Wal-Mart, the combined company looks set to cause major problems for the world's largest retailers.

The synergies between Carrefour and Promodes are readily apparent. Both companies began as family firms. Together they have a presence in 26 countries and, say some analysts, are in front of Wal-Mart in terms of international presence. Senior managers from each of the businesses have declared their joint intention to make the most of strong growth prospects to do battle for the world-wide retail market. In all, the group has 9,000 stores and employs nearly a quarter of a million people. With 680 hypermarkets and 3,200 discount stores, sales estimates for 1999 were a massive 54 billion Euros.

The benefits of the merger have been clearly stated by those involved. For the newly combined business, there is the potential for increased profitability, with a three-year doubling of net profits sought. The attraction to the shareholders is obvious, as those with a stake in the business will become part of one of the largest businesses on the Paris stock exchange. Meanwhile employees are also looking forward to the excellent range of career opportunities which the merger will create. Carrefour is optimistic that customers, too, will enjoy the improvements brought about by the extra resources which will be aimed at everything from service initiatives and product innovation to marketing, quality and food safety.

It is interesting to consider what impact the Carrefour–Promodes link-up will have on the competitive environment. Major player Wal-Mart has watched developments with particular interest. With such excellent international coverage, the newly merged business is bound to cause concern for the US giant. Indeed, it seems that the only weak areas for Carrefour and Promodes are in Germany and the US, although both of these regions are strongholds for Wal-Mart. Although the US-based retailer remains silent about its future plans, it seems that more expansion is on the cards. The company's acquisition of UK retailer Asda seems a clear signal of intent. Some analysts predict that within five years overseas earnings may generate one quarter of Wal-Mart's earnings. This would represent an 18 per cent increase on current figures and would almost certainly involve further attempts to reduce overseas operating costs. Only time will show whether the friendly merger between Carrefour and Promodes reaps the benefits both parties are seeking. However, it seems that the move is likely to promote a flurry of other acquisitive moves within the global retailing sector.

As Carrefour moves forward into the new Millennium, the situation in its saturated domestic market will become more entrenched. With the maturing of other retail markets around the world, competition will increase further and the industry's obsession with low price will further impinge upon the bottom line. Through a range of activities Carrefour has already started addressing the difficulties which this situation imposes. The business continues to be committed to global expansion. Initiatives in the Pacific Rim and Central Europe are the current focus. Since Carrefour moved into Asia via Taiwan, the retailer has acquired interests in seven different Pacific Rim nations. Now a major push into the Japanese market is underway, with a number of outlets already planned. Although the Japanese market has traditionally been hostile to outsiders, the retailer believes that recent financial upheavals in the Pacific Rim are changing consumers' attitudes. In particular, the company believes that consumers are becoming more receptive to foreign brands and that there is definitely room for a hypermarket offering based around good value. Despite the difficulties associated with entering the Japanese market, Carrefour's previous global experiences, positive and negative, should help the retailer to make the most of this opportunity. It seems likely that Carrefour will follow its usual approach of modifying its outlets to suit local needs, recruiting and training the necessary personnel from the local area. Initially Carrefour will also work with local distributors, combining consumer requirements for local products with the careful introduction of foreign brands.

Carrefour's interest in Central Europe is not surprising. This region offers good growth prospects and competition is not so heavy as in Western Europe. Poland, Hungary, the Czech Republic and Slovakia are just some of the countries to which Carrefour has become committed. Extracts from a recent interview with the managing director of the retailer's Czech subsidiary Carrefour Ceska Republika provide an interesting insight into the venture.

■ *How well has Carrefour been accepted?*

Shopping malls that also house hypermarkets are a fairly new phenomenon for the Czech client and consumer, especially in the provinces. He has to progressively familiarize himself with it, and has to learn how to direct himself in such an immense shopping area. However, all those who have opened this type of shopping mall before us, and especially in the capital, could see that the Czech client does very much appreciate the concept.

■ *Have you had to adapt your assortment? Your merchandising?*

Our intention was to offer 60,000 products right from the beginning, just as we did in France. In order to do this, we had to widen the non-food range. The average local shopping basket contains fewer foodstuffs than in France. We have also adopted the principle, very new here, of seasonal rotation. For example, last year, we started selling toys very early, way before the end of the year. The same for winter sporting goods. This strategy has been very important for us. As a matter of fact, each season, we present a new assortment.

■ *Have you established any co-operation with local producers?*

The part of locally product foodstuffs is very important. We sometimes develop channel agreements, as we have done for apples. The client/supplier relationships are interesting for both parties. For example, we buy flour from a producer in Plzen. We also buy freshwater fish such as trout and carp. I think that there is a sort of fear here concerning foreign companies, imports and supernational companies. However, with these types of agreements, everybody comes out winning.

(Source: M. Laurent Noel, 'Carrefour has Czech mate', *Chain Store Age*, August 1999, 75 (8), pp. 44–48.)

And Finally …

There is no question that retailing has entered a period of dynamic change. New store formats, changing consumer profiles and the advent of Internet and home shopping are just some of the developments which Carrefour is facing. It remains to be seen whether or not the hypermarket will be sufficiently flexible to adapt to the changing market place. What is clear is that in markets which are saturated, growth will continue to be achieved through acquisition and by investing in new services and offerings. Carrefour's reputation as a ruthless controller of costs also looks set to continue as the business continues to wage its war to improve profit margins by increasing its control over the supply chain and margins.

Carrefour's commitment to international development has been unstinting. In the words of Carrefour's Chairman: 'Internationalization is a difficult learning curve which is expensive at the outset. After setting up the basics, it becomes necessary to be patient enough to fine-tune the concept and to await profitability, which may be quite distant. Internationalization represents long-term investment'.

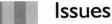

Issues

Carrefour is one of the most successful retailers in the world, now active in Asia Pacific, South America, much of Europe and is even competing in Wal-Mart's home market of North America. Through organic growth and acquisition, Carrefour has grown to become one of the world's leading retailers, but such international expansion has not always been trouble-free.

International marketing

What are the options available to a business such as Carrefour when devising plans for international expansion? Which approaches did Carrefour adopt? Has this strategy proved to be the optimum way forward?

What are the barriers to expansion posed by the forces of the international marketing environment? Which impacted on Carrefour?

Competitive strategy

Has Carrefour's strategy taken account of its competitive arena? Was the French retailer wise to enter the North American market?

Product development

How has Carrefour modified its product to take account of its international expansion? Should a business such as Carrefour strive for global homogeneity in its trading proposition?

Relevant Theory Notes

T16: International Marketing, pp. 297–301
T7: Competitive Strategy, pp. 237–245
T2: The Marketing Environment and Competition, pp. 199–204
T8: The Marketing Mix: Products and Product Management, pp. 246–254

Part IV
Theory Notes

This section contains theory notes that provide an overview of the fundamental concepts and frameworks of modern marketing.

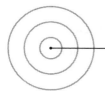

Theory Note 1:   What is Marketing?

Definitions

Marketing is not a science: there is no single correct definition or approach to undertaking marketing. There are, though, common themes. The most important are (a) the ability to satisfy customers, (b) the identification of favourable marketing opportunities, (c) the need to create an edge over competitors, (d) the capacity to make profits or financial surpluses to enable a viable future for the organization, (e) that resources are utilized shrewdly to maximize a business's market position, (f) the aim to increase market share in priority target markets. If the 'right' opportunities are pursued, customers are thoroughly understood, the 'right' customers targeted with a marketing proposition designed to give a business an edge over its rivals, it is likely that customers will be satisfied, market share will rise in core target markets and profitability will accordingly support a viable future. Conversely, if a business develops a product or service which fails to reflect customer expectations and needs, is no better than competing offers and takes no account of evolving market conditions, the business is unlikely to enjoy a prosperous future.

Peter Drucker, one of the gurus of modern business thinking, defined marketing thus,

> The aim of marketing is to make selling superfluous. The aim is to know and to understand the customer so well that the product or service fits him/her and sells itself.

This is perhaps one of the most famous definitions in marketing. If the business researches its market and its customers so well that it exactly understands the product attributes required by its customers, the desired point of purchase, pricing, promotional imagery and selling methods, customer service and brand identity, then the product should be so in line with the desired needs and expectations of targeted customers that it sells itself. The two key points to Drucker's definition are then that marketing should make selling superfluous – or at least the 'hard sell', and that the basic task of marketing management is to develop an excellent understanding of the customer.

The UK's Chartered Institute of Marketing (CIM) views marketing as,

> The management process responsible for identifying, anticipating and satisfying customer requirements profitably.

This definition takes Drucker's ideas further, adding the element of profitability. This is true for all organizations, not just those such as retailers, banks or manufacturers seeking high profitability. Even utilities, public sector organizations and not-for-profit organizations such as charities seek to create a surplus of revenue over costs.

The American Marketing Association (AMA) and market leading text *Marketing: Concepts and Strategies* by Dibb *et al.* define marketing as,

> Marketing consists of individual and organisational activities that facilitate and expedite satisfying exchange relationships in a dynamic environment through the creation, servicing, distribution, promotion and pricing of goods, services and ideas.

Marketing is indeed dynamic. The solution to a marketing problem – declining sales, poor brand awareness, competitor hostility or distributor hesitance, for example – found to be effective one week may no longer be relevant a few weeks or months later. Customers are fickle and perpetually seek more from a product or service, competitors alter their sales and marketing activity, market trends and broad political, economic, social and technological forces constantly change, all impacting on a marketer's proposed solution to a problem or emerging opportunity. The second half of the AMA/Dibb definition introduces two additional concepts. First, the creation, servicing, distribution, promotion and pricing ingredients are the tactical decisions made by marketers to persuade customers to prefer their proposition. This set of tactical issues is termed the *marketing mix*, often referred to as the '5Ps' of marketing: product, people, place, promotion and pricing. This is the toolkit that marketers manipulate in order to stay ahead of competitors, anticipate market forces and satisfy targeted customers. Another facet of the AMA's definition is that marketing is just as applicable for services and ideas as it is for tangible products, such as Heinz beans, Kellogg's cereals, or Kodak film. It is too easy when reading many marketing texts to believe that marketing is only relevant to consumer goods, specially fast moving consumer goods (FMCGs) such as beans, cereals and film. Marketing is as prevalent in industrial, services and even public sector markets as it is in consumer goods. Whether it is Persil washing powder, Ford cars, JCB diggers, Raytheon power units, Barclays financial services, Direct Line insurance, BUPA healthcare, easyJet flights, Tony Blair's voter focus groups or Warwick Business School's MBA programme, marketing is an every-day occurrence.

Clearly the definitions of Drucker, the CIM, AMA/Dibb *et al.* focus on a variety of aspects of marketing. To some extent, this also sums up the nature of marketing. There is an element of science inherent in many of the tools in the marketer's toolkit, but compared with finance, operational research, quantitative methods, engineering or scientific research, marketing is more subjective and open to wide-ranging interpretation. There is never only one approach to tackling a marketing problem, nor a single correct solution. Marketing is about understanding customers, anticipating future requirements, and tailoring a business's marketing mix to satisfy targeted customers, to provide an edge over competitors and adequate financial returns.

The Birth of Marketing

It is a widely held belief that marketing has evolved, growing up in the 1960s in America, led by the major consumer goods businesses such as Heinz, Kellogg's, and Kodak. Many business authors present a sequence of eras through which commercial activity passed as the twentieth century unfolded:

Production era: 1850s–1920s

> The Industrial Revolution occurred, followed by mass production and rigidly structured jobs. Products were developed without too much thought for finding customers or creating an edge over rival propositions. There were sufficiently few products to risk swamping customers and little competition.

Sales Era: 1920s–1950s

> The focus for businesses was on personal selling and advertising. Sales were seen as the major means for increasing profits. Products were handed over to the sales force who persuaded customers to want them.

Marketing Era: 1950s–present

> A customer orientation replaced the 'hard sell' of the sales-led era as companies determined the needs and wants of customers before introducing their products or services.

Relationship Marketing Era: 1990s

> Some business experts believe that the marketing era has recently shifted from being *transaction-based* to focusing on *relationships*. The argument is that marketing's focus used to be on attracting new customers or orders, but that businesses have now recognised it is just as important to hang on to such new customers so that they become repeat buyers and long-term loyal customers. As such, marketers devote their attention to both winning new customers – transaction marketing – and to building up positive on-going relationships to maintain their loyalty and custom – relationship marketing.

At the start of the twentieth century, products were developed by inventors and then sold into the marketplace. As more companies entered emerging and growing markets, the level of competition forced greater emphasis on aggressive selling. As customers became more sophisticated, product choice greater and competitive activity more intense, successful businesses turned to marketing to properly identify and anticipate customer needs, gearing up design and production accordingly. This was the birth of marketing. As the last century drew to a close, the emphasis on customer-first thinking encouraged marketers to plan programmes designed to maintain customer loyalty and create on-going customer relationships.

Marketing is not Selling

Many student surveys asking passers-by in the street to define marketing return the same answers:

> 'Marketing is selling', 'It's advertising' or the uncharitable view that 'Marketing is conning people to buy what they don't want!'.

In fact, as should by now be clear, marketing is none of these. If a business through its marketing activity properly understands its customers' expectations and wants, its products or services should genuinely be able to satisfy a customer's need. The product-first, hard selling of the 1960s and 1970s may well have on occasions led hard-pressed sales personnel and company executives to deceive prospective customers, but the ethos of marketing is far removed from such views. Advertising is the 'sharp end' of marketing witnessed daily by consumers watching television, listening to the radio, reading a newspaper or magazine, going to the cinema, or travelling on public transport. As will be described in subsequent chapters, advertising is part of marketing, but it is only one small facet of the tactical marketing mix toolkit.

Figure IV.1 illustrates the distinction between selling and marketing. Under selling, the product is first produced, then sold and the consumer is only involved in the process in terms of being the final element in the chain – the purchaser or consumer. Profits arise from volume sales. Under the marketing philosophy, customers are consulted at every stage of the process, the marketing mix being adjusted accordingly. Profits or financial surpluses stem from customer satisfaction. Personal selling is deemed to be a component of the promotional mix, itself just one ingredient of the marketing mix. Marketers identify the most attractive market opportunities, hone a business's product or service proposition to reflect customers' wishes and competitors' offers, developing a distinctive brand identity and awareness. They therefore guide and support the efforts of their colleagues in the sales force.

Figure IV.1	*Selling and Marketing*

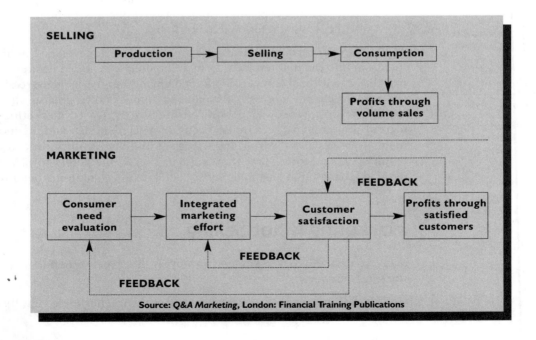

Source: *Q&A Marketing*, London: Financial Training Publications

Key characteristics

Selling Philosophy	Marketing Philosophy

Selling Philosophy
- Sales oriented
- One-way process
- Little adaptation to external marketing environment forces
- Narrow view of consumer needs
- Emphasis on the single customer in the selling situation
- Output 'sold' to customers overtly
- Short-run goals and sales targets
- Sales volume oriented
- Informal planning and feedback

Marketing Philosophy
- Consumer oriented
- Two-way interactive process
- Adaptation to the external marketing environment
- Broad view of consumer needs
- Emphasis on groups of consumers or target market segments
- Marketing research impacts on outputs
- Longer-term goals and plans
- Profit and market share oriented
- Integrated planning and feedback

The Marketing Process

For many years in too many organizations, marketing was confined to promotional activity, such as advertising, and occasional marketing research. There are still many businesses which wrongly view marketing as the function tasked only to develop a marketing mix – product, people, place, promotion and price – in splendid isolation of strategic thinking and analysis of the marketplace. Only a few organizations have strategic planners, so corporate strategy tends to be developed by the senior management team. Marketers should be talking to customers, monitoring market trends and studying competitors, and therefore need to be involved in corporate strategic decision-making. Very few businesses have a discrete market analysis function, so what understanding there is of market trends, competitor moves and evolving customer requirements, comes from those tasked with marketing. Market-oriented, customer-focused businesses utilize the expertise of marketers in this way, drawing on their analyses and strategic thinking, rather than leaving marketers only to tweak the marketing mix ingredients of their tactical programmes. For a marketing function in a business to be effective, it must be fully conversant with the marketing ethos and process.

The definitions of marketing provide a *raison d'être*, and clearly put customer satisfaction as the primary requirement, but by themselves such definitions do not make marketing *happen*. Marketing is a way of thinking and acting: looking outside a business to examine changes in the marketplace, customers' ever-evolving expectations and to anticipate competitors' actions. Marketing requires (a) understanding and analysis, (b) objective thinking and strategic decision making, (c) implementation programmes and controls to ensure the determined strategic recommendations are actioned. The marketing strategy should reflect the marketplace and any forecast changes. Strategy cannot be determined until adequate marketing analyses have been undertaken. Only once the analyses have fed into strategy formulation should the tactical marketing mix be specified and internal controls put in place to implement the desired marketing strategy. This is a simple but very important process: *A-S-P* – *a*nalysis first, then *s*trategic thinking and only then the formulation of tactical sales and marketing *p*rogrammes intended to action the recommended strategy. Figure IV.2 summarizes the *A-S-P* process of marketing, designed to ensure marketing is more than a one-dimensional text book definition.

Figure IV.2	*The Analysis, Strategy and Programmes Process of Marketing*

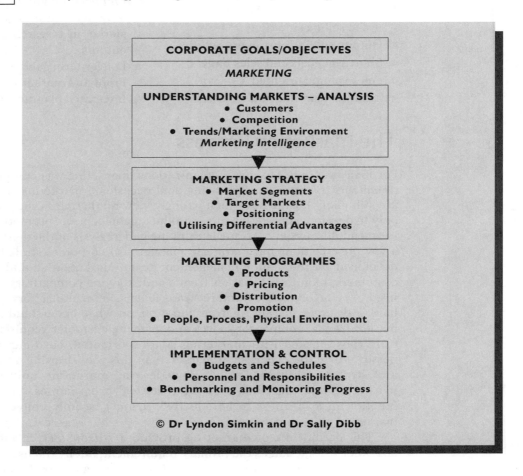

© Dr Lyndon Simkin and Dr Sally Dibb

A business cannot determine a viable strategy or specify tactical programmes without first *a*nalysing its marketplace: customers, competitors, marketing environment forces and trends, plus its capabilities to tackle such opportunities and threats. Managerial experience, instinct and ability occasionally may prove sufficient in analysing the marketplace, but more than likely there will be the need to supplement such thoughts with marketing research to provide adequate marketing intelligence for decision-making. The marketing *s*trategy stage requires the identification of which customer groups or market segments should be prioritized, with what proposition, brand positioning and competitive edge or differential advantage. Once a business has determined its target market strategy it should ensure its marketing mix tactical programmes match the expectations of those customers deemed priority targets, emphasize the determined brand positioning, maximize any edge over rivals while differentiating the product or service in the marketplace. Internal controls will be required to facilitate the roll-out of such programmes. If the 'nuts and bolts' of marketing – the product, people, place, promotion and pricing ingredients of the marketing mix – fail to reflect the issues identified in the marketing analyses or the requirement of the marketing strategy, it is unlikely the product or even the company in question will have a healthy future. Each of these *A-S-P* stages of marketing is examined in subsequent chapters.

Useful References

Baker, M. (1999) 'The Nature and Scope of Marketing' in the *IEBM Encyclopedia of Marketing*, (ed. MJ Baker), London: Thomson Learning. Not light bed-time reading but a very thorough reference resource for marketers.

Baker, M. (1999) 'What is Marketing?' in *The Marketing Book* (ed. MJ Baker), Oxford: Butterworth-Heinemann. *The Marketing Book* is a good collection of readings by leading academics covering most facets of marketing.

Dibb, S., Simkin, L., Pride, W. and Ferrell, OC (2001) *Marketing: Concepts and Strategies*, Boston: Houghton Mifflin. This is the market leading mainstream marketing textbook adopted by most business schools to explore and to explain the subject of marketing.

Doyle, P. (1998) *Marketing Management and Strategy*, London: Pearson. Not an introductory reader, this insightful examination of strategic marketing is a good read for serious marketers.

Levitt, T. (1960) 'Marketing Myopia', *Harvard Business Review*, 38 (4), pp. 45–56. Possibly where modern marketing began: Levitt lambasted the inward-looking, product-led, aggressive selling of 'US Inc'!

Lynch, J. (1994) 'What is Marketing?' in *Effective Industrial Marketing* (ed. N Hart), London: Kogan Page. Industrial products and services are marketed, too, as described well in this book of collected readings.

Weekly Trade Magazines

- *Marketing Week*, London: Centaur Communications
- *Marketing*, London: Haymarket Publishing
- *Campaign*, London: Haymarket Publishing

While oriented more to consumer markets than industrial, business-to-business markets, these three magazines keep readers up-to-date with the latest concepts, ideas, tools, brands, product and campaign launches, with the gossip typical of most trade journals. *Campaign* is focused on the world of advertising. They are all readily available at larger newsagents in London and the conurbations, or to order on subscription. Major 'breaking' stories tend to be covered by all of these titles, so there is no need to purchase all three.

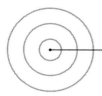

Theory Note 2: The Marketing Environment and Competition

Definition

> The marketing environment is defined as those external trading forces that directly or indirectly influence an organisation's acquisitions of inputs and generation of outputs.

The forces of the marketing environment are trading forces over which a business has little or no control such as economic recession, EU bureaucracy, technological innovation or social trends, but they are forces that tangibly affect the way in which the company can do business and how it performs. Unfortunately, because these forces are external to a business, all too often senior managers and marketers choose to ignore them. The result of such neglect is that opportunities arising from external change are missed and threats caused by external pressures are allowed to impede performance when prompt attention may have pre-empted any such problems.

For instance, the greening consumer has created an opportunity for Calor Gas to provide energy for 'environmentally friendly' low-emission Vauxhall and Volvo cars. Had Calor's marketers not been monitoring their marketing environment, they may not have identified such an opportunity at an early stage, enabling competitors to gain a head start in this evolving market. Another example is the EU's overhaul of the retailing practices for car showrooms. Some manufacturers recognized the need to build relationships with franchised dealerships to maintain their loyalty, while other car manufacturers failed to recognize the freedom granted to dealerships by the new EU regulations and the threat posed to the manufacturers' existing exclusive showroom arrangements.

To monitor changes in the marketing environment, marketers must scan and analyse continuously. Many companies have individual marketing managers or committees whose function is to collect and collate data related to trends in the market and aspects of the marketing environment. *Environmental scanning* is the process of tracking information from observation, secondary sources – such as the press, trade journals, government reports, information libraries – and from marketing research. Company intranets increasingly are facilitating the sharing of snippets of information concerning the forces of the marketing environment.

The components of the marketing environment are variously defined. Many economists refer to the *PEST analysis*: political, economic, social and technological forces. Marketers tend to examine more forces than these four and have come to identify two categories of forces: macro and micro. The macro forces are the very broad market forces which affect all companies operating in a particular market and therefore also all consumers. The micro forces are still outside a business's direct control, but will have a much more variable and 'localized' impact on different companies active in a market as they relate to competitive, supplier and buyer issues.

The Macro Marketing Environment

The macro marketing environment forces are broad, market-wide issues (see Figure IV.3):

- *Legal Forces.* Many laws influence marketing activities. For example, procompetitive legislation and consumer protection laws.

- *Regulatory Forces.* Interpretation of laws is important, but so is an understanding of the enforcement by various government and non-government regulatory bodies. For example, government ministries, local authorities and councils, trade and professional bodies all introduce restrictions on trading practices and procedures which must be followed by businesses.

- *Political Forces.* Many marketers view the actions of government as beyond influence, while others successfully lobby and influence policy-making and legislating bodies of central and local governments. There must be, though, ethical behaviour and lobbying should be above-board and within accepted procedures. Even where a business is unable or unwilling to practice lobbying, it is still very much the case that awareness of impending policy changes enables pre-emptive measures to be put in place.

- *Societal or Cultural Forces.* These are the dynamics and workings of society: groups and individuals often ignore the activities of companies and marketers until then infringe – usually negatively – on their lifestyles and choices. Current consumer pressure on companies to produce products which are less harmful to the earth's physical environment is an example of such external forces.

- *Technological Forces.* Technological expertise with which to accomplish tasks is quickly evolving and changing, affecting how people satisfy their needs and lead their lives. It also affects what products marketers can bring to the marketplace and how these items are presented to the consumer. A few years ago, direct PC-based home shopping or banking seemed unrealistic, but now retailers and banks are re-thinking their trading formats and strategies to move with the times.

- *Economic Forces.* General economic conditions – recession or boom – will impact on any market, as will consumer demand and spending behaviour. Such conditions are prone to dramatic changes, patterns and fashions and must be considered when developing target market strategies and marketing plans.

| Figure IV.3 | *The Macro and Micro Forces of the Marketing Environment* |

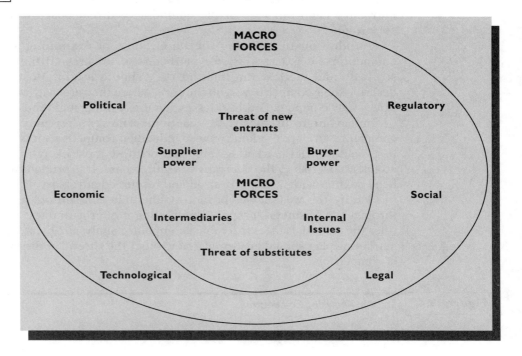

The Micro Marketing Environment

These forces are still outside a business's direct control, but their impact is more company-specific than the very broad macro marketing environment forces. Michael Porter summarized these as direct rival, new entrant and substitute competitive forces, plus the competitive impact of buyers and suppliers. Increasingly marketers consider also the role of channel intermediaries and even their internal company marketing environment.

Competitive forces

Most businesses are aware of direct (similar) competitors, but few are geared up in advance to the arrival in a market of new rivals or to the impact of alternative solutions to customers' problems provided by non-similar competitors or substitutes. For example, Daewoo's entry into the small car market in Europe had a significant and detrimental impact on Rover's small car sales. Environmental scanning would have forewarned car manufacturers and enabled them to develop pre-emptive measures such as new model launches of their own, branding initiatives, customer loyalty programmes and dealer training. Daewoo's appearance could not have been avoided, but its impact on existing manufacturers could have been limited if the new entrant had been anticipated. JCB's diggers dig trenches for pipes and cables. Iseki's tunnelling moles lay pipes and cables remotely underground, reducing the need for a digger's trench. Iseki is not a manufacturer of construction equipment and without an awareness of the micro forces in the marketing environment, JCB may have been unaware of the competitive threat posed from this unlikely substitute.

In addition to realizing the importance of examining all categories of competitors, it is necessary for marketers to understand the detailed level of strategic and tactical information they should attain. Most companies can describe their competitors: who they are, where they are, with what products and prices they compete. Few businesses genuinely understand their rivals' strategies or endeavour to predict their reaction to moves they may make. Very few companies attempt to identify those individual competitors it is sensible to avoid in a head-to-head marketing campaign or those most likely to be vulnerable to attack at low risk to the company's resource base. It is prudent to avoid head-to-head conflict with a similarly sized and resourced adversary. It is more desirable to identify the weaknesses of more vulnerable competitors and address these through the business's proposed marketing mix programmes. Figure IV.4 identifies the essential stages in a robust competitor analysis. No marketing strategy or marketing plan should be formulated without the shrewd and systematic analysis of competitors.

Figure IV.4	*Steps in Analysing Competitors*

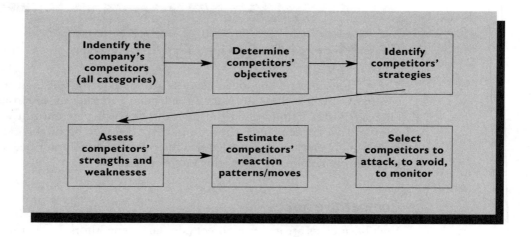

Supplier and buyer forces

Most businesses source raw materials, components or supplies from third parties. Without the understanding and co-operation of these other organizations, a business would fail to deliver a quality product or service which satisfies its customers' needs. Marketers must be aware of these supplier forces, such as supplier innovations; deals with rivals; supply shortages, delays or quality concerns; strikes or recruitment difficulties; legal actions or warranty disputes; supply costs and price trends; new entrants into the supply chain; or anything prone to altering the business's receipt of its required supplies. Buyers also have a variable impact on a business. In business-to-business markets, the merchandising director of a large retailer may have favourite suppliers. A new manager may alter the status quo and source from alternate suppliers. In consumer markets, the fickleness of consumers alters brand loyalty and will also have a variable impact on the fortunes of marketers. This theme is discussed more fully in the next chapter.

Intermediary forces

Some businesses sell directly to their targeted customers. Most, though, utilize the skills, network and resources of intermediaries to make their products available to the end-user customer. Intermediaries include resellers – such as retailers, wholesalers, agents, brokers, dealers – plus physical distribution companies responsible for logistical needs, providers of marketing services such as advertising agencies or packaging design consultancies, and financial facilitators of credit lines and export guarantees. Without the smooth co-operation of such intermediaries, a business is unlikely to be able to deliver its products as required by its customers. Failure to pick up on any problems with intermediaries may result in a loss of business.

The internal marketing environment

It is necessary when creating and implementing marketing strategies and marketing mix programmes to consider the reaction, attitudes and abilities of the *internal* environment: top management, finance, research and development, purchasing, manufacturing, sales and marketing, logistics. The marketing function's recommendations must be consistent with senior management's corporate goals, be conveyed to other functions within the business and reflect colleagues' views, input, concerns and abilities to implement the desired marketing plan. Marketers must be aware of these organizational factors, monitor them and modify their actions accordingly to ensure internal take-up of their ideas and plans. Therefore, it is increasingly common for marketing decision-makers to consider their internal marketing environment when developing marketing plans and recommendations.

The Marketing Environment and Strategic Opportunities

When changes occur in the marketing environment they can trigger major developments. If large enough, such changes are called *strategic windows* or paradigm shifts. If market leaders have failed to spot the underlying development or evolutionary change, rivals may have an opportunity to gain an advantage over established companies and brands by 'stepping through the open window'. The established company must strive to 'close the window' with its own proposition speedily enough to pre-empt competitors' in-roads. Failure to monitor the marketing environment and take appropriate action invariably results in a business being unable to react quickly enough to the change to keep out competitors. Marketing strategists believe there are six broad causes of strategic windows opening:

- *New technology.* Duracell utilized lithium technology to overtake market leader EverReady.

- *New markets.* Security company Securicor identified the potential of the mobile 'phone market in its early days, taking a lucrative majority share in Cellnet.

- *New distribution channels.* Vodaphone was first to recognize some cellphone buyers' reluctance to deal with salespeople in specialist mobile 'phone shops, developing self-service displays for Halford's and Woolworth's.

- *Market re-definition.* NCR used to make cash registers for retailers. It spotted the EPoS data needs of retailers and switched to supplying full EPoS and cash register system solutions for its retailer customers.

- *New legislation and regulation.* The EU's 'open skies' policy has enabled smaller airlines such as easyJet or Virgin Express to access routes.

- *Political and financial shocks.* Government policy towards the railways has placed greater pressure on operators such as Virgin Trains to improve performance, while fluctuations in central bank interest rates in 1999 caused a boom in housing prices and for the estate agency sector.

Useful References

Brownlie, D. (1994) 'Organising for Environmental Scanning: Orthodoxies and Reformations', *Journal of Marketing Management*, 10 (8), pp. 703–724. A good summary of analysis techniques.

Dibb, S., Simkin, L., Pride, W. and Ferrell, O.C. (2001) *Marketing: Concepts and Strategies*, Boston: Houghton Mifflin; chapters 2 and 21. A more thorough examination of the macro and micro marketing forces, strategic implications and competitor intelligence.

Drucker, P. (1981) *Management in Turbulent Times*, London: Butterworth-Heinemann/ Pan. Dated but insightful explanation of the importance of understanding the external trading environment.

Peattie, K. (1995) *Environmental Marketing Management*, London: Pitman. All there is to know about marketing environmental (green) issues.

Porter, M. (1979) 'How Competitive Forces Shape Strategy', *Harvard Business Review*, March–April, pp. 137–145. The birth of modern competitive strategy in marketing.

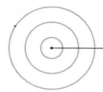

Theory Note 3:   Buying Behaviour

Definitions

> Consumer buyer behaviour focuses on the decision processes and acts of individuals (you and me) involved in buying and using products.
>
> Organizational – or business-to-business – buyer behaviour is the purchase behaviour of producers, re-sellers, government units, and institutions.

At the heart of the principle of effective marketing is the need to satisfy customers. This cannot be achieved without a sound understanding of them: their needs and wants, buying behaviour and the influences which impact on their purchasing decision-making. This is true whether the customer is an end-user consumer buying groceries from a supermarket or hi-fi products from an electrical superstore, or if the customer is a business such as BMW purchasing components from Bosch or parts from Lucas Verity. Marketers must strive to 'get into the heads' of their existing and prospective customers. This is *buyer behaviour* in marketing terms. This understanding gives an insight into how best to influence their buying activities and can result in the development of a more suitable marketing mix (product, price, promotion, distribution, people) for the customers targeted.

Consumer Buying Behaviour

There are various types of decision-making. *Routine response* is where familiar, non-risky items are bought without much deliberation, such as milk, cigarettes, newspapers. Instances where there is some existing knowledge but the consumer supplements it with some information gathering and consideration are occurrences of *limited decision-making*. If the purchase involves unfamiliar, expensive or infrequently bought products, such as cars, holidays, houses or personal pensions, there is usually *extensive decision-making*. By contrast, *impulse buying* involves no conscious planning but a powerful urge to instantaneously buy!

There have been many attempts to model the ways in which people buy. Figure IV.5 illustrates a typical consumer buying process model.

(i) *Problem Recognition.* This is the point where the consumer realises that a purchase is required. For example, a household appliance such as a washing machine that is broken beyond repair must be replaced.

(ii) *Information Search.* At this stage in the buying process, the consumer begins searching for information to help with the required purchase. Information may be gleaned from many sources, such as talking with friends, family and colleagues; magazines; advertising; brochures; sales assistants; or surfing the web. During this stage a list of criteria is implicitly drawn up together with a number of alternative product/service options.

(iii) *Evaluation of Alternatives.* This is where the consumer must choose between the alternatives (sometimes referred to as the *evoked set*) by measuring the different product/service options against the criteria selected. In some cases, insufficient information will have been collected, causing the consumer to return to the information search stage.

(iv) *Purchase.* The complexity of purchase varies according to the type of product being bought. Compare for instance the simple act of buying a newspaper with the complexity of a house purchase.

(v) *Post-Purchase Evaluation.* After any purchase, particularly one which is expensive, there will be a period of post-purchase evaluation. This is where the consumer tries to judge the success of the purchase made. The result will have an impact on future purchases, as the evaluation feeds back into subsequent decision-making.

| **Figure IV.5** | *The Consumer Buying Decision Process and Influencing Factors* |

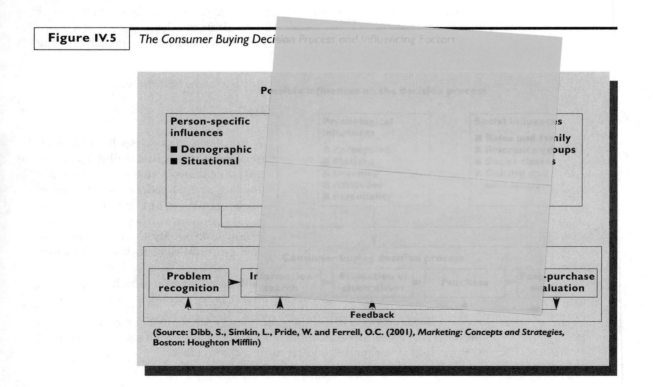

(Source: Dibb, S., Simkin, L., Pride, W. and Ferrell, O.C. (2001), *Marketing: Concepts and Strategies,* Boston: Houghton Mifflin)

There are a number of factors which influence the way in which people buy:

■ *Person-Specific Influences.* These relate to demographic issues (age/sex/occupation) and situational factors (external conditions which exist when a purchase is made).

■ *Psychological Influences.* Different consumers have different perceptions, motives and attitudes towards what and how they purchase. Other factors, such as the level of knowledge about a particular item and personality, often have an impact.

■ *Social Influences.* All consumers are influenced by social factors when they buy. For example, tastes tend to be influenced by social class and culture, and behaviour is radically affected by family roles and *reference groups* (friends/colleagues), as well as by exposure to messages in the media.

Models of buyer behaviour are beneficial to marketers, bringing an understanding of the factors which impact on people's buying decisions. In addition, by appreciating the processes which consumers go through, marketers can decide what kind of marketing effort to target at consumers as they pass through the different stages. For instance, some of the car advertisements appearing on television are aimed at stimulating brand awareness so that when consumers recognize a need to buy a new car, they may consider a particular brand as advertised. Later on in the buying process, the car manufacturers must be prepared to provide detailed information about product offerings together with test drives.

As with any models representing reality, buyer behaviour models are subject to criticisms. A number of difficulties are readily apparent:

■ Different products are bought in different ways.

■ The length of the buying process varies according to the type of buying decision: routine response, limited decision-making, or extended decision-making.

■ For some products, stages are omitted altogether: buying a newspaper is a routine activity with little information search.

The appropriateness of the model also depends on whether a product has been purchased before. Is the product a *routine re-buy*, *modified re-buy* or completely *new buy*?

Business-to-Business or Organizational Buying Behaviour

Organizational business-to-business markets can be classified into:

■ *Industrial or producer markets.* These companies buy products for use in the manufacture of other products or to support that manufacture. For example, food producer Nestlé buys glucose syrup, cocoa powder, sugar, etc.

■ *Re-seller markets.* Companies in this category buy goods for re-sale to customers. Generally they do not alter the physical nature of those goods. For example, wholesalers or retailers, such as Booker, Marks and Spencer, Carrefour or IKEA.

These companies deal in physical goods.

- *Institutional markets.* Companies in this category include charities, libraries, hospitals, educational establishments, etc.

- *Government markets.* This category includes both local and national government.

These organizations are generally involved with the handling of services.

This distinction into organizational type is important: it may affect the characteristics of the buying process. For instance, government markets are known for their bureaucratic buying processes – often operating through a series of committees seeking tenders and taking many months.

Various attempts have been made to model the organizational buying decision process – see Figure IV.6:

(i) *Recognize Problem.* This is the stimulus for the purchase of a new product or service. It can come from inside the organization such as when an existing piece of equipment breaks down or supplies run out, or from outside, perhaps as a result of technological advances.

(ii) *Establish Product Specification to Solve Problem.* Here the organization must decide exactly what attributes it is looking for from the products/services or supplier sought. The length of time taken to do this will depend on whether the item is a routine re-buy, modified re-buy or new buy.

(iii) *Search for Products and Suppliers.* Buyers may choose to patronize existing suppliers or search for new suppliers by referring to information from trade shows, journals, databases, web pages and personal contacts.

(iv) *Evaluate Products Relative to Specifications.* Supplier offerings are compared with the specification drawn up and comparisons made.

(v) *Select and Order Most Appropriate Product.* This may follow on naturally from the evaluation of products relative to specifications, but on occasions further information is required before a decision can be made.

(vi) *Evaluate Product and Supplier Performance.* An important stage of the process: it will impact on the decisions which are made in the future.

As with consumer buying, there is a range of factors which impact on decision-making and the buying process:

- *Environmental.* Laws, regulations, economic conditions, competitive forces, technological change and social forces. For example, EU regulations have a strong effect on how the process takes place.

- *Organizational.* Including company objectives – which may be short- or long-term, purchasing policies – such as 'Buy non-GM modified ingredients', resources and the structure of the buying centre.

- *Interpersonal.* Anyone involved in buying for an organization understands the power of relationships, conflict and co-operation which can impact – for better or worse – on the decisions made.

- *Individual.* As with consumer buying, individual factors such as age, education level and job status of those managers involved will have an impact on the choices which are made.

| **Figure IV.6** | *The Organizational Business-to-Business Buying Process* |

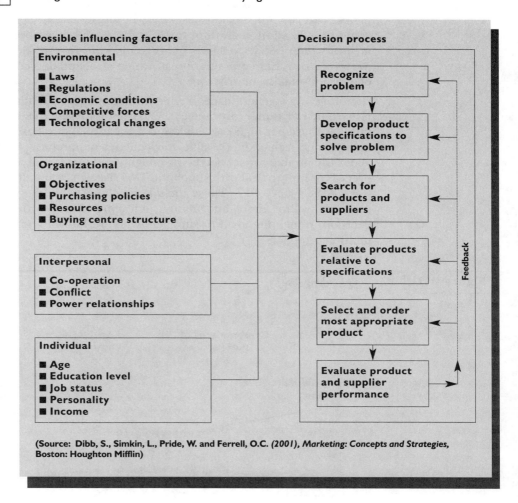

(Source: Dibb, S., Simkin, L., Pride, W. and Ferrell, O.C. (2001), *Marketing: Concepts and Strategies*, Boston: Houghton Mifflin)

Contrasts Between Business-to-Business and Consumer Buyer Behaviour

The marketing concept applies to both consumer and organizational markets: it is an organization's aim to define the needs of target markets and adapt products/services to satisfy those needs in a more effective way than its competition. There are, however, a number of obvious contrasts between consumer buying behaviour and the behaviour exhibited by organizations. These can be shown by highlighting the particular characteristics of organizational buyer behaviour.

■ *Group Activity.* Generally more people are involved in organizational buying behaviour than in consumer buying behaviour. Those involved in buying in an organizational situation are collectively referred to as the *buying centre*.

The roles within the buying centre include those of buyers, users, influencers, technologists, gatekeepers, policy makers and deciders. The number of people carrying out these roles varies by organization, and also within the same organization according to the type of purchase being made. Other factors which impact on how many people are involved in buying include perceived risk, time pressure, organization size, and degree of centralization of decision-making or ordering.

■ *High Risk.* As a general rule, buying for organizations tends to be more high risk than consumer purchase. This is not to say that some consumer purchases are not high risk. Risk in organizational purchases can come from high product value, the possible consequence of purchase, lack of knowledge about the product or service being bought, and uncertainty about the buying process or how to deal with suppliers. This risk can be handled in a number of ways – see Figure IV.7. These include involving other people in the buying process, seeking more information, engaging in trial orders, deferring the decision, remaining loyal to suppliers who are known and trusted, or using multiple suppliers.

Figure IV.7	*Ways of Handling Risk*

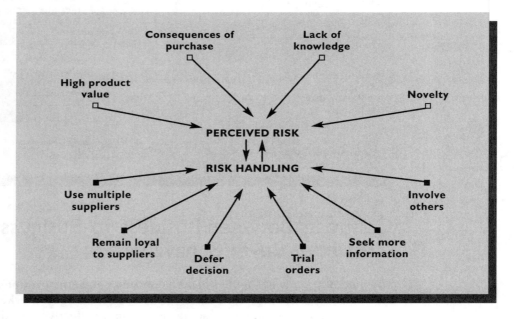

■ *Fewer and Larger Buyers.* FMCG – fast moving consumer goods – companies tend to aim their products at large markets. By contrast many companies in organizational markets are reliant on relatively few customers. This has two impacts: (a) there is a tendency for long-term relationships to be developed, which reduce risk while building trust, mutual adaptation, time saving and the definition of clear roles and tasks; (b) there is more use of personal selling – face-to-face contact – especially in high-risk situations. Figure IV.8

illustrates the exchange which takes place in personal contact between buying and selling organisations. The length of time taken to swap information, products, finance and to interact socially will be dependent on the nature of purchase.

- *Formal Buying Process.* In organizations, buyers are often restricted by certain company rules or procedures and have a fairly limited say in the purchase which is made. Some organizations are particularly bureaucratic. Generally, there is extensive use of formal quotes, tenders and negotiation in business-to-business purchases.

- *Nature of Demand.* Demand in organizational markets is *derived* from demand for products or services in consumer markets. This means it tends to fluctuate according to the level of demand for consumer goods. For example, the demand for car components is affected by the demand for cars. A characteristic of derived demand is that it also leads to elastic demand in organizational markets, because a reduction in the price of components or raw materials is unlikely to lead to a radical change in primary demand.

- *Geographic Concentration of Buyers.* There is a tendency for concentration of certain industries to occur in different areas. For example, in the UK, shipbuilding was concentrated in the North East while the textile industry grew up around Manchester; information technology (IT) is now centred on the M4 corridor.

| **Figure IV.8** | *Personal Contact and Buyer/Seller Exchange* |

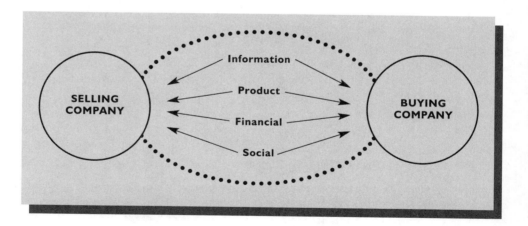

Useful References

Assael, H. (1998) *Consumer Behaviour and Marketing Action*, Boston. Kent. Not light bed-time reading, but very thorough.

Engel, J.F., Blackwell, R.D. and Miniard, P.W. (1997) *Consumer Behaviour,* Fort Worth: West. For generations of qualitative marketing researchers, this text has been the guiding light.

Ford, D. (1997) *Understanding Business Markets*, London: Academic Press. For many, the mainstay of UK business-to-business buyer behaviour texts.

Ford, D., Hakansson, H. and Turnbull, P. (1998) *Managing Business Relationships*, Chichester: Wiley. A slightly unusual perspective: relationship marketing meets buyer behaviour in organizational markets.

Foxall, G., Goldsmith, R.E. and Brown, S. (1998) *Consumer Psychology for Marketing*, London: Thomson Learning. Very much psychology to the fore, an intriguing addition to the UK-authored buyer behaviour literature.

Hutt, M.D. and Speh, T.W. (1998) *Business Marketing Management: Strategic View of Industrial and Organisational Markets*, Fort Worth: Dryden Press. As Engel, Blackwell and Miniard are to consumer buyer behaviour tutors, Hutt and Speh are in organizational markets.

Lambkin, M., Foxall, G.R., Van Raaij, F. and Heilbrunn, B. (eds) (1998) *European Perspectives on Consumer Behaviour*, London: Pearson. Claimed to be the definitive collection of European readings regarding consumer buying behaviour.

Peter, J.P. and Olson, J.C. (1998) *Consumer Behaviour and Marketing Strategy*, Homewood, Illinois: Irwin. Well explained, simple and nicely laid out, similar coverage to Assael or Engel *et al*.

Powers, T.L. (1991) *Modern Business Marketing*, St Paul, Minnesota: West. This book addresses more than just business-to-business buying behaviour and for those interested in organizational markets, should be core reading.

Theory Note 4: Marketing Research

Definition

A formalised means of obtaining and collecting information to be used to make sound marketing decisions.

(Tull and Hawkins 1990)

From the basic definition of marketing, it is clear marketers must understand their customers (see T3) – their characteristics, needs, preferences, product choices, behaviour. In addition, in order to develop strategies and implement marketing programmes, marketers must know about market trends and the forces of the marketing environment (see T2), competition (T2, T7) and company capabilities (T14). Long-serving managers when handling non-risky, routine decisions may base their thinking on their previous experiences or intuition. Where there is less pre-existing knowledge or the issue is more far reaching – such as the launch of a new product, creation of a new brand name or advertising campaign, entry into a new target market or marketing channel – it is highly likely marketers will turn to marketing research to provide sufficient information for astute decision-making.

Marketing Intelligence, Marketing Research and the MIS

Students should be aware of three inter-related key terms:

- *Marketing research.* The collection of data/information, often in an *ad hoc* fashion, to solve specific problems. In other words, a situation arises where the marketing department feels uncomfortable at making a decision with the available marketing intelligence/understanding, and instigates the collection of additional information with the purpose of assisting in the specific decision-making in question. All businesses conduct marketing research at some point in time, whether it is a survey of customer satisfaction, testing out a new product concept or reviewing managers' perceptions of an operational problem.

- *Marketing intelligence.* All of the data and ideas available within a system, such as a company or marketing department. This may be formally documented or computerized, or held informally as ideas or experiences in the heads of key managers.

■ *Marketing information systems (MIS).* Framework for managing and accessing internal and external data. The Marketing Information System – known as the MIS – can be as simple as a directive from a board of directors to each of its key departments to share information. At the other extreme and more usually, it could be in the form of an IT solution using state of the art data processing, retrieval, transmission technology. Both marketing intelligence and marketing research form the key elements of a marketing information system (see Figure IV.9).

| **Figure IV.9** | *Marketing Research and Marketing Intelligence in the MIS* |

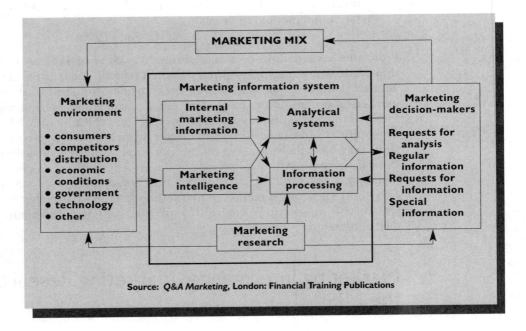

Source: *Q&A Marketing*, London: Financial Training Publications

Research and Intuition in Marketing Decision-Making

If every decision made by a marketer were to be based purely on formal marketing research, very few decisions would ever be made quickly enough to be of any use. Marketing by its very nature is in a dynamic, ever-changing environment. On a daily basis, marketers have to make decisions about changes in product attributes, pricing, promotional activity, distribution, sales support, competitive activity and customer attitudes. Usually, such decisions are made using any information to hand plus the general experience/intuition of the managers in question. Where the risk of making the wrong decision is large and there may be severe ramifications for the company's well-being (and the marketer's job!) marketing research will often form the basis for a more rigorous appraisal and decision-making process.

Marketing research is by nature more formally planned than judgements based on intuition, with clear goals and research methodology. Marketing research tends to be used to confirm hypotheses or to carry out systematic surveys and classifications. Intuition, on the other hand, is preference-based, depending on managers' personal feelings and experience. Such intuitive decisions can be shown to have been correct or wrong within a very short space of time. By demonstration, if experience is shown to be inadequate, the marketer can simply change his/her mind. Therefore, intuition is useful for addressing more minor problems that need to be solved quickly. A marketer's experience and awareness of some of the more obvious practical consequences can often be sufficient. More thought-provoking, risky, new or complex issues are addressed through marketing research, combined with the decision-maker's experience.

The Marketing Research Process

Figure IV.10 shows the five stages of the marketing research process. Understanding and respecting these stages helps foster a much more systematic and reliable approach to tackling marketing research.

Figure IV.10	*The Five Stages of the Marketing Research Process*

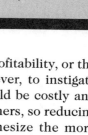

➤ **Define and locate problems to be researched**
➤ **Develop research hypotheses**
➤ **Collect relevant data**
➤ **Analyse and interpret research findings**
➤ **Report research findings**

The overall problem may be a sudden drop in market share or profitability, or the impending launch of a competitor's innovative product. However, to instigate marketing research on such a vague, widely defined, basis would be costly and wasteful of resources. In order to focus the efforts of the researchers, so reducing time and budgets, it is necessary for the marketer to hypothesize the more specific aspects which need to be examined. For example, is the product simply obsolete or is it over-priced, or is the competitor's new channel of distribution superior? It is important to consider the final two steps in the process before embarking on the third step, actually collecting the data. A great deal of time and money are wasted when data are collected without a thorough understanding of how they will be stored, analysed and interpreted. Costly recoding and convoluted statistical analyses can easily result. Similarly, it is important to know how a particular programme of research will be reported and to whom, so that the level of information can be fine-tuned to suit the understanding of the target audience – marketing colleagues, board of directors or distributors.

Data Collection

Marketing researchers work with *quantitative* or *qualitative data*. Research findings which can be analysed and expressed numerically are quantitative. Information based on value judgements that is difficult to quantify is qualitative. Generally, qualitative data are used to produce hypotheses or test-out managerial judgements, while more extensive quantitative data collection is used to verify understanding and confirm proposed actions. Data collection techniques fall into two categories: *primary data* collection and *secondary data* collection. Despite its name, primary data collection should not be the initial concern. Secondary data – 'second-hand' information – is, as the name suggests, already in existence. It is therefore readily available, probably at little or no cost. However, it will also, by default, be out-of-date and will not directly address all of the issues currently to be researched. It is possible that when coupled with managerial instinct and experience, secondary sources will provide adequate insights for the decision-makers. The increasing availability of marketing information on the Internet is assisting marketers in this respect. If secondary sources are insufficient, primary data collection – the collection of bespoke/customised information to tackle the specific issue at hand – will be necessary to address the gaps in understanding in a bespoke manner.

Secondary data

There are two types of secondary information:

- *Internal Sources.* This is information already available within the organization or company, such as accounting records, marketing information, R&D reports, sales force returns, previous marketing research findings or consultants' reports, etc.
- *External Sources.* These can be census information, EU or DTI libraries, embassies, press and periodicals, trade reports, web site information, investment broker reports, etc.

Primary data collection

There are two key types of primary data collection:

- *Observation.* Personal or Mechanical. For example, supermarket managers watching the behaviour of queues, patterns of trolley pushing and manipulating store layout accordingly, or video cameras in fast-food restaurants monitoring customer behaviour.
- *Surveys.* Mail/Postal, Telephone, Personal or Internet. For most marketing researchers, these surveys are at the heart of their activity.

Primary Data Collection Surveying

Mail surveys

The two key advantages of mail surveys are their economy and lack of interviewer bias. Potentially, the lowest cost per response. Costs include typing, photo-copying/printing and postage. Because there is no face-to-face contact, there can be no bias from the interviewer to the respondent. However, there are significant deficiencies with the technique. It is a particularly inflexible research tool. The questionnaire must be short, easy for respondents to complete, with no probing questions to cause offence/non-response. In addition, there is often a long lead-time in terms of mailing out, following up, and receiving responses. Respondent rates can be quite disappointing. Obtaining up-to-date mailing lists is notoriously difficult, even from the professional mailing houses, and many questionnaires end up in the waste bin. Researchers work on the basis that 25 per cent of addresses on a mailing list become obsolete every 12 months. A response rate in consumer marketing of 30 per cent is believed to be very favourable, but typically in business-to-business situations response rates can be as low as 1–2 per cent. A great deal of research has been undertaken to find out whether or not response rates can be improved by adding incentives such as a 50p piece for coffee from a vending machine, a free pen, or whether coloured paper may improve response rates. The additional cost incurred in amending the questionnaire along these lines has not been deemed worthy of their further consideration. However, in certain situations incentives such as prize draws – bottles of champagne/whisky, holidays – have been seen to significantly improve response rates. Personalizing the questionnaire is also known to significantly improve the chances of gaining a response: it is important to find out the name of the person to whom the ques-tionnaire should be sent rather than just the job function title. If in doubt, the 'Managing Director' should be the choice: questionnaires sent to a 'junior' will rarely be passed upwards to a more senior member of staff. Mail questionnaires are often utilized in quantitative studies.

Telephone surveys

These avoid interviewers' travel expenses, but – typically because outside agencies often need to be sub-contracted – are more expensive than postal ques-tionnaires. Telephone surveys are more flexible than mail shots because interviewers can ask certain probing questions and can build some rapport, thus encouraging respondents to answer. However, because most research agencies pay their telephonists on a piece rate, telephonists are often reluctant to extend interviews with unnecessary explanation and discussion. There is some anonymity, but it may be hard for interviewers to develop trust over the phone with respondents, particularly with the growing use of teleselling. With the increasing ownership of telephones, sample bias is less of a problem than in the past. Telephone interviewing is very popular, particularly in large-scale quanti-tative studies. Touch screen technology and light pens for the interviewers, instant data trapping and analysis, the turn-around of findings in only a few days or even hours, plus the growing professionalism of the leading call-centre research houses, have assisted in this technique's popularity amongst marketers. For business-to-business marketing research there is a significant problem in terms of gatekeeping: if the target for the telephone interviewer is a senior manager, it is highly likely that the call will not get past the secretary. Nevertheless, busy managers are more prone to answer questions posed in telephone surveys than they are in face-to-face interviews. *Internet surveys* are in many ways an extension of this approach, with most businesses' web sites now attempting to capture customer views. Until web addresses are as easily available as commercial lists to researchers, the tool cannot replicate the hypothesis-led surveys common in telephone-based marketing research. Telephone and Internet surveys are often utilized in quantitative studies.

Personal interviews

There are four types of personal interviews:

- *In-home interview*. Extremely detailed, good response rates, paid for, honest answers as respondents are on home territory, but very expensive and time consuming. Once very popular, but now replaced by the following face-to-face personal interview activities. More likely to be used in qualitative than quantitative studies.

- *Quali-depth interviews*. A relatively new innovation, whereby 25-minute interviews are conducted in hired halls/meeting rooms, for example close to the high street, for a minimal incentive. Available time restricts coverage, but face-to-face contact permits more complex issues to be examined than by mail or telephone, plus stimulus materials – product, packaging, advertising – can be shown to respondents. Utilized in both qualitative and quantitative studies.

- *Shopping mall intercept*. The researcher with the clipboard on the street corner or outside the shop's exit. Three or four minutes' worth of questions, with some chance to build rapport, explain questions, follow up answers, but relatively limited scope to get a detailed understanding of the issues. Identifying the 'correct' survey target respondent is a problem. Can be used in qualitative studies, but more commonly are utilised in quantitative studies.

- *The focus group*. These are 1½-hour – or occasionally 2½-hour – discussion groups, typically with eight respondents, generally one sex, held in a hotel room, studio, or relevant retail outlet. Such discussions, led by a moderator from a marketing research agency, tend to start with a general free-flow discussion, before focusing on the product, market, brand or advertising concept in question (hence the term focus). Focus groups are one of the most useful and commonly used marketing research techniques, particularly where it is necessary to probe at length to really 'get under the skin' of a problem. The most popular form of qualitative research.

Of all the survey techniques, personal interview surveys are the most expensive, and of the personal interviews, in-home interviewing is the most costly because of the interviewer's time, with an average of one interview per evening. Face-to-face interviewing is the most flexible technique in that respondents can react to visual material, researchers can assist in filling out questionnaires, follow up responses, and interrogate in more detail. There is the potential advantage of the interviewer building up a rapport with respondents. The personal attributes of the interviewers may, though, bias respondents' answers and responses.

Respondents' co-operation is not generally a problem, particularly as for certain types of in-home interviewing and focus group interviewing there is usually a cash incentive. For shopping mall intercepts, many people may refuse to participate, but generally interviewers are in busy thorough-fares and there are many potential target consumers to approach. Because the numbers of respondents are generally much lower in the survey design than for telephone or mail surveys, sampling is a potential pitfall and must be carefully orchestrated. For example, in the marketing research industry it is a widely held belief that eight focus groups well structured around the country, mixing different social classes, can represent the whole of the country's population: the opinions of 64 people may form the basis for a product launch or promotional strategy. It should be remembered, however, that all too often important marketing decisions are made by managers who have not talked to their targeted customers and who themselves do not purchase the product being marketed. In such cases, the views of just a few interviewees or focus groups would be very useful.

Sampling

There are three types of *probability* sampling:

i.   *Random.* Everyone in the population has an equal chance of being included in the sample.
ii. *Stratified.* Each separate group identified in the population gets proportionate representation in the sample.
iii. *Area.* Typically geographic units; sampling of people or units in the specified area.

The main type of *judgemental* sampling is *quota.* Based on specified criteria, typically age, sex, education, race – simple demographics, interview targets are pre-selected by interviewers, typically based on appearance. For example, a researcher may be told to interview 50 ladies aged between 40 and 55, all of whom are from 'a good background'. The interviewer cannot ask his/her targets their age/social status, but must make a judgement based on the person's appearance and manner. There is significant room for error in this approach, particularly as often such researchers are part-time, sub-contractors paid on piece rates, and the sooner their quota is met the sooner they can go home!

Marketing Research Pre-Requisites

Marketing research must match key criteria:

- *Reliability.* Were the research to be repeated with a similar sample frame and survey design soon after the original survey, the results should be similar.
- *Validity.* The survey findings must be in line with the research problems and hypotheses.
- *Robustness.* The research programme and statistical analysis techniques should not crash through poor design.
- *Communication.* The research findings must be capable of communication to the client and client audiences.

Worth Remembering

- Information is always needed in marketing, but circumstances may mean formal marketing research is not possible or completely necessary.
- It is often possible to reach a compromise between intuition and formal research.
- Secondary sources of information should be scanned prior to conducting primary research.
- There is a sliding scale of accuracy in survey techniques from face-to-face interviewing, through telephone interviewing, to mail surveys.
- In most marketing situations a mix of research techniques is used in the research programme, rather than just one approach.
- Despite the emphasis in textbooks on consumer marketing, marketing research is not just orientated to consumer research. Trade marketing research – particularly examining competitors, distributors, customer service initiatives, or new product development ideas – is very important.
- It is important to have a clear brief for any researcher which addresses the marketer's problem and relates to the proposed hypotheses.
- Any selected marketing research technique should be tested out before large surveys are rolled out.

Useful References

Birn, R. (1999) *The Effective Use of Market Research,* London: Kogan Page. A nice, down-to-earth introduction to marketing research.

Chisnall, P.M. (1997) *Marketing Research,* Maidenhead: McGraw-Hill. Of the UK texts, probably the most impressive and certainly very thorough.

McQuarrie, E.F. (1996) *The Market Research Toolbox: a Concise Guide for Beginners*, London: Sage. The title is self-explanatory: a welcome addition to the bookshelf.

Parasuraman, A. (1991) *Marketing Research,* Reading, Massachusetts: Addison-Wesley. One of the most authoritative US texts.

Tull, D.S. and Hawkins, D.I. (1990) *Marketing Research,* New York: Macmillan. The old favourite of several generations of marketing lecturers.

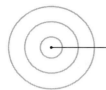

Theory Note 5: Forecasting

Forecasting in Marketing

In marketing, forecasts of sales, market size and market share are required to enable marketers to:

- estimate market attractiveness;
- monitor performance;
- allocate resources effectively;
- gear up production to meet demand;
- plan stocks – excess stocks cost money/use resources; too low production leads to missed sales/customer and distributor unease.

Forecasting Models

The following types of models are available to marketers seeking to achieve a better understanding of market size and share.

- Product Class Sales Model (or Industry Sales Model)
  This type estimates the total number of units of a product category purchased by the population of all spending units.
- Brand Sales Model
  Here, the total number of units is estimated of a particular brand bought by the population of all spending units.
- Market Share Model
  This model assesses the relative number of units of a particular brand purchased by the total population; i.e. relative to the total number of units of the product class.

Methods of Forecasting

Other than astrology and the occult, there are basically three categories of forecasting for sales/marketing issues:

- Judgemental
- Time series and projection
- Causal.

Judgemental

SALES FORCE COMPOSITE

This is simply where sales representatives/field managers are asked to estimate their sales. The overall forecast is then arrived at by summing up their forecasts.

Advantages:

- Widely used.
- Relatively accurate over the short-term (one or two quarters).
- Inexpensive.
- Gives customer-by-customer records of expected sales per field representative in business-to-business industrial markets. This is particularly useful for monitoring and evaluating the sales force.

Problems:

- It is difficult to motivate sales representatives/field managers to take the time to be conscientious in forecasting.
- Individual pessimistic/optimistic biases come to the fore.
- Group/company biases are not ruled out. It is therefore necessary to make allowances for biases.

The sales force/field managers tend to be highly aware of changes in likely customer purchases in the short-term – the next few months – but often are unaware of broad economic trends or movements which are likely to affect customers' industries or clients. Therefore, this judgemental technique is weak in the longer-term and in identifying turning points in underlying market trends.

EXPERT CONSENSUS

This is a jury of experts who offer opinions. Experts include marketers, marketing researchers, company executives, consultants, trade association officials, trade journal editors, and in some cases government agency officials. This is a very widely used technique. There are basically three types of expert consensus: point forecasts, interval forecasts, probability distribution forecasts.

- *Point.* Sales forecasts are for a specific amount of sales (i.e. an absolute amount with no room for mistakes or margin of error). Taken in isolation, particular point forecasts – for example, a group of managers stating categorically that in one specific territory sales of a particular product will be 80,000 units over the next three months – can be prone to bias and error. It is therefore better to have several points forecast by different groups of managers and to aggregate their predictions.
- *Interval forecasts.* This is where a particular measure of confidence in the forecast is given. In other words, the managers above could be 80 per cent confident that 80,000 units will be sold in the three-month period.
- *Probability forecasts.* In this case, different forecasts for the same product in the same market are given with percentage accuracies attached. For example,

the managers above could be 80 per cent confident that sales of 80,000 units could be achieved, only 50 per cent confident that sales of 100,000 could be achieved, and only 10 per cent confident that 110,000 units could be achieved. This option allows the 'best' and 'most pessimistic' forecasts to be clearly identified.

The problem with using a jury of expert opinion is that there is a need to 'weight' the value of each expert's forecast. There are four methods for *weighting*:

i   Use of equal weights – the simple averaging of all experts' forecasts, giving each expert equal prominence.

ii Assigning weights proportional to an assessment of each expert's level of expertise/knowledge/common sense.

iii Assigning weights proportional to a self-assessment of expertise – allowing each expert to give a measure of his/her expertise.

iv Use weights proportional to the relative accuracy of past forecasts – i.e. looking at how accurate each expert's forecasts have been in the past and making allowances for the new forecasts accordingly.

There is no evidence that any one of these four methods of weighting is better than the others.

DELPHI

This is a commonly used approach and one recommended by many marketing researchers and consultants. The simple steps are as follows:

i   Participants – e.g. field managers – make separate, individual forecasts.

ii Central analyst – e.g. at head office – independently aggregates these forecasts.

iii A revised forecast is returned to each separate participant in the field.

iv Participants then make revised forecasts in the context of the new 'picture'.

v   The analyst at head office then centrally pulls the forecast together to produce the final overall forecast.

The Delphi technique avoids the weighting problems discussed above. The median of the group's overall response will tend to move towards a truer answer. This technique is useful for short-, medium- and long-term forecasts, and also for new product developments where there is no historical information on which to base a forecast.

Time series models

Time series models involve a set of observations being evaluated to identify trends. In many cases this involves the use of simple graphs. For example, sales in units against time: typically then, sales per month or per quarter or per year over a particular period of time. The assumption is that past patterns/changes can be used to predict the future. Figure IV.11 gives an example of a time series graph.

It is important to identify the underlying trend, *standardised* for cyclical, seasonal and random variation (statistical noise). It is therefore common to use data which have been averaged-out over time.

| **Figure IV.11** | *Example of a Time Series Graph* |

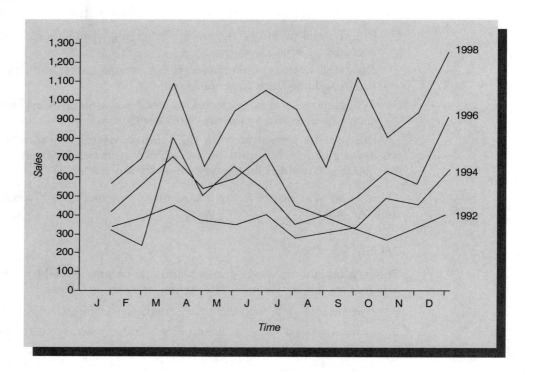

This approach is characterized by a reliance on the last period's sales as a basis for forecasts for the next period's sales. It is only useful if the underlying trend of sales is flat rather than at a particular peak or trough (in which case, a particularly good or bad period of sales would be used to forecast the next period's sales, even though the underlying trend may show that there is in reality no relationship between the two neighbouring periods). Typical use is for forecasting monthly or quarterly sales. There are several approaches:

MOVING AVERAGES

This is where the *average* of the values for the last X periods is taken into account and updated – 'moved' – each period. In other words, were sales figures available for eight periods, the newest sales figures would be added to make nine periods in total. The average would be then taken for the most recent eight periods, dropping the initial period (period number 1). Typically, eight periods – 'the recent past' – are used.

> **'Sales for the next period would be equal to the average sales
> for the average last X [say eight] periods'**

Forecasts generated using this method would probably need adjusting by a seasonal index figure. For example, around –5 per cent for a known trough, or around +8 per cent for a known high point in the seasonal pattern. It is important to remember that this is a forecast suitable for predicting only one sales period in advance – one month or one quarter. Its main use, therefore, is for inventory control.

EXPONENTIAL SMOOTHING

This method uses a 'weighted' moving average. The more recent the period, the heavier the weight given. In other words, the more recent the period, the greater the importance regarding the prediction. This assumes that more recent sales are a better indication of future sales. This approach tends to be computer based, using complicated algorithms and statistical packages. There are various derivatives of this technique, such as *Double Exponential Smoothing*, *Adaptive Smoothing*, *Winter's Extended Exponential Smoothing*.

STATISTICAL TREND ANALYSIS

This is the determination of the underlying trend or pattern of growth, stability or decline in a series of data. It is typically based on simple regression analysis of *Time* versus *Sales*. The approach is oriented towards statistical computer packages, although some graphics and spreadsheet packages can also undertake this task.

BOX-JENKINS

Major economic cycles are inherent in sales patterns. With such cycles, most of the above techniques have been proved to be unhelpful – they do not pick up the cycles. There is a need, therefore, for a *Box-Jenkins* routine: a specially designed statistical routine requiring computer support. A major drawback is that there needs to be a minimum of 45 sales periods of information, although the routine can consider underlying cycles inherent in trends.

It is important to remember that:

- Clearly, there is a need to have managers' knowledge of expected market changes in any forecasting.
- Before choosing a particular forecasting technique, it is important first to examine a plot of sales data and to visually 'eyeball' the *pattern/trends* before deciding how far back in the data set to proceed and which technique to use.
- Typically, it is better to use a combination of forecasting techniques and to aggregate the various forecasts to come up with one overall prediction of sales.

Causal forecasting

These forecasting approaches look at changes in sales due to fluctuations in one or more market variables – such as competitor activity, price, etc. – other than simply time.

BAROMETRIC

This method relies on changes in one variable predicting a rise or fall in another. For example, marketers of baby food may argue that sales depend on levels of births. In construction, sales of backhoe diggers depend on the number of housing starts. Therefore it is important to attain data on sectors/industries relevant to a particular product's sales, and correlate this information with product sales. The problem is mainly one of false messages and of using several different indicators at once. Still, this is a useful technique for helping to explain some of the trends and patterns, or even helping to validate predictions resulting from some of the above *time series* or *judgemental* techniques.

BUYER INTENTIONS – SURVEYS

Here, surveys obtained through marketing research of buyer intentions are used. If these surveys are undertaken at regular points in time, a plot can be made of the customer survey expectations of purchase intent against real sales occurring during similar periods. Over time, through graphs and simple correlation, the overall pattern can be identified and therefore the value/error of the predictions made from marketing research surveys can be quantified. These surveys can then be used on a regular basis knowing the expected margin of error to put on the claim for customer expectations of purchases. In other words, the evaluation of past surveys' results against real sales, gives a weighting to future surveys' findings and their accuracy.

CAUSAL REGRESSION

This is the most widely used causal model of forecasting. A multivariable regression equation relates sales to various predictor variables such as disposable income, price relative to competitors, levels of advertising, numbers of products on the market, etc.

The Multiple Regression Process:

i.   Identify the *dependent variable*, which is what is to be predicted, such as sales.

ii. Identify – through discussions with management, previous research studies, etc. – the relevant predictor *independent variables*.

iii. Collect *time series* or *cross-sectional* data. Time series data give the same information collected for various points in time: an historical record/trend. Cross-sectional data give a snapshot in time: a 'one-off hit'.

iv. Identify whether the relationship between sales and predictor variables is *linear* (a straight line), or *curvilinear* (with various peaks and troughs).

v.   Use regression on a standard computer package such as SPSS or Minitab to attain the *coefficients* (each individual independent variable's weighting or relative impact) and percentage of accuracy. In other words, each of the predictor variables such as disposable income, price, etc., will have a different impact on sales and until all of the relevant predictor/independent variables have been identified there will not be a high percentage level of accuracy for predictions (known as the R^2). In other words, if key market characteristics which determine sales are omitted, the level of accuracy will be low.

vi. Repeat steps i to iv adding in additional predictor variables until the overall R^2 – the level of predictive ability usually measured as a percentage – is 'good' (say, over 70 per cent).

ECONOMETRIC MODELS

These models apply mathematical analogues and equations using multivariate statistical techniques similar to regression but which are somewhat more complicated, such as AID, factor analysis, etc.

Which Technique?

Overall, experts believe that the *causal* techniques are more effective than the *judgemental*. Within the judgemental category, no one technique has been proved to be better than the others, although the *Delphi* technique is extremely popular and widely used. Within the causal approaches, it is again hard to prove that one technique is better than others. The *barometric* approach and *buyer intention survey* are both widely used and can be extremely useful in explaining/describing forecasts made using the more statistical techniques or *time series graphs*. Of the statistical techniques, *causal regression* – taking into account many marketing variables – has been shown to be a very useful technique.

The overall conclusion is that it is better to use a mixture of forecasting techniques rather than just one. The *Delphi* technique is an extremely useful one to consider, supported in the first place by simple *time series graphs* and the *moving averages* approach. In order to explain some of these trends, it is useful then to look at the *barometric* approach – specifically looking at how sales of products compare with customers' sales; for example, housing starts if supplying construction equipment. Often owing to resources, in the slightly longer-term it is a beneficial exercise to develop a simple *multiple regression* model which once developed will typically run on a very straightforward spreadsheet such as Lotus 123.

Useful References

Diamantopoulos, A. and Schlegelmilch, B.B. (1997) *Taking The Fear Out of Data Analysis*, London: Thomson Learning. Marketers discover quantitative methods!

Harvard Business Review (1991) *Accurate Business Forecasting,* Boston: Harvard Business Review Paperbacks. A good summary of suitable techniques.

Hooley, G.J. and Hussey, M.K. (1994) *Quantitative Methods in Marketing*, London: Thomson Learning. A selection of articles examining key quantitative methods and their use in marketing.

Lilien, G.L. and Kotler, P. (1983) *Marketing Decision Making*, New York: Harper and Row. A modelling-based view of marketing decisions.

Naert, P. and Leeflang, P. (1978) *Building Implementable Marketing Models*, Leiden: Martinus Nijhoff. For the more numerate marketer! Dated, but a superb guide. This text has been revised as *Building Models For Marketing Decisions*, by Leeflang, S.H., Wittink, D.R., Wedel, M. and Naert, P., published by Kluwer in 2000.

Tull, D.S. and Hawkins, D.I. (1990) *Marketing Research*, New York: Macmillan. Covers the basic forecasting techniques with typical thoroughness and clarity.

Theory Note 6: Market Segmentation

Definitions

Market segmentation is the act of grouping customers in markets with some heterogeneity into smaller, more similar or homogeneous segments.

Targeting is the task of prioritizing on which segment or segments a business is to focus its sales and marketing activities.

Positioning is the process of creating an image and identity for a product or service in the minds of targeted customers.

In marketing, the market segmentation process involves these three activities: the sub-division of a market's customers into separate market segments, the identification of which segment(s) should be targeted, and the determination of a positioning for the product or service in the targeted segments.

Segmentation

High-growth companies succeed by identifying and meeting the needs of certain kinds of customer – not all customers – for special kinds of products and service – not all products or all services. Business academics call this market segmentation. Entrepreneurs call it common sense.

(Clifford and Cavanagh 1985)

Customers have different product needs and wants yet it is usually unrealistic for companies to customize their products for each individual. However, if organizations only offer one, mass-market-type product, they are unlikely to adequately satisfy many customers' needs. For this reason companies are increasingly moving towards a target marketing strategy where the focus is on a particular group, or groups, of customers. This identification of target customer groups is *market segmentation*. In a room of 20 students, each individual may well aspire to a model of car not cited by the others. It would be difficult, though for a car manufacturer to provide 20 different products. Out of the 20 students, 5 may aspire to an expensive, status symbol, two-door sports coupé, while 6 others desire a more functional 4x4 off-roader. These sub-groups are worth targeting and may be the basis for segments.

Market segmentation allows companies to go some of the way towards satisfying the diversity of needs while maintaining certain scale economics. Customers are aggregated into groups with similar requirements and buying characteristics.

The business decides which group or groups to target with its sales and marketing activity. The *marketing mix* (see T8–T11) is constructed around the specific requirements of the targeted group(s) or segment(s) of customers. The product or service is then positioned directly only at the targeted consumers. This positioning takes into consideration customer attitudes and the offerings of competing organizations within the same segment.

The segmentation process

The market segmentation process consists of three distinct stages, as illustrated in Figure IV.12:

Figure IV.12 | *Market Segmentation Process*

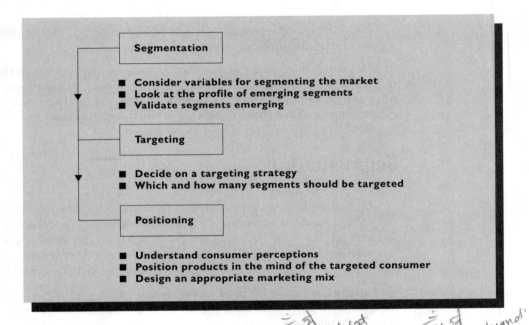

The benefits of a market segmentation approach to companies are many:

- Better understanding of customer needs and wants. This can result in a more carefully tuned and effective marketing mix programme being devised. This should improve customer satisfaction and even loyalty to a brand.

- Improved understanding of the competitive situation. Such additional insights can help companies develop and maintain a differential advantage or competitive edge over competing products and brands.

- More effective resource allocation. To target 100 per cent of a market is not usually realistic. Focusing on certain segments allows organizations to make the best of their resources.

Conducting segmentation

There are two fundamental steps:

i. Segmentation variables – also called *base variables* – are used to divide markets up into groups of customers with *similar product needs*. Many different segmentation bases can be used (see Figure IV.13 for those often used in consumer segmentation), but the key is to select bases which effectively distinguish between different product requirements.

In industrial or business-to-business markets, the list of potential base variables includes:

- *Personal characteristics of the buyers.* Demographics, personality and lifestyles of those in the buying centre (see T3). → वही A Buying behaviour
- *Situational factors.* Urgency of purchase or size of order.
- *Purchasing approach.* Buying centre structure, buying policies, balance of power amongst decision-makers.
- *Operating variables.* The technologies applied or the manner in which products are used.
- *Company demographics.* Company age, location, industry, sector (SIC code), size, competitive set, etc., will alter product and purchasing requirements.

ii. Once segments have been identified using one or a combination of these base variables, as much as possible must be done to understand the characteristics of the customers in those segments. This understanding will make it easier for the marketer to design a marketing mix programme which will appeal to the segment targeted. Building up a fuller picture of the segments is called *profiling* and uses *descriptor variables*. Descriptors can include variables relating to customer characteristics or product-related behavioural variables. In fact, the more extensive the picture, the better.

Uses of effective segmentation

Shrewd market segmentation can help companies to take advantage of marketing opportunities which might otherwise be missed:

i. *Market penetration:* increasing percentage of sales in present markets by taking sales from competitors.

ii. *Product development:* offering newer, improved products to current markets, through the expansion of the product range.

iii. *Market development:* selling existing products to new markets by finding new applications.

iv. *Diversification:* moving into new markets by offering new products.

In addition to these strategic options, developed by Ansoff, market segmentation should lead to:

- Increased customer satisfaction owing to the more astute and bespoke segment-specific marketing mix.

■ Prudent use of resources to target priority segments with well-honed marketing mix programmes.

Figure IV.13 | *Base Variables for Segmenting Consumer Markets*

BASIC CUSTOMER CHARACTERISTICS

Because of the ease with which information concerning basic customer characteristics can be obtained and measured, the use of these variables is widespread.

DEMOGRAPHICS

Age/Sex/Family/Race/Religion
The family life-cycle concept is an imaginative way of combining demographic variables.

SOCIO-ECONOMICS

Income/Occupation/Education/Social class
Different income groups have different aspirations in terms of cars, housing, education, etc.

GEOGRAPHIC LOCATION

Country/Region/Type of urban area (conurbation/village)/Type of housing (affluent suburbs/inner city)

PERSONALITY, MOTIVES AND LIFESTYLE

Holiday companies often use lifestyle to segment the market: young singles or tours catering especially for senior citizens or centres for young families.

PRODUCT-RELATED BEHAVIOURAL CHARACTERISTICS

PURCHASE BEHAVIOUR

Customers for tinned foods, like baked beans, may be highly brand loyal to Heinz or HP or may shop purely on the basis of price.

PURCHASE OCCASION

A motorist making an emergency purchase of a replacement tyre, while on a trip far from home, is less likely to haggle about price than the customer who has a chance to 'shop around'.

BENEFITS SOUGHT

When customers buy toothpaste they seek different benefits: fresh breath and taste, or for others fluoride protection is the key.

CONSUMPTION BEHAVIOUR AND USER STATUS

Examining consumption patterns can indicate where companies should be concentrating their efforts. Light or non-users are often neglected. The important question to ask is why consumption in these groups is low.

ATTITUDE TO PRODUCT

Different customers have different perceptions and preferences of products offered. Car manufacturers from Skoda to Porsche are in the business of designing cars to match customer preferences, changing perceptions as necessary.

(Source: Dibb, S., Simkin, L., Pride, W. and Ferrell, O.C. (2001) Marketing: Concepts and Strategies, Boston: Houghton Mifflin)

Essential qualities for effective segments

Whatever choices are made it is essential that segments which are to be implemented satisfy a number of key criteria:

- *Measurable.* The segments must be able to be delimited and measured/ assessed for market potential.

- *Substantial.* In order to warrant marketing activity, the identified segment must be large enough to be viable and therefore worthwhile targeting with products/services.

- *Accessible.* Having identified a market segment, and checking on its potential viability, the marketer must be able to action a marketing programme with a finely developed marketing mix aimed at targeted consumers. Occasionally, although there are sufficient consumer similarities for consumers to have been grouped together in an identified market segment, the similarities are not sufficient to enable a marketer to implement full marketing programmes.

- *Stable.* There must be an assessment of a segment's short-, medium-, and long-term viability, particularly in the light of competition and marketing environmental changes (see T2). Introducing a segmentation scheme is time-consuming and costly, requiring changes to the sales force and distribution, so the scheme must be robust in at least the medium-term.

- *Useful.* The segmentation scheme developed must bring clear benefits and lead to a better relationship with targeted customers and prudent use of sales and marketing resources.

Targeting

Once segments have been identified decisions about how many and which customer groups to target must be made. The options include:

- *Mass marketing strategy.* Offering one product/retail concept to most of the market, across many market segments. Although scale economies can be achieved, there is the risk that few customers will be adequately satisfied.

- *Single segment strategy.* Concentrating on a single segment with one product/ retail concept. This is relatively cheap in resources, but there is a risk of putting 'all eggs in the one basket' – if the segment fails the company's financial strength will rapidly decline.

- *Multi-segment strategy.* Targeting a different product/retail concept at each of a number of segments. Although common, this approach can spread the risk of being over-committed in one area, it can be extremely resource hungry.

No business, even the huge US corporations like Ford or General Motors, targets every segment in a marketplace. Which target segment strategy a company adopts will be dependent on their attractiveness, which is affected by a wide range of market, product and competitive factors. Each of these must be carefully considered before a decision is made about segments to be targeted:

i. Company's existing market share and market homogeneity – a company's knowledge of an existing market.

ii. Product homogeneity – a company's expertise, on which to build, in an existing product field.

iii. Likelihood of production and marketing scale economies.

iv. Level of competition.

v. Capability and ease of matching customer needs.

vi. Segment attractiveness in terms of size and structure.

vii. Available company resources.

viii. Anticipated profitability and market share

Positioning

■ *Product Positioning.* The decisions and activities directed towards creating and maintaining a company's intended product concept in customers' minds. The creation of a product's perceived image.

■ *Brand Positioning.* Creating a clear and distinctive image for the brand.

■ *Market Positioning.* Arranging for a product or brand to occupy a clear, distinctive and desirable place – relative to competing products or brands – in the minds of targeted customers.

Positioning relates to the attributes normally ascribed to a product or brand by the consumer: its standing, quality, type of people using it, strengths and weaknesses, any unusual or memorable characteristics, price, value and intended use or function.

The product must be perceived by the selected target customers to have a distinct image, *vis-à-vis* competitors. This image must be in line with their own desires/expectations. The whole of the marketing mix is important in developing an effective positioning. This is because the product and customer service attributes must be consistent with the targeted customers' expectations and needs, as must the associated price points and channels of distribution. However, promotional activity is central to establishing an effective positioning as it is through the promotional mix (see T11) that the positioning is communicated to the target audience.

[handwritten note: Marketing Mix Base]

Determining a positioning plan

There are a number of steps involved in determining a positioning plan:

i. Define the segments in a particular market.

ii. Decide which segment or segments to target.

iii. Understand what the target consumers expect and believe to be most important when deciding on a purchase (see T3).

iv. Develop a product or retail brand which caters specifically for these needs and expectations (see T8).

v. Evaluate the positioning and images, as perceived by the target customers, of competing products/retail concepts in the selected market segment or segments.

vi. With the understanding achieved in steps ii. to iv. (knowledge of a product/ brand, the needs and expectations of target customers, their perception of competing brands' positioning), select an image that sets the product or brand apart from the competing brands. Ensure the chosen image matches the aspirations of the target customers. The selected positioning and imagery must be credible and have longevity.

| **Figure IV.14** | *A Perceptual Map for the UK Furniture Industry* |

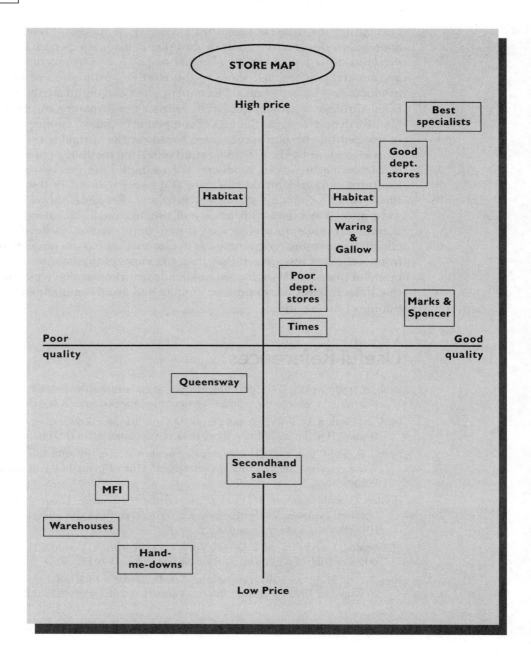

vii. Communicate with the targeted consumers about the product using the promotional element of the marketing mix as well as making the product readily available at the right price and place. This necessitates the associated development of the full marketing mix. The ingredients of the marketing mix must all reflect the desired positioning image.

Perceptual maps

Perceptual mapping is based on a variety of mathematical and subjective approaches designed to place or describe consumers' perceptions of brands or products on one or a series of 'spatial maps'. It is a means of visually depicting consumers' perceptions, showing the relative positionings of different brands, products or even companies. The core product and brand attributes must be identified through consumer research. Further confirmatory research should then identify the relative positionings of competing brands or companies. These should be plotted on the perceptual map, based on the variables (attributes) deemed most important by the consumers and reflecting their views of the relative merits of competing brands or products. For example, the perceptual map of the UK furniture market depicted in Figure IV.14, as produced in the late 1980s, identified 'value for money' as the key attribute. Research showed that consumers were most concerned with price and product quality. Understanding the positioning of brands on such a spatial map helps marketers develop realistic and effective marketing programmes. It is essential such perceptual maps are derived from consumer research, rather than the views of marketers responsible for the brand in question. Marketers should endeavour to develop a positioning strategy that differentiates their brand or product and avoids emulating the existing positioning of a competitor.

Useful References

Dibb, S. and Simkin, L. (1996) *The Market Segmentation Workbook*, London: Thomson Learning. A 'how to do' market segmentation process aimed at marketing managers.

Dibb, S., Simkin, L., Pride, W. and Ferrell, O.C. (2001) *Marketing: Concepts and Strategies,* Boston: Houghton Mifflin. A more in-depth explanation of this chapter's content.

Frank, R. and Wind, Y. (1971) *Market Segmentation,* Englewood Cliffs N.J.: Prentice-Hall. Where market segmentation first began! Out of print but still available in many libraries.

Hooley, G. and Saunders, J. (1993), *Competitive Positioning: The Key to Market Success*, London: Pearson. While emphasizing warfare strategies in competitive analysis, this UK text also examines positioning.

McDonald, M. and Dunbar, I. (1995) *Market Segmentation*, London: Macmillan. Similar in ethos to Dibb and Simkin's *Market Segmentation Workbook*.

Ries, A. and Trout, J. (1981) *Positioning: The Battle for Your Mind,* New York: McGraw-Hill. Reissued in 1993 by Warner Books. A superb examination of brand positioning.

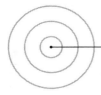

Theory Note 7:   Competitive Strategy

Definition

> Competitors are generally viewed by a business as those companies that market products similar to, or substitutable for, its products when aimed at the same target market.

Competing products, services and brands are those which a targeted customer could select as an alternative to a business's own product or service. As discussed in T2, companies are not always very good at monitoring their competitive environment. In addition to understanding the nature of the competitive threat posed, marketers must develop marketing strategies which strive to effectively combat rivals' marketing mixes and target market strategies. Competitive strategy is a core ingredient of marketing.

A Competitor Orientation

Decisions about marketing strategy must take into consideration the competitive situation in which companies operate. It is often argued that success is dependent upon becoming 'competitor oriented'. Understanding competitors' relative strengths and weaknesses, market shares and positionings is essential. Taken in conjunction with an appreciation of key customer needs, companies should have an indication where to position their product offerings, now and in the future. In addition to planning its own marketing activity, a business should be aware of its rivals' activities, current strategies, likely future proposals and even how key competitors will react to its own proposed marketing mix programmes. David Aaker proposed a set of questions marketers should be able to address when examining competitors – Figure IV.15.

Various approaches have been proposed for analysing the competitive environment. One of the most widely quoted is that of Michael Porter. Other competitive strategy experts discuss competitiveness in terms of warfare strategies – offensive and defensive – based on military analogies.

Porter's Competitive Strategy

The competitive arena

Porter believes the competitive arena to consist of competing organizations 'jockeying for position' in an environment determined by a number of outside forces – see Figure IV.16.

| Figure IV.15 | *Aaker's Competitive Issues* |

- ■ **WHO**
  - – **'Usual' rivals, but also those less intense yet still serious, and makers of substitute products?**
  - – **Categorization of rivals in terms of assets, skills, strategies, level of activity / threat?**
  - – **Any new entrants? Barriers to entry? Possibility of strengthening these barriers?**
- ■ **EVALUATION**
  - – **Their strategies? Their level of commitment?**
  - – **Successes / failures over time? Track record?**
  - – **Their strengths / weaknesses? Assets / skills?**
  - – **Their leverage points over this business? Any strategic weaknesses, customer problems, unmet needs which rivals could exploit?**

| Figure IV.16 | *Industry Forces in the Competitive Arena* |

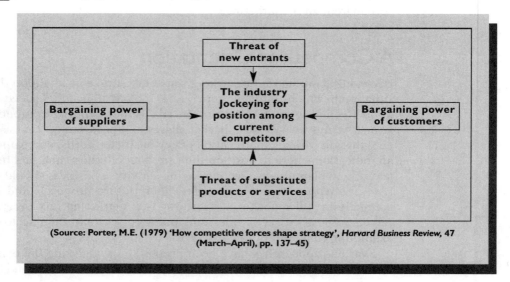

(Source: Porter, M.E. (1979) 'How competitive forces shape strategy', *Harvard Business Review*, 47 (March–April), pp. 137–45)

- ■ *Bargaining Power of Suppliers.* The impact of the supplier depends on the availability of alternative suppliers and product substitutes. In monopoly situations the bargaining power of the supplier is particularly high. This can result in high prices and inflexible, poor quality, product offerings. At the other extreme, in industries with many suppliers and much substitution, there is often relatively low bargaining power for supplying companies.
- ■ *Bargaining Power of Buyers.* High buyer bargaining power usually occurs in industries where suppliers' power is low. Where buyers purchase large

volumes of standardized items which can readily be sourced elsewhere if necessary. Often these items form only a part of the final product.

■ *Threat of Substitute Products or Services.* A proliferation of substitute products within an industry can significantly limit the growth potential and long-term profits. Competing companies have less control over price and can even face problems of over-capacity.

■ *Threat of New Entrants.* New entrants in a market lead to increased capacity which can limit the market share or profits of existing competitors. The likely impact of new entrants is determined in part by the barriers to entry which prevail. Typical barriers to entry include the presence of strongly branded competitors, economies of scale, control of distribution and high capital requirements. In markets where barriers are high, the number of new entrants will be limited.

The generic strategies

Porter identified three *generic competitive strategies* which, he claims, can result in success for companies competing for position in any particular market. These are *cost leadership, differentiation* and *focus* (see Figure IV.17). The dangers of trying to adopt a mix of these strategies can result in companies becoming 'stuck in the middle', with no real competitive advantage.

| **Figure IV.17** | *Porter's Generic Strategies* |

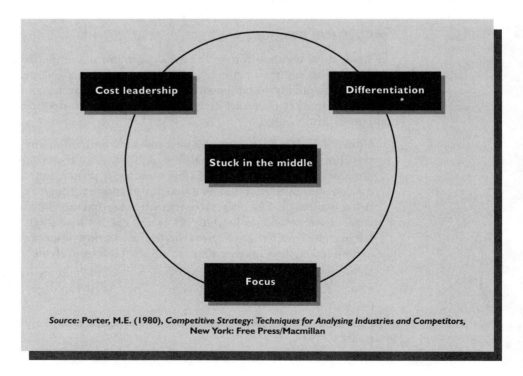

Source: Porter, M.E. (1980), *Competitive Strategy: Techniques for Analysing Industries and Competitors,* New York: Free Press/Macmillan

- *Cost Leadership.* Involves developing a low cost base, often through economies of scale associated with high market share, to give high contribution. This can then be used to further develop the low cost base. Very tight cost controls are essential to the success of this strategy.

- *Differentiation.* Companies adopting a differentiation strategy strive to offer a product/marketing effort which has a distinct advantage or is different to that offered by competitors. Differentiation can be achieved on a number of fronts: creative and innovative product or brand design are possibilities, as are novel distribution channel, pricing and customer service policies.

- *Focus.* Focused companies must maintain close links with the market so that product and marketing effort can be designed with a particular target group in mind. Often of small size, unable to achieve cost leadership or maintain significant differentiation, such companies succeed by effectively meeting customer needs which may be being missed by larger players in the market. Many such players are niching.

It is not generally possible to follow all three generic strategies simultaneously, but it is common for businesses to gain cost leadership while also differentiating their proposition – Direct Line in the insurance market, for example. While it is also possible to seek a focused and differentiated approach, such as Porsche. Failure to follow any of the three will result in the lack of competitive advantage and probable commercial disaster.

Warfare Strategies

Competitive positions

The analysis of competition and the development of competitive strategies have been linked to military principles. Under this scenario, competing companies represent the enemy to be defeated. The principles are based upon the concept that in any market there are five different types of *competitive position* which companies can occupy:

- *Market Leader.* This is the highest market share company which retains its position either (a) by trying to expand the total market (market development), perhaps by finding new uses for a product, or (b) by increasing market share (market penetration), for example through an aggressive advertising campaign. The aggressive measures are balanced by a desire to protect current market share. In many ways, the market leader has the most difficult job in that it has to help to grow the overall market, improve its own share and defend its existing market share against attack from rivals.

- *Market Challenger.* One or more non-market leaders which aggressively attack for additional market share. They seek rapid growth and one day perhaps market leadership.

- *Fast Mover.* These are smaller players which are unlikely to remain minor rivals.

■ *Market Follower.* These are low share competitors without the resources/ market position/R&D/commitment to challenge or seriously contend for market leadership.

■ *Market Nicher.* Companies which specialize in terms of market/product/ customers by finding a safe, profitable market segment. As markets mature, increasing competitiveness tends to mean large companies become more interested in such segments which then for a niche-only company are more difficult to retain.

Different marketing strategies are appropriate for companies which occupy the various competitive positions within markets, including aspects of attack and defence.

Strategies for competitive positions

PRINCIPLES OF DEFENSIVE WARFARE

The skill to adopt a defensive position is important if companies are to protect their existing market share. However, defence should not be regarded solely as a negative activity. Strong defence involves striking a balance between waiting to be attacked and parrying that attack. In general, key basic rules apply:

■ Only the market leader should consider adopting a defensive role. Even in these circumstances it is necessary to combine defensive with offensive strategies.

■ Don't sleep behind high walls – they won't be high enough! Companies adopting a myopic view of their market position are readily open to attack from aggressive market challengers.

■ The best defensive strategy is the courage to attack.

■ It is essential that strong competitive moves are blocked.

Adopting a defensive position does not necessarily mean remaining static. Companies should be ready to move and respond to aggressive marketing effort from competitors – see Figure IV.18:

■ *Build walls around strong positions.* This requires companies to fully under- stand their true strengths (for example brand name), and to be proactive in their attempts to retain that strength.

■ *Protect weak areas.* Attention on weak areas can sometimes be diverted by marketing tactics which focus on other aspects of the product/marketing offering.

■ *Be mobile and ready to move.* Companies should be quick to exploit new markets, products and opportunities.

■ *Withdrawal from market/product if absolutely necessary.* It can be sensible to consolidate in areas which are strong, thus focusing resources. Such action should not leave weak areas which might allow competitors access to key markets.

Figure IV.18	*How to Defend*

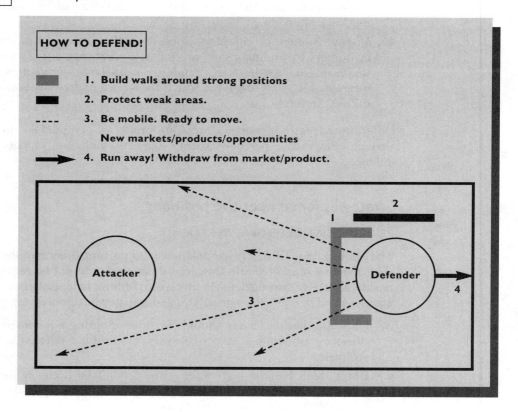

PRINCIPLES OF OFFENSIVE WARFARE

These principles apply particularly to companies in a non-market leading position, which are challenging aggressively for additional market share. It is often regarded as low risk to attack market followers and market nichers rather than the market-leading organization. Key issues include:

- The strength of the leader's position. It is essential to be aware of the dangers of antagonizing the powerful, resource-rich market leader.

- Finding a weakness in the leader's strength and attacking at that point. When a decision is made to attack the leader, this should always be in an area which the challenger feels able to sustain. The decision should consider the challenger's cost structure and resources.

- Launching the attack on as narrow a front as possible. Being focused in challenging ensures that resources are not spread too thinly.

There are several ways in which to attack – see Figure IV.19:

- *Head-to-head.* This full-frontal method of attack is in many ways the most difficult to sustain. The challenger tries to match the market leader blow by blow on some aspect of the marketing programme, for example price or promotional spend. Challengers which attempt this approach often fail!

- *Attack weak points.* A common sense approach, but it requires an understanding of rivals' strengths and weaknesses, plus the development of a more robust marketing proposition than theirs.

- *Adopt a multi-pronged strategy.* It can be appropriate to overwhelm competitors, thus diluting their ability to respond.

- *Guerrilla attack.* This type of challenging is not large scale and prolonged. The intention is to annoy and wound competitors with unpredictable and periodic attacks.

Figure IV.19	*How to Attack*

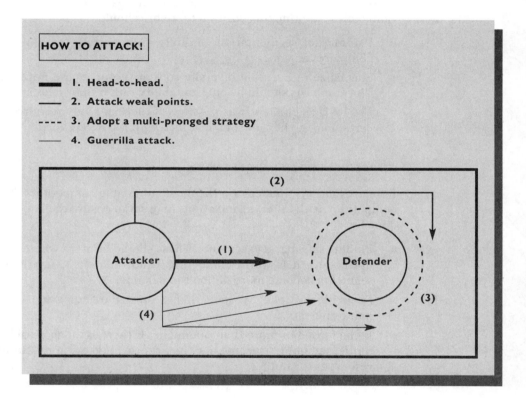

STRATEGIES FOR FAST MOVERS

These are smaller players which are unlikely to remain minor rivals, taking the stance of market followers. Instead, they have every intention of growing in size and importance and must be carefully watched. All too often marketers monitor only like-for-like competitors and the major players in a market, failing to identify rising star fast movers until it is too late to effectively combat them or to knock them out of the market before they become a significant threat. If a business is a fast mover it must:

- Grow at the expense of more minor rivals in the market so as not to antagonize the market leader and aggressive challengers who could turn their guns on the upcoming 'upstart' before it is capable of defending itself.
- Ensure it has a differential advantage and is in tune with its targeted customers, providing a well received proposition.
- Quickly establish distribution channels and a loyal customer base in preparedness for eventual attack.

STRATEGIES FOR MARKET FOLLOWERS

Although there are opportunities for followers in markets, companies occupying these positions are often vulnerable to attack from their larger competitors. Companies adopting this position therefore should:

- Use market segmentation carefully. Concentrate only on areas where the company can cope.
- Specialize rather than diversify so that resources are not spread too thinly. The emphasis should be on profitability rather than sales growth.
- Use R&D as efficiently as possible. If there are only resources to compete in certain areas they must be matched with the R&D effort.

STRATEGIES FOR MARKET NICHERS

In many markets, nichers are the most vulnerable competitors. They must avoid competition with other organizations in order to ensure their success. This can be done by:

- Finding safe market segments. These should be areas where big companies do not believe it is worth competing. Unfortunately, as markets mature, such segments become more difficult to defend.
- Securing a niche by specializing on a particular market, customer or marketing mix.
- Being strong in more than one niche. If there is an aggressive attack on one niche segment, this means that there may be opportunities to switch resources to another.

Applying The Marketing Mix

As they develop their marketing programmes, companies in different competitive positions have at their disposal the full range of the extended (7Ps) marketing mix (see T13):

- Price can be used through discounting or offering other payment methods and terms.
- Product can be varied through product innovation, proliferation or repositioning.

■ Promotion can be used on many fronts. Advertising, sales promotion, personal selling, public relations, sponsorship, direct mail and the Internet are all at the disposal of competing organizations with different requirements, targets and promotional budgets.

■ Distribution can be improved by seeking out innovative ways in which the customer can be reached.

■ People, Process and Physical Evidence, sometimes regarded as the elements of the *services marketing mix* (T13), are an important consideration for companies wishing to improve or differentiate these aspects of their marketing efforts.

Differential Advantage

In developing a marketing mix, marketers should strive to identify and maintain a differential advantage. This goes further than determining a business's strengths. A differential advantage is unique to one brand, product or organization: it is an attribute which is not yet matched by rivals but which is highly desired by the target market's customers. If emphasized in the marketing mix, it should appeal to the targeted customer while providing the business with an edge over its competitors. Inevitably, such an advantage will be short-lived, but it should (a) bring financial rewards in the short-term, (b) improve standing with customers, and (c) make it that much more difficult for rivals to emulate the overall proposition being marketed. In the insurance market, Direct Line's direct selling, telephone-based, discounted service cornered the marketplace and brought rich rewards for its management.

Useful References

Davidson, J.H. (1972) *Offensive Marketing,* New York: Penguin. A superb warning: understand the competition!

Hooley, G. and Saunders, J. (1993) *Competitive Positioning: The Key to Market Success*, London: Pearson. The nuances of warfare and developing competitive strategies.

O'Shaughnessy, J. (1995), *Competitive Marketing: a Strategic Approach*, London: Thomson Learning. Marketing management with a good examination of competitive strategy.

Porter, M.E. (1979) 'How competitive forces shape strategy', *Harvard Business Review,* 47 (March–April), pp. 137–45. Where many marketers first heard about their competitive arena.

Porter, M.E. (1980) *Competitive Strategy: Techniques for Analysing Industries and Competitors*, New York: Free Press/Macmillan. How to become competitive.

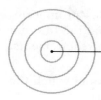

Theory Note 8:   The Marketing Mix: Products and Product Management

Definitions

Product: everything – both favourable and unfavourable – received in an exchange. A product is a complexity of tangible and intangible attributes, including functional, social and psychological utilities or benefits. A product may be a good, a service, or an idea.

Product Management: a form of marketing management where the marketing function and department are orientated around individual products, brands or product portfolios. Product management has a proactive, strategic view of the role of marketing.

The product ingredient of the marketing mix has to be right if customers are to be enticed to buy and ultimately satisfied by their purchase decision. In managing products, marketers undertake several key product management tasks, including:

- branding decisions;
- portfolio management;
- modifying/deleting/developing products;
- product positioning;
- the development of marketing programmes (marketing mixes);
- marketing research/MIS.

The *marketing mix* is the tactical 'toolkit' of product, people, place, price and promotion that a company can control in order to satisfy its customers. Product is a core ingredient of the marketing mix and is at the heart of a company's proposition as offered to the target market.

Products

As one of the basic elements of the marketing mix, product is the foundation stone for a marketing programme. Without first having a product defined it is difficult to develop the rest of the marketing mix. Marketing philosophy would dictate that consumer needs have been adequately identified so that the products are developed in line with such requirements. There are three core categories of products:

■ *Consumer products.* These are products all readers of this book will buy from shops, mail order or via the Internet for their use as consumers:

    ■ *Convenience goods:* products bought quickly, frequently, typically with little shopping around; such as soap powder, cigarettes, newspapers, some food items.

    ■ *Shopping goods:* consumers tend to shop around comparing quality and price; clothing, furniture, electrical appliances.

    ■ *Speciality goods:* usually pre-selected by brand, with consumers searching for suitable outlets stocking the chosen brand; Porsche car, B&O hi-fi, Gucci designer fashions.

    ■ *Unsought goods:* goods about which initially the customer is unaware or for which he/she has not recognized a need – until stimulated by promotional activity: smoke detectors, CD in its early days, life insurance.

■ *Service products.* As discussed under services marketing in T13, service products tend to be more intangible in their make-up, often requiring the active participation of the consumer in the production process. Services include:

Tourism	Professional Services
Catering	Some Retail
Travel	Legal
Healthcare	Maintenance
Sports/Recreational/Leisure	Personnel
Entertainment	Business Consultancy
Education	Media
Financial	Computing Support
Personal Services	Government/Administration
	Non-Profit/Voluntary/Charitable

■ *Industrial products.* These are products purchased by other companies in order to produce their products or services for their customers:

    ■ Raw materials: cotton, crude oil, iron ore, etc.

    ■ Component parts: manufactured materials and parts used as components in subsequently produced products.

    ■ Capital items: installations such as factories, offices, heavy machinery, plant.

    ■ Accessory equipment: PCs, desks.

    ■ Consumable supplies: paint, cleaning fluids, pencils, photocopying paper, inkjet cartridges, etc.

    ■ Services: maintenance, repair, legal or consultancy.

To the customer, there are *three levels of product*:

■ *Core Product.* The level of a product that provides the perceived real core benefit or service.

■ *Actual Product.* A composite of the features and capabilities offered in a product: quality and durability, design and product styling, packaging and brand name.

■   *Augmented Product.* Support aspects of a product, including customer service, warranty, delivery and credit, personnel, installation and after-sales support.

In mature markets, those with many competing products of a similar nature or where the product is viewed as a commodity, marketers are increasingly turning to the augmented product to build customer loyalty and develop a competitive edge over rivals.

Branding Decisions

For nearly all products, there is now a brand – the obvious exception being pharmaceutical generics. Many marketers believe that product differentiation is the name of the game. *Product differentiation* is the use of the marketing mix to differentiate a company's products from its competitors' products, with the hope of establishing the superiority and desirability of its products relative to competing brands. A brand, therefore, is essential to the effective marketing of many products in order to create a unique identity for a particular product. A *brand* is a name, term, symbol, design, or combination of these that identifies a seller's products and differentiates them from competitors' products.

For any product, service or idea there is a need to determine whether or not to have a brand. In most cases, the answer is affirmative and therefore there are key branding decisions for the marketer, discussed below:

The need for brands

The brand should 'say' something about the product and make it more distinctive. Brands make shoppers more efficient: many shoppers go out with specific brands on their 'shopping list', so reducing time spent in distributors/retail outlets. Brands facilitate product differentiation – the real key to marketing.

Types of brands

■   *Manufacturer.* Heinz, Ford, IBM, JCB, Abbey National are manufacturer brands.

■   *Private/own label.* Retailers' own labels, such as St Michael in Marks and Spencer, Saisho in Dixons, No. 7 in Boots, George clothing in Asda; or simply the retailer's name as the branding foundation: Sainsbury's, Tesco, Debenhams own-label products.

■   *Generic:* Currently very few examples as there is little scope for product differentiation, but many pharmaceutical products are not overtly associated with a specific manufacturer, being instead known by their pharmacy description.

Quality

All products have an in-built life-cycle/quality threshold often determined by the R&D researchers. Frequently consumer research is fed by marketers into the development of products and their associated quality levels. Every brand and product has a pre-determined quality.

Family branding

Here there are three choices for a company:

a. *Individual brand names for each separate product.* For example, Procter and Gamble – P&G – separately brands Tide and Bold; Mars separately brands Snickers, Mars Bar, Bounty.

b. *Blanket family name.* Here the company attaches its own name and identity to every product in its portfolio – the Del Monte approach.

c. *The company name combined with individual brand name.* A very popular approach in marketing whereby individual products are given their own identity, but the company name is also attached to create the overall brand name and identity. For example, Kellogg's Rice Krispies or Kellogg's Raisin Splitz; the Ford Focus or Ford Mondeo.

Brand extension and multi-branding

Marketers must decide between *brand extension and multi-branding.* Under *brand extension,* a product is launched and given the identity of an existing product which will also carry on in production. The new product must have similar attributes and psychological values to the existing product. For example, when Fairy Liquid – previously only a washing-up detergent – was chosen to name Procter and Gamble's new attack on Unilever's clothes washing powder Persil, it was deemed that both washing-up detergent and washing powder/liquid were bought by the same member of the household, from the same part of the same type of retail outlet, and used in the same room of the house, the kitchen. Hence, the new washing powder/washing liquid was named Fairy. In retaliation, Unilever launched a washing-up detergent named Persil. For brand extension, it is essential that the attributes of the products in question are similar.

Or, the company can opt for *multi-branding.* Here, every product is given its own identity. For example, most toothpastes, washing powders, cleaning detergents are in fact produced by only a handful of companies. Each company has a host of separate brands and most consumers would not know that they were all produced by only two or three different companies. Similarly, in confectionery and petfood, two or three companies dominate the market. However, these companies go to great lengths to create separate identities for their products, often giving them separate production bases, distribution channels, and marketing teams as well as their own brand identities.

Although there is an element of cannibalization within a company's portfolio with several competing products all vying for consumers' attention, the companies that practise this technique believe that overall it gains them market share and shelf space. If such companies launch a new product they appreciate the product will cut the market shares of their existing brands, but these companies hope to steal shares from competitors' brands so that overall the company has a net gain. In addition to gaining overall shelf space, the companies therefore hope to gain brand loyalty for each separate brand, and perhaps creating in-company competition keeping their management teams on their toes. It also facilitates product differentiation, one of the key bases of modern marketing.

Naming of the product

Some companies have poorly chosen names and make them part of their marketing tactics — 'great unpronounceables of our time' introduces the press advertising for Bunnahabhain, 'unspeakably good malt'. However, most companies wish to be more circumspect in their selection of brand name. The choosing of the brand name is essential to effective marketing, and the name should:

- Say something about the product.
- Be easy to say/reproduce.
- Be distinctive.
- Translate into languages.
- Be suitable for legal protection in home and overseas markets.

However, as the once successful and market leader slimming aid chocolate brand will testify, despite all the careful research and plans of marketing managers, occasionally the broader marketing environment (see T2) plays a role: Aydes was the victim of the increasing awareness of HIV's AIDS.

Packaging/labelling

Packaging and labelling are very much part of the marketing process. Not just the *primary* packaging – the immediate container, but also the secondary packaging – the shipping packaging. The packaging and labelling must reflect the brand image, identity, and intended attributes of the product within.

Customer service

Whether it is after-sales, warranty provisions, ease of communication channels between consumers and customer service personnel, or follow-up tracking consumer attitude research, conscious decisions must be made by the marketing team responsible for a product or brand in terms of the provision of customer service. Too little will alienate customers and leave opportunities open to competitors. The provision of 'too much' customer service will be wasteful for the company's resources. Consumers and business-to-business customers increasingly expect higher levels of customer service.

Product mix decisions

In Europe, Mars – trading in the UK as Pedigree Petfoods – has 8 of the 10 leading petfood brands: Whiskas, Pedigree, Cesar, Sheba, Brekkies, Frolic, Kitekat, Pal.

Most companies have a *portfolio* of products, and whether each product has a separate marketing team or one marketing team is handling the whole portfolio, it is necessary to be aware of the ramifications for the strategy and marketing programme of one product in a company's portfolio on the remaining products.

The product portfolio approach to marketing attempts to manage the *product mix* – the composite of products an organization makes available to consumers – in an attempt to create specific marketing strategies to achieve a balanced mix of products aimed at producing maximum long-run profits. There are various product portfolio management techniques available, the most famous being the BCG Growth-Share Matrix and the Directional Policy Matrix (DPM) or GE Model (see Product Portfolio in the Glossary in Part V). It is important for marketing managers to regularly evaluate the relative strengths and weaknesses of the products in their portfolio. This helps determine which products should receive additional resources, which products to phase out, and on which products to depend for cash generation.

Positioning

One of the key tenets of marketing is effective positioning. As discussed in T6, product positioning results from decision activities directed towards trying to create and maintain the company's intended product concept in customers' minds. It is the creation of a product's perceived image and standing. Branding is often instrumental as the identifier for such imagery/positioning.

The Product Life Cycle (PLC)

Figure IV.20 illustrates the typical stages of the product life cycle: *introduction, growth, maturity* and *decline.* All products and markets pass through such a cycle, although an individual product may be at a different point in the life cycle than the overall market. For example, a company entering late into a market may have its brand or products at the introduction or growth stage, when in fact the overall market is in maturity or even decline.

Industry profits peak ahead of industry sales, as earlier on in the life cycle there tends to be a lower level of competition and higher pricing. As a product moves through these stages, the strategies relating to competition, product development, pricing, promotion, distribution and market information must be evaluated and modified.

Managing The Product Mix

A host of techniques is used to identify products that have good potential/growth/ future sales; those with only relatively little potential; and products for which there are severe problems and no obvious future. These techniques include the Boston Consultancy Group's Growth-Share Matrix and the Directional Policy Matrix. In this context, three of the key facets of product management are:

Figure IV.20	*The Product Life Cycle*

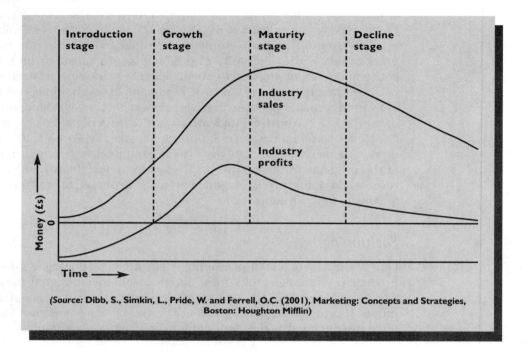

(Source: Dibb, S., Simkin, L., Pride, W. and Ferrell, O.C. (2001), **Marketing: Concepts and Strategies,**
Boston: Houghton Mifflin)

- *Modifying existing products.* Marketing managers frequently become aware through feedback from the salesforce/dealers, or consumer research, that a particular product's sales have declined because it needs updating/revising. With perhaps only relatively minor changes in the quality, function or style aspects of the product, or pricing, there can be a prolonged life and viability for the product.

- *Deleting products.* One of the hardest tasks in marketing is to delete a product. Those blatantly at the end of their life cycle may once have been the star performers in a company and certain executives may harbour desires to see such success re-kindled. For other products, potential has never been reached but executives may believe there is still the chance. All companies and organisations have products in their portfolio that should have been deleted many years previously. There are three options for deleting products:

  - *Phase out*: long-term planning identifies a point in time when a particular product or brand will be deleted and replaced with a new product offer – very common in the car market, for example.

  - *Run out*: a decision is made to curtail production of the product and so cease ordering components and supplies. However, existing stocks will be worked out into finished products to be sold.

  - *Immediate drop*: the performance of a product is particularly catastrophic, often using up scarce resources, with no benefits to the company whatsoever. The decision is made to drop the product immediately, often with associated financial write-offs of inventory and marketing effort, and with the risk of alarming consumers and dealers. However, the financial burden of carrying on producing such a product outweighs the potential pitfalls.

■ *Developing new products.* Marketing depends on identifying consumers' needs and wants. These are forever changing (see T3), with the result that marketers must perpetually update their product portfolios. There are key stages in the development of new products:

i. *Idea Generation.* From marketing research, in-company suggestion boxes, media coverage, managerial brain-storming, competitors' developments, customer complaints, dealer feedback, etc.

ii. *Idea Screening.* Only a small proportion can be investigated further.

iii. *Business Analysis.* Does the proposed product fit with the current product mix?
Is there demand for the new product and will it last?
Will its introduction harm/help the short-term company performance?
Are there future marketing environment/competitive changes which will impact on this product's performance?
Can the company's R&D, engineering, production cope?
If new facilities are needed, how much will they cost and when will they be required?
Is money available for the full product launch?

iv. *Product Development.* Is the product technically feasible?
What marketing mix will be required?

v. *Test Marketing.* The full-scale trial of a product in the marketplace: actually sold through selected distribution channels and supported as an existing product in a portfolio. Typically, in one ITV television region where promotional effort can be constrained and made cost effective, and the merits of the marketing programme/sales can be adequately reviewed.

vi. *Commercialization.* If test marketing is successful, full-scale production is instigated, with a full market launch and the development of a bespoke marketing mix and support programme.

Useful References

Baker, M.J. (1999) *The Marketing Book,* London: Butterworth-Heinemann/CIM. A comprehensive reader, including much on products and product management.

De Chernatony, L. and McDonald, M. (1998) *Creating Powerful Brands*, Oxford: Butterworth-Heinemann. As the title implies, tips on branding!

Dibb, S., Simkin, L., Pride, W. and Ferrell, O.C. (2001) *Marketing: Concepts and Strategies,* Boston: Houghton Mifflin. Several chapters devoted to brands and product management.

Doyle, P. (1998) *Marketing Management and Strategy*, London: Pearson. A superb insight into brand issues.

Macrae, C. (1996) *The Brand Chartering Handbook*, London: Addison-Wesley. Essential reading for those interested in branding.

Rosenau, M.D., Griffin, A., Castellion, G. and Anschuetz, N. (eds) (1996) *The PDMA Handbook of New Product Development*, New York: John Wiley. A useful guide for new product development.

Wind, Y. (1982) *Product Policy: Concepts, Methods and Strategy,* Reading, Massachusetts: Addison-Wesley. The staple text on many marketing lecturers' shelves.

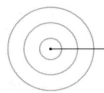

Theory Note 9:　The Marketing Mix: Place – Distribution and Marketing Channels

Definitions

Distribution – the 'place' element in the marketing mix – is the selection of a distribution or marketing channel.

A marketing channel is a channel of distribution, a group of interrelated intermediaries which direct products to consumers.

There are two major types of marketing intermediaries: merchants which take title to merchandise and resell; or agents and brokers, which receive a fee or commission for expediting exchanges. For most products and services – with the exception of some factory and farm shops or those sold directly by some catalogues or e-commerce – intermediaries are used in order to simplify the producers' selling and marketing efforts, and the consumers' purchasing. For example, were 5 producers and 5 buyers in a market, all dealing separately and directly with each other, there would need to be 25 transactions for them all to communicate with each other. If in the same market there was a major middleman or intermediary – such as a wholesaler – there would only have to be 5 channels between the producers (one each) and the wholesaler, and 5 channels between the buyers and the wholesaler (one each), or 10 transactions in total. In most product categories, it is simply not financially viable for suppliers to deal directly with all of their target customers: they require third-party channel intermediaries to help expedite the distribution of their goods and services.

Selecting Distribution Channels

When a company is selecting a distribution channel for a particular product or range of products, it has to take into account:

- its organizational objectives and resources;
- market characteristics;
- consumer behaviour;
- product attributes;
- environmental forces.

In particular, the company has to make a conscious decision regarding the desired *intensity of market coverage.* Here, there are three options:

- *Intensive.* Many outlets with relatively small catchment areas and significant levels of competition. Common for convenience products (see T8).
- *Selective.* For more expensive shopping goods, where the customer base and catchment area must be larger.
- *Exclusive.* Where prestigious products are deliberately restricted in terms of the numbers of distributors, such as Chanel perfume or Riva sports boats, or when a company's resources limit the number of distribution outlets it can support, as in the case of Porsche or Saab cars.

Marketing Channels

Figure IV.21 illustrates the typical, conventional market channel, as well as a vertical marketing system, showing the functions handled at each stage.

| **Figure IV.21** | *Examples of Channels* |

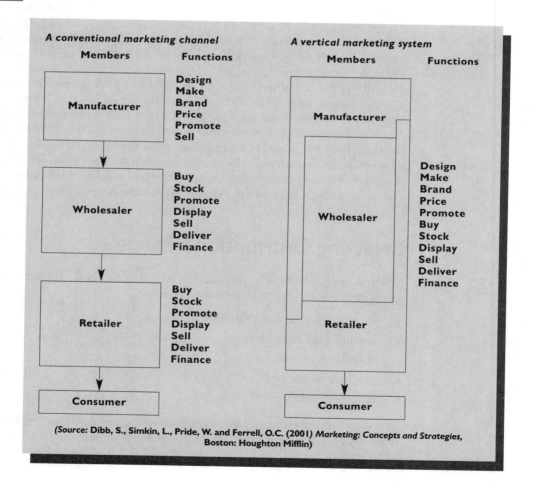

(Source: Dibb, S., Simkin, L., Pride, W. and Ferrell, O.C. (2001) *Marketing: Concepts and Strategies,* Boston: Houghton Mifflin)

There are differences between the channels for industrial/business-to-business goods and consumer products (see Figure IV.22).

| **Figure IV.22** | *Channels for Industrial/Business-to-Business Goods and Consumer Products* |

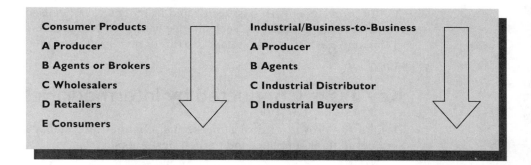

Consumer Products	Industrial/Business-to-Business
A Producer	A Producer
B Agents or Brokers	B Agents
C Wholesalers	C Industrial Distributor
D Retailers	D Industrial Buyers
E Consumers	

Consumers

Not all products pass through such a convoluted distribution channel involving all of these stages, although many items of fashion clothing and certain food items such as biscuits often do. Fruit and vegetables and most other clothing miss out stage B, passing directly from producers to wholesalers. Non-process foods, electricals, DIY goods and furniture typically pass straight from producers to retailers, missing out stages B and C. There are relatively few examples of stages B, C and D being missed but, in farm shops and factory shops, plus some e-commerce, produce and merchandise pass directly from producer to consumer.

Business-to-business/industrial

Exported cars and construction equipment frequently move through all four stages of this marketing channel, with agents shipping vehicles and distributors selling them. Mainframe computer equipment often passes from agents to industrial buyers, with agents required to help sell, display and advise consumers, with there being no need for industrial distributors. Where there is relatively little selling involved, but more repeat ordering, there is often no need for agents – items such as gears, components and parts, passing directly from producers to industrial distributors, missing out step B. For very large plant and equipment, such as turbines, there is no marketing channel as manufacturers deal directly with industrial buyers.

Direct marketing

As described in T12, a current trend is towards direct marketing, where producers and suppliers cut out subsequent channel members and sell directly to the target market. For example, book publishers supply Amazon, which in turn cuts out retail shops by selling directly to its customers over the Internet. Direct marketing involves a decision by a company's marketers to select a marketing channel which avoids dependence on marketing channel intermediaries. Instead marketing communications activity is focused on promotional mix ingredients that directly contact targeted customers. These include direct mail, telemarketing, direct response television advertising, door-to-door/personal selling and the Internet. Its growth has been rapid in recent years, caused largely by home shopping and e-commerce. Such change has provided marketers with a new set of options in selecting a channel for distribution.

Key Tasks Conducted by Intermediaries

Despite the growth of direct marketing, channel intermediaries provide many services to their suppliers and to their customers:

- *Sorting out:* classification of heterogeneous supplies to homogeneous groups.
- *Accumulation*: developing a bank or stock of homogeneous products to provide aggregate inventory/stock.
- *Allocation*: breaking down homogeneous stocks or inventories into smaller units.
- *Sorting*: combining products into collections, assortments or ranges that buyers want.

Classification of Channel Participants

There are two key groups of channel participants: those which actually participate in negotiations within the distribution process and those which simply facilitate the distribution chain.

Facilitating agencies

These are organizations which enable the exchange to take place:

- Transportation
- Storage and warehousing
- Advertising agencies
- Financial and insurance firms
- Trade shows and trade markets
- Marketing research houses

Member participants: contractual organizations

- Producers and manufacturers

■ Intermediaries:

> Retailers
> Wholesalers
> Distributors

■ Final users:

> Organizations/Businesses

Channel Leadership

Two of the key desires in marketing are control and power within marketing channels. Organizations at different levels in a particular channel are to some extent dependent upon co-operation and mutual understanding, but similarly will be vying for channel leadership so as to be able to dictate strategies and policies relating to their products and their product areas.

Determinants of channel leadership include:

■ *Economic sources of power*:

– Control of resources – ownership or indirect control may preclude others becoming active in a market.
– Size of business – the largest players in a market often exert their will over channel members and smaller competitors.

■ *Non-economic sources of power*:

– Reward power — the provision of financial benefits rivals fail to offer.
– Expert power — when other channel members believe the leader provides special expertise required for the channel to function effectively.
– Referent power/opinion leadership — emerges when other channel members emulate the leader.
– Legitimate/genuine leader — a superior-subordinate relationship.
– Coercive power — the leader's ability to punish other channel members.

These elements pull together to determine a particular overall level of power for each organization or player within a marketing channel. The overall position of power for a company or organization in the marketing channel depends on the roles and positions of the other channel members and willingness to lead. A significant change in recent years has been the move to what is popularly referred to as *relationship marketing* (see T1). The priority for most sales and marketing managers used to be on winning 'the order'. While clearly still important, marketers have realized that once won over, a customer should be cajoled into remaining loyal and building up an on-going relationship. In terms of channel 'politics', this has meant much more co-operation than before in many instances. *Partnershipping programmes* often see manufacturers and their immediate channel members sharing marketing intelligence, developing marketing programmes together, seeking mutually beneficial long-term contracts and security of operations.

Useful References

Christopher, M. (1997) *Marketing Logistics*, Oxford: Butterworth-Heinemann. A specialist text examining logistical issues.

Christopher, M. (1998) *Logistics and Supply Chain Management*, London: Pitman. An insightful UK examination of marketing channels.

Dibb, S., Simkin, L., Pride, W. and Ferrell, O.C. (2001) *Marketing: Concepts and Strategies,* Boston: Houghton Mifflin. Several chapters devoted to channels in marketing.

Fernie, J. (ed.) (1990) *Retail Distribution Management: Strategic Guide to Developments and Trends,* London: Kogan Page. An overview of channel options.

Powers, T.L. (1991) *Modern Business Marketing,* St Paul, Minnesota: West. Coverage of all aspects of business-to-business marketing, including the selection of channels.

Rosenbloom, B. (1999) *Marketing Channels: A Management View*, Fort Worth: Dryden. A thorough US examination of marketing channel management.

Shipley, D. (ed.) (1989) 'Industrial distribution channel management', special edition, *European Journal of Marketing* 23 (2) Bradford: MCB. Interesting selection of papers addressing distribution in marketing.

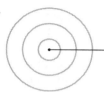

Theory Note 10: The Marketing Mix: Pricing

Definition

Price is a value placed on that which is exchanged (the good, the idea or service).

The Impact of the Competitive Arena

Companies must set prices which are consistent with the competitive situation operating in the particular market. There are several competitive situations:

■ *Pure monopoly*: a single seller only.

■ *Pure competition*: many sellers – and buyers – selling similar goods or services, each with only some influence on demand. Market conditions and market forces set price.

■ *Oligopolistic competition*: few sellers which are highly susceptible to each other's actions. Price fixing often in collusion.

■ *Monopolistic competition*: despite the name given to such a situation, there are many sellers – and buyers – offering different products over a range of prices.

Factors Affecting Pricing Decisions

Companies do not have a completely free hand when determining pricing levels. There is a range of factors which warrant careful consideration before such decisions can be made:

■ *Organizational and marketing objectives*. Prices must be consistent with company objectives. Companies requiring a rapid increase in market share will have different pricing strategies – for example, price cutting – than those requiring very high profitability in the short-term, where margins need to be maintained.

■ *Elements of the marketing mix*. Price levels must not be determined in isolation of other marketing mix elements. Each element must be consistent with the others so that a cohesive mix is developed. A product with an 'up-market' image and promotional campaign requires an appropriately 'high' price rather than a discount price, as well as a select channel of distribution and selling programme!

- *Costs.* Although in the short-term companies may set prices that do not recoup production, distribution and marketing costs, long-term survival depends on the costs being fully met of producing and selling an item.

- *Channel member expectations.* Each player in the marketing channel (see T9) needs to be able to 'mark-up' sufficiently to make adequate profits for their own business fortunes.

- *Competition.* A marketer cannot set prices without knowing competing products' pricing. Target market customers will be aware of rivals' prices and often overtly compare prices and payment terms.

- *Customer perceptions.* Companies must understand the importance which customers place on price. This will vary according to the market and target segment under consideration.

- *Legal and regulatory issues.* National and local governments sometimes impose controls which impact on prices. In addition, consumer legislation exists to protect customers from unreasonable or unfair pricing.

Stages for Establishing Prices

Develop pricing objectives

A variety of both short- and long-run objectives shape the pricing decisions which are made. These include cash flow, survival, profit, RoI (Return on Investment), market share, maintaining status quo and product quality.

Assess target market's ability to purchase and evaluation of price

The sensitivity of different customers to price is variable. Companies must understand whether target markets will tolerate high prices and to what degree these customers will be prepared to 'shop around'. Customer tolerance will relate to income, economic conditions and perception of value.

Determine level of demand and analyse the relationship with cost and profit

Companies need to consider how many of an item will be purchased at different price levels. This involves analysing the elasticity of demand, i.e. the effect of a small price change on numbers purchased – see Figure IV.23. The price elasticity of demand is calculated using the formula:

$$\textbf{Price Elasticity of Demand} = \frac{\% \text{ Change in Number Demanded}}{\% \text{ Change in Price}}$$

For items which have highly inelastic demand, a shift in price leads to a very small change in quantity demanded. For items which have highly inelastic demand, a shift in price leads to a very small change in quantity demanded.

| **Figure IV.23** | *The Elasticity of Demand* |

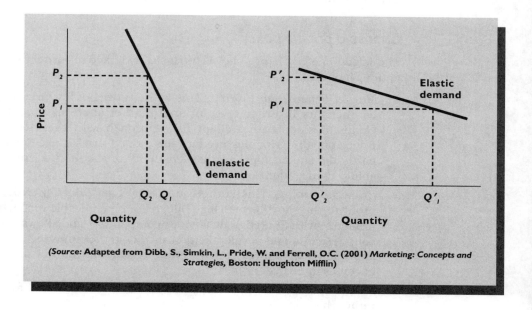

(Source: Adapted from Dibb, S., Simkin, L., Pride, W. and Ferrell, O.C. (2001) Marketing: Concepts and Strategies, Boston: Houghton Mifflin)

Understanding the relationship between profit, revenue and costs is essential if realistic prices are to be set. Calculating total costs determines the minimum price which can be charged to ensure profitability.

P (Profit) = R (Revenue) – C (Total Costs)

TC (Total Costs) = FC (Fixed Costs) + VC (Variable Costs)

Fixed costs are costs which remain constant irrespective of the number of items produced, such as rent and rates. Variable costs, such as raw materials and wages, do change as the number of items produced alters. Usually the variable cost of producing an item is the same for each item.

Marginal cost (MC) is the additional cost a company incurs when one more item is produced.

The point at which total costs are equal to the revenue generated is termed the *break-even point*. Calculating the break-even point at a number of different pricing levels allows a company to understand better the relationship between costs and revenue, and indicates the likely impact of different pricing alternatives.

Break-even points= $\dfrac{FC}{P - VC}$

Evaluate competitive pricing

Understanding how competitors set prices for their products and knowing their prices, helps companies determine the parameters within which price levels should be set. Such understanding also indicates the importance which customers place on price and highlights key direct competitors. This is a particularly important consideration in markets where price competition is common.

Choose a pricing policy

The selection of a pricing policy is intrinsically linked to corporate objectives. The options include:

- *Market Penetration Pricing.* This is the setting of low prices relative to key competitors in order to gain large market share as quickly as possible. Companies sometimes adopt this approach with the intention of raising prices once a particular product has gained market acceptance. Success is partly dependent on the price sensitivity of the market and the company's ability to meet demand.

- *Price Skimming.* This is the use of very high prices in order to maximise profit in the short-term. This policy is only applicable for highly innovative products, with limited or no obvious competitors, and allows companies to recoup research and development costs quickly. Despite the attractions of this approach, companies usually have to exit the market once competition becomes intensive.

- *Psychological Pricing.* Here, price levels are determined for psychological rather than rational reasons. Perceived value pricing is based on what buyers believe the product to be worth. For example, customers would expect the price of a full English breakfast at a five-star deluxe hotel to differ from that at a transport café, although the basic offering may be similar. *Odd-even pricing* involves trying to attract customers using odd number prices. The idea is that more customers will purchase an item priced at £9.99 than at £10.00.

- *Promotional Pricing.* This approach to pricing involves the use of special price levels to increase sales in the short-term. This can involve the use of *special-event pricing*, linked perhaps to a national public holiday. In other circumstances companies, such as retail outlets, use a small number of low-priced items – *price leaders* or *loss leaders* – to attract custom.

Select a pricing method

This refers to the mechanical process through which price is set:

- **Cost-Driven Pricing** (*Cost-plus pricing*): prices are set at a level to allow a certain percentage profit once all costs have been met.

- **Competition-Driven Pricing** (*Going-rate pricing*): prices are fixed after consideration of competitors' pricing levels. Decisions about whether to price above, below or at the same level as competing brands can then be made. In very competitive markets, where one or a small number of companies dominates, there may be a standard or 'going-rate' price.

- **Demand-Driven Pricing** (*Variable pricing*): commonly used in markets where demand is variable over time. This approach allows companies to make extra profits at peak times while ensuring some sales when demand is low. Leisure attractions, such as Madame Tussaud's, commonly adopt such an approach.

Decide on a specific price

The price which is ultimately set will depend on how companies manipulate their overall marketing mixes. This element of the mix – *price* – has more flexibility than other aspects because it can be altered very quickly.

Value

When determining prices, the management discussion should not focus purely on the actual monetary value/price to be set. Payment terms, such as interest free credit or ninety days to pay in some business-to-business markets, also may be of great importance to the targeted customer. Of significant interest should be the customer's perception of value. *Value for money* is the benefit customers perceive to be inherent in a product or service – or its consumption – weighed against the price demanded. This perception of value will be influenced by the customer's previous experiences, product quality, the augmented product (see T8), brand image, purpose, anticipated usage, overall appeal, competing propositions and other demands on disposable income. Marketers are increasingly realizing the importance of value as opposed to raw price in the marketing mix. The decisions marketers take regarding pricing must also reflect their brand positioning strategy, as price and value are strongly linked with brand image (see T6).

Useful References

Diamantopoulos, A. and Mathews, B.P. (1995) *Making Pricing Decisions: a Study of Managerial Practice*, London: Thomson Learning. How to set prices in marketing.

Dibb, S., Simkin, L., Pride, W. and Ferrell, O.C. (2001) *Marketing: Concepts and Strategies,* Boston: Houghton Mifflin. Several chapters devoted to pricing in the marketing mix.

Monroe, B.K. (1990) *Pricing: Making Profitable Decisions,* New York: McGraw-Hill. Essential reading for marketers involved in pricing decisions.

Nagle, T. (1994) *Strategy and Tactics of Pricing*, London: Pearson. Profitable decision-making explored.

Nagle, T. and Holden R.K. (1995) *The Strategy and Tactics of Pricing*, Englewood Cliffs: Pearson. A very thorough exploration of pricing issues in marketing.

Winckler, J. (1983) *Pricing for Results*, Oxford: Butterworth-Heinemann. Dated but thorough in explaining the economics of pricing.

Theory Note 11: The Marketing Mix: Promotion

Definitions

Promotion in the marketing mix is the communication with individuals, groups or organizations in order to facilitate exchanges by informing and persuading the audience to accept the business's products or services.

Communication is a sharing of meaning through the transmission of information.

The Marketing Communications Process

Effective marketing depends on the exchange of goods, services and ideas, and thereby is heavily dependent on effective communications. In marketing, marketing communications is the communication of information which facilitates or expedites the exchange process between supplier and target customer or marketing channel member.

The communications process is instigated by the *source,* which will be the company with the product or service to offer. The source develops a *coded message* – the promotional campaign message – which passes through a chosen *medium* of transmission – such as print, broadcast, personal selling or the Internet – through to the *target audience* or receiver of the message. The target audience will be the key customers in a target market segment. In marketing, the elements of the *promotional mix* are used to facilitate the communications process: advertising, personal selling, PR and publicity, sales promotion, direct mail, sponsorship, and the Internet. As explored in T12, many of these ingredients are utilized in the in-vogue application of *direct marketing*: notably direct mail, the Internet, door-to-door selling and telesales.

In any market there will be a mix of consumers (or business-to-business customers) in terms of *product adoption.* The *innovators* who are the minority of consumers first to take a new product or idea, through the *early adopters,* the *early majority,* the *late majority* and finally to the *laggards.* Promotional activity and communications effort aimed at the innovators and early adapters must explain the nature of the product and create a market, as such consumers will have no previous experience or information of such products. By the time, at the other extreme, the laggards in the market are seeking to make a purchase, overall market size will be quite large and awareness of such products high. When CD players were launched, Sony and Philips spent a great deal of money promoting the generic benefits of CDs over vinyl records and turntables in order to establish a need for the product in the target market's eyes. Now a mature market, the typical promotional activity is very much brand-specific and assumes most consumers know about the product category.

Product Adoption and Promotion

As the level of adoption progresses, promotional tactics will need to change. Consumers must first be *aware* of a product or service, develop an *interest* so as to wish to *evaluate* it against competing product offers, before *trying* the product or service in order to fully *adopt* (purchase) the product in question – see Figure IV.24. An effective promotional campaign cannot be developed without first understanding at which stage(s) the target audience has reached in the product adoption process or which stages the specific promotional execution must address.

| **Figure IV.24** | *The Stages of Product Adoption* |

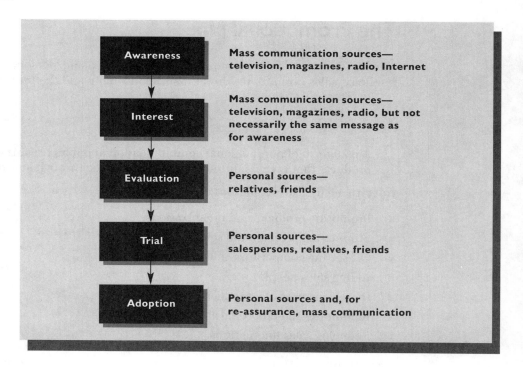

The Five Communications Effects

There are five key communications effects:

- *Category Need.* It is important for targeted customers to understand that there is a market, with products in existence, to meet perhaps previously unrealized customer needs. They must accept they want or need the general product category.

- *Brand Awareness*. Once targeted customers realize there is a need for a particular category of product, marketers must concentrate promotional effort on enforcing specific brand awareness.

- *Brand Attitude*. There will be numerous competing brands on offer, so targeted customers must be made aware of a brand and they must have a favourable attitude to the brand to keep their interest.

- *Brand Purchase Intention*. The favourable attitude to a brand must be stimulated so as to encourage targeted customers to experience the product and consider making a purchase.

- *Purchase Facilitation*. Once brand awareness, brand attitude and purchase intention have been created, the elements of the marketing mix other than promotion play an important role in making the product or service available for purchase/consumption.

The Promotional Mix

The key elements of the promotional mix are advertising, personal selling, PR and publicity, sales promotions, direct mail, sponsorship and the Internet:

Advertising

A paid form of non-personal communication about an organization and/or its products that is transmitted to a target audience through a mass medium.

Advertising uses are numerous:

- Promoting products and organizations.
- Stimulating primary and selective demand.
- Off-setting competitors' advertising.
- Aiding sales people.
- Increasing uses of a product.
- Reminding and enforcing attitudes.
- Reducing sales fluctuations.

Advertising can target a large audience or, by carefully selecting media, a specific group. It is generally the most expensive element in a company's marketing budget, but because it tends to be through mass media and hits a large number of people, it is a relatively low per capita cost. However, actual expenditure in real terms is very high. Feedback is slow and its effectiveness is hard to measure.

An advertising campaign is a series of advertisements, utilizing various media, to reach a particular target audience. There are eight stages in developing an advertising campaign:

i.   Identification of the target audience.

ii.   Definition of clear campaign objectives.

iii. Determination of a distinctive platform or advertising proposition.

iv.   Specification of the advertising budget.

v.   Development of the media plan (which print or broadcast titles, etc.).

vi.   Creativity – the production of the advertising messages.

vii. Execution of the campaign.

viii. Evaluation of advertising effectiveness.

Personal selling

Personal selling is a process of informing customers and persuading them to purchase products through personal communication in an exchange situation.

Personal selling is the passing on of information and persuasion with face-to-face communication, and can be narrowly focused at a few individuals, with immediate feedback. It is expensive – salesforce time, cars and salaries – but significantly more specific and has greater impact than advertising. *Telesales* – sales and marketing over the telephone – has emerged to support face-to-face selling, while reducing the fieldforce cost. Personal selling depends heavily on language:

- Verbal.
- Kinesic – body language.
- Proxemic – distance.
- Tactile – physical contact.

The personal selling process involves key stages:

i.   Prospecting and evaluating.

ii.   Preparation.

iii. Approaching the customer.

iv.   Making the presentation.

v.   Overcoming objections.

vi.   Closing the deal.

vii. Following up.

PR and publicity

Public relations (PR) is the planned and sustained effort to establish and maintain good will and mutual understanding between an organisation and its publics. Publicity is non-personal communication in news story form, regarding an organisation and/or its products, which is transmitted through a mass medium at no charge.

Target publics include customers, employees, shareholders, trade bodies, unions, suppliers, government officials, journalists and society in general.

'No charge' is perhaps a little misleading. For advertising there is an overt charge for column centimetres in the press or seconds of air time on TV or radio. PR releases and material are used in news bulletins and the media with no obvious billing cost. However, there is an associated cost in resources. For example, it may be necessary to use a PR agency or internal PR manager. Sometimes publications using PR material also expect an organization to place its advertisement in the same publication.

Types of publicity:

- Press release: one page, less than 300 words, contact name.
- Feature article: 1,000 words for specific publication.
- Captioned photograph.
- Press conference.
- Editorials.
- Films and tapes.
- In-company publications.
- Interview techniques.
- VIP links.
- Visits/seminars/meetings.
- Third party endorsement/seal of approval.
- Associations with influential groups or personalities.

Uses of PR:

- Awareness of products, brands, activities, personnel.
- Maintain level of positive public visibility.
- Enhance/shift a particular image/perception.
- Overcome negative imagery/publicity.

Golden rules for PR:

- Must be a continuous programme.
- Person/department/agency accountable.
- On-going working relationships with media personnel.
- Well-produced material matching target media's exact requirements.
- Evaluation of PR and publicity efforts.

Good PR does not happen overnight. It is a continuous activity, requiring clear policies, commitment, accountability, the development of long-term links with journalists and the media, and the understanding of targeted media's publication/ broadcast criteria and requirements, plus on-going evaluation of the PR activity.

PR in Crisis Management:

- Identify key targets to receive messages.
- Do not cover up – have a policy ready to implement.
- The company should report facts itself.
- Do not discourage news coverage – give immediate access.

If journalists deem a story newsworthy it will be featured whether or not a company co-operates. It is preferable to be 'in control'; to identify who needs to hear the company's account – specific media, certain customers, distributors, regulatory bodies, etc.; to present selected facts and to 'assist' journalists. In this manner there is far greater opportunity to input into or 'slant' the story, and therefore for 'damage limitation'.

Sales promotion

Activity and/or material inducing sales through added value or incentive for the product to resellers, sales people, or consumers.

Sales promotions on the whole do not grow a market. Instead, they are usually offering an incentive such as a price reduction, free merchandise, give-away or competition entry. As a result, they persuade regular purchasers of the particular brand to simply bring forward their purchase. Sales promotion is a very useful technique for evening-out sales troughs and/or helping short-term cash flow problems.

Types of sales promotion:

- Trade promotion, from manufacturer to distributors.
- Salesforce promotion, from manufacturer to sales force.
- Consumer promotion, from manufacturer to end-user consumers.
- Retail/distributor promotion, from distributors to consumers.

Examples of sales promotion:

- *Consumer*: coupons, free samples, demonstrations, competitions, loyalty cards, frequent-user incentives, trading stamps.
- *Trade:* at wholesalers, retailers and sales people: sales competitions, free merchandise, buy-back allowances, point-of-sale displays, trade shows and conferences.

The UK spends half as much on sales promotions as advertising, and therefore sales promotions are very important marketing activities. The recent growth in loyalty cards such as Tesco's Clubcard and of frequent-user schemes such as Air Miles, has led to a significant rise in the use of sales promotions. Sales promotions are usually instigated to supplement personal selling or advertising and are rarely used in isolation. Because they induce sales, many sales promotions are often irregular in use, aimed at short-term sales increases.

Direct mail

Direct mail is printed advertising material delivered to a prospective customer's or donor's home or work address.

Direct mail to many is known as 'junk mail'. It is a very well used ingredient of the promotional mix for consumer goods and services, but also in business-to-business marketing communications.

Direct mail requires:

- Attention-giving flashes.
- The direct mail package – mailing envelope, explanatory letter, response and return devices.
- Up-to-date and bespoke mailing lists.
- Effective copy writing.

Sponsorship

Sponsorship is the financial or material support for an event, activity, person, organization or product by an unrelated organization or donor. Funds will be made available to the recipient of the sponsorship deal in return for the prominent exposure of the sponsor's name or brands.

Sponsorship is utilized by many businesses to increase brand awareness or improve target audience perceptions. The arts, sports and even television programmes are sponsored. It is essential the target audience has an affinity with the recipient of the sponsorship. Reputable partnerships must be maintained: if the image of sponsor or recipient is tarnished, it will reflect detrimentally on the other.

The Internet

The Internet is a chain of computer networks linking computers to the web sites of commercial businesses, not-for-profit organizations, information providers, public bodies, private individuals and social groups. Increasingly it is used for e-commerce.

Until recently, only computer enthusiasts accessed the Internet for information searches or on-line discussions. The growth of home and office PCs has created a new media opportnuity for businesses communicating with certain target audiences. In turn, this has led to the explosion in *e-commerce*, home shopping and *direct marketing* – see T12.

Selecting a Promotional Mix

There are key considerations that shape the creation of a promotional mix:

- *Companies' objectives*: Is a company wishing to create awareness, educate customers or increase sales?

- *Budget and resources*: Television advertising is more expensive than local press advertising, while both can prove more costly than PR activity. Available resources will strongly direct the choice of which ingredients of the promotional mix to utilize.

- *Type of market*: FMCG/consumer/industrial/service. For example, trade shows and catalogues are commonly used by business-to-business marketers, while consumer goods are more likely to appear in glossy magazine or television advertising.

- *Policy – push or pull*: Under a 'push' policy, each member of the marketing channel promotes to the next member of the marketing channel with the intention of pushing a product or service down through the marketing channel. Under a 'pull' policy, promotion is aimed directly at the end-user of the particular product or service with the intention of the end-user demanding distributors stock the particular product. In most markets, the two policies are not mutually exclusive: using different promotional techniques and campaigns, they are often tackled simultaneously.

- *Nature of the target market*: Market size, geographic spread, demographics all impact on the viability of promotional mix and media choices.

- *Product characteristics*: Industrial/consumer/service; seasonality; price; product life cycle; product use, must all be taken into consideration when selecting the campaign message, media and promotional mix ingredients.

- *Market coverage*: Intensive/selective/exclusive – see T6.

- *Cost and availability of media slots*: Some options inevitably prove to be cost prohibitive, while suitable television slots, press space or print capacity may be booked up when desired.

Useful References

Belch, G. and Belch, M. (1998) *Advertising and Promotion: An Integrated Marketing Communications Perspective*, New York: McGraw-Hill. One of the key US texts.

Douglas, T. (1988) *The Complete Guide to Advertising,* London: Macmillan. Dated but lively and revealing examination of the practicalities of advertising.

Engel, J.F., Warshaw, M.R. and Kinnear, T.C. (1994) *Promotional Strategy: Managing the Marketing Communications Process*, Homewood, IL: Irwin. Very thorough US examination of managing promotion.

FitzGerald, M. and Arnott, D. (2000) *Marketing Communications Classics*, London: Thomson Learning. A super collection of readings on most aspects of marketing communications from most key authors.

Jefkins, F. and Yadin, D. (1998) *Public Relations,* London: Pearson Professional. In the UK, Jefkins has been essential reading for those interested in PR for over two decades.

Kitchen, P.J. (ed.) (1998) *Marketing Communications: Principles and Practice*, London: Thomson Learning. A welcome addition to the bookshelf: very good coverage of all aspects of managing the promotional mix.

Kitchen, P.J. (1997) *Public Relations: Principles and Practice*, London: Thomson Learning. A sound alternative to the work of Jefkins.

Rapp, S. and Collins, T. (1987 and 1999) *MaxiMarketing*, New York: McGraw-Hill. An intriguing deployment of the promotional mix toolkit.

Rossiter, J.R. and Percy, L. (1997) *Advertising, Communications and Promotion Management*, New York: McGraw-Hill. A rigorous examination of advertising and notably sales promotions.

Shimp, T.A. (1997) *Advertising, Promotion and Supplemental Aspects of Integrated Marketing Communications*, Fort Worth: Dryden Press. A core US text on most marketing lecturers' shelves.

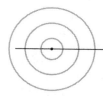

Theory Note 12: Direct Marketing and the Internet

Definitions

Direct marketing is a decision by a company's marketers to select a marketing channel which avoids dependence on marketing channel intermediaries, and to focus marketing communications activity on promotional mix ingredients which contact directly targeted customers.

(Simkin, 2001)

The Internet is a chain of computer networks stretching across the world, linking computers of different types to the web sites of commercial businesses, not-for-profit organisations, public bodies, private individuals and social groups. Increasingly it is used for e-commerce – the use of the Internet for commercial transactions. Intranets are internal, in-company Internet networks for routine communications, fostering group communications, providing uniform computer applications, distributing the latest software, or informing colleagues of marketing developments and new product launches.

(O'Malley, Patterson and Evans, 1999)

Direct Marketing

Direct marketing is one of the current 'hot topics' in marketing. First derived in the 1960s, until recently, the term 'direct marketing' described the most common direct marketing approaches such as direct mail and mail order. Now direct marketing is deemed to include all the communications tools which enable a marketer to deal directly with the targeted customers: direct mail, telemarketing, direct response television advertising, door-to-door/personal selling and the Internet.

Direct marketing is more than part of the promotional mix, however. It involves a decision by marketers to (1) select a marketing channel that does not depend on marketing channel intermediaries such as wholesalers, retailers or distributors, and (2) focus marketing communications activity on promotional mix ingredients which deal directly with targeted customers.

Direct marketing evolved from the mail order industry, typified by businesses such as Littlewoods, GUS, or Grattan, that developed catalogues and mail shots to customers in order to sell direct from their warehouses, avoiding the use of retail outlets and showrooms. They were joined by a diverse mix of businesses, ranging from factory outlets, machine tool companies to specialist food producers, that wished to sell direct. These businesses had to devise promotional mixes which attracted sufficient numbers of the right types of customers to deal directly with them, rather than buying from the more traditional marketing intermediaries in the marketing channel. These traditional intermediaries were then cut out of the distribution channel. Although mail order declined in the 1980s, towards the end of that decade the major operators revitalized their fortunes and were joined by mail order operations from major retailers such as Next with its *Next Directory*. Ubiquitous telephone access has helped facilitate mail order operations and the recent rapid growth in home computer Internet access has provided a further growth spurt.

Direct marketing is now adopted by a host of businesses ranging from fast moving consumer goods companies, business-to-business marketers, charities and even Government departments. Of all elements of the promotional mix, it is reported to be the fastest growing, but this is partly a reflection of the large number of promotional mix ingredients that it includes, such as direct mail, tele-selling and the Internet.

Various factors have contributed to this growth:

i. The desire by marketers to identify alternative media and promotional tools.

ii. The need to improve targeting of potential customers.

iii. Improvements in marketing data and databases.

iv. Advances in technology and systems permitting cost effective direct and interactive contact with certain types of consumers.

For the promotional mix, there are several key implications:

■ Direct mail is on the increase. Of the largest 1500 UK companies 83 per cent expect to deploy more direct mail in the new millennium, with the bulk focusing on prospecting for sales rather than responding to direct response advertising requests for brochures or catalogues.

■ Telemarketing has grown but this will continue as more businesses turn to direct marketing aided by advances in automated call centres.

■ Personal selling has suffered in the past from poorly identified sales targeting, but better geodemographic targeting and improved analysis of direct marketing responses are enabling more focused use of personal selling.

■ Door-to-door selling and leaflet dropping are also on the increase and are visible forms of direct marketing encountered by most householders.

■ In 1989 *direct response advertising* – containing a call for action within the advertisement either by coupon or telephone – accounted for less than a fifth of advertising revenue. The figure is closer to a third now as marketers increasingly utilize direct marketing. This is supported by the growth in satellite and cable television channels which enables more direct response television advertising.

■ The most obvious implication is for use of the Internet to communicate with current and prospective customers. As more and more consumers hook up to the Internet either at home or at work, the opportunity is growing for marketers to communicate directly with consumers with increasingly bespoke messages.

However, as with all marketing propositions and promotional mix executions, to be welcomed by targeted customers and effective in terms of generating sales, the deployment of any direct marketing campaign must strive to reflect targeted customer behaviour, needs and perceptions; provide a plausible proposition which is clearly differentiated from competitors' propositions; and match an organization's corporate goals and trading philosophy. Direct marketing is not a substitute for marketing practice, nor for the traditional promotional mix. Direct marketing is an increasingly popular deployment of marketing. It results from certain marketers' strategic choices about marketing channels and because particular promotional mix tactics are seen as the best ways to contact prospective customers.

The Internet

Not too long ago only computer enthusiasts accessed the Internet on a regular basis, mostly for on-line discussions or to search for information. Although these are still popular activities, the world wide web is now a major focus of attention for marketers of consumer goods, services, charities and industrial products. Companies as diverse as Ford, Sony and JCB provide product and company details on their web pages. These web sites tended initially to be for information purposes rather than overtly for promotional tools or selling opportunities. BMW was one of the first businesses to spot the opportunity for selling on the web, creating a directory of used cars available from its network of independent dealerships. Consumer concern about the security of making purchases on-line, divulging credit card details or bank account numbers held back progress, but investment by the web hosts and credit card companies to instigate scrambling and coding of confidential information has led to massive growth in e-commerce. Tesco and Iceland make grocery shopping available on the net, the National Exhibition Centre sells concert tickets, charities take donations and most brands can be sourced via the Internet.

As more and more households connect to the Internet, confidence in using this medium for transactions is growing. This is not uniform across all consumers. Just as with any new product (see T8), there are innovators, early adopters and the early majority, while others are resistant to this new way of conducting business or simply do not have the equipment, expertise or available resources to hook-up. Research indicates that there are signs that older consumers, the less affluent and less educated are now accessing the web.

As an ingredient in the promotional mix there is no doubt the Internet is of growing importance. While this is not true in all countries, it is a trend expected to continue with the associated rapid growth of e-commerce. Few major brands do not have their own web pages. Most television and press advertisements direct consumers to web addresses for further information or ordering facilities. Packaging for many consumer products signals the presence of a web site.

The Internet enables frequent and customized changes of messages targeted at specific consumers. If linked to e-mail it enables the consumer to have ready access to the site host, providing an on-going and evolving relationship between marketer and customer. Internal in-company marketing has turned to the web, with *intranet* in-company Internet networks facilitating routine and group communications, providing uniform computer applications, and distributing the latest software or information about market developments and new product launches.

There is a clear process for developing a web site:

i.   Planning the site's goals.

ii.   Analysis of the required content.

iii. Designing and building of the site.

iv.   Implementation using hypertext mark-up language (HTML).

v.   Monitoring to ensure that once up and running the site reflects user views and is regularly up-dated.

Far from being a minor task, marketers have realized that web site design is a specialized activity which requires the skills of a qualified *web master* and the careful design of material to reflect the characteristics of the product, the brand and of the intended consumer. To be an effective web site, key characteristics are vital:

- Targeted customers must be prepared and able to access the Internet.

- The site has to contain information that is relevant and interesting for targeted customers.

- The pages of the site need to be stylish, eye-catching, quick to open, while easy to interpret.

- The web site design should be memorable and distinctive.

- Web site branding and imagery must be consistent with the brand positioning of existing products, the product's packaging and other promotional mix executions such as advertising and sales promotion materials.

- The web site's ethos should not contradict the work of the rest of the marketing mix or the product's heritage.

- The information on the web site has to be regularly and accurately up-dated and tailored carefully to reflect the buying behaviour of the targeted customer.

- User feedback should be sought to continually up-date the web site, just as with any other service or product.

Useful References

Adams, N.R., Dogramaci, O., Gangopadhyay, A. and Yesha, Y. (1999) *Electronic Commerce: Technical, Business and Legal Issues*, New Jersey: Pearson. Not the most accessible of reads, but thorough coverage.

December, J. and Randall, N. (1996) *The World Wide Web Unleashed*, Indianapolis: Sams Publishing. The dos and don'ts of building web sites.

Dibb, S., Simkin, L., Pride, W., Ferrell, O.C.(2001) *Marketing Concepts and Strategies,* Boston: Houghton Mifflin.

Evans, M.J., O'Malley L. and Patterson, M. (1996) 'Direct Marketing Communications in the UK: a Study of Growth, Past, Present and Future', *Journal of Marketing Communications*, 2, pp. 51–65. Dated, but a straightforward review of essential steps.

McGoldrick P. (1997) *Retail Marketing*, Maidenhead: McGraw-Hill. This leading retail marketing text contains a good explanation of direct marketing's evolution and role in marketing channels.

O'Malley, L., Patterson, M. and Evans, M. (1999) *Exploring Direct Marketing*, London: Thomson Learning. A thorough explanation of direct marketing and the Internet's role.

Schwartz, E.I. (1997) *Webonomics: Nine Essential Principles for Growing Your Business on the World Wide Web*, New York: Broadway Books. E-commerce explained.

Theory Note 13: The Marketing of Services

Definition

A service is the result of applying human or mechanical efforts to people or objects. Services are intangible products involving a deed, a performance or an effort which cannot be physically possessed.

The marketing of consumer goods, and to some extent industrial goods, is made simpler by the fact that there is a tangible product, be it a tin of Heinz Baked Beans, a Sony Walkman or a JCB backhoe digger. However, for a fast food restaurant what exactly is the product? Is it the burger in a bun, the environment, or the provision of a meal? Is it the service level, friendliness, atmosphere or efficiency with which food is delivered to the consumer? Similarly, for travel, tourism, financial services, legal, sports and recreational, entertainment, personal services, healthcare, education, the public sector and charities, computing advice, business consultancy and media services, personnel and catering, exactly what is the product? For most services, the product is somewhat intangible and therefore more difficult both to brand and to market. Services tend to be an event or a 'happening', which when repeated on another occasion will be different, no matter how slightly.

Classification of Services

There are three broad categories of services:

■ Profit-making services (e.g. financial, tourism, entertainment, catering, personal).

■ Non-profit making services (voluntary organizations, charities).

■ Public services and state utilities (central and local government services, health, and in many countries telecommunications, water and power).

The Importance of Services

GDP % of Services	
Europe	58%
USA	67%
Japan	58%

      Employment in Services

Europe	60%
UK	67%

The reasons for such a major proportion of gross domestic product (GDP) and employment stemming from the service sector are mainly increased affluence and more leisure time, demographic and psychographic factors, and a desire to avoid fixed costs and to delegate tasks to specialists:

- Marginal utility of goods has declined, particularly of food and many consumer durables. After World War II, many now 'basic' goods and services were seen as luxuries. Throughout the 1980s and 1990s, the consumer's desire was for more interesting and leisure-oriented products.

- Smaller families led to more time to fill and greater disposable income.

- More leisure time. Services consume time and are actively sought, particularly in the entertainment/tourism sectors.

- There is a desire for self-fulfilment: experience rather than ownership, therefore people buy-in outside services.

- Increasing affluence has led to mundane activities being contracted out.

- More and more technology has created a need for specialist services to maintain many everyday household and office objects. These are provided by services businesses.

- Political: there is electoral competition to offer better claimed levels of services.

For non-consumer services there are three key reasons why, in business situations, service provision has grown in the economy:

- Specialization: delegation of non-core tasks to external specialists, such as advertising, marketing research, head-hunting.

- Technology: the need for knowledgeable organizations, including consultants, IT advisers, etc.

- Flexibility: the need to avoid fixed overheads. For example, much marketing research expertise is bought-in on an *ad hoc* basis; maintenance, cleaning and catering contracts go to external suppliers.

The Four Characteristics of Services

The marketing of services is quite different in nature and complexity from the marketing of consumer goods or industrial products for four important reasons:

i. *Intangibility.* Services cannot be touched, stored or acquired. They are an experience or process.

ii. *Direct Organisation – Client Relationship.* The buyer generally meets the company's representative. Therefore, very often the production of the service and its consumption are inseparable.

iii. *Consumer Participates in the Production Process.* Service quality depends partly on the knowledge and co-operation of the consumer.

iv. *Complexity*. Service management has to cope with complex systems, largely through the importance of the direct interface with customers and the integral role of the service provider's personnel.

The Differences: Implications for Marketers

The marketing mix

The key difference for the marketing of services is the revised marketing mix for services. The standard marketing mix is the '4Ps':

- product
- price
- place (distribution)
- promotion.

The characteristics of services mean the '4Ps' are no longer sufficient. In addition, services marketers have added three more ingredients to produce the '7Ps' of services marketing:

- people
- physical evidence/ambience
- process.

PEOPLE

In a bank, the clerk is very much part of the product; in a restaurant the chef and the waiter are fundamental to the offer of the service. Operational staff often perform the task and sell the product. Employee selection, training and motivation are crucial. The famous quote by Leo Burnett of the leading advertising agency Leo Burnett Inc. sums up the importance of this additional element of the marketing mix: 'Every evening, all our assets go down the elevator'.

PHYSICAL EVIDENCE

The environment – layout, decor and lighting, etc. – and ambience/'feel' are very much a part of the product offer. For example, the facilities, cleanliness, upkeep and mood in the restaurant, hospital, sports club or whatever.

PROCESS

Friendliness of staff and flows of information affect the consumer's perception of the product offer. Appointment/queuing/payment systems become part of the product offer. All are operational matters which directly affect customer perceptions and are important marketing elements.

The implications are that there are problems in creating a differential advantage or competitive edge in services marketing – more so than in the marketing of consumer or industrial products. This is because of the character-istics of services, the intangibility of the product and the extended marketing mix.

Creating a differential advantage

A core aim of marketing is achieving product/brand differentiation with a real or perceived differential advantage/competitive edge (see T7). For any product this is difficult, but in services it is even more difficult. Once achieved, it is hard to sustain. The reasons are simple but varied:

i.   No product differentiation.

ii. No patent protection.

iii. Few barriers to entry: easy for competitors to enter and to copy.

iv. Difficult to control the customer interface.

v.   Problems of growth: key personnel can only be spread so far.

vi. Irregular service quality, largely resulting from human activity.

vii. Difficult to improve productivity and lower the cost to the consumer.

viii. Problems in innovation. Services can be copied and are 'people-based'.

ix. Restrictive regulations, particularly in the professions.

The key implication is that marketing in services has had to adopt all the key practices from consumer and industrial marketing. In particular there has been significant work in developing branding in services and clear product differenti-ation, through promotional imagery and brand identity. This has been true for many years in the financial services sector and tourism industry, but is growing in other sectors, ranging from leisure and health through to education and government units. Branding, distinctive positioning *vis-à-vis* rivals and control of personnel are pivotal to the success of most services businesses.

Useful References

Berry, L. (1995) *On Great Service*, New York: The Free Press. The essentials of controlling service quality.

Dibb, S., Simkin, L., Pride, W. and Ferrell, O.C. (2001) *Marketing: Concepts and Strategies,* Boston: Houghton Mifflin. Several chapters address the differences between the marketing of services and consumer products.

Donnelly, J.H. and George, W.R. (1981) *Marketing of Services,* AMA Proceedings Series, Chicago: American Marketing Association. Dated, but the source of many current tips regarding services marketing.

Glynn, W.J. and Barnes, J.G. (1995) *Understanding Services Management, Integrating Marketing, Organisational Behaviour, Operations and Human Resource Management*, Chichester: Wiley. People are at the heart of most services and of this text.

Gronroos, C. (1990) *Service Management and Marketing*, Lexington, MA: Lexington Books. A more thorough and academic read than the concise guides on services marketing. Still in good libraries.

Lovelock, C.H. (1992) *Managing Services,* Englewood Cliffs: Pearson. To many academics, Lovelock's work is the single most important reference point on services marketing.

Lovelock, C.H. (1996) *Services Marketing,* Englewood Cliffs: Pearson. Essential reading!

Palmer, A. (1998) *Principles of Services Marketing*, Maidenhead: McGraw-Hill. A popular UK text.

Payne, A. (1993) *The Essence of Services Marketing*, Hemel Hempstead: Pearson. A UK-based view of services marketing.

Zeithaml, V. and Bitner, J. (1996) *Services Marketing*, New York: McGraw-Hill. A good US text, co-authored by one of the founders of services marketing thinking.

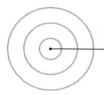

Theory Note 14: Industrial, Business-to-Business Marketing

Definition

An industrial market consists of individuals, groups and organizations that purchase a specific kind of product for direct use in producing other products or for use in their day-to-day operations.

Industrial marketing involves activities – exchanges – between industrial or business customers of industrial products. Companies produce goods which are used by other companies to produce other products. Their customers are companies, government departments or institutions, *not* the general public as consumers. Industrial marketing used to be the most common term adopted for marketing of business-to-business goods, along with organizational marketing. Business-to-business marketing is currently the popular term.

Products

Industrial or business-to-business markets include several categories of products:

- Raw materials: cotton, crude oil, iron ore, etc.
- Major equipment: installations, heavy equipment, plant.
- Component parts: manufactured materials and parts used as components in subsequently produced products/services.
- Accessory equipment: PCs, desks, etc.
- Process materials: used in the production of other goods – supplies, materials, ingredients.
- Supplies/services: maintenance, repair, cleaning, legal, consultancy, etc.
- Consumable supplies: paint, cleaning fluids, pencils, photocopying paper, inkjet cartridges, etc.

Target Marketing

Many texts claim that industrial target marketing is straightforward. In most countries there is significant industrial census data collected for government purposes, known in the UK and USA as SIC – Standard Industrial Classification – data. With this information it is possible to identify for any product the number of units sold and to which markets or customer groups, all coded through SIC codes. It is therefore possible to estimate market sizes, potential market sizes, key customer groups and major competitor organizations. It is also possible to determine purchase potential by:

i.   identifying number of units sold from SIC data; and

ii.   producing such information as a ratio to the number of customers in a market from the entries in a trade directory.

Unfortunately, life is not always so simple: many SIC codes are too broad to be useful in this way. However, given the relatively small number of customers in many business-to-business markets, compared with millions in some consumer markets, it is reasonable to argue that target marketing is sometimes *relatively* more straightforward than for targeting consumer goods or services.

Market segmentation (see T6) is often poorly practised in industrial markets, where historically businesses have classified their customers by industry sector or the product group purchased, rather than the customer need and behaviour base variables utilized in market segmentation. Increasingly, more businesses are adopting customer-focused segmentation as they develop proper target marketing strategies and strive to gain a competitive edge over their rivals.

It is important to remember that the buying behaviour of businesses as customers differs from the buying behaviour of consumers, as explained in T3. The buying process is more formalized and includes more stages, there are different influencing factors, and typically more personnel are involved in the purchase decision.

Marketing Mix Variations

Compared with the marketing of consumer products, there are relatively few variations in the marketing practices for industrial products. In services marketing (T13), owing to the nature of the intangible product, there is a more convoluted and extended marketing mix. For industrial or business-to-business marketing, the core marketing mix as deployed in consumer markets holds more or less firm, although there are some important caveats.

Product and service

The product is more broadly defined than the actual component or finished good being sold on from one company to another. Very often *service* – as part of the overall 'product' proposition – is very important. Key elements, in addition to the core and actual product, of importance in industrial marketing are:

■   On-time delivery.

■   Quality control.

■   Custom/bespoke design.

- Technical advice before a sale.
- Product specification advice.
- Installation application support.
- On-going maintenance and warranties.
- Parts distribution.

Distribution channels

Depending on the product in question and the target market's characteristics, when compared with the distribution of consumer goods, there often are not as many stages in the marketing channel. Direct marketing channels or carefully selected distributors are common. This can be because of the significant levels of technical advice which are required during the product specification stage, supply, process and installation. Occasionally agents are used in order to field enquiries and handle general administration, particularly for seasonal products. However, many business-to-business companies prefer to control the channel directly as quality control for agents (and distributors) can be a problem. Distributors fulfil similar roles to agents, but they sell under their own name, carry stocks and have their own expert staff; they may not be totally dependent on a sole supplying company.

Promotion

This is very different from consumer marketing. In particular, the utilization of the ingredients of the promotional mix differs:

PERSONAL SELLING

This is the dominant element of the promotional mix (see T11 and T12) in much business-to-business marketing:

- Fewer customers, often making mass media communications financially unviable, and direct contact more feasible.
- Technical products often require detailed explanations.
- High cost products require a re-assurance element from the personal selling process.
- Repeat purchases are common and the sales force follows up leads/builds rapport with regular customers.

However the cost of personal selling is high – salaries, expenses, cars – so recently *telemarketing* – telephone selling – has emerged as a significant element in the promotional mix in business-to-business marketing.

ADVERTISING

There is relatively little advertising when compared with consumer marketing, but it is used to create general awareness, brand identity and to support a personal selling effort or sales promotion campaign. Through technical journals, trade directories and trade associations, advertising can be quite specifically targeted. Trade adverts tend to be 'wordy' and detailed. They tend not to be the persuasive/emotive advertisements typically deployed for consumer products. Indeed, branding in business-to-business markets is usually more for ease of identification than for image-building.

SALES PROMOTION

This is very important in industrial marketing, particularly through catalogues and print material, sample merchandising and trade shows. It is often tied to personal selling and the activities of the sales force. *Direct mail* is a very popular ingredient of the promotional mix for many business-to-business products.

PR, SPONSORSHIP AND THE INTERNET

Public relations is utilised by marketers of all types. Business-to-business marketers, notably through the support of sports events and theatre productions, have frequently used sponsorship. The growth of direct marketing has led to rapid take-up of the Internet in these businesses' promotional mixes (see T12).

Price

Legal and economic constraints are quite prevalent in many industrial markets. For example EU agreements prohibit price fixing, low price imports and dumping of discounted obsolete products. Low pricing used to be the fundamental selling platform in industrial marketing, but now the need to create a differential advantage (see T7) is the focus. This sometimes helps to justify an above-average market price. The common pricing methods are:

- pre-set or administered pricing;
- bid pricing with invitations to tender;
- negotiated pricing, when business-to-business customers expect to be able to negotiate on price.

Payment terms, such as 90 days' credit, are particularly important to most business-to-business customers.

Differential Advantage or Competitive Edge

Increasingly, marketers for industrial products are seeing the need to develop marketing strategies similar in complexity to those instigated by FMCG and consumer goods companies. Business-to-business companies are no longer in the market simply to supply raw materials/components/services to other producing/service businesses as a base price operation. There is a need to steal an edge in terms of product innovation and selling techniques over competitors, and to perpetually update positioning and product imagery. The creation of a differential advantage, either through selling/distribution methods or through product innovation, is very much a focus for most industrial companies. Many have turned to *customer service* and the building of on-going, mutually beneficial relationships as a means of creating an edge over rivals.

Useful References

Chisnall, P. (1995) *Strategic Business Marketing*, London: Pearson. A good overview of industrial marketing.

Ford, D. (1997) *Understanding Business Markets*, London: Academic Press. One of the best examinations of business-to-business marketing.

Hart, N. (1994) *Effective Industrial Marketing*, London: Kogan Page. A good selection of readings addressing industrial marketing issues.

Hutt, M.D. and Speh, T.W. (1998) *Business Marketing Management: Strategic View of Industrial and Organisational Markets,* Forth Worth: Dryden Press. One of the leading works explaining organizational buying behaviour.

Moriarty, R.T. (1983) *Industrial Buying Behaviour*, Lexington: Lexington. An alternative to the work of Hutt and Speh.

Powers, T.L. (1991) *Modern Business Marketing,* St Paul, Minnesota: West. A thorough insight into marketing in businesses.

Webster, F.E. (1995) *Industrial Marketing Strategy,* New York: John Wiley. One of the original authors focusing on business-to-business markets.

Theory Note 15: Marketing Planning

Definitions

Marketing planning is a systematic process involving assessing marketing opportunities and resources, determining marketing objectives and developing a plan for implementation and control.

The marketing plan is the written document or blueprint for implementing and controlling an organization's marketing activities related to a particular marketing strategy.

The aims of good marketing planning echo much of best marketing practice:

- Serving the 'best' target customers.
- Beating the competition.
- Keeping abreast of market developments.
- Maximizing returns for the organization.
- Using resources to best advantage.
- Minimizing threats.
- Recognising the organization's strengths and weaknesses.
- Having a clear plan of action and operational controls.

These days, most larger businesses deploy marketing planning in order to formalize their thinking, understanding of their marketplace and to specify their marketing activities.

The Marketing Planning Process

There is a logical and straightforward approach to marketing planning:

- Analysis of markets and the trading environment.
- Determination of core target markets.
- Identification of a differential advantage (competitive edge).
- Statement of specific goals and desired brand positioning.
- Development of marketing mix programmes (the tactics) to implement the plans and recommended strategies.
- Determination of required budgets and allocation of marketing tasks.

The analysis of target markets (see T6), of key current and up-coming competitors (T7), and of the marketing environment (T2) creates a firm foundation for decision-making. Without an understanding of customer segments, trends and competitors, the recommended marketing tactics – the marketing mix programmes – have no clear strategic basis. The marketer must determine a basis for competing or a differential advantage (T7) in each of the targeted market segments. The selection of target markets and the determination of a differential advantage should take into account the company's *marketing assets*, and its strengths and weaknesses. Marketing assets can be *customer based,* including the strength and reputation of the brand; *distribution based*, such as channel control and distribution coverage; or *internal* assets, including skills and resources.

To implement the planned strategy, a marketing mix programme must be formulated which takes the product or service to the targeted customers in the most effective manner. The marketer must calculate the costs associated with implementing this marketing programme and justify them with accurate sales forecasts (T5). To ensure implementation of the recommended marketing strategy and the marketing mix tactics, tasks must be costed, allocated to individual managers and scheduled. There must also be on-going performance monitoring and benchmarking against key rivals' endeavours.

The process

Leading exponents of marketing planning recommend a sequential process: (i) analysis, then (ii) strategic thinking utilizing feedback from the analysis stage, and (iii) the development of tactical marketing mix programmes to facilitate implementation of the recommended strategy, coupled with the specification of internal controls to ensure the marketing plan is actioned. This is the *A-S-P* process – see Figure IV.25.

Figure IV.25	*The A-S-P Essential Stages of Marketing Planning*

Analysis
 ➤ **Opportunities/Trends/Customers' Needs & Perceptions/Market Segments/Brand Positionings/Competitive Activity/Company Capabilities/Product Portfolio Performance**

Strategy
 ➤ **Core Target Markets/Basis for Competing/Desired Positioning/Marketing Objectives & Sales Targets**

Programmes for Implementation
 ➤ **Marketing Mix Tactics: Product/Service Levels/Customer Care/Distribution/Promotion & Communication/Pricing & Payment Conditions**
 ➤ **Specification of Tasks/Scheduling/Budgets/On-going Work/Benchmarking & Performance Monitoring**

(Source: Dibb, S., Simkin, L., and Bradley, J. (1996) The Marketing Planning Workbook, London: Thomson Learning)

The planning cycle

As Figure IV.26 depicts, marketing planning never ceases: it is an on-going analysis/planning/control process or cycle. Many organizations update their marketing plans annually, presenting the key recommendations to all senior managers. Most commonly, there is a three-year timeframe to the proposed marketing plan.

Figure IV.26	*The Marketing Planning Cycle*

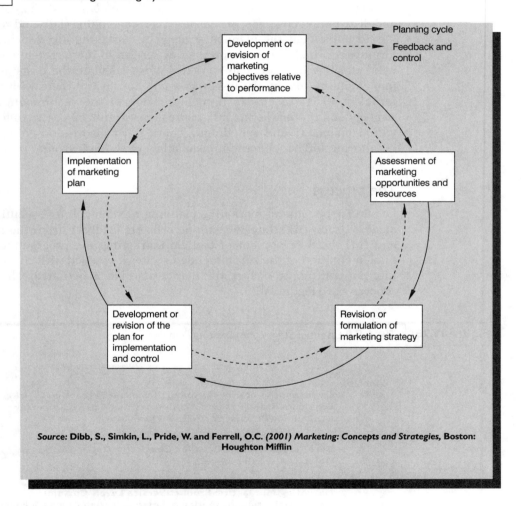

Source: Dibb, S., Simkin, L., Pride, W. and Ferrell, O.C. *(2001) Marketing: Concepts and Strategies,* Boston: Houghton Mifflin

The Marketing Plan Report

The written marketing plan document:

■ Offers a 'road map' for implementing a business's strategies and achieving its objectives.

- Assists management in controlling and monitoring the implementation of strategy.

- Informs new participants of the business's plan, their role and responsibilities.

- Specifies how best to (re)allocate resources.

- Stimulates thinking.

- Assigns responsibilities, tasks and timing.

- Makes participants aware of deficiencies, problems, opportunities and threats.

Presentations to marketing colleagues and to senior directors may complete the planning process, but the written report is the subsequent action plan and reference point. This document must be well written and clear, with full supporting evidence in the analysis section to explain its conclusions and recommendations. There are various formats, but a popular structure is shown in Figure IV.27.

| **Figure IV.27** | *The Marketing Plan Document Structure* |

Section	Content	No. Pages
1	Management Summary	2–3
2	Objectives	1
	Company Mission Statement	
	Detailed Company Objectives	
	Product Group/Brand Goals	
3	Product/Market Background	2–3
	Product Range and Explanation	
	Market Overview and Sales Summary	
4	SWOT Analysis	1–2*
5	Marketing Analyses	8–12*
	Marketing Environment & Trends	
	Customers	
	Competition & Competitors' Strategies	
6	Strategies	3–4
	Core Target Markets	
	Basis for Competing/Differential Advantage	
	Desired Product/Brand Positioning	
7	Statement of Expected Results/Forecasts	1–2
8	Marketing Programmes	8–12*
	Marketing Mixes	
	Tasks, Responsibilities, Schedules	
9	Financial Implications/Budgets	1–2
10	Operational Implications	1–2
11	Appendices	20+
	SWOT Details	
	Background Data and Information	
	Research Findings	
	References	

* Likely to be supported with material in appendices

- *The Management Summary, or Executive Summary,* should be a concise overview of the entire report, including key aims, overall strategies, fundamental conclusions and salient points regarding the suggested marketing mix programmes. Not many people read an entire report, tending to 'dip in' here and there, so the Management Summary should be good, punchy and informative.

- *Objectives* are for the benefit of the reader, to give perspective to the report. Aims and objectives should be stated briefly.

- *Product/Market Background* is a necessary section. Not everyone will be fully familiar with the products and their markets. This section 'scene-sets', aiding the reader's understanding of the marketing plan.

- The *SWOT Analysis* is an important foundation for any marketing plan, helping to produce realistic and meaningful recommendations. The section in the main body of the report should be kept to a concise overview, with detailed market-by-market or country-by-country SWOTs – and their full explanations – kept to the appendices.

- *The Marketing Analyses* section is the heart of the marketing planning exercise: if incomplete or highly subjective the recommendations are likely to be based on an inaccurate view of the market and the company's potential. This section gives a sound foundation to the recommendations and marketing programmes. It includes analyses of the marketing environment, market trends, customers, competitors, competitor positions and competitors' strategies.

- *Strategies* should be self-evident if the analyses have been objective and thorough: which target markets are most beneficial to the company, what is to be the differential advantage or competitive edge in these markets, and what is the desired product or brand positioning. This strategy statement must be realistic and detailed enough to action.

- Having highlighted the strategic thrust and intention, it is important to explain the *Expected Results* and sales volumes, to show why the strategies should be followed.

- *Marketing Programme Recommendations* are the culmination of the various analyses and statement of strategies: exactly what needs to be done, how and why. This is the detailed presentation of the proposed marketing mixes designed to achieve the goals and implement the strategies. The required implementation issues must also be addressed: who will be responsible and when.

- An indication is required of the necessary resources (budgets) to roll-out implementation of the proposed plans of action. The *Financial Implications* must be given.

- These strategies and marketing programmes may have ramifications for other product groups, sectors or territories, for R&D, for engineering/production, etc. *The Operational Implications* must also, therefore, be flagged up.

- The report should be as concise as possible. The document must, though, tell the full story and include evidence and statistics which support the strategies and marketing programmes being recommended. The use of *Appendices* – so long as they are fully cross-referenced in the main body of the report – helps to keep the report concise and well focused.

The SWOT Analysis

The SWOT (or TOWS) analysis is one of the most commonly implemented analyses in marketing. A simple format for its presentation is illustrated in Figure IV.28. It is important the SWOT is not merely a collection of managers' hunches. It must be based on objective facts and on marketing research findings. Managers often produce SWOT grids for each leading competitor and for separate markets, revealing a company's relative strengths and weaknesses and ability to face the identified threats and opportunities. The SWOT analysis is a mix of internal and external issues, with Strengths and Weaknesses principally relating to in-company issues and Opportunities and Threats arising from external factors identified in the core marketing analyses of customers, competitors, market trends and crucially the forces of the marketing environment.

| **Figure IV.28** | *The SWOT Grid* |

Issues: external environment – threats/opportunities

- Social/Cultural
- Regulatory/Legal/Political
- Technological
- Economic Conditions
- Competition:

Intensity of rivalry	Bargaining power of buyers
Ability	Bargaining power of distributors
Threat of entry	Bargaining power of suppliers
Pressure from substitutions	

- Market's customer needs

Issues: internal environment – strengths/weaknesses

■ *Marketing*

Product	Distribution/Distributors
Service	Promotion
People	Branding and Positioning
Pricing	Marketing Information/Intelligence

■ *Engineering and Product Development*

Often of peripheral importance, but with more formalised input from marketing – as marketing planning takes off – this often changes.

■ *Operations*

Production	Marketing
Sales	Processing orders/Transactions, etc.

■ *People*

R&D	Skills
Sales	Wages/benefits
Distributors	Training/development
After-Sales	Methods/conditions/staff turnover
Marketing	Motivation
Processing/Customer Service	

All are central to the successful implementation of the marketing philosophy and the marketing function.

■ *Management*

A sensitive and often contentious area, but sometimes management structures and philosophies need altering to facilitate the successful implementation of a marketing plan.

■ *Company Resources*

People	Communications
Finance (Budgets)	IT Systems
Time	Marketing Information

Useful References

Crowner, R.P. (1991) *Developing a Strategic Business Plan with Cases*, Homewood, IL: Irwin. A US view of business planning.

Dibb, S., Simkin, L., and Bradley, J. (1996) *The Marketing Planning Workbook*, London: Thomson Learning. One of the leading UK texts examining, from a practitioner's perspective, the stages of undertaking marketing planning.

Jain, S.C. (1999) *Marketing Planning & Strategy*, Cincinnati, OH: South Western. A core US reader addressing at length the philosophy of marketing planning.

Lehmann, D.R. and Winner, R.S. (1994) *Analysis for Marketing Planning*, Burr Ridge, Ill: Irwin. A good, easy to follow US text.

McDonald, M.H. (1999) *Marketing Plans*, Oxford: Butterworth-Heinemann. A solid guide to marketing planning.

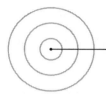

Theory Note 16: International Marketing

Definition

International marketing is marketing activity performed across national boundaries.

(Vern Terpstra 1978)

Levels of Involvement in International Markets

When marketers first began discussing international marketing they had a simple view. At one extreme there was exporting almost by accident, in an unplanned manner. An alternative approach was to purposefully plan activity seeking out marketing opportunities outside the domestic market. While these two options still are in evidence, the understanding of how businesses should address international markets has evolved to include five core options:

- *Domestic marketing.* Home market involvement only.
- *Export marketing.* This is an attempt to create sales without significant changes in a business's products, other marketing mix ingredients and overall operations. There is an active effort to exploit foreign markets for existing products.
- *International marketing.* Greater commitment to international markets. Overall planning deliberately encompasses international marketing activities. Direct investment in non-domestic markets is likely and products may be sourced outside the home market.
- *Multinational marketing.* Further steps are taken to adapt to local tastes. The marketing mix is modified to appeal to local target market needs.
- *Global marketing.* A total commitment to international marketing which involves utilizing a business's assets, experience and products to develop and maintain marketing strategies on a global scale. There is a global marketing strategy with adaptation to reflect local needs.

The Nature of International Marketing

Irrespective of the scale of international involvement, businesses identify a need for marketing intelligence addressing their non-domestic opportunities. Secondary sources have improved significantly, led by governments seeking to encourage companies to exploit overseas markets and the growth of web-based information sources. In most situations, businesses find they also require some primary information gathering (see T4), notably of cultural differences which affect their target customers' expectations and also regarding the selection of marketing channels for sales and distribution.

The forces of the marketing environment provide a sensible framework for marketers addressing international markets. As explained in T2, all marketers need to monitor and understand the marketing environment. This is just as true when tackling international markets. Cultural and social; economic and competitive; political, regulatory and legal; plus technological forces must all be examined. Tariffs, quotas and non-tariff barriers, such as rules, regulations or taxes, are active in many international markets, affecting trading conditions and marketing practices. Regional trade alliances play a major role in the way many businesses are permitted to do business, to what extent and where.

The European Union (EU), European Free Trade Association (EFTA), European Economic Area (EEA), Commonwealth of Independent States (CIS) in the former Soviet Union, Association of South East Asian Nations (ASEAN), Asia Pacific Economic Co-operative (APEC), and the North American Free Trade Agreement (NAFTA), are just some of the more important regional alliances which stipulate trading regulations and conditions for companies seeking international marketing opportunities. Indeed, many of these associations operate tariffs, quotas, non-tariff barriers and bureaucracy aimed to protect their member state companies from external commercial activity.

Arrangements for Handling International Marketing

There are several market entry strategies possible, depending largely on a business's level of commitment. One option is occasional casual exporting, while at the other extreme, a company could expand its overall production and marketing operations into other countries.

- *Exporting*. The lowest level of commitment and the most flexible approach to international marketing. A channel intermediary such as an agent may handle most of task. Minor changes to packaging, labelling style or colour will be the extent of any product adaptation.

- *Licensing*. When production, technical assistance and marketing know-how are required across national boundaries, licensing is an alternative to direct investment. The licensee pays commissions or royalties on sales or supplies. Very popular for smaller manufacturers wanting to more widely distribute a successful brand.

- *Franchising*. A form of licensing, franchising also avoids direct overseas investment by granting the right to use trade names, brand names, designs, patents, copyright, production and marketing processes to locally based third-party businesses.

- *Joint Ventures.* A partnership between a domestic company and a foreign business or government is a joint venture in international marketing. Very popular when hefty investment is required or extensive resources are needed in production. National protection policies may create the need for a joint venture as governments strive to protect their native businesses, employment and resources.

- *Strategic Alliances.* An extension of the joint venture concept, where partnerships are formed to create competitive advantage on a world-wide basis. The partners retain their own identities, but each brings a unique set of competencies to the combined operation.

- *Trading Companies.* These provide a link between buyers and sellers in different countries. A trading company is not involved in manufacturing nor does it own production-based assets. Instead it buys in one country and sells to buyers in another country. Trading companies take over ownership of products bought and undertake all of the sales and marketing activity required to move the products from the domestic country to foreign markets.

- *Foreign Direct Investment.* Once a business is committed to an overseas country or market which it views as stable and offering longer term potential, direct ownership of a foreign subsidiary or division becomes a viable option. *Multinational enterprises* are companies with operations or subsidiaries located in many countries.

The International Marketing Mix

Marketing in a non-domestic environment requires an understanding of the marketing environment. With this intelligence it is likely that some or total modification of the marketing mix will be required to satisfy target market expectations in the international market.

Product and promotion

There are five possible options:

i. *Keep product and promotion the same world-wide*, as in the case of Coca-Cola or Pepsi. This approach reduces costs and simplifies controls over the marketing mix, but assumes homogeneity between non-domestic markets and the home market, which is not always possible.

ii. *Adapt promotion only.* As with McDonald's, the product is largely unchanged country to country, but different means of promotion are deployed reflecting local practices, competitor activity and available media opportunities.

iii. *Adapt product only.* If promotion is unchanged but the product is modified to reflect local conditions, the assumption is that the altered product will still serve the same purpose and satisfy the same customer need. For example, Lever Brothers modifies its detergents to reflect local water types and washing appliance characteristics, but the detergent still washes clothes.

iv. *Adapt both product and promotion*. If a product serves a new function or is used differently in a foreign market, both the product and promotional ingredients in the international marketing mix must be modified. When P&G launched Cheer in Japan the company promoted the washing powder as being effective in all temperatures. Most Japanese washed their clothes in cold water, so the promotional message was inappropriate, while they added large amounts of fabric conditioner. P&G had to add fabric conditioner and re-launch Cheer.

v. *Invent new products*. This is quite an extreme option, but reflects the identification of large latent demand which warrants such investment and innovation. Colgate developed a plastic hand-operated washing machine for developing countries lacking ready access to electricity. The successful product led to large sales of the company's washing powders.

Distribution and pricing

Government and regulatory bodies often impose restrictions to prevent dumping of heavily discounted products in non-domestic markets and parallel importing of low-priced products from other countries, through non-official channels, on what is known as the 'grey market'. Marketers must be aware of such regulatory forces. In multinational enterprises, transfer pricing between sites and factories will also be an issue.

There are four basic options in terms of determining the distribution and price ingredients of the international marketing mix:

i. Same pricing policies, but no control over distribution.

ii. Pricing policies changed for international markets, but no control over distribution.

iii. New marketing channels established, but same price policies used.

iv. New marketing channels established, and new pricing policies.

Indecision leads to ineffective marketing activity: marketers must plan and action one of these options.

People

The cultural differences inherent in international markets often encourage the recruitment of personnel with local knowledge and expertise. Channel members such as agents can help in this respect. Marketing personnel must also exhibit a sound understanding of the regulatory and political environment in order to facilitate a business's activities in its non-domestic markets.

Useful References

Bradley, F. (1998) *International Marketing Strategy*; Hemel Hempstead: Pearson. One of the few leading international marketing texts not authored in North America.

Jeannet, J.-P. and Hennessey, D. (1997) *Global Marketing Strategies*; Boston: Houghton Mifflin. Thorough and well written with many good examples and insights.

Keegan, W. (1989) *Global Marketing Management*; Englewood Cliffs: Pearson. To many, the most comprehensive explanation of international marketing.

Paliwoda, S.J. and Thomas, M.J. (1998) *International Marketing*, Oxford: Butterworth-Heinemann. An authoritative UK text addressing international marketing.

Terpstra, V. and Sarathy, R. (2000) *International Marketing*; Hinsdale, Fort Worth: Dryden Press. Perhaps the book that first explored the nuances of marketing across national boundaries.

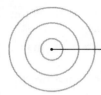

Theory Note 17: Ethics and Social Responsibility in Marketing

Definitions

Marketing ethics are the moral principles that define right and wrong behaviour in marketing.

Social responsibility is an organisation's obligation to maximise its positive impact and minimise its negative impact on society.

OC Ferrell

Marketers should be aware of the ethical and social responsibility issues arising from their activities. While controversial, such issues can cause significant harm to a brand or company, enabling competitors to gain an edge. Poor handling of ethical issues may lead to customer dissatisfaction, while increasingly the public expects businesses to operate in a way which at the very least does no harm to the natural environment. It is far better to routinely behave ethically and for the greater good, than to have to face consumer and media outrage if disreputable practices come to light.

Ethical Issues in Marketing

Moral philosophies are the rules which guide individuals and help determine their behaviour:

1. *Utilitarianism* focuses on maximizing the greatest good for the largest number of people. Under this approach it would be unethical to act in a manner which brings personal gain at the expense of society in general. An airline's reaction to a bomb threat or a car manufacturer's response to news of faulty components may result in managers opting to take no action, with decisions being operationally-driven and cost-focused. Or such managers could accept disruption to operations and associated costs and act to safeguard their customers by taking precautionary measures. For example, in the autumn of 1999 Daewoo publicized a product alert in the national press for a small number of its GB20T8ST televisions, requesting purchasers contact its helpline. Although only a small number of units were affected and the risk to users was very slight, Daewoo acted responsibly in safeguarding its consumers, despite the costs of press advertising, staffing the helpline and rectifying any possible product defects.

2. *Ethical formalism* takes a different stance: rules for behaviour are based on whether an action can be taken consistently as a general rule without

concern for alternative options. Most marketers are influenced by their colleagues' attitudes, senior managerial practices, corporate codes of conduct and by the prevalent corporate culture: values, beliefs, goals, norms, rituals. Poor practices commonplace in one business may never occur in a direct rival owing to its culture and ethical ethos.

Marketers are daily faced with ethical dilemmas. If risks are not disclosed in connection with a product's use or true value, ethical issues arise. If it is known that a new washing powder may actually do damage, as with Persil Power, it is correct to withdraw the product rather than maintain either indifference to the problem or continue to promote it to the target market. In promotion, marketers frequently face ethical constraints and forces, notably in advertising with exaggerated claims, concealed facts or outright lying. The monitoring of personal selling is notoriously difficult, with unscrupulous sales personnel deliberately misleading customer prospects, bribing them or lying about rivals' products. Hidden costs can become an issue, with unwitting customers discovering that the actual price to be paid is much higher than the 'excluding VAT and delivery' cost advertised. In distribution, channel members often facilitate the flow of goods. Excessive pressure by suppliers, bribery, over-generous bonuses, misleading information concerning competing products, deliberately restricted deliveries, all occur from time to time as attempts are made to control channel intermediaries, yet these are far from ethical practices. Codes of ethics and of practice are important in pre-empting these problems, but these codes must be supported by incisive and public management action to remedy deficiencies in the behaviour of a company's personnel.

Social Responsibility

While ethics relate to separate decisions and the acts of individual managers, social responsibility in marketing refers to a business's obligation to strive to have a positive impact on society. The Newsprint & Newspaper Industry Environmental Action Group's endeavours mean 40 per cent of raw materials used in producing daily newspapers are from waste paper and the timber comes from managed forests. This trade body has acted responsibly for the greater good of society, rather than purely for its members' commercial interests. Perhaps the operator of the National Lottery should reduce prizes to prevent a gambling culture taking hold or to encourage increased charitable donations. Retailers refusing to stock GM-modified foods, factory farmed meat or CFC-containing aerosols, are examples of commercial organizations acting not only in their own interests, but instead attempting to take a longer term perspective that is for the benefit of the natural environment. Current US Government moves are putting significant pressure on the tobacco industry to be more concerned for the broader population and the humanitarian consequences of their products.

Social responsibility and ethical decision-making are closely linked and in both there is a fine line between striving to be responsible and seeking commercial benefit from societal and trading issues. For example, the 1999 advertising and lobbying campaign undertaken by airline British Midland claimed to be putting the interests of the traveller first. This campaign sought 'An Open Skies Policy' for transatlantic flights out of London airports, removing the existing treaty permitting just two US and two British airlines to compete for passengers from Heathrow. According to British Midland, this outmoded treaty resulted in fares up to £1,500 more expensive than on other equivalent European routes to New York. This campaign was pitched as being socially responsible and caring for the greater good, but such utilitarianism in British Midland's decision-making could be questioned when the commercial benefits for British Midland of such a policy change are considered. While a laudable attempt to win a better deal for the traveller, the cynical observer may be alienated by British Midland's lobbying.

There are several considerations which should be addressed under social responsibility in marketing:

- *Consumer Issues.* Consumer movements strive to protect the rights of individuals and groups of consumers through lobbying of policy-makers and the media. Such pressure has led to safer cars and playgrounds, better working conditions in heavy industry, and much legislation aimed to safeguard consumers.

- *Community Relations.* Marketers are part of a broader community and are expected to satisfy the well-being of this broader community. McDonald's has a scheme equipping family facilities close to children's hospitals, IBM reduces prices to educational establishments and Tesco allows shoppers to collect vouchers enabling local schools to purchase discounted computer equipment. While all such schemes undoubtedly are designed to increase the public's goodwill towards the businesses concerned, they do also have a positive impact on the local community.

- *Green Marketing.* This is the development and sale of products which specifically do not harm the natural environment. Natural resources should not be ravaged, production processes must not pollute, consumption should not be wasteful or poisonous, while waste disposal must aim to be safely controlled. Unfortunately, some businesses make 'green' claims for their products which simply are not true. While such practice is unethical, it is also far from being socially responsible.

Reactions for Dealing with Social Responsibility Issues

There are four basic strategies for handling social responsibility in marketing:

1. *Reaction Strategy.* A business adopting such a strategy permits a problem to go unresolved until the public finds out. The business then has a *reactive strategy*, denying responsibility and dealing with individual cases to quell disquiet, while continuing to trade normally.

2. *Defence Strategy.* Attempts to minimize or avoid additional obligations once a problem has arisen are a *defensive strategy*. Legal manoeuvres, lobbying or manipulation of the press are common defensive ploys.

3. *Accommodation Strategy*. A much better approach is an *accommodation strategy*, whereby a business assumes responsibility for its actions. Lever Brothers and P&G have become actively involved in recycling initiatives and seeking alternative technologies which are less harmful to the natural environment. Instead of 'pretending' their products and production processes are faultless, such companies have overtly decided to work with their detractors in identifying better practices and solutions.

4. *Proactive Strategy*. Under a *proactive strategy* a company assumes responsibility for its actions and responds to external criticisms without outside pressure or government intervention. BMW voluntarily set up plants for the recycling of old cars and promotes the less harmful disposal of car waste products.

Useful References

Charter, M. (1999) *Greener Marketing*, Sheffield: Greenleaf Press. Green issues. Slightly quirky but very informative.

Donaldson, T. (1992) *The Ethics of International Business*; New York: Oxford University Press. A dated but revealing insight into the practices of corporate decision-making.

Ferrell, O.C. and Fraedrich, J. (2000) *Business Ethics*; Boston: Houghton Mifflin. Written by two of the initial proponents of ethics in marketing.

Goldberg, M.E., Fishbein, M. and Middlestadt, S.E. (eds) (1997) *Social Marketing: Theoretical and Practical Perspectives*, New Jersey: Lawrence Erlbaum Associates. Marketing with social responsibility explored in depth.

Manley II, W.W. (1992) *The Handbook of Good Business Practice*; London: Routledge. A step-by-step approach to avoiding the key pitfalls in striving to behave well. Out of print but still in good libraries.

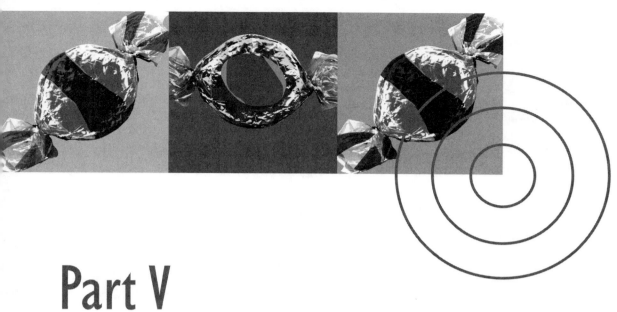

Part V

Glossary of Key Terms

This section contains a glossary explaining over 100 key marketing terms, with full cross-referencing for their appearance – and more comprehensive discussion – in the associated theory notes.

Key terms from the Part IV theory notes, with page references

Advertising – A paid form of non-personal communication, about an organization and/or its products or services, that is transmitted to a target audience through a mass medium (p. 268).

Base Variables – In Market Segmentation these are variables used to form the basis for identifying homogeneous groups of customers in a market: *demographic, geographic, psychographic and behaviouralistic* variables in consumer markets; *geographic location, type of organization, customer characteristics, product usage* in organizational, business-to-business markets (p. 232).

Brand – Established product name, term, symbol, design, wholly of a proprietary nature, usually officially registered. There are three types: *Manufacturer, Private/Own Label, and Generic* (p. 248).

Brand Awareness – Once *Category Need* is established, consumers must be aware of the specific brand if they are ever to adopt the particular brand (p. 268).

Brand Extension – A newly launched product or service is given the identity or name of an existing product, but only if the product has an affinity with the new product (p. 249).

Brand Management – Product Management (p. 248).

Break-Even Point – When total costs are equal to the revenue generated from a product or service (p. 263).

Business-to-Business Marketing – Activities and exchanges between companies. The customer is another business or organization (not an end-user private consumer) that in turn produces goods or services to be marketed to its own customers (p. 285).

Buyer Behaviour: Consumer – The decision processes and acts of individuals involved in buying and using products or services (p. 205).

Buyer Behaviour: Organizational/Business-to-Business – The purchase behaviour of producers, re-sellers, government units and institutions (p. 205).

Buyer Behaviour Influences – *Consumer*: person specific, psychological, social. *Organizational:* business environment, company aims/policies/ resources, personal relationships, characteristics of personnel (p. 207).

Buyer Behaviour Process: Consumer – Problem recognition; information search; evaluation of alternatives; purchase; post-purchase evaluation (p. 205).

Buyer Behaviour Process: Organizational/Business-to-Business – Problem recognition; product specification; product/supplier search; evaluation of options; selection of product/supplier; evaluation of product/supplier performance (p. 207).

Campaign – Organized course of action, planned carefully to achieve pre-determined goals. Can relate to sales drives or any part of the Promotional Mix, but typically is applied to Advertising (p. 268).

Campaign – The weekly trade magazine published in London by Haymarket Publishing; news and features primarily from the advertising industry, with updates on the rest of the marketing communications industry (p. 197).

Category Need – To be potential customers, consumers must first realize a particular product or service exists and that they have a need for such a product (p. 267).

Causal Forecasting – This set of techniques includes *Barometric, Surveys of Buyer Intentions, Regression Analysis,* and various *Econometric Models.* These tools examine changes in sales due to fluctuations in one or more market variables (p. 226).

Channel – *A Marketing Channel* is a channel of distribution, a group of interrelated intermediaries that direct products to consumers (p. 255).

Channel Intermediaries – Members of a *marketing channel* that provide key services to their suppliers and customers: *sorting out, accumulation, allocation, sorting* (p. 258).

Channel Participants – *Facilitating agencies* or *contractual organisations* (p. 258).

Channel Leadership – Control over a marketing channel through *economic sources of power* or *non-economic sources* (p. 259).

Communications Effects – Category Need; Brand Awareness; Brand Attitude; Brand Purchase Intention; Purchase Facilitation (p. 267).

Competition-Driven Pricing – *Going-rate pricing*, when prices are fixed after consideration of competitors' pricing levels (p. 264).

Competitive Edge – Differential Advantage (p. 288).

Competitive Positions – *Warfare Strategy* believes an organization must know its position in a market relative to its competitors. A **Market Leader** has market share leadership in a market and must grow its market by finding new applications for its products or services, by market development, or by market penetration, while defending its position against rival challengers. A **Challenger** is aggressively attacking the market and the market leader to gain market share. A **Fast-Mover** is a smaller player, perhaps a relative new-comer, that is intending to grow quickly its market share at the expense of rivals, but is not large enough to challenge for market leadership. A **Market Follower** has low market share and few resources to contend for market leadership. A **Nicher** specializes in terms of market/product/customers by finding a small, safe, non-competitive niche (p. 240).

Competitors – These are generally viewed by an organization as those rival organizations which market similar or substitutable products or services to the same Target Market (p. 237).

Cost-Driven Pricing – *Cost-plus pricing,* when prices are set at a level to allow a certain percentage profit once all costs have been met (p. 264).

Costs: Fixed – Costs which remain constant irrespective of the number of items produced, such as rent and business rates (p. 263).

Costs: Marginal – The additional cost an organization incurs when one more item is produced (p. 263).

Costs: Variable – Costs, such as raw materials and labour, which vary as the number of items produced fluctuates (p. 263).

Demand-Driven Pricing – *Variable pricing*, commonly used in markets where demand is variable over time (p. 264).

Differential Advantage – If a Marketing Mix is developed which is exactly in line with the targeted consumers' needs and expectations, which is a superior marketing mix to those offered by direct competitors, then there is a real or perceived *differential advantage:* something a product or an organization has, desired by consumers and not matched by competitors (p. 245). See also Porter's *Generic Strategies*, (p. 239 and p. 240).

Direct Mail – Printed advertising material delivered to a prospective customer's or donor's home or work address (p. 272).

Direct Marketing – A decision by a company's marketers to select a *marketing channel* which avoids dependence on marketing channel intermediaries, and to focus marketing communications activity on Promotional Mix ingredients which contact directly targeted customers – door-to-door selling, the Internet, direct mail, telemarketing (p. 275).

Distribution – In the Marketing Mix, the 'Place' element; the selection and control of a *Marketing Channel* (p. 255).

Domestic Marketing – Home market involvement only (p. 297).

E-commerce – the use of the *Internet* for commercial transactions (p. 275).

Environmental Scanning – The process of tracking information about the *Marketing Environment* from observation, secondary sources and primary research (p. 199).

Export Marketing – This is an attempt to create sales without significant changes in a business's products, other marketing mix ingredients and overall operations. There is an active effort to exploit foreign markets for existing products (p. 297).

Exporting – The lowest level of commitment and the most flexible approach to international marketing. A channel intermediary such as an agent may handle most of task. Minor changes to packaging, labelling style or colour will be the extent of any product adaptation (p. 298).

Family Branding – Three choices for an organization naming and branding its products or services: *Individual Brand Names* for each separate product; *Blanket Family Name* across the portfolio; *Company Name* combined with *Individual Brand Name* for each product or service (p. 249).

Foreign Direct Investment – Once a business is committed to an overseas country or market which it views as stable and offering longer term potential, direct ownership of a foreign subsidiary or division becomes a viable option (p. 299).

Focus Group – Between 6 and 8 people, usually single sex, who – for a small fee or product sample – take part in 1.5- or 2.5-hour group discussions. These discussions commence generally, before focusing on a specific product field, brand or advertising application (p. 218).

Forecasting – Predicting future events on the basis of historical data, opinions, trends, known future variables. Principally there are three categories of forecasting models in marketing: *Judgmental, Time Series Projections,* and *Causal* (p. 221).

Franchising – A form of licensing, franchising also avoids direct overseas investment by granting the right to use trade names, brand names, designs, patents, copyright, production and marketing processes to locally based third party businesses (p. 298).

Global Marketing – A total commitment to international marketing which involves utilising a business's assets, experience and products to develop and maintain marketing strategies on a global scale. There is a global marketing strategy with adaptation to reflect local needs (p. 297).

Industrial Market – *An Industrial Market* consists of individuals, groups, organizations which purchase a specific kind of product for direct use in producing other products or for use in day-to-day operations (p. 285).

Influencing Factors: Consumer Buying Behaviour – The factors influencing the way in which people buy: *Person-Specific; Psychological; Social* (p. 207).

Influencing Factors: Organizational or Business-to-Business – The range of factors impacting on decision-making and the buying process: *Environmental; Organizational; Interpersonal; Individual* (p. 208).

Intermediaries – In *Marketing Channels,* these are agents or brokers, wholesalers or retailers for consumer goods, and agents or distributors for industrial goods. They *sort out, accumulate, allocate goods* (p. 203).

International Marketing – Greater commitment to international markets. Overall planning deliberately encompasses international marketing activities. Direct investment in non-domestic markets is likely and products may be sourced outside the home market (p. 297).

International Strategic Alliances – An extension of the joint venture concept, where partnerships are formed to create competitive advantage on a world-wide basis. The partners retain their own identities, but each brings a unique set of competencies to the combined operation (p. 299).

Internet – A chain of computer networks linking computers to the web sites of commercial businesses, not-for-profit organisations, information providers, public bodies, private individuals and social groups, increasingly used for e-commerce (p. 275).

Intranets – Internal, in-company *Internet* networks for routine communications, fostering group communications, providing uniform computer applications, distributing the latest software, or informing colleagues of marketing developments and new product launches (p. 275).

Intuition – In many situations managers have neither time nor resources to access Marketing Intelligence or commission Marketing Research in order to address a problem; instead they make decisions based on their experience and understanding of their market (p. 215).

Joint Ventures – A partnership between a domestic company and a foreign business or government is a joint venture in international marketing. Very popular when hefty investment is required or extensive resources are needed in production. National protection policies may create the need for a joint venture as governments strive to protect their native businesses, employment and resources (p. 299).

Judgemental Forecasting – Subjective opinions of managers, aggregated and averaged: *Sales Force Composite* seeks the views and predictions from the fieldforce; *Expert Consensus* includes the opinions of industry experts; *Delphi* attains forecasts from the fieldforce, centrally collates and revises them before returning the updated forecasts to the fieldforce for further modification and opinion (p. 222).

Licensing – When production, technical assistance and marketing know-how are required across national boundaries, licensing is an alternative to direct investment. The licensee pays commissions or royalties on sales or supplies. Very popular for smaller manufacturers wanting to more widely distribute a successful brand (p. 298).

Marginal Cost – The additional cost a company incurs when one more item is produced (p. 263).

Market Coverage – the Intensity of Market Coverage presents three options: *Intensive* with many distribution outlets; *Selective* with fewer outlets but with larger catchments; *Exclusive* with deliberately restricted and limited distribution (p. 255).

Market Penetration Pricing – This is the setting of low prices relative to key competitors in order to gain large market share as quickly as possible (p. 264).

Market Segmentation – The identification of target customer groups where customers are aggregated into groups with similar expectations, requirements and buying characteristics (p. 229).

Market Segmentation Process – Segmentation; Targeting; Positioning. How does the market break down? Which segment should be targeted? How should the product be offered to the targeted market? How should it be positioned relative to competitors' products? (p. 230).

Market Segment Qualities – *Measurable; Substantial; Accessible; Stable; Useful* (p. 233).

Marketing – Marketing consists of individual and organizational activities that facilitate and expedite satisfying exchange relationships in a dynamic environment through the creation, distribution, promotion and pricing of goods, services and ideas. It is the management process responsible for identifying, anticipating and satisfying customer requirements profitably – (p. 192).

Marketing – The weekly trade magazine published in London by Haymarket Publishing; news and features from the world of practising marketers (p. 197).

Marketing Assets – Properties or features which can be used to advantage in the marketplace: *Customer-based,* such as image and reputation, brand name; *Distribution-based; Internal Assets,* including skills and experience, economies of scale, technology (p. 291).

Marketing Audit – A systematic examination of the objectives, strategies, organization, and performance of an organization's marketing unit (p. 291).

Marketing Communications – The communication of information that facilitates or expedites the exchange process (p. 266).

Marketing Environment – Those external forces that directly or indirectly influence an organization's acquisitions or inputs and generation of outputs. The *macro marketing environment* includes legal, regulatory, political, societal, technological and economic forces. The *micro marketing environment*, made famous by Porter's work examining the forces of competition, includes direct competition, substitute competition, supplier influences, buyer power, the influence of intermediaries and internal issues (p. 199).

Marketing Ethics – The moral principles that define right and wrong behaviour in marketing (p. 302).

Marketing Information System (MIS) – This is a *framework* for managing and accessing internal and external data, including Marketing Intelligence and Marketing Research information (p. 214).

Marketing Intelligence – The data and ideas available within a system, such as a marketing department (p. 213).

Marketing Mix – The tools available to the marketing manager, often referred to as 'the 4Ps': *product, place (distribution), promotion, and pricing* (p. 192). For the marketing of services, the 4Ps are extended to 'the 7Ps', with the addition of *people, process, and physical environment (ambience)* (p. 282). Increasingly, marketers of consumer goods and industrial products are including aspects of the *extended marketing mix* in their work.

Marketing Plan – The written document or blueprint for implementing and controlling an organization's marketing activities related to a particular marketing strategy (p. 292).

Marketing Planning – A systematic process involving assessing marketing opportunities and resources, determining market objectives, and developing a plan for implementation and control (p. 290).

Marketing Research – A formalized means of obtaining/collecting information to be used to make sound marketing decisions in addressing specific problems (p. 213).

Marketing Research Process – Define and locate the problem (task); develop hypotheses; collect data; analyse and interpret findings; report research findings and conclusions (p. 215).

Marketing Strategy – A plan for selecting and analysing a Target Market; developing and maintaining a Marketing Mix (p. 195).

Marketing Week – The weekly trade magazine published in London by Centaur Communications; news and features from the marketing and agency world (p. 197).

Medium/Media. – Choice of *medium* of transmission for a promotional campaign: print, TV/radio, cinema, posters, personal selling, Internet, etc. (p. 266).

Monopolistic Competition – despite the name given to such a situation, there are many sellers – and buyers – offering different products over a range of prices (p. 261).

Moral Philosophies – The rules which guide individuals and help determine their behaviour: (a) *Utilitarianism* focuses on maximizing the greatest good for the largest number of people; (b) *Ethical Formalism* takes a different stance – rules for behaviour are based on whether an action can be taken consistently as a general rule without concern for alternative options (p. 302).

Multi-Branding – Each product or service in an organization's portfolio is given its own unique name and brand identity (p. 249).

Multinational Enterprises – Companies with operations or subsidiaries located in many countries (p. 299).

Multinational Marketing – Extensive steps are taken to adapt to local tastes. The marketing mix is modified to appeal to local target market needs (p. 297).

New Product Development (NPD) – As products or services are deleted from the Product Mix, replacement products must be launched. The **NPD Process** includes: *Idea Generation; Idea Screening; Business Analysis; Product Development; Test Marketing; Commercialization* (p. 253).

Oligopolistic Competition – few sellers which are highly susceptible to each other's actions. Price fixing often in collusion (p. 261).

Perceptual Maps – Based on a variety of mathematical and qualitative research tools, *Perceptual Mapping* describes consumers' perceptions of brands or products, and their attributes, on 'spatial maps' (p. 235).

Personal Selling – A process of informing customers and persuading them to purchase products through personal communication in an exchange situation (p. 269).

PEST analysis – A definition of the marketing environment as: political, economic, social and technological forces (p. 199).

Porter's Competitive Strategies – The competitive arena is affected by outside forces: *direct like-for-like rivals; bargaining power of suppliers; bargaining power of buyers; threat of substitute products or services; threat of new entrants* (p. 237). Otherwise known as the forces of the *Micro Marketing Environment* (p. 252).

Porter's Generic Strategies – Three generic strategies resulting in success and competitive advantage for organisations competing for position in any particular market: *Cost Leadership; Differentiation; Focus* (p. 239).

Positioning – Part of the Market Segmentation process. *Product Positioning* refers to decisions and activities intended to create and maintain a firm's product or service concept in customers' minds. *Market Positioning* arranges for a product or service to occupy a clear, distinctive and desirable place – relative to competing products or services – in the minds of targeted customers. *Brand Positioning* creates a distinctive and differentiated image for a brand. (p. 234).

Price – As an element of the Marketing Mix, *Price* is a value placed on anything which is exchanged; a good, service or idea. *Price* is influenced by the competitive situation, the Marketing Environment, organizational policies, objectives, cost structures, the other elements of the Marketing Mix, and consumer needs and expectations (p. 261).

Price Elasticity of Demand – $\dfrac{\text{\% Change in Number Demanded}}{\text{\% Change in Price}}$ (p. 262).

Price Skimming – The use of very high prices in order to maximize profit in the short-term (p. 264).

Primary Data Collection – In Marketing Research this is the act of collecting bespoke information for specific research requirements. There are two types: observation (mechanical or personal) and surveys (mail/postal, telephone, Internet or personal) (p. 216).

Product – Everything (both favourable and unfavourable) received in an exchange: a product is a complexity of tangible and intangible attributes, including functional, social and psychological utilities or benefits. A product may be a good, service or an idea (p. 246).

Product Adoption Process – *Awareness; Interest; Evaluation; Trial; Adoption* (Purchase and Consumption) (p. 267).

Product (Brand) Management – A form of marketing management where the marketing function is oriented around individual products/brands or product portfolios. *Product Management* is proactive, taking responsibility for both Marketing Strategy and the implementation of Marketing Mixes; it is not marketing as a service or ancillary resource (p. 246).

Product Deletion – *Phase Out, Run Out* or *Immediate Drop*; through whichever mechanism, products and services reach obsolescence and need to be deleted from the Product Mix (p. 252).

Product Levels – *Core Product*: the level of a product that provides the perceived real core benefit or service; *Actual Product*: a composite of the features and capabilities offered in a product – quality and durability, design and product styling, packaging and brand name; *Augmented Product*: support aspects of a product, including customer service, warranty, delivery and credit, personnel, installation and after-sales support (p. 247).

Product Life Cycle (PLC) – *Introduction; Growth; Maturity; Decline.* Most products, services and markets pass through this sequence. Marketing Strategies must be altered accordingly (p. 251).

Product Mix – The range of products controlled by one organization. Often broken into product categories when the organization is active in numerous, unrelated markets. The *Product Mix* is dynamic and requires manipulation: *Product Deletion; Product Modification; New Product Development* (p. 251).

Product Modification – Products need revising and updating periodically to remain competitive and in the Product Mix (p. 252).

Product Portfolio – The *Portfolio* approach to marketing attempts to manage the Product Mix so as to balance short-term gains with longer term profitability. There are various analytical tools available to assist in this management process: *The Boston Consultancy Group* (**BCG**) *Growth-Share Matrix* and the *Directional Policy Matrix* (**DPM**) are the most popular for analysing the relative attraction and positions of an organization's various products or brands (p.251).

Products: Consumer – Goods consumed by the general public; consumers as private individuals: *Convenience Goods, Shopping Goods, Speciality Goods, Unsought Goods* (p. 247).

Products: Industrial – Supplies used in the manufacture of other products: *Raw Materials, Component Parts, Capital Items, Accessory Equipment, Consumable Supplies, Ancillary Services* (p. 247).

Products: Services – Service products tend to be intangible, requiring the participation of the consumer in their production and consumption: *Tourism, Catering, Travel, Health, Leisure, Entertainment, Education, Financial, Consultancy, Retailing, Government/Administration, Non-Profit/Voluntary/Charitable service products* (p. 247).

Profit – Revenue less Total Costs (p. 263).

Promotional Mix – The core elements of promotional activity: traditionally *Advertising, Sales Promotion, Personal Selling* and *Public Relations/Publicity*, with the more recent additions of *Sponsorship, Direct Mail* and the *Internet* (p. 268).

Promotional Pricing – An approach to pricing involving the use of special price levels to increase sales in the short-term. This can involve the use of *special-event pricing*, linked perhaps to a national public holiday (p. 264).

Psychological Pricing – Price levels are determined for psychological rather than rational reasons. Perceived value pricing is based on what buyers believe the product to be worth (p. 264).

Public Relations – The planned and sustained effort to establish and maintain good will and mutual understanding between an organization and its publics (p. 269).

Publicity – Non-personal communication in news story form, regarding an organization and/or its products or services, which is transmitted through a mass medium at no charge (p. 269).

Publics – *Target publics* for *public relations* include customers, employees, shareholders, trade bodies, unions, suppliers, government officials, journalists and society (p. 270).

Pure Monopoly – a single seller only (p. 261).

Pure Competition – Many sellers – and buyers – selling similar goods or services, each with only some influence on demand. Market conditions and market forces set price (p. 261).

Quali-Depth Interviews – A relatively new Marketing Research approach: 20–25-minute interviews conducted in halls or meeting rooms close to, for example, a high street (p. 218).

Qualitative Research – Deals with information too difficult or expensive to quantify; value judgements typically involving group discussions or personal interviews (p. 216).

Quantitative Research – Research findings which can be analysed and expressed numerically; often large sample surveys from mailed questionnaires or telephone interviewing, or analysis of sales data and market forecasts (p. 000).

Relationship Marketing – The move from *transaction-based* marketing to seeking on-going *relationships*. Marketers devote their attention to both winning new customers – transaction marketing – and to building up positive on-going relationships to maintain their loyalty and custom – relationship marketing (p. 193).

Sales Promotion – Activity and/or material inducing sales through added value or incentive for the product to resellers, sales people or consumers. There are *Trade Promotions, Consumer Promotions* and *Retail/Distributor Promotions* (p. 271).

Sampling – In Marketing Research, except in industries with few customers or competitors, it is not cost effective to survey whole populations. Instead, samples are selected which represent their total populations or target markets. **Probability** sampling can be *random, stratified* or *area*. **Judgemental** sampling is more subjective and often is *quota* based (p. 219).

Secondary Data – In Marketing Research this is 'second-hand' information previously collected or published for another purpose, but readily available to consult. There are two types: internal sources (information within an organization) and external sources (in libraries, publications) (p. 216).

Selling – A process of persuasion leading to a continuing trading arrangement, initiated and perpetuated at either a personal or an impersonal level but commonly confined to oral representation supported by visual aids. The focus is off-loading goods, services or ideas; is one-way with little customer feedback into the marketing mix (p. 194).

Services – *A Service* is the result of applying human or mechanical efforts to people or objects. Services are intangible products involving a deed, a performance or an effort which cannot be physically possessed or stored (p. 280).

Services Marketing Mix – This is extended from the '4Ps' to the '7Ps': *Product, Price, Place (Distribution), Promotion; plus, People, Physical Evidence (Ambience), Process* (p. 282).

Services Characteristics – *Intangibility, Direct Organization-Client Relationship, Consumer Participation in Production, Complexity* (p. 281).

Shopping Mall Intercept – Typified by the market researcher on a street corner or in a shopping centre, with a clipboard and three or four minutes' questions (p. 218).

Social Responsibility – An organization's obligation to maximize its positive impact and minimize its negative impact on society. Consideration of (a) *Consumer Issues* – consumer movements strive to protect the rights of individuals and groups of consumers through lobbying of policy-makers and the media; (b) *Community Relations* – marketers are part of a broader community and are expected to satisfy the well-being of this broader community; (c) *Green Marketing* – the development and sale of products that specifically do not harm the natural environment (p. 303).

Social Responsibility Strategies – (a) *Reaction Strategy* – a business permits a problem to go unresolved until the public finds out, when it then reacts; (b) *Defence Strategy* – minimization or avoidance of additional obligations once a problem has arisen; (c) *Accommodation Strategy* – a business assumes responsibility for its actions; (d) *Proactive Strategy* – a company assumes responsibility for its actions and responds to external criticisms without outside pressure or government intervention (p. 304).

Sponsorship – The financing or partial funding of an event, personality, activity, programme or product in order to gain consumer awareness and media coverage from the association; most commonly in sports, the arts and entertainment (p. 272).

SWOT Analysis – Central to Marketing Planning, the SWOT is an analysis of an organization's Strengths, Weaknesses, Opportunities and Threats, product group by product group market by market. The Strengths/Weaknesses are internal considerations, while the Opportunities/Threats relate to the market and the Marketing Environment (p. 295).

Target Audience – Group of people or a market segment at which a specific Promotional Campaign is aimed (p. 266).

Targeting – Part of the Market Segmentation process, *Targeting* is the act of identifying which market segments (or sectors) on which to concentrate resources and marketing activity: *mass marketing, single segment,* or *multi-segments*. Targeting criteria include existing market share, market homogeneity and market knowledge; product homogeneity; production and marketing scale economies; the level of competition; capability of satisfying customers' needs; segment size and structure; available company resources; anticipated profitability and market share (p. 233).

Time Series Forecasts – A set of observations, such as monthly or annual sales returns, examined and extrapolated to produce predictions for future figures. The main approaches are: *Naive, Moving Averages, Exponential Smoothing, Statistical Trend Analysis,* and *Box- Jenkins* (p. 223).

Total Costs – Fixed Costs + Variable Costs (p. 263).

Trading Companies – These provide a link between buyers and sellers in different countries. A trading company is not involved in manufacturing nor does it own production-based assets. Instead it buys in one country and sells to buyers in another country. Trading companies take over ownership of products bought and undertake all of the sales and marketing activity required to move the products from the domestic country to foreign markets (p. 299).

Value for money – The benefit customers perceive to be inherent in a product or service – or its consumption – weighted against the price demanded (p. 265).

Warfare Strategies – The analysis of competition linked to military warfare strategies. These include: *principles of Defensive Warfare; principles of Offensive Warfare;* strategies for *Market Leaders, Challengers, Followers, Nichers* (p. 241).

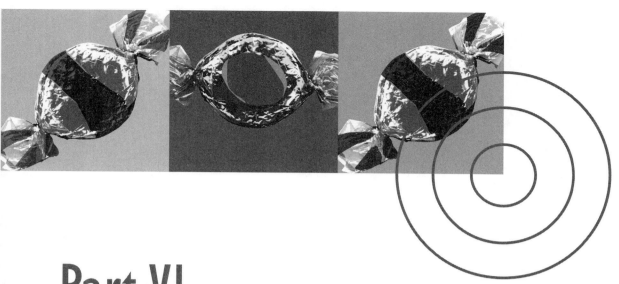

Part VI
Further Readings

This section contains the key recommended further readings from each theory note.

Adams, N.R., Dogramaci, O., Gangopadhyay, A. and Yesha, Y., (1999) *Electronic Commerce: Technical, Business and Legal Issues*, New Jersey: Pearson. Thorough but highly American view of e-commerce.

Assael, H. (1998) *Consumer Behaviour and Marketing Action,* Boston: Kent. Not light bed-time reading, but very thorough.

Baker, M.J. (1999) *The Marketing Book,* London: Butterworth-Heinemann. *The Marketing Book* is a superb collection of readings by leading academics covering most facets of marketing.

Baker, M.J. (1999) *Encyclopaedia of Marketing*, London: Thomson Learning. Not light bed-time reading but a very thorough reference resource for marketers.

Belch, G. and Belch, M. (1998) *Advertising and Promotion: An Integrated Marketing Communications Perspective*, New York: McGraw-Hill. Very popular in North America.

Berry, L. (1995) *On Great Service*, New York: The Free Press. The essentials of controlling service quality.

Birn, R. (1999) *The Effective Use of Market Research,* London: Kogan Page. A nice, down-to-earth introduction to marketing research.

Bradley, F. (1998) *International Marketing Strategy*; Hemel Hempstead: Pearson. One of the few leading international marketing texts not authored in North America.

Brownlie, D. (1994), 'Organising for Environmental Scanning: Orthodoxies and Reformations', *Journal of Marketing Management*, 10 (8), pp. 703–724. The processes for tackling environmental scanning.

Charter, M. (1999) *Greener Marketing*, Sheffield: Greenleaf Press. Green issues. Quirky but informative look at green marketing.

Chisnall, P. (1995) *Strategic Business Marketing*, London: Pearson. A good overview of industrial marketing.

Chisnall, P. (1997) *Marketing Research*, Maidenhead: McGraw-Hill. Of the UK marketing research texts, probably the most impressive and certainly very thorough.

Christopher, M. (1997) *Marketing Logistics*, Oxford: Butterworth-Heinemann. A specialist text examining logistical issues.

Christopher, M. (1998) *Logistics and Supply Chain Management*, London: Pitman. Marketing channels comprehensively examined.

Crowner, R.P. (1991) *Developing a Strategic Business Plan with Cases*, Homewood, IL: Irwin. A US view of business planning

Davidson, J.H. (1972) *Offensive Marketing,* New York: Penguin. A superb warning: understand the competition!

December, J. and Randall, N. (1996) *The World Wide Web Unleashed*, Sams Publishing. The dos and don'ts of building web sites.

De Chernatony, L. and McDonald, M. (1998) *Creating Powerful Brands*, Oxford: Butterworth-Heinemann. As the title implies, tips on branding!

Diamantopoulos, A. and Mathews, B.P. (1995*) Making Pricing Decisions: a Study of Managerial Practice*, London: Thomson Learning. A rare but welcome exploration of pricing decisions.

Diamantopoulos, A. and Schlegelmilch, B.B. (1997) *Taking The Fear Out of Data Analysis*, London: Thomson Learning. Quantitative methods for marketers.

Dibb, S., Simkin, L., and Bradley, J. (1996) *The Marketing Planning Workbook*, London: Thomson Learning. One of the leading UK texts examining, from a practitioner's perspective, the stages of undertaking marketing planning.

Dibb, S., Simkin, L., Pride, W. and Ferrell, O.C. (2001) *Marketing: Concepts and Strategies*, Boston: Houghton Mifflin. This is the market-leading mainstream marketing textbook adopted by most business schools to explore and to explain the subject of marketing.

Dibb, S. and Simkin, L. (1996) *The Market Segmentation Workbook*, London: Thomson Learning. A 'how to do' market segmentation process aimed at marketing managers.

Donaldson, T. (1992) *The Ethics of International Business*; New York: Oxford University Press. A dated but revealing insight into the practices of corporate decision-making.

Donnelly, J.H. and George, W.R. (1981) *Marketing of Services,* AMA Proceedings Series, Chicago: American Marketing Association. Dated, but the source of many current tips regarding services marketing.

Doyle, P. (1998) *Marketing Management and Strategy*, London: Pearson. Not an introductory reader, this insightful examination of strategic marketing is a good read for serious marketers.

Drucker, P. (1981, reprinted in 1993) *Management in Turbulent Times*, London: Butterworth-Heinemann/Pan. Dated but insightful explanation of the importance of understanding the external trading environment.

Engel, J.F., Warshaw, M.R. and Kinnear, T.C. (1994) *Promotional Strategy: Managing the Marketing Communications Process*, New York: McGraw Hill/Irwin. Very thorough US examination of managing promotion.

Engel, J.F., Blackwell, R.D. and Miniard, P.W. (1997) *Consumer Behaviour,* Fort Worth: The Dryden Press. For generations of qualitative marketing researchers, this text has been the guiding light.

Evans, M.J., O'Malley, L. and Patterson, M. (1996) 'Direct Marketing Communications in the UK: a Study of Growth, Past, Present and Future', *Journal of Marketing Communications*, 2, pp. 51–65. A straightforward review of essential steps.

Ferrell, O.C. and Fraedrich, J. (2000) *Business Ethics*; Boston: Houghton Mifflin. Written by two of the initial proponents of ethics in marketing.

Fernie, J. (ed.) (1990) *Retail Distribution Management: Strategic Guide to Developments and Trends,* London: Kogan Page. An overview of channel options.

FitzGerald, M. and Arnott, D. (2000) *Marketing Communications Classics*, London: Thomson Learning. A super collection of readings on most aspects of marketing communications from most key authors.

Ford, D. (1997), *Understanding Business Markets*, London: Thomson Learning. One of the best examinations of business-to-business marketing.

Ford, D., Hakansson, H. and Turnbull, P. (1998) *Managing Business Relationships*, Chichester: Wiley. Relationship marketing interfaces with business-to-business buying behaviour.

Foxall, G., Goldsmith, R.E. and Brown, S. (1998), *Consumer Psychology for Marketing*, London: Thomson Learning. Very sound UK consumer buying behaviour text.

Frank, R. and Wind, Y. (1971) *Market Segmentation,* Englewood Cliffs N.J.: Prentice-Hall. Where market segmentation first began!

Glynn, W.J. and Barnes, J.G. (1995) *Understanding Services Management, Integrating Marketing, Organisational Behaviour, Operations and Human Resource Management*, Chichester: Wiley and Dublin: Oak Tree Press. People are at the heart of most services and of this text.

Goldberg, M.E., Fishbein, M. and Middlestadt, S.E. (eds) (1997), *Social Marketing: Theoretical and Practical Perspectives*, New Jersey: Lawrence Erlbaum Associates. US Marketing with a conscience.

Gronroos, C. (1990) *Service Management and Marketing*, Lexington, MA: Lexington Books. A more thorough and academic read than the many concise guides on services marketing.

Hart, N. (1994) *Effective Industrial Marketing*, London: Kogan Page. A good selection of readings addressing industrial marketing issues.

Harvard Business Review (1991) *Accurate Business Forecasting,* Boston: Harvard Business Review Paperbacks. A wonderful summary of suitable techniques.

Hooley, G.J. and Hussey, M.K. (1999), *Quantitative Methods in Marketing*, London: Thomson Learning. Multivariate techniques explored through a collection of far-reaching readings.

Hooley, G. and Saunders, J. (1993) *Competitive Positioning: The Key to Market Success*, London: Pearson. The nuances of warfare and developing competitive strategies.

Hutt, M.D. and Speh, T.W. (1998) *Business Marketing Management: Strategic View of Industrial and Organizational Markets,* Forth Worth: Dryden Press. As Engel, Blackwell and Miniard are to consumer buyer behaviour tutors, Hutt and Speh are in organizational markets.

Jain, S.C. (1999) *Marketing Planning & Strategy*, Cincinnati, OH: South Western. A core US reader addressing at length the philosophy of marketing planning.

Jeannet, J.-P. and Hennessey, D. (1997) *Global Marketing Strategies*; Boston: Houghton Mifflin. Thorough and well written with many good examples and insights.

Jefkins, F. and Yadin, D. (1998) *Public Relations*, London: Pearson Professional. In the UK, Jefkins has been essential reading for those interested in PR for over two decades.

Keegan, W. (1989) *Global Marketing Management*; Englewood Cliffs: Pearson. To many, the most comprehensive explanation of international marketing.

Kitchen, P.J. (ed.) (1998) *Marketing Communications: Principles and Practice*, London: Thomson Learning. A welcome addition to the bookshelf: very good coverage of all aspects of managing the promotional mix.

Kitchen, P.J. (1997) *Public Relations: Principles and Practice*, London: Thomson Learning. A sound alternative to the work of Jefkins.

Lambkin, M., Foxall, G.R., Van Raaij, F. and Heilbrunn, B. (eds) (1998) *European Perspectives on Consumer Behaviour*, London: Pearson. Claimed to be the definitive collection of European consumer buying behaviour papers.

Lehmann, D.R. and Winner, R.S. (1994) *Analysis for Marketing Planning*, Burr Ridge, Ill: Irwin. A good, easy to follow US text.

Levitt, T. (1960) 'Marketing Myopia', *Harvard Business Review*, 38 (4), pp. 45–56. Possibly where modern marketing began: Levitt lambasted the inward-looking, product-led, aggressive selling of 'US Inc'!

Lilien, G.L. and Kotler, P. (1983) *Marketing Decision Making,* New York: Harper and Row. A modelling based view of marketing decisions.

Lovelock, C.H. (1996) *Services Marketing,* Englewood Cliffs: Pearson. Essential reading!

Lovelock, C.H. (1992) *Managing Services,* Englewood Cliffs: Pearson. To many academics, Lovelock's work is the single most important reference point on services marketing.

Lynch, J. (1994) 'What is Marketing?' in *Effective Industrial Marketing* (Ed N Hart), London: Kogan Page. Industrial products and services are marketed, too, as described well in this book of collected readings.

Macrae, C. (1996) *The Brand Chartering Handbook*, London: Addison-Wesley. Essential reading for those interested in branding.

McDonald, M. and Dunbar, I. (1995) *Market Segmentation*, London: Macmillan. Similar in ethos to Dibb and Simkin's *Market Segmentation Workbook*.

McDonald, M.H. (1999) *Marketing Plans*, Oxford: Butterworth-Heinemann. A solid guide to marketing planning.

McGoldrick, P. (1997) *Retail Marketing*, Maidenhead: McGraw-Hill. This leading retail marketing text contains a good explanation of direct marketing's evolution and role in marketing channels.

McQuarrie, E.F. (1996), *The Market Research Toolbox: a Concise Guide for Beginners*, London: Sage. The title is self-explanatory: a welcome addition to the bookshelf.

Monroe, B.K. (1990) *Pricing: Making Profitable Decisions,* New York: McGraw-Hill. Essential reading for marketers involved in pricing decisions.

Moriarty, R.T. (1983) *Industrial Buying Behaviour*, Lexington: Lexington. An alternative to the work of Hutt and Speh.

Nagle, T. (1994) *Strategy and Tactics of Pricing*, London: Pearson. Profitable decision-making explored.

Nagle, T. and Holden R.K. (1995) *The Strategy and Tactics of Pricing*, Englewood Cliffs: Pearson. Pricing in marketing extensively explained and analysed.

Naert, P. and Leeflang, P. (1978) *Building Implementable Marketing Models,* Leiden: Martinus Nijhoff. For the more numerate marketer! Dated, but a superb guide. This text has just resurfaced as *Building Models For Marketing Decisions,* by Leeflang, S.H., Wittink, D.R., Wedel, M. and Naert, P., published by Kluwer in 2000.

O'Malley, L., Patterson, M. and Evans, M. (1999) *Exploring Direct Marketing*, London: Thomson Learning. A thorough explanation of direct marketing and the Internet's role.

Manley II, W.W. (1992) *The Handbook of Good Business Practice*; London: Routledge. A step-by-step approach to avoiding the key pitfalls in striving to behave well.

O'Shaughnessy, J. (1995), *Competitive Marketing: a Strategic Approach*, London: Thomson Learning. Marketing management with a good examination of competitive strategy.

Paliwoda, S.J. and Thomas, M.J. (1998) *International Marketing*, Oxford: Butterworth-Heinemann. A welcome UK view of international marketing issues.

Palmer, A. (1998) *Principles of Services Marketing*, Maidenhead: McGraw-Hill. A popular UK services marketing introduction.

Parasuraman, A. (1991) *Marketing Research,* Reading, Massachusetts: Addison-Wesley. One of the most authoritative US texts.

Payne, A. (1993) *The Essence of Services Marketing*, Hemel Hempstead: Pearson. A UK-based view of services marketing.

Peattie, K. (1995) *Environmental Marketing Management*, London: Pitman. All there is to know about environmental (green) issues in marketing.

Peter, J.P. and Olson, J.C. (1998) *Consumer Behaviour and Marketing Strategy,* New York: McGraw Hill/Irwin. Well explained, simple and nicely laid out, similar coverage to Assael or Engel *et al*.

Porter, M.E. (1979) 'How competitive forces shape strategy', *Harvard Business Review,* 47 (March–April), pp. 137–45. Where many marketers first heard about their competitive arena.

Porter, M.E. (1980) *Competitive Strategy: Techniques for Analysing Industries and Competitors,* New York: Free Press/Macmillan. How to become competitive.

Powers, T.L. (1991) *Modern Business Marketing,* St Paul, Minnesota: West. A thorough insight into marketing in businesses.

Rapp, S. and Collins, T. (1999) *MaxiMarketing,* New York: McGraw-Hill. An intriguing deployment of the promotional mix toolkit.

Ries, A. and Trout, J. (1981) *Positioning: The Battle for Your Mind,* New York: McGraw-Hill. Reissued in 1993 by Warner Books. A superb examination of brand positioning.

Rosenbloom, B. (1999) *Marketing Channels: A Management View*, Fort Worth: Dryden. Detailed North American view of distribution channels in marketing.

Rosenau, M.D., Griffin, A., Castellion, G. and Anschuetz, N. (eds) (1996) *The PDMA Handbook of New Product Development*, New York: John Wiley. A well explained examination of new product development.

Rossiter, J.R. and Percy, L. (1997) *Advertising Communications and Promotion Management,* New York: McGraw-Hill. A rigorous examination of advertising and notably sales promotions.

Schwartz, E.I. (1997) *Webonomics: Nine Essential Principles for Growing Your Business on the World Wide Web*, New York: Broadway Books. E-commerce explored.

Shimp, T.A. (1997) *Advertising, Promotion and Supplemental Aspects of Integrated Marketing Communications*, Fort Worth: Dryden Press. A core US text on most marketing lecturers' shelves.

Shipley, D. (ed.) (1989) 'Industrial distribution channel management', special edition, *European Journal of Marketing* 23 (2) Bradford: MCB. Interesting selection of papers addressing distribution in marketing.

Terpstra, V. and Sarathy, R. (2000) *International Marketing*; Fort Worth: Dryden Press. Perhaps the book that first explored the nuances of marketing across national boundaries.

Tull, D.S. and Hawkins, D.I. (1990) *Marketing Research,* New York: Macmillan. The old favourite of several generations of marketing lecturers.

Webster, F.E. (1995) *Industrial Marketing Strategy,* New York: John Wiley. One of the original authors focusing on business-to-business markets.

Winckler, J. (1983) *Pricing for Results*, Oxford: Butterworth-Heinemann. Dated but thorough in explaining the economics of pricing.

Wind, Y. (1982) *Product Policy: Concepts, Methods and Strategy,* Reading, Massachusetts: Addison-Wesley. The staple product management text on many marketing lecturers' shelves.

Zeithaml, V. and Bitner, J. (1996) *Services Marketing*, New York: McGraw-Hill. A good US examination co-authored by one of the founders of modern services marketing.

Index

Note: Page references in *italics* indicate tables and figures; those in **bold** indicate the glossary. *Italics* are also used for the names of companies treated in full in the case studies.